NARRATIVES

OF

CONVERSIONS AND REVIVAL INCIDENTS.

NARRATIVES

OF

REMARKABLE CONVERSIONS

AND

REVIVAL INCIDENTS:

INCLUDING

A REVIEW OF REVIVALS,

FROM THE DAY OF PENTECOST TO THE GREAT AWAKENING IN THE LAST CENTURY—CONVERSIONS OF EMINENT PERSONS—INSTANCES OF REMARKABLE CONVERSIONS AND ANSWERS TO PRAYER—AN ACCOUNT OF THE RISE AND PROGRESS OF THE

GREAT AWAKENING OF 1857-'8.

BY WILLIAM C. CONANT.

WITH AN INTRODUCTION

BY HENRY WARD BEECHER.

"The powers of the world to come."—HEB. vi. 5.

NEW YORK:
DERBY & JACKSON, 119 NASSAU STREET.
1858.

ENTERED according to Act of Congress, in the year 1858, by
DERBY & JACKSON,
In the Clerk's Office of the District Court of the United States, for the Southern District of New York.

W. H. TINSON, Stereotyper.

GEO. RUSSELL, & Co., Printers.

CONTENTS.

1*

INTRODUCTION.

All the histories of the Human Race have, as yet, been external and physical. That part in which man's distinctive nature dwells,—his mind and heart,—has either been passed by entirely, or empirically handled. Neither is the time yet come for doing what the time past has failed even to attempt. Men do not even know what the mind is, what are its constituent powers, what are those faculties which produce the endless results of human experience. The body has been explored; every function watched, and the organs closely studied. The nerves have been traced, the veins and arteries have been mapped down accurately, the most secreted passages and tissues have been revealed, and all those silent changes which are going on in the dark laboratory of Vital Forces have been guessed or found out. It is no longer what a man performs that is known, but what *it is that performs.* Effects have been traced back to their causes, and thus these causes have been studied in all their history, both by induction and by experiment.

Not even what the Mind *does* is yet studied. But what

are the primary forces which produce the endless phenomena of mentality, men are only beginning to inquire. When each of the constituent powers of the human mind shall have been scientifically ascertained; its laws, its combinations, its modifications registered, then a new era will dawn upon the Science of History. The History of Man, not alone the external elements of his life, but the life and history of each faculty of the human mind, as they have been developed in every period of time, from the earliest dawn to the present; under all diversities of climate, civil institution, social usage, secular occupation, under all methods of teaching, of restraint, of incitement, will yet be written. And the history of the development of each faculty of the human Soul will be the highest ground of true history, and the last to be occupied. When that day shall arrive, the most profoundly affecting chapter will be the history of man's Religious nature. The blind outreaching of the human soul toward purity, toward rest, toward strength; the aspirations of earnest men for divine life, their conflicts with fear, with doubt, with passions, will constitute a history in the presence of which all outward events, all changes of kingdoms, or movements of commerce, of art, or diplomacy, will be both coarse and tame. The single record of the struggles of great souls with a legitimate doubt, will be a history of itself. In every church, in every age, there have been men who made their way up out of error, formalism, or death, as seeds do, lifting up the dirt and forcing their way to the light by the irresistible might of growth. The conflicts of such, usually accompanied by reproach without, and by pains and deep sufferings within, would be more profoundly affecting than the most touching history of disappointed love, or of any of those passions of which Dramas are made.

As man's religious nature is his highest, so the real history of the soul's religious struggles and developments is to be the crowning attainment of future historic periods.

The book which is here presented to the reader, does not pretend to any philosophical method, nor, indeed, has it any philosophic end in view. It neither proposes to group its materials around any theory or principle, nor to give the reader any elements of judgment by which he may measure and decide the value of the materials collected. It has just this merit: that it has collected from different sources, materials hitherto widely scattered, and often inaccessible to ordinary readers, and presented them in a compact form, at a reasonable price, to the common reader. This is all. There is no more rubbish, probably, than will be found in any other approved religious reading. That there is a good deal of chaff; that many things narrated imply great mistakes; that many things carry with them, either by statement or implication, mistakes, and even sometimes untruths, cannot be doubted. That there are exaggerations; that there are morbid experiences; that there are special truths erected into general truths; that there are peculiar personal experiences, idiosyncratic, set forth authoritatively for the imitation of all men, is also undeniable. But what then? Is there any field of wheat without straw and without chaff? What if it were better to give clean wheat, who, yet, knows how to winnow the recorded religious experiences of the world? There are few that could do it, however much they wished. There are fewer yet that would dare to do it, however able they might be. The world is very jealous of its religious ignorance, and embalmed mistakes are sacred as ancient idols. No man has ever carried a people one march nearer the promised land, without being in danger, repeatedly, of being stoned. No man has ever purified the life of an age, without substantially laying down his own for that sake. And there are few men that love their fellows as Paul did his, or who can adopt that highest expression of love ever uttered by human lips, "*And I will very gladly spend and be spent for you, though the more abundantly I love you the less I be loved.*" And Paul himself, I think, only in moments of sublime intensity, could utter that other and climacteric desire, "*For I could wish that myself were accursed from Christ, for my brethren, for my kinsmen according to the flesh!*"

For a long time, then, much must remain in confusion, much that is indifferent must continue to be held as sacred, and much that is sacred must be disregarded or sacrificed.

There are a few points which may be presented, and which, it is hoped, will prevent some evil which might arise from many of these narratives, and secure some good. For, those who will not be in danger of being misled by these histories, are generally those who the least need to read them; while those who need them most, are, as a class, most in danger of being injured by them.

1. It is very important that young persons, and persons who are just entering upon a Christian life, should be taught not to try themselves by other people's evidences. It is supposed that if religion is of God, it will, of course, be just the same in all men. But, in fact, religion is the right

using of the whole mind and life. Men are different one from another. They were meant to be. The strength of some lies in the feelings, of others in their intellect, of others in their stability and will. Some men are calm, others excitable. Some are imaginative, and others literal and practical. Some are nervous and quick, others phlegmatic and slow. Besides these constitutional differences, men have had widely different teaching and training, and all these circumstances conspire to make their religious developments personal and peculiar! God leads every soul according to what that soul is, and what its history has been. And although Love is the one central experience in all, and is that grand and characteristic element which makes all men alike Christians; yet love developes itself in different degrees in different men—in some gradually, in others suddenly; in some, it is transfused with the imagination, in others it is a very plain and homely emotion. It rushes like a mountain torrent from some hearts; in others it is like a silver spring in a meadow—silent, gentle, and almost invisible.

No man should try to produce in himself another man's experience, unless he first *becomes* that other man. In an orchestra, the flute, the violin, the clarionet, the horns, all give forth music. But music is not the same sound, nor of the same quality in each of them as in the other. Love God and love men with *your* nature. And do not lose comfort and growth in grace by waiting to feel like some other Christian. Be a Christian. Consecrate *your* heart and *your* life to Christ's service, and then the greater the difference between you and other Christians the better; just as in a flower-garden, the summer is rich, not by having all flowers just like each other, but by having as many different varieties as is possible.

2. Many persons are stumbled by the doctrine of instantaneous conversion. That there is an instantaneous influx of spiritual influence upon the hearts of men, which becomes the cause and beginning of an active change in their life and feelings, cannot reasonably be doubted by those who take the pains to examine the facts of actual life. *Character* is not changed suddenly. Habits die out gradually. Habits form gradually. The Christian character continues to be progressive. But the question is simply this, Do not men suddenly, instantly, *enter* upon this Christian career? Do they not change the direction of their will, the aim of their lives, and the desires of their hearts, suddenly? The causes which prepare the way may have been gradually accumulating, and the full results to which they point may be long in ripening. But the *point of beginning*, whether the person is conscious of the fact, or not, is instantaneous. And the teaching of this truth will, in the long run, give great decisiveness to minds which, upon any other view, would give way to procrastination, upon a vain hope of becoming gradually good. Men *do* become good gradually. But they never *begin* gradually. That is instant and decisive!

3. But it does not follow, that men are not converted; that they have not truly come under the influence of the Divine Mind, because they are not conscious of the day and hour in which they began to live anew. The sun may come up behind clouds, it may not shine out till noon, nor even

until its going down. A disease may pass its crisis, and for hours and days one may not be conscious of it.

My own observation has led me to the conclusion that more persons become true, spiritual Christians without sudden joy, and without the consciousness, *at the time* of transition, of a great change, than with it.

In robust and impetuous natures; in persons who have lived in violent or great sins, who are brought under very powerful religious influences, we should expect to find a change which came with powerful sensation, and a clear consciousness. But when moral persons, of an even disposition, well taught in religious truths, especially if of a mild and restrained habit of feeling, are converted, we should look for no such evidences.

Those who read this book should also be put upon their guard against waiting for *deep convictions of sin.* There may be more feeling than is good, as well as less. That is feeling enough which is strong enough to turn a man away from evil. Neither should men suppose it needful to sound conviction that the preliminary experiences should occupy a long time. When a man knows that he is wrong, it is a shame to him to be a great while in forsaking it. An honorable mind should turn instantly from evil. A period of conviction, running through weeks, is to be deplored. It is neither wise nor morally wholesome. It is contrary to Scripture precept, and to the results which followed the first preaching of the Gospel. Men should not lie in a bath of conviction as clothes lie in a dyeing vat, until they are thoroughly struck through. They should rather be like ships, which, having run upon one tack, put about at once, without waiting, and without losing headway.

But after all cautions, after all instructions, after all experiences have been set forth for the instruction of others, every one must, in the end, find his own way to a vivid realization of faith in Christ. It is the divine work in man's soul. And though men may lessen the obstacles, and greatly expedite the work, no teaching and no human influence can do all. There is a passage into which the soul comes, where only it and God stand together. In that face to face wrestling, the issue is simply, submission to God! And the human will must meet that decisive question, unhelped, save by the gracious strivings of God's loving Spirit!

REVIEW OF REVIVALS.

THE history of the Gospel is the real record of the Supernatural in this world. We deny that "the age of miracles is past;" and this humble volume—humble, yet of transcendent contents—shall sustain the denial. The miraculous system of Divine Revelation, far from having ceased, has advanced to a sublimer stage of development, suitable to the higher susceptibilities it has engendered in man. Forty centuries of laborious education, with line upon line, precept upon precept, symbol upon symbol, and wonder upon wonder, reiterated upon the crude and sensuous susceptibilities of human nature, had but sufficed to introduce the glorious revelation of Omnipotence and Grace which we name the Era of our Lord. In the fullness of times, CHRIST came: and the supernatural wonders which attest the operation of God, took on thenceforth the spiritual nature and pure moral glory of his kingdom. Then first the Spirit of God was manifested as the occupant of the human soul; the tabernacle of God was with men, and he descended to "dwell" among us; spreading abroad the wonders of his power in a universal largess unto and upon all that believe. "When he ascended up on high, he led captivity captive and gave gifts unto men." Likened to a rushing, mighty wind, the Holy Ghost came down, surcharging even the common channels of life and intelligence in man; bursting forth as with excess and exuberance of power, in sensible as well as spiritual prodigies, for a time.

And when the day of Pentecost was fully come, they were all with one accord in one place. And suddenly there came a sound from heaven as of a rushing, mighty wind, and it filled all the house where they were sitting. And there appeared unto them cloven tongues like as of fire, and it sat upon each of them. And they were all filled with the

Holy Ghost, and began to speak with other tongues, as the Spirit gave them utterance.

And there were dwelling at Jerusalem Jews, devout men, out of every nation under heaven. Now, when this was noised abroad, the multitude came together, and were confounded, because that every man heard them speak in his own language. And they were all amazed and marvelled, saying one to another, Behold, are not all these which speak Galileans? And how hear we every man in our own tongue, wherein we were born? Parthians, and Medes, and Elamites, and the dwellers in Mesopotamia, and in Judea, and Cappadocia, in Pontus, and Asia, Phrygia, and Pamphylia, in Egypt, and in the parts of Libya about Cyrene, and strangers of Rome, Jews and proselytes, Cretes and Arabians, we do hear them speak in our tongues the wonderful works of God. And they were all amazed, and were in doubt, saying one to another, What meaneth this? Others mocking said, These men are full of new wine.

But Peter, standing up with the eleven, lifted up his voice, and said unto them, "Ye men of Judea, and all ye that dwell at Jerusalem, be this known unto you, and hearken to my words: For these are not drunken, as ye suppose, seeing it is but the third hour of the day. But this is that which was spoken by the prophet Joel: 'And it shall come to pass in the last days, saith God, I will pour out of my Spirit upon all flesh: and your sons and your daughters shall prophesy, and your young men shall see visions, and your old men shall dream dreams: and on my servants and on my handmaidens I will pour out in those days of my Spirit: and they shall prophesy: and I will show wonders in heaven above, and signs in the earth beneath; blood, and fire, and vapor of smoke: the sun shall be turned into darkness, and the moon into blood, before that great and notable day of the Lord come: and it shall come to pass, that whosoever shall call on the name of the Lord shall be saved.'

"Ye men of Israel, hear these words: Jesus of Nazareth, a man approved of God among you by miracles, and wonders, and signs, which God did by him in the midst of you, as ye yourselves also know: Him, being delivered by the determinate counsel and foreknowledge of God, ye have taken, and by wicked hands have crucified and slain: whom God hath raised up, having loosed the pains of death: because it was not possible that he should be holden of it. Therefore, being by the right hand of God exalted, and having received of the Father the promise of the Holy Ghost, he hath shed forth this which ye now see and hear."

Now, when they heard this, they were pricked in their heart, and said unto Peter and to the rest of the apostles, Men and brethren, what shall we do? Then Peter said unto them, "Repent, and be baptized every one of you, in the name of Jesus Christ, for the remission of sins, and ye shall receive the gift of the Holy Ghost. For the promise is unto you, and to your children, and to all that are afar off, even as many as the Lord our God shall call." And with many other words did he testify and exhort, saying, Save yourselves from this untoward generation.

Then they that gladly received his word were baptized; and the same day there were added unto them about three thousand souls. And they continued steadfastly in the apostles' doctrine and fellowship, and in breaking of bread, and in prayers. And fear came upon every soul; and many wonders and signs were done by the apostles. And all that believed were together, and had all things common: and sold their possessions and goods, and parted them to all men, as every man had need.

And they, continuing daily with one accord in the temple, and breaking bread from house to house, did eat their meat with gladness and singleness of heart, praising God, and having favor with all the people. And the Lord added to the church daily such as should be saved.

Thus was the new order of supernatural manifestations initiated by the Holy Ghost. The primitive Revival was prolonged and extended until, within a brief period, the mighty accumulation of converts at Jerusalem threatened to preponderate over the sects that had hitherto shared the dominion of that religious metropolis, and alarmed them into desperate and furious persecution. The martyrdom of Stephen was the signal of a general onslaught, in which Saul of Tarsus took a conspicuous if not a leading part. The unresisting flock were dispersed before their enemies like chaff, and thus in the wisdom of Divine Providence, wide regions were at once overspread by a fugitive but witnessing church, and more than ever "mightily grew the word of God, and prevailed:"

"And they were all scattered abroad throughout the regions of Judæa and Samaria, except the apostles. As for Saul, he made havoc of the church, entering into every house, and haling men and women, committed them to prison. Therefore they that were scattered abroad went everywhere preaching the word."

"I verily thought," says Paul in his defence before Agrippa—

"I verily thought with myself, that I ought to do many things contrary to the name of Jesus of Nazareth. Which thing I also did in Jerusalem: and many of the saints did I shut up in prison, having received authority from the chief priests; and when they were put to death, I gave my voice against them. And I punished them oft in every synagogue, and compelled them to blaspheme; and being exceedingly mad against them, I persecuted them even unto strange cities.

"Whereupon as I went to Damascus with authority and commission from the chief priests; at midday, O king, I saw in the way a light from heaven, above the brightness of the sun, shining round about me, and them which journeyed with me. And when we were all fallen to the earth, I heard a voice speaking unto me, and saying in the Hebrew tongue, Saul, Saul, why persecutest thou me? it is hard for thee to kick against the pricks. And I said, 'Who art thou, Lord?' And he said, 'I am Jesus whom thou persecutest. But rise, and stand upon thy feet: for I have appeared unto thee for this purpose, to make thee a minister and a witness both of these things which thou hast seen, and of those things in the which I will appear unto thee; delivering thee from the people and from the Gentiles, unto whom now I send thee, to open their eyes, and to turn them from darkness to light and from the power of Satan unto God, that they may receive forgiveness of sins and inheritance among them which are sanctified by faith that is in me.' "

Speaking before his countrymen, he adds:

"And they that were with me saw the light, and were afraid; but they heard not the voice of him that spake to me. And I said, 'What shall I do, Lord?' And the Lord said unto me, 'Arise, and go into Damascus; and there it shall be told thee of all things which are appointed for thee to do.'

"And when I could not see for the glory of that light, being led by the hand of them that were with me, I came into Damascus. And one Ananias, a devout man according to the law, having a good report of all the Jews which dwelt there, came unto me, and stood, and said unto me, 'Brother Saul, receive thy sight.' And the same hour I looked up upon him. And he said, 'The God of our fathers hath chosen thee, that thou shouldst know his will, and see that Just One, and shouldest hear the voice of his mouth. For thou shalt be his witness unto all men of what thou hast seen and heard. And now why tarriest thou? arise, and be baptized, and wash away thy sins, calling on the name of the Lord.' "

And the following connected particulars are added by Luke:

"And he was three days without sight, and neither did eat nor drink. And there was a certain disciple at Damascus, named Ananias; and to him said the Lord in a vision, 'Ananias.' And he said, 'Behold, I am here, Lord.' And the Lord said unto him, 'Arise, and go into the street which is called Straight, and inquire in the house of Judas for one called Saul, of Tarsus: for, behold, he prayeth, and hath seen in a vision a man named Ananias coming in, and putting his hand on him, that he might receive his sight.' Then Ananias answered, 'Lord, I have heard by many of this man, how much evil he hath done to thy saints at Jerusalem: and here he hath authority from the chief priests to bind all that call on thy name.' But the Lord said unto him, 'Go thy way: for he is a chosen vessel unto me, to bear my name before the Gentiles, and kings, and the children of Israel: for I will shew him how great things he must suffer for my name's sake.' And Ananias went his way, and entered into the house; and putting his hands on him said, 'Brother Saul, the Lord, even Jesus, that appeared unto thee in the way as thou camest, hath sent me, that thou mightest receive thy sight, and be filled with the Holy Ghost.' And immediately there fell from his eyes as it had been scales: and he received sight forthwith, and arose, and was baptized. And when he had received meat, he was strengthened."

From this time forth and by this Apostle, the Gospel was proclaimed and the churches of Christ were planted, confirmed, and established, throughout Asia Minor and the islands and shores of the Mediterranean, embracing the whole world of intellect, letters, arts, commerce, and empire, at that day. No obstruction stayed the triumphant progress of that Gospel, so witnessed and thus delivered to the charge of faithful successors. Repeated and overwhelming persecutions proved but flood-tides that swept it onward to universal dominion. Nothing stayed it, till it reached the fatal eminence of imperial power. Thence to its next great revival, is a dark interval of a thousand years, in which the eye pauses on no resting place.

That the Spirit of God, and He who said to his church, "Lo, I am with you ALWAY," were inactive or inefficient during this millennium of desolation, it were impiety to conceive. Great preparatory processes, commensurate with this great extent of time, though perhaps inscrutable as yet to our philosophy, were doubtless wrought in secret and disguise, under all the dark history of Romanized Europe in the Middle Ages. For out of that mysterious laboratory of the Holy Spirit and Divine Providence, "in the fullness of time," sprang the stupendous spiritual movement of the REFORMATION—not, indeed, of any virtue in the chaotic materials, but by virtue of an indwelling Spirit who, far from having forsaken the Church, had doubtless never for one hour suspended His all-wise and almighty work, though lost to human view, and almost forgotten by man, until the offspring of the wondrous task was ready for the birth.

Darkness covered the earth, and gross darkness the people—deepening as if to endless night. If a star or two appeared, it was only to be quenched apparently in clouds of devastating war. None could see a harbinger or promise of returning day, at the period when the secret work of Providence was ripe, and the morning watch came on unperceived—and GOD said, Let there be light! Then Wicliffe, the morning star of the Reformation, arose before the dawn, in the fourteenth century, clothed in the light of a reöpened BIBLE. Soon after, in the beginning of the fifteenth, John Huss caught the reflection, and added to it the flame of his martyrdom. The revival of letters advanced. Twenty-four universities arose in less than a hundred years. In the midst of this movement, the art of printing was given, imparting an impetus to literature, which had been otherwise inconceivable, and providing the swift and subtle agent by which the infant Reformation was to surprise and overpower its great adversary unawares. At the same juncture the Mohammedan power, overwhelming the Eastern metropolis, swept the remnant of Greek learning into Europe. Finally, in and about the last quarter of the same memorable century, Luther, Zuinglius, Cranmer, Melanchthon, Knox, and Calvin, with other mighty champions of the truth, were born. Little thought the simple mothers what they had in their cradles. But God's time was at hand, and the final preparations for his work were now masked under the form of a few poor men's babes.

O GOD! when thou wentest forth before thy people; when thou didst march through the wilderness; the earth shook, the heavens also dropped, at the presence of GOD! . . . . The LORD gave the word: great was the company of those that published it. In the beginning of the sixteenth century the unlooked-for heralds came, proclaiming free salvation by Christ crucified: first, Lefevre, Farel, Briçonnet, Chatelain, and their friends, in France; then Zuinglius, in Switzerland, and almost at the same moment the giant of the Reformation, MARTIN LUTHER, in Germany—each attended by a host of zealous and able coadjutors, both in church and state—Ecolampadius, Melanchthon, Calvin—preachers, scholars, princes, and nobles: soon Tyndale, with his printed English Testament, in England; Patrick Hamilton, George Wishart, and John Knox, in Scotland; John Taussen, in Denmark; John Laski, in Poland; Olaus Petri and Laurentius, in Sweden, and humbler names without number, in every quarter; all these arose at once, or within little more than a quarter of a century, by the mysterious spirit and providence of God, filled Europe with their doctrine, and triumphantly established the truth of the Gospel in the countries now Protestant, within periods varying from ten to fifty years from the date of this marvellous uprising.

Much, indeed, of what is commonly called the Reformation, belongs to a kingdom that is only of this world. Political power and ambition, political alliance and protection, political means and appliances, were the bane of its spirituality and purity, and while these elements seemed indeed to preserve it from extinction, it is probable that in some cases, as in France, they were also its ruin. The struggle for liberty, beginning in the struggle for divine truth, was long identified with it, and fastened its changing fortunes upon the cause of the gospel. The progress of the kingdom of Christ through this stormy chaos of good and evil, is what all can witness, but none can clearly trace, save the All-wise Being who directs both the operation and the result. Now, however, the confusion is measurably cleared. The vexed elements have gradually settled and separated; the contradiction in nature which severs the heavenly from all earthly kingdoms, begins to be apprehended; and we can contemplate the Reformation proper, in distinction from the mere politico-religious changes attached to it. To contemplate this pure heavenly object, we must seek it in the hearts of God's people. Eminent illustrations of its power and quality will be found in another part of this volume, exhibiting the essence of the Reformation, which history cannot represent. So much of the historical Reformation was the mere creation or rather fiction, of law, that the measure of true religious improvement effected in the Protestantized churches is often left extremely dubious. But here in the inner life whose records are preserved to us, we have a veritable, unambiguous substance. Here is the revived power of the doctrine of the Cross of Christ; here is the secret of a revolution equal, and we may hope more than equal, to that which in a similar length of time (three centuries) had at first broken the power of paganism as that of popery is now broken, and placed Christianity on the throne of the Cæsars. Here is once more a supernatural wonder, an operation of the Holy Ghost, in common language a *revival*, a restoration of life, a spiritual resurrection, of the most amazing and glorious character. Scarcely less sudden and overwhelming than the descent of Pentecost, with the subsequent general spreading of the gospel by Paul, and perhaps hardly inferior to the same in the multitude of its converts and the number and piety of its martyrs, while to all appearance beyond comparison with it in the permanence of its impulse and the magnitude of its immediate fruits—it is identified with the primitive revival in its central principle, Christ crucified, and closely resembles it as a spiritual springtime awakening at the word of God out of the profoundest depth of wintry desolation, but not without a patient sowing of precious seed long previous, and an unconscious softening and preparation of the common heart by Divine Providence. The reforming preachers came to a people long involved in night; but it had been a night of storm and tempest—no stagnant, putrescent, Asiatic calm. The mass of men were strangers to leisure for luxurious vices and corrupt philosophies: their minds were vigorous, simple, and earnest. Neither were they hardened by habit to a disregarded gospel. The excessive wickedness in high places which had almost blotted out the memory of true Christianity, had saved the common people from that most deadly, depraving and indurating form of sin, the disbelief and contempt of revealed truth and a crucified Saviour. The news of such a Saviour once announced, flew like the winds among "a people prepared for the Lord" more perfectly perhaps than we can guess, by the very miseries of their state; and being welcomed with exultation, were cherished with a tenacity which death and torture could not relax.

The great and only apostasy foretold by the apostles having passed, we naturally look for a steady forward movement of the kingdom of Christ from thence; and to this day we are not disappointed. Successive epochs of revival have continued to develop a growing freedom and fullness in the Gospel, as apprehended by its votaries, with enlarged designs and advanced methods of union and effort for the evangelization of mankind. It will be found remarkable, upon a slight examination, that the Gospel was first offered in the simple, concrete form, of adherence to the person of Jesus of Nazareth as the Messiah, leaving the religious exercises and doctrines involved in this act of submission and faith, to be developed progressively in the practice of religion, by the teachings of the

Holy Spirit. The fact of Christ's resurrection, was the single symbol of faith presented to the people by the Jewish apostles on the day of Pentecost. "God hath made that same Jesus whom ye have crucified, both Lord and Christ." In every subsequent demonstration of the Spirit, the person of Christ crucified has been in like manner the centre of faith and attraction, but with some special and explicit disclosure of the mode of salvation by Him, demanded by the times, and leading to important practical enlargement and advance. The great development and elucidation of the mode of salvation, given through the apostle of the Gentiles, was such as to lead naturalizing philosophers who are ignorant of the common source of life in the person of Christ, to suppose that it was nothing less than another gospel, and a doctrinal schism from the church at Jerusalem, of which Paul was the leader! The substance of his teaching was, "that a man is justified by faith [in Christ as his Saviour] *without the works of the law;*" and in this shape the gospel filled the old Roman world. The form in which the same gospel revived at the Reformation, was justification by faith in Christ, not only without the works of the law, but *without the observances of religion—without*, in neither case signifying *in the absence of*, the works or observances referred to, but simply that such works or observances, however obligatory, contribute nothing to the justification of sinners. The old Jewish notion of sacerdotal *mediums* of grace, against which Paul began the contest, had taken and held possession of the church in a modernized form, which the Reformation was (or rather is) to eradicate we trust finally. We come now to a new revival epoch, in which the fact of *regeneration* was to be brought out prominently into the Christian consciousness, in connection with the gift of faith in the Lord Jesus Christ.

Up to the present time, we have little further to say of continental Europe, as touching the direct and marked advance of Christianity. The time is not yet come. Turning to Britain and America, we find one more great period of this kind to examine and understand. Here the Reformation, having been less speedily settled, had time and occasion, through protracted conflict, to develop fully its distinguishing feature, which we have defined as justification by faith, independent of the observances of religion, or in other words, of the church. On the Continent, the Reformation, wherever it was successful, was settled by law, within the lifetime of a single generation at farthest; and therefore stopped very near its starting-point, of justification independent of *the Church of Rome.* The genius of British liberty admitted of no such incomplete and inconsistent conclusion. Although the accession of Elizabeth early terminated the political sway of Rome, yet the conflict with Romish church principles at home, continued, bitter and bloody, down to the period of the Revolution, about a century later. All that period embracing the reigns of Elizabeth, James, and the two Charleses, was marked by seasons of furious persecution, even to the death, of those who claimed an absolute justification in Christ, and openly rejected the intervention of the church as the channel of atonement. Such was the substance of what was called Nonconformity, and such was the substance of the quarrel between it and the established church, notwithstanding that many more superficial questions were often made perhaps unnecessarily prominent as occasions of dispute. The names of Baxter and Bunyan, and the history of the Scottish Covenanters, need only to be mentioned in illustration of the character and sufferings of the true Protestants of this period. Their strength and their importance to the spiritual condition and future of Britain, are illustrated by the fact that no less than two thousand ministers in a then small kingdom, sacrificed their places by refusing to obey the Act of Uniformity under the second Charles. There is reason, however, to believe that the exodus of Nonconformists to America, may yet prove to have been the most important of the many inestimable fruits of that great conflict.

The English church had been "reformed" by act of Parliament under Edward VI., counter-reformed in the same way under Queen Mary, and re-reformed by Queen Elizabeth—the great body of the clergy holding fast their benefices with unscrupulous tenacity throughout these vicissitudes. Nineteen-twentieths of Queen Mary's clergy became Queen Elizabeth's clergy without compunction, and certainly without conversion. The Reformation was not in *them,* assuredly. It is not surprising therefore, that generally speaking both religious knowledge and morals, among people and clergy, remained at the lowest ebb; and that the church, after being purged of the most of its piety and learning by the Act of Uniformity, continued to descend in the moral scale, carrying the people with it, until, after the accession of the House of Hanover, the scandalous condition of the country was perhaps unequalled in Europe. Bishop Burnet says that candidates for ordination were commonly quite unacquainted with the Bible, and unable even to give an account of the statements in the church catechism. When they re-appeared before him to obtain institution to a living, it was still apparent in many that they had not "read the Scriptures nor any other good book since they were ordained." "Of all the ministers of religion he had seen in the course of his extensive travels—Papists, Lutherans, Calvinists, and Dissenters—they were the most remiss in their labors, and the least severe in their lives."

A writer of the time refers to family prayer as "a custom entirely neglected by men of any business or station." Lady Mary Wortley wrote in 1710, that there were "more atheists among the fine ladies than among the loosest sort of rakes." Ignorance and drunkenness, it is stated, were the predominant qualities of the working classes; licentiousness and infidelity of the higher. Montesquieu, who visited England in 1729–31, protested that the English had no religion at all. "If any one," he said, "spoke of it, everybody laughed." Low as religion had sunk in France, he confessed that he himself had not enough of it to satisfy his countrymen; and yet he found that he had too much to suit English society. Of the clergy, even as late as 1781, Cowper could write without fear of contradiction:

> Except *a few* with Eli's spirit blest,
> Hophni and Phineas may describe the rest!*

In the American colonies, although for obvious reasons, these wretched extremes of impiety were not to be looked for, yet from their intimate connection with the mother country, it was but natural that an unprecedented dearth of religion and deterioration of morals should prevail at this time. Such was the condition of the English people, on both sides the Atlantic, on the eve of the Great

* London Quarterly Review, No. cciv., pp. 253–255.

Awakening of the 18th century. "It is time for THEE, Lord, to work: for they have made void Thy law."

It is affecting to review the part which fell to the Evangelical Protestants of Britain, in the 17th century, especially. The commanding political elements of the Reformation lent visible dignity and hope to the Protestant party, in the most worldly eyes, and cheered the natural man with constant exercise and achievement throughout all vicissitudes. All was otherwise after the legal Reformation was settled, and the battle remained to be fought with spiritual weapons alone, in political helplessness, social contempt, and the absence of every support and resource upon which men can naturally depend. Stripped and emptied of everything but Christ, the believers of this time became preëminent in faith and patience, in the midst of overwhelming wickedness. Nor was it given them to see aught with eyes of the great issue of their weak and despised toils. They were sternly tried to the end. Their place in the history of the church was of the first order, their influence was to be momentous, their life and teaching was the seed from which God would raise up the church of Britain and America, which we now see and shall see; and affliction and oppression could neither be withheld nor relaxed, for *them*, until the severely winnowed wheat was all sown of pure *faith*, unmixed with any elements of mere nature which ruin itself could crush out. They sowed in tears, and but for Christ in despair; wasting and diminishing they sowed on, while the seed fell into the ground and died, the wintry autumn grew more desolate and sere, and one by one they closed their eyes on frozen fields of buried grain which seemed to mock the hope of resurrection.

Thus they left it, at the period of unprecedented profanity and lewdness, which we have described as occurring in the first quarter of the eighteenth century. Who could have thought that the springtime was at hand, and the harvesters of God were already preparing to go forth to the greatest ingathering of souls that English eyes had ever seen? The sacred poet, Watts, survived in mellow age, like the apostle John, an unscathed relic of ruthless times that seemed to have respected in spite of themselves the rapt serenity of his life, and left it uninvaded. Philip Doddridge, a younger man, almost a child of that century, was entering a career of popularity and usefulness as a dissenting minister; destined to welcome and promote, though he had no immediate share in originating, the new order of things in religion which was about to arise. Besides these two, we recall no eminent men of God then surviving to link the new revival personally with that period of patience and faithfulness unto death, which had waned to such a cheerless close in the almost undisputed wickedness of the time.

About a quarter of the century had passed away, when a boy at Oxford, Charles Wesley by name, began to be concerned about the conscientious improvement of his time, which had before been lost in idle diversions, and commenced diligently to observe the *method* of study prescribed by the statutes of the University. Others joined him, forming a little society, distinguished by observance of the method of study and of the sacramental observances and means of grace. A thing so extraordinary in that day as serious attention to study and religious worship, even on the part of a handful of boys, could not pass without observation and ridicule, and young Wesley and his friends, from their regard to the method of study, soon went by the slang epithet of "the Methodists." John Wesley, who was five years older than Charles, now four years a serious and devout clergyman of the Church of England, at this time returned to Oxford as a tutor, and joining the little society of "Methodists," became a master-spirit among them. Their earnestness and austerity in religion deepened to a wonderful extent, and exhibited itself in unbounded self-denials, charities, fastings, prayers, and labors, in all which they found no spiritual peace, yet persevered in spite of opposition, defamation, and contempt.

Four or five years had thus passed over the heads of these young devotees, when an indigent student entered as a *servitor*, defraying his college expenses by performing menial offices in the rooms of the wealthier young men in the University. This was George Whitefield, then eighteen years of age, both by nature and grace marked as the greatest beyond comparison of those among whom he moved as a menial. He was strongly attracted towards the Wesleys and their associates, by their earnest religious life, but from the poverty of his station dared not intrude himself upon their notice. But having been named to Charles Wesley by a poor woman whom he had employed on an errand of charity, he was sought out, and introduced to the little brotherhood, of which he became one of the most zealous members. It was among their rules, for example, frequently "to interrogate themselves whether they have been simple and recollected, whether they have prayed with fervor, on Monday, Wednesday, Friday, and Saturday noon; if they have used a collect at nine, twelve, and three o'clock; duly meditated on Sunday, from three to four, on Thomas à Kempis; mused on Wednesday and Friday, from twelve to one, on the Passion," etc. "I now began," says Whitefield, "like them, to live by rule, and to pick up every fragment of my time, that not a moment of it might be lost. Like them, having no weekly sacrament at our college, although the rubric required it, I received it every Sunday at Christ Church. I joined with them in keeping the stations, by fasting Wednesdays and Fridays, and left no means unused which I thought would lead me nearer to Christ. By degrees, I began to leave off eating fruits and such like, and gave the money I usually spent in that way to the poor. Afterwards, I chose the worst sort of food, though my place furnished me with variety. My apparel was mean. I thought it unbecoming a penitent to have his hair powdered. I wore woollen gloves, a patched gown, and dirty shoes. It was now suggested to me that Jesus Christ was among the wild beasts when he was tempted, and that I ought to follow his example; and being willing, as I thought, to imitate Jesus Christ, after supper I went into Christ Church walk, near our college, and continued in silent prayer nearly two hours, sometimes lying on my face, sometimes kneeling upon my knees. The night being stormy, gave me awful thoughts of the day of judgment. The next day, I repeated the same exercise at the same place. After this, the holy season of Lent came on, which our friends kept very strictly, eating no flesh during the six weeks, except on Saturdays and Sundays. I abstained frequently on Saturdays also, and ate nothing on the other days (except Sunday) but sage tea without sugar, and coarse bread. I constantly walked out in the cold mornings till one part of my hands was quite black."

This truly Romish course of penance and austerity finally exhausted nature, and threw him into an alarming illness which lasted seven weeks. This sickness Whitefield calls, in his journal, "a glorious visitation." The constant brotherly attentions of his fellow-ascetics, the Wesleys, with their maxims and citations, were ineffectual now, to comfort or direct his mind. His course of externals, with the energy of the natural man which had much to do in prompting and sustaining it, was effectually broken up, and his thoughts communed with his own heart and the word of God. He spent much of his time in reading the Greek Testament, and in prayer. He gained more clear, truthful, and affecting views of his own sinfulness, and saw how hopeless was the effort to remove a sense of guilt by religious observances. "One day," he informs us, "perceiving an uncommon drought and noisome clamminess in my mouth, and using things to allay my thirst but in vain, it was suggested to me that when Jesus Christ cried out '*I thirst*,' his sufferings were near over. Upon this I threw myself on the bed, and cried out, *I thirst, I thirst!* Soon after, I perceived my load to go off; a spirit of mourning was taken from me, and I knew what it was truly to rejoice in the Lord." "When I said those words, *I thirst, I thirst*, my soul was in an agony; I thirsted for a clear discovery of my pardon through Jesus Christ, and the seal of the Spirit. I was at the same time enabled to look up with faith to the glorious Lord Jesus as dying for sinners, and for some time I could not avoid singing psalms wherever I was."

Whitefield was now, like the apostle whose life his own most resembles, ready for action. Though strongly restrained by a humble diffidence, his scruples were providentially overcome, and he was speedily ordained and commenced his career as an Evangelist, at the age of twenty-one. "The discovery of a complete and gratuitous salvation filled with ecstasy a spirit prepared to appreciate it, and, from their great, deep breaking, his affections thenceforward flowed, impetuous and uninterrupted, in the one channel of love to the Saviour. He traversed England, Scotland, and Ireland, for four and thirty years, and crossed the Atlantic thirteen times, proclaiming the love of God and his great gift to man. A bright and exulting view of the atonement's sufficiency was his theology; delight in God and rejoicing in

Christ Jesus were his piety ; and a compassionate solicitude for the souls of men was his ruling passion." Delivered like Paul from the sorest bondage of the law, he became like him, in an eminent sense, Christ's freeman ; he loved all who loved his Saviour, with an equal affection ; and his expanded spirit, incapable of a narrow conception, added another beautiful parallel to the earnestness with which Paul trampled upon every thought of a party for himself, "sent not to baptize but to preach the Gospel," and thankfully washing his hands of any possible imputation of that leadership which lesser good men supposed it important to secure.

The conversion of the Wesleys was deferred till after a longer, if perhaps less acute, experience of the law. "I was convinced more than ever," says John Wesley, "of the exceeding height and breadth and depth of the law of God. The light flowed in so mightily upon my soul that everything appeared in a new view. I cried to God for help, and resolved not to prolong the time of obeying him, as I had never done before. And by my continued endeavor to keep his whole law, inward and outward, to the best of my power, I was persuaded that I should be accepted of him, and that I was even then in a state of salvation." In 1735, he went to Georgia as a missionary to the Indians, where he "spent his whole time in works of piety and mercy, and distributed his income so profusely in charity that for many months together he had not one shilling in the house. In the prosecution of his work he exposed himself to every change of season, frequently slept on the ground under the dews of night in summer, and in winter with his hair and clothes frozen to the earth. On his homeward voyage, the language of his still restless heart was : 'I went to America to convert the Indians ; but, oh ! who shall convert me ? Who is he that will deliver me from this evil heart of unbelief ? I have a fair summer religion ; I can talk well ; nay, I believe myself safe, while no danger is present ; but let death look me in the face, and my spirit is troubled ; nor can I say, To die is gain.' A few days after his arrival in London, he met with Peter Böhler, a minister of the Moravian Church, 'by whom,' he says, 'in the hand of the great God, I was clearly convinced of unbelief, of the want of that faith whereby alone we are saved with the full Christian salvation,' and 'who amazed me more and more, by the accounts he gave of the fruits of living faith, and the holiness and happiness which he affirmed to attend it.' On the 24th of May, 1738, Wesley emerged out of his darkness into marvellous light, and experienced for the first time the full liberty of the sons of God. 'In the evening,' he says, 'I went, very unwillingly, to a society in Aldersgate street, where one was reading Luther's Preface to the Epistle to the Romans. About a quarter before nine, while he was describing the change which God works in the heart through faith in Christ, I felt my heart strangely warmed. I felt I did trust in Christ, Christ alone for salvation; and an assurance was given me that he had taken away my sins—even mine—and saved me from the law of sin and death.'"

"His brother Charles was also made partaker of the same grace. They had passed together through the briers and thorns, through the perplexities and shadows, of the legal wilderness, and the hour of their deliverance was not far separated. Böhler visited Charles in his sickness at Oxford; but the 'Pharisee within' was somewhat offended when the honest German shook his head at learning that his hope of salvation rested upon 'his best endeavors.' After his recovery, the reading of Haliburton's Life produced in him a sense of his want of that faith which brings peace and joy in the Holy Ghost. Böhler visited him again in London; and he began seriously to consider the doctrine which he urged upon him. Luther on the Galatians then fell into his hands; and on reading the preface he observes, 'I marvelled that we were so soon removed from him that called us into the grace of Christ, unto another gospel. Who would believe that our church had been founded on this important article of justification by faith alone?'

"On Whitsunday, May 21st, Charles Wesley awoke in hope and expectation of soon obtaining the object of his wishes, the knowledge of God reconciled in Christ Jesus. In reading various portions of Scripture on that day, he was enabled to view Christ as set forth to be a propitiation for his sins through faith in his blood; and he received that peace and rest in God which he so earnestly sought."

Nor were these three the only Apostles whom God raised up from the little circle of "methodical" devotees at Oxford. There were Ingham, and Broughton, and Habersham afterwards of

Georgia, among them, with others who afterwards became useful in the great work, according as the Lord gave to every one. Romaine was at Oxford then, but avoided and despised them for their "singularity." Benjamin Ingham filled an important part, both directly and indirectly, leading to the conversion of one of the most efficient laborers in this period, the celebrated Countess of Huntington. Full of ardent zeal, he accompanied the Wesleys to Georgia, and with them returned to proclaim the new-found gospel in his native country of Yorkshire, where he preached "with marvelous power," and was speedily shut out from the pulpits of the Establishment by ecclesiastical censure. Lady Margaret Hastings heard of his fame and invited him to Ledstone Hall, where his good news were joyfully received. She was a sister of the Earl of Huntington, whose gifted lady was among the many whose hearts the Lord had touched in secret and awakened to the claims of his holy law, before there were any to direct them to the Saviour. Lady Huntington's heart had been thus touched from early childhood, and at the very time when the Oxford "Methodists" were groping anxiously in their cloister for righteousness by the works of the law and the church, she, a young bride in the midst of the splendors and excitements of the highest society, was striving in a similar manner after the same thing, with prayers, fastings, charities, and scrupulous devotion to every duty and ordinance. When her sister, Lady Margaret, unfolded her new religious experience, and said "Since I have known and believed in the Lord Jesus Christ for salvation, I have been as happy as an angel," Lady Huntington was astonished and alarmed. She knew nothing of such peace, although she supposed that she had neglected nothing that could tend to holiness and the satisfaction of the conscience. She fell under keener conviction of sin, and the intense conflict that ensued in her soul was the occasion of severe illness, which superadded the terrors of death to the alarm of a guilty conscience, and broke down her spirit in helpless despair at the feet of Jesus. "Then it was that the words of Lady Margaret came laden with wonderful meaning. 'I too will wholly cast myself on Jesus Christ for life and salvation,' was her last refuge; and from her bed she lifted up her heart to God for pardon and mercy through the blood of his Son. With streaming eyes she cast herself on her Saviour : 'Lord, I believe ; help thou mine unbelief.' Immediately the scales fell from her eyes ; doubt and distress vanished ; joy and peace filled her bosom. With appropriating faith, she exclaimed, 'My Lord, and my God!' From that moment her disease took a a favorable turn ; she was restored to health, and what was better, to newness of life. On her recovery, she sent for John and Charles Wesley, then in London, and also newly converted to a lively faith, to come and visit her, expressing a warm interest in their labors, and bidding them God speed in the great and glorious work of urging men to repentance and to heaven. This was in the year 1739, and Lady Huntington was at the age of thirty-two." The character of her life thenceforward is epitomized in the following energetic passage from one of her letters to Doddridge.

"I hope you will never care about the ceremony of time in your letters to me, but just when attended with greatest ease to yourself, for we both agree that the one thing worth living for must be, proclaiming the love of God to man in Christ Jesus. As for me, I want no holiness he does not give me ; I can wish for no liberty but what he likes for me, and I am satisfied with every misery he does not redeem me from, that in all things I may feel, 'without him I can do nothing.'"

Lady Huntington appears to have been the leading lay instrumentality in the great religious movement of her day. She devoted her life and fortune to the gospel, with the zeal and singleness of an apostle. Her high station, adorned by a consistency and fidelity which never quailed before the scoff or the malice of a dissolute aristocracy, became incalculably influential in promoting the spread of truth. Her prayer-meetings among ladies of her own rank ; her fortitude in braving their scorn by personal expostulation ; her mansion thrown open for a preaching-station to the despised "Methodists ;" her powerful staff of chaplains, with some of whom, accompanied by her family and friends, she made repeated and extended tours of evangelism in destitute or darkened regions—usually taking her summer recreation, or travelling for health, in this way ; in her widowhood, her retrenchment of the expenses deemed indispensable to the dignity of her station, in order to meet the demands of an insatiable liberality in the support of the gospel; the numerous chapels built, and preachers supported by her own means, in different parts of the country; a prosperous college established and supported for the training of godly ministers; her prompt secession from the Church of England, when forced to choose between this painful step and the silencing of certain of her chaplains, who then preached in no less than sixty-seven chapels of "Lady Huntington's connection;" these and many other works of which we can give no impression here, prolonged to the very end of nature in her eighty-fourth year, and crowned with humble renunciation of herself and all her works, are among the deathless traits of her ever-glorious and solitary example.

The rising work of grace was early signalized by the conversion of desperate reprobates who were seized in the very van of the audacious ungodliness of the day, and carried over in triumph by the mighty power of God, to a stand of like prominence on the side of holiness and the gospel. Of such was the celebrated Colonel Gardiner, whose astonishing conversion and reformation, from ten to fifteen years before the date of those just recounted, will be found in another part of this volume. Like wonders fitly accompanied this work of omnipotence in its progress through an age chiefly distinguished by gross impiety. The scoffing Walpole wrote truly, "the Methodists love your great sinners, and truly they make an abundant harvest." The *regenerating* power of a living faith in Christ, wrought by the Holy Spirit, appropriately came out in a glorious prominence in such an age, both in the miracles of the Spirit and in the preaching of His witnesses. Whitefield says of his preaching: "the doctrine of the new birth made its way like lightning into the hearers' consciences." This doctrine had become very generally lost to the Christian consciousness itself, both in Old and New England, and was now commonly treated by the religious classes as a wild and dangerous vagary of enthusiasm. Even in New England, it was scarcely recognized as a condition of church membership. The work of the time was therefore to give it a practical demonstration, and a root in the heart of the church, which could never be shaken.

At the very moment when these mighty instruments of the Spirit were being forged in the fires of conviction and tempered by the baptism of the Holy Ghost, in England, a "surprising work of God" was witnessed in the then colony of Massachusetts, under the leading instrumentality of President Edwards. "The Great Awakening," as it has been commonly designated, doubtless the most important event in American history, both in its spiritual and temporal consequences, first appeared in power at Northampton, about 1735. Upwards of a year of growing seriousness, heightened by a succession of solemn events in the little community, had passed; "and then it was," continues President Edwards, "in the latter part of December (1734), that the Spirit of God began extraordinarily to set in, and wonderfully to work among us; and there were, very suddenly, one after another, five or six persons who were, to all appearance, savingly converted, and some of them wrought upon in a very remarkable manner.

"Presently upon this a great and earnest concern about the great things of religion and the eternal world became universal in all parts of the town, and among persons of all degrees and all ages; the noise among the dry bones waxed louder and louder; all other talk but about spiritual and eternal things was soon thrown by; all the conversation in all companies, and upon all occasions, was upon these things only, unless so much as was necessary for people carrying on their ordinary secular business. Other discourse than of the things of religion would scarcely be tolerated in any company. Religion was with all classes the great concern, and the world was a thing only by the by. The only thing in their view was to get the kingdom of heaven, and every one appeared pressing into it: the engagedness of their hearts in this great concern could not be hid; it appeared in their very countenances. There was scarcely a single person in the town, either old or young, that was left unconcerned about the great things of the eternal world. Those that were wont to be the vainest and loosest, and those that had been most disposed to think and speak slightly of vital and experimental religion, were now generally subject to great awakenings. And the work of conversion was carried on in a most astonishing manner, and increased more and more; souls did, as it were, come by flocks to Jesus Christ.

"This work of God, as it was carried on, and the number of true saints multiplied, soon made a glorious alteration in the town; so that in the spring and summer following, anno 1735, the town seemed to be full of the presence of God: it never was so full of love, nor so full of joy, and yet so full of distress as it was then. There were remarkable tokens of God's presence in almost every house; parents rejoicing over their children as new born, and husbands over their wives, and wives over their husbands. In all companies, on whatever occasions persons met together, Christ was to be heard of and seen in the midst of them. And even at weddings, which formerly were occasions of mirth and jollity, there was now no discourse of anything but the things of religion, and no appearance of any but spiritual mirth.

"So far as I, by looking back, can judge, this work appears to me to have been at the rate at least of four persons in a day, or near thirty in a week, take one with another, for five or six weeks together. If I may be allowed to declare anything that appears to me probable in a thing of this nature, I hope that more than three hundred souls were savingly brought home to Christ in this town, in the space of half a year (how many more I don't guess), and about the same number of males as females.

"In the month of March the people in South Hadley began to be seized with deep concern about the things of religion, which very soon became universal; and the work of God has been very wonderful there, not much, if anything, short of what it has been here, in proportion to the size of the place. About the same time it began to break forth in the west part of Suffield (where it has also been very great), and it soon spread into all parts of the town. It next appeared at Sunderland, and soon overspread the town; and I believe was for a season not less remarkable than it was here. About the same time it began to appear in a part of Deerfield, called Green River, and afterwards filled the town, and there has been a glorious work there: it began also to be manifest in the south part of Hatfield, in a place called the Hill, and after that the whole town, in the second week in April, seemed to be seized, as it were at once, with concern about the things of religion; and the work of God has been great there. There has been also a very general awakening at

West-Springfield and Long Meadow; the same in Enfield, Springfield, Westfield, Hadley, Northfield, and a large number of the towns of Connecticut.

"But this shower of Divine blessing has been yet more extensive: there was no small degree of it in some parts of New Jersey; especially the Rev. Mr. William Tennent, a minister, who seemed to have such things much at heart, told me of a very great awakening of many in a place called the Mountains, under the ministry of one Mr. Cross; and of a very considerable revival of religion in another place, under the ministry of his brother, the Rev. Mr. Gilbert Tennent; and also at another place, under the ministry of a very pious young gentleman, a Reformed Dutch minister, whose name was Frelinghuysen."

We have already seen that while the Awakening was breaking out in Northampton, Whitefield was entering on his wonderful career in the mother country. He preached his first sermon in 1736, and drove fifteen of his hearers mad, according to the account reported to the bishops, by the scandalized and astonished observers. "In preaching that men of all ages and conditions must be 'born again' or never 'see the kingdom of heaven,' though there were some in the land who believed it, he found himself practically alone, going forth as the herald of a doctrine which the public agreed to consider as new." Critics of a later day have discovered, to their astonishment, that the sermons which then turned the world upside down, were composed of but common thoughts, simply expressed, even to tameness. But it has been well retorted, What has made those thoughts common? They were not common when he began to utter them, but astonishing, especially in England, and to a considerable extent in this country also. The effect which God wrought by them, through the consecrated genius of this wonderful orator, was certainly tremendous, both immediately and remotely. Whitefield was an organ for the truth, expressly fitted to this day and to his own country, where his great work was performed. The means and circumstances of the revival differed noticeably and not unaccountably, in the old country, with its dissolute Establishment, its gay and voluptuous aristocracy, and its ignorant common people, from those of the same work among the sober, educated, and self-governing people of New England. For the former, popular eloquence seemed an indispensable means of grace, which in the latter have been much less in request, and have been attended with much less beneficial results. The same difference is observable in a remarkable instance at the present day.

Whitefield's first sermon was preached in his native parish at Gloucester, in his twenty-second year. He then went to London, where the success of the "boy preacher," as he was called, was instantaneous, and unprecedented among persons of all ranks. In many of the city churches he proclaimed the glad tidings of great joy to multitudes, who were powerfully affected. Lord and Lady Huntington constantly attended wherever he preached, and Lady Anne Frankland became one of the first fruits of his ministry, among the nobility of the metropolis. While at London, such multitudes assembled that it was necessary to place constables at the doors, both within and without, and on Sunday mornings in the latter months of the year, long before day, you might have seen the streets filled with people going to hear him, with lanterns in their hands.

Leaving London in about two months, he went down to labor for a friend, among a poor and illiterate people in Hampshire, where he was reached by a missionary call from the Wesleys, in Georgia, which he enthusiastically accepted. While preparing for his departure, and taking leave of his friends in Bristol, Bath, and other places, he continued to preach with increasing power and fame.

In Bristol, where he preached five times a week, "It was wonderful," he says, "to see how the people hung upon the rails of the organ loft, climbed upon the leads of the church, and made the church itself so hot with their breath, that the steam would fall from the pillars like drops of rain. Sometimes almost as many would go away for want of room as came in, and it was with great difficulty I got into the desk to read prayers or preach. Persons of all ranks gave me private invitations to their houses, and many made me large offers if I would not go abroad." When he came to London, those who had heard him before compelled him to preach almost incessantly. He preached nine times a week, and thousands went away from the largest churches, unable to gain admittance.

Whitefield had undoubtedly a dramatic genius of the most extraordinary power, but disclosed and called into play by nothing less than the glorious gospel of the blessed God. "He had a voice of rich compass, which could equally thrill over Moorfields in musical thunder, or whisper its secret in every private ear; and to this tuneful voice he added a most expressive and eloquent action. Improved by conscientious practice, and instinct with his earnest nature, this elocution was the acted sermon, and by its pantomimic portrait enabled the eye to anticipate each rapid utterance, and helped the memory to treasure up the palpable ideas. . . . His thoughts were possessions, and his feelings were transformations; and if he spoke because he felt, his hearers understood because they saw. They were not only enthusiastic amateurs, like Garrick, who ran to weep and tremble at his bursts of passion, but even the colder critics of the Walpole school were surprised into momentary sympathy and reluctant wonder. Lord Chesterfield was listening in Lady Huntingdon's pew when Whitefield was comparing the benighted sinner to a blind beggar on a dangerous road. The beggar's little dog gets away from him when skirting the edge of a precipice, and he is left to explore the path with his iron-shod staff. On the very verge of the cliff this blind guide (the staff) slips through his fingers and skims away down the abyss. All unconscious, its owner stoops down to regain it, and stumbling forward—'Good Good! he is gone!' shouted Chesterfield, who had been watching with breathless alarm the blind man's movements, and who jumped from his seat to save the catastrophe. But the glory of Whitefield's preaching was its heart-kindled and heart-melting gospel. But for this all his bold strokes and brilliant surprises might have been no better than the rhetorical triumphs of Kirwan and other pulpit dramatists. He was an orator, but he only sought to be an evangelist." Hear him entreat:

"I beseech you, in love and compassion, to come to Jesus. Indeed, all I say is in love to your souls. And if I could be but an instrument of bringing you to Jesus, I should not envy, but rejoice in your happiness, however much you were exalted. If I was to make up the *last* of the train of the companions of the blessed Jesus, it would rejoice me to see you above me in glory. I could willingly go to prison or to death for you, so I could but bring one soul from the devil's strongholds, into the salvation which is by Christ Jesus. Come then to Christ, every one that hears me this night. Come, come, my guilty brethren; I beseech you, for your immortal soul's sake, come to Christ. Methinks I could speak till midnight unto you. Would you have me go and tell my Master that you will not come, and that I have spent my strength in vain? I cannot bear to carry such a message to him. I would not, indeed, I would not be a swift witness against you at the great day of account; but if you will refuse these gracious invitations, I must do it."

In this spirit, not very prevalent even now, Whitefield began his ministry. On his return from Georgia, 1739, "the clergy had begun to perceive that either his doctrine or theirs, concerning the new birth and the way of a sinner's justification before God, must fall. The bishops received him coldly. In two days, the use of five churches was denied him. Pamphlets were published against his sermon on regeneration, and sermons were preached against him, his doctrines, and his proceedings. But he was busy in attending prayer-meetings and preaching in the few churches that were still open, and awakenings and conversions multiplied. At Bristol he had the use of the churches at first, but in a short time all were closed against him. Already at London, seeing the crowds around the doors and windows, unable to hear, he had thought of preaching to them in the open air; but both he and his friends hesitated and prayed before taking so bold a step. While at Bristol, he made the attempt. The colliers in the vicinity were numerous, rude, and ignorant. When provoked, they were the terror of the city; and at all times it was thought dangerous to go among them. Whitefield went one day to Hannam Mount, and preached to about a hundred of them. The news spread rapidly among the colliers, and his audience soon increased to twenty thousand. The gospel was indeed 'good *news*' to them, for they had never heard preaching before. Having no righteousness of their own to renounce, they were glad to hear of a Jesus who was a friend to publicans, and who came not to call the righteous, but sinners, to repentance. The first discovery of their being affected was, to see the white gutters made by their tears, which plentifully fell down their black cheeks, as they came out of their coal-pits. Hundreds and hundreds of them were soon brought under deep convictions, which, as the event proved, happily ended in sound and thorough conversion. At this time he made two excursions into Wales, where a revival of religion had commenced several years before, under the ministry of the Rev. Griffith Jones, and was now carried on by the ministry of Mr. Howel Harris, a man of strong mental powers, great Christian zeal, and considerable learning.

"Intent on the advancement of his orphan-house in Georgia, Whitefield soon went to London, passing on his way through Oxford. At both places he found opposition, and in London was shut out of the churches. He preached to thousands in Islington churchyard, and now resolved to give himself to the work in the open air. The spots on which Whitefield now began, in his own language, 'to take the field,' and publicly to erect the standard of the Redeemer's cross, are well known. Moorfields, then a place of general rendezvous and recreation from the crowded city, Kennington Common then about two, and Blackheath about five miles from London, were the favorite sites to which he loved to resort, and 'open his mouth boldly' to listening thousands, in honor of his crucified and glorified Lord. Recording his first engagement of this kind in his diary of Sabbath evening, April 29, 1739, he writes, 'Begun to be yet more vile this day, for I preached at Moorfields to an exceeding great multitude; and at five in the evening went and preached at Kennington Common, where upwards of twenty thousand were supposed to be present.' For several successive months these places were his chief scenes of action. At a moderate computation, the audience frequently consisted of twenty thousand. It is said that the singing could be heard two miles, and the voice of the preacher nearly one."

"While one day preaching on Blackheath, there passed along the road t some distance, an old man and 'Mary' his wife, with their ass and his oaded panniers, returning from London to their home in Kent. Atracted alike by the crowd and the preacher's voice, the old man and his rife turned a little out of their way to hear 'what the man was talking bout.' Whitefield spoke of somewhat which occurred eighteen hundred ears ago, and the old man said, 'Mary, come along, it is only something hich happened a long while ago;' but Mary's attention had been rrested, and she wished to stay a minute or two longer. They were oth soon in tears, and the inquiry was excited in their hearts, 'What iall we do to be saved?' On their way home, the old man recollected s neglected Bible, and asked, 'Why, Mary, does not our old book at me say somewhat about these things?' They went home, and examined the old book with new light. 'Why, Mary,' asked the old man, 'is this indeed our old book? why, everything in it seems quite new.' So true is it, that the teaching of the Spirit gives new discernment as to the truths of divine revelation."

"A fact illustrating the children's love to the evangelist may be here mentioned. In his open-air preachings, especially in and about London, he was usually attended by many of them, who sat round him, in and about the pulpit, and handed to him the notes of those who desired his counsels and prayers. These children were exposed to the missiles with which he was often assailed, but however terrified they might be, or even hurt, they seldom shrunk; 'but,' says he, 'on the contrary, every time I was struck, they turned up their little weeping eyes, and seemed to wish they could receive the blows for me.'"

At his first preaching in Moorfields, Gillies says:

"The thing being strange and new, he found, on coming out of the coach, an incredible number of people assembled. Many told him that he would never come out of that place alive. He went in, however, between two friends, who by the pressure of the crowd were soon parted from him entirely, and obliged to leave him to the mercy of the rabble. But these, instead of hurting him, formed a lane for him, and carried him along to the middle of the fields, where a table had been placed. This, however, having been broken by the crowd, he mounted a wall, and preached to an exceeding great multitude in tones so melting, that his words drew tears and groans from the most abandoned of his hearers. Thirty thousand people sometimes gathered together to hear him."

A cheaply constructed tabernacle was eventually run up for him in Moorfields, and of the close of one day's preaching he records:

"We then retired to the Tabernacle, with my pockets full of notes from persons brought under concern, and read them amidst the praises and spiritual acclamations of thousands, who joined with the holy angels in rejoicing that so many sinners were snatched, in such an unexpected, unlikely place and manner, out of the very jaws of the devil. *Three hundred and fifty awakened souls were received in one day;* and I believe the number of notes exceeded a thousand."

Scarcely had Whitefield completed the tabernacle, when he was earnestly solicited to hold public services at the west end of the city, and Long-Acre chapel, then under the charge of a dissenter, was offered for his use.

"An unruly rabble there endeavored to drive the preacher from his post; but a running fire of brickbats, broken glass, bells, drums, and clappers, neither annoyed nor frightened the intrepid evangelist; nor did an interference on the part of the hierarchy, which followed soon after, prohibiting his preaching in an incorporated (dissenting) chapel. 'I hope you will not look on it as contumacy,' said Whitefield to the bishop, 'if I persist in prosecuting my design until I am more particularly apprised wherein I have erred. I trust the irregularity I am charged with will appear justifiable to every lover of English liberty, and, what is all to me, be approved at the awful and impartial tribunal of the great Bishop and Shepherd of souls.' Writing to Lady Huntingdon, he says, 'My greatest distress is so to act as to avoid rashness on the one hand and timidity on the other;' and this shows, what indeed was proved in his whole life, an entire absence of that malignant element of fanaticism which courts opposition and revels in it."

"Determined not to be beaten from his ground, yet hoping to escape some of its annoyances, Whitefield resolved to build a chapel of his own. Hence arose Tottenham Court-road chapel, which went by the name of 'Whitefield's Soul-trap.' 'I pray,' said he, 'the Friend of sinners to make it a soul-trap indeed to many wandering creatures. My constant work is preaching fifteen times a week. Conviction and conversion go on here, for God hath met us in our new building.' It was completed and dedicated in November, 1756, and within two years of its opening, not only did the congregation build a parsonage-house for their minister, but twelve almshouses for as many poor widows."

"About this time Joseph Periam, a young man in London, who had read his sermon on 'regeneration,' became deeply impressed by it; he sold all he possessed, and prayed so loud and fasted so long, that his family supposed him deranged, and sent him to the Bedlam madhouse, where he was treated as 'methodistically mad,' and as 'one of Whitefield's gang.' The keepers threw him down, and forced a key into his mouth, while they drenched him with medicine. He was then placed in a cold room without windows, and with a damp cellar under it. Periam, however, found some means of conveying a letter to Whitefield, requesting both advice and a visit. These were promptly given. The preacher soon discovered that Periam was not mad; and taking a Mr. Seward and some other friends with him, he went before the committee of the hospital to explain the case. Seward so astounded the committee by quoting Scripture, that they pronounced him to be as mad as Periam. The doctors frankly told the deputation that, in their opinion, Whitefield and his followers were 'really beside themselves.' It was, however, agreed, that if Whitefield would take Periam out to Georgia, his release would be granted. Thus the conference ended, and the young man went out as a schoolmaster at the Orphan-house, where he was exemplary and useful."

The dignitaries of the Church (to return) now took the field against him. The Bishop of London published a pastoral letter aimed against "enthusiasm," by which was intended the doctrines of regeneration, and justification by faith, without the works of the law or the Church either as a ground or a condition precedent; which Whitefield defended in a reply.

"The ideas of Whitefield and his opponents were now fairly drawn out and embattled against each other, and it was to be decided, whether a truly spiritual religion should be allowed to subsist in the Church of England. On these vital points of doctrinal and practical religion, Whitefield found sympathy among the Dissenters. He had some pleasing interviews with Watts, Doddridge, and other leading Congregationalists; but, as he preferred to labor in the Church to which he belonged, and as they were afraid that his enthusiasm and irregularities would work mischief in the end, there was no public coöperation between them. Watts cautioned him against giving heed to 'impressions,' supposed, but not proved, to be from the Holy Spirit; warned him of the danger of delusion and imprudence, and gave him credit for sincerity and zeal, but doubted his 'extraordinary call to some parts of his conduct.' Doddridge called him a very honest man, but weak, and 'a little intoxicated with popularity.' [At a later day however, these excellent men obtained very different impressions, and became warm friends of the revivalist and the revival.] Whitefield in these controversies and labors, was executing no plan of his own, but simply doing the duty which the circumstances of each day demanded. He had come to England, to receive priest's orders, and collect money for his orphan-house. An embargo, caused by the commencement of a war with Spain, unexpectedly detained him, and he was neither willing nor permitted to be idle. He preached to a few hearers in a private room, or to thirty thousand on Kennington Common: attended a little prayer-meeting, gave advice to an anxious sinner, heard good advice from Watts and Doddridge, or engaged in controversy with the Bishop of London, just as one occasion after another called him to do. And now, the embargo being raised, and the care of the colliers and some other affairs being transferred to Wesley, whom he had induced to commence field-preaching, this pastor of a little parish in Georgia embarked, August 14, 1739, for Philadelphia, on his return to the people of his charge."

Nearly simultaneous with the conversion of the Wesleys, occurred that of David Brainerd—an event of recognized importance, particularly in its relation to the missionary movement which was to become such a leading and vital element of the religious activity of the period now inaugurated, and which already manifested itself with singular energy in the earliest impulses of the young Oxford apostles. The Indians were then the prominent objects of the missionary spirit, which, descending to a later generation, has expanded, in less than a century, to the compass of the globe. The experience of David Brainerd is a beautiful parallel to that of President Edwards (inserted in another place), as will be seen from the following narrative, and might be still more noticeably illustrated if we had room for a more extended quotation:

"After a considerable time spent in similar exercises and distress, one morning, while I was walking in a solitary place, as usual, I at once saw that all my contrivances and projects to effect or procure deliverance and salvation for myself were utterly in vain; I was brought quite to a stand, as finding myself totally lost. I had thought many times before, that the difficulties in my way were very great; but now I saw, in another and very different light, that it was forever impossible for me to do anything toward helping or delivering myself. I then thought of blaming myself, that I had not done more, and been more engaged while I had opportunity—for it seemed now as if the season for doing was for ever over and gone—but I instantly saw, that let me have done what I would, it would no more have tended to my helping myself, than what I had done; that I had made all the pleas I ever could have made to all eternity; and that all my pleas were vain. The tumult that had been before in my mind was now quieted, and I was somewhat eased of that distress which I felt while struggling against a sight of myself, and of the divine sovereignty. I had the greatest certainty that my state was forever miserable, for all that I could do, and wondered that I had never been sensible of it before.

"I continued, as I remember, in this state of mind from Friday morning till the Sabbath evening following (July 12, 1739), when I was walking again in the same solitary place where I was brought to see myself lost and helpless, as before mentioned. Here, in a mournful, melancholy state, I was attempting to pray; but found no heart to engage in prayer or any other duty. My former concern, exercise, and religious affections were now gone. I thought that the Spirit of God had quite left me; but still was not distressed, yet disconsolate, as if there was nothing in heaven or earth could make me happy. Having been thus endeavoring to pray—though, as I thought, very stupid and senseless—for near half an hour; then, as I was walking in a dark, thick grove, *unspeakable glory* seemed to open to the view and apprehension of my soul. I do not mean any *external* brightness, for I saw no such thing; nor do I intend any imagination of a body of light, somewhere in the third heavens, or anything of that nature; but it was a new inward apprehension or view that I had of God, such as I never had before, nor anything which had the least resemblance of it. I stood still, wondered, and admired! I knew that I never had seen before anything comparable to it for excellency and beauty; it was widely different from all the conceptions that ever I had of God, or things divine. My soul rejoiced with joy unspeakable, to see such a God, such a glorious divine Being; and I was inwardly pleased and satisfied, that he should be God over all for ever and ever. My soul was so captivated and delighted with the excellency, loveliness, greatness, and other perfections of God, that I was even swallowed up in him; at least to that degree that I had no thought as I remember, at first, about my own salvation, and scarce reflected, that there was such a creature as myself.

"Thus God, I trust, brought me to a hearty disposition to *exalt him*, and set him on the throne, and principally and ultimately to aim at his honor and glory, as King of the universe. I continued in this state of inward joy, peace and astonishment, till near dark, without any sensible abatement, and then began to think and examine what I had seen, and felt sweetly composed in my mind all the evening following. I felt myself in a new world, and everything about me appeared with a different aspect from what it was wont to do.

"At this time the *way of salvation* opened to me with such infinite wisdom, suitableness, and excellency, that I wondered I should ever think of any other way of salvation; I was amazed that I had not dropped my own contrivances, and complied with this lovely, blessed, and excellent way before. If I could have been saved by my own duties, or any other way that I had formerly contrived, my whole soul would now have refused. I wondered that all the world did not see and comply with this way of salvation, entirely by the *righteousness of Christ*."

Three or four years later, we find Brainerd engaged in his heavenly mission of mercy to the poor heathen of the forest in New Jersey. On his removal to Crossweeksung, in New Jersey (1745), his labors were visited with an outpouring of grace so marvellously divine as justly to be included among the great manifestations of the time we are now dwelling on. His preaching appears, especially at this time, to have been much imbued with the tender and winning elements of the gospel. His text, on the 6th of August, 1745, preaching to about forty Indians who could understand him, was, "Herein is love."

"They seemed eager of hearing; but there appeared nothing very remarkable, except their attention, till near the close of my discourse; and then Divine truth was attended with a surprising influence, and produced a great concern among them. There were scarcely *three* in *forty* who could refrain from tears and bitter cries. They all as one seemed in an agony of soul to obtain an interest in Christ; and the more I discoursed of the love and compassion of God in sending His Son to suffer for the sins of men; and the more I invited them to come and partake of his love, the more their distress was aggravated, because they felt themselves unable to come. It was surprising to see how their hearts seemed to be pierced with the tender and melting invitations of the gospel, when there was not a word of terror spoken to them.

"There were this day two persons who obtained relief and comfort; which, when I came to discourse with them particularly, appeared solid, rational, and scriptural. After I had inquired into the grounds of their comfort, and said many things which I thought proper to them, I asked them what they wanted that God should do farther for them. They replied, 'they wanted Christ should wipe their hearts quite clean,' etc.

"*Aug.* 8. There were now six in all, who had got some relief from their spiritual distresses; and five whose experience appeared very clear and satisfactory. There was much visible concern among them while I was discoursing publicly; but afterward, when I spoke to one and another more particularly, whom I perceived under much concern, the power of God seemed to descend upon the assembly '*like a mighty rushing wind*,' and with an astonishing energy bore down all before it. I stood amazed at the influence which seized the audience almost universally; and could compare it to nothing more aptly than the irresistible force of a mighty torrent, or swelling deluge, that with its insupportable weight and pressure bears down and sweeps before it whatever is in its way. Almost all persons of all ages were bowed down with concern together, and scarcely one was able to withstand the shock of this surprising operation. Old men and women who had been drunken wretches for many years, and some little children not more than six or seven years of age, appeared in distress for their souls, as well as persons of middle age. It was apparent that these children, some of them at least, were not merely frightened with seeing the general concern, but were made sensible of their danger, the badness of their hearts, and their misery without Christ, as some of them expressed it. The most stubborn hearts were now obliged to bow. They were almost universally praying and crying for mercy in every part of the house, and many out of doors; and numbers could neither go nor stand. Their concern was so great, each one for himself, that none seemed to take any notice of those about them, but each prayed freely for himself. Those who had lately obtained relief, were filled with comfort at this season. They appeared calm and composed, and seemed to rejoice in Christ Jesus. Some of them took their distressed friends by the hand, telling them of the goodness of Christ, and the comfort that is to be enjoyed in him; and thence invited them to come and give up their hearts to him. I could observe some of them, in the most honest and unaffected manner, without any design of being taken notice of, lifting up their eyes to heaven, as if crying for mercy, while they saw the distress of the poor souls around them. There was one remarkable instance of awakening this day which I cannot fail to notice here. A young Indian woman, who, I believe, never knew before that she had a soul, nor ever thought of any such thing, hearing that there was something strange among the Indians, came, it seems, to see what was the matter. In her way to the Indians she called at my lodgings, and when I told her that I designed presently to preach to the Indians, laughed, and seemed to mock; but went, however, to them. I had not proceeded far in my public discourse before she felt effectually that she had a soul; and before I had concluded my discourse, was so convinced of her sin and misery, and so distressed with concern for her soul's salvation, that she seemed like one pierced through with a dart, and cried out incessantly. She could neither go nor stand, nor sit on her seat without being held up. After public service was over she lay flat on the ground, praying earnestly, and would take no notice of, nor give any answer to, any who spoke to her. I hearkened to what she said, and perceived the burden of her prayer to be, '*Have mercy on me, and help me to give you my heart.*' Thus she continued praying incessantly, for many hours together."

This extraordinary influence continued for many months of constant seriousness and tenderness, with repetitions at intervals, of the mighty operations of the Spirit above described, and frequent instances of blissful conversion, and wonderful reformation on the part of persons before given to the worst of crimes. Indeed the Divine presence seems never after to have left the people among whom he labored, until his final sickness removed the youthful apostle from them, in his twenty-ninth year. In the course of eleven months, about forty of this small congregation were brought into the church of Christ, on as unequivocal evidence of regeneration, perhaps, as it is possible for human judgment to obtain. We quote only one example, indicating what seems to have been the usual type of experience among these converts :

"She now appeared in a heavenly frame of mind, composed and delighted with the divine will. When I came to discourse particularly with her, and to inquire of her how she obtained relief and deliverance from the spiritual distresses which she had lately suffered, she answered, in broken English, '*Me try, me try save myself; last, my strength be all gone* (meaning her ability to save herself); *could not me stir bit further. Den last me forced let Jesus Christ alone send me hell, if he please.*' I said, 'But you was not willing to go to hell, was you?' She replied, '*Could not me help it. My heart, he would wicked for all. Could not me make him good*' (meaning, she saw it was right she should go to hell, because her heart was wicked, and would be so after all she could do to mend it). I asked her how she got out of this case. She answered still in the same broken language, '*By by, my heart be glad desperately.*' I asked her why her heart was glad. She replied, '*Glad my heart, Jesus Christ do what he please with me. Did not me care where he put me; love him for all,*' etc. She could not readily be convinced but that she was willing to go to hell if Christ was pleased to send her there; although the truth evidently was, that her will was so swallowed up with the divine will that she could not frame any hell in her imagination which would be dreadful or undesirable, provided it was the will of God to send her to it."

The rekindling of the missionary spirit in this great awakening was not observable only in the Oxford "Methodists," and Brainerd. Results of similar character to those that attended his brief career, were enjoyed at other Mission stations at the same period. Among the Indians on Long Island, thirty-five adults and forty-four children were baptized by Mr. Horton, in two years from his arrival in 1741. Soon after, there were numerous conversions among the Indians near Stonington ; and a visit from these Christian Indians, was the means of awaking those in Westerly, Rhode Island, where over sixty were admitted to the Church, about 1744, and heathenism appears to have been completely extinguished. Brainerd's career was scarcely begun ere it was ended, but he being dead yet speaketh—one of the first and master spirits of modern Missions. Simultaneously with these efforts and Divine manifestations among the North American heathen, in October 1744, leading revivalists in Scotland, seconded by Edwards and others in America, were prompted first to suggest the Monthly Concert of prayer for the conversion of the world ; now attached, a blessed institution, to the churches of Christ almost universally.

Whitefield arrived in Philadelphia, in the fall of 1739. Of his incidental labors there, Dr. Franklin says :

"The multitudes of all sects and denominations that attended his sermons in Philadelphia, were enormous. It was wonderful to see the change soon made in the manners of our inhabitants. From being thoughtless and indifferent about religion, it seemed as if all the world was growing religious; so that one could not walk through the town in an evening without hearing psalms sung in different families in every street.

"I computed that he might well be heard by more than thirty thousand people. I refused to contribute to his orphan-house in Georgia, thinking it injudiciously located. Soon after, I happened to attend one of his sermons, in the course of which I perceived he intended to finish with a collection, and I silently resolved he should get nothing from me. I had in my pocket a handful of copper money, three or four silver dollars, and five pistoles in gold. As he proceeded, I began to soften, and determined to give the copper. Another stroke of his oratory made me ashamed of that, and determined me to give the silver; and he finished so admirably, that I emptied my pocket wholly into the collector's dish, gold and all. At this sermon there was also one of our club, who, being of my sentiments respecting the building at Georgia, and suspecting a collection might be intended, had, by precaution, emptied his pockets before he came from home. Towards the conclusion of the discourse, however, he felt a strong inclination to give, and applied to a neighbor, who stood near him, to lend him some money for the purpose. The request was made to, perhaps, the only man in the company who had the firmness not to be affected by the preacher. His answer was, 'At any other time, friend Hodgkinson, I would lend to thee freely ; but not now, for thee seems to be out of thy right senses.' "

"Look where I would," says an eye-witness, "most were drowned in tears." Among other very striking conversions in Philadelphia, at this period, was that of a young lady, who had for several years made a public profession of Christianity, but now became fully convinced that "she was totally unacquainted with vital piety." It is stated that she once walked twenty miles to hear Whitefield preach. She became a woman of eminent godliness.

"An aged man who was living in 1806, and who well remembered the scenes he witnessed, bore testimony that after this visit of the great evangelist, public worship was regularly celebrated in Philadelphia twice a day for a whole year; and that on the Lord's day it was celebrated three, and frequently four times in each church. He said there were not less than twenty-six societies regularly held for prayer and Christian conference.

"Such was the influence of Whitefield, not only in Philadelphia, but throughout the colony of Pennsylvania, that in the city attention to commerce was suspended, and in the country the cultivation of the land for the time being was abandoned, that people might hear him proclaim the gospel of the Lord Jesus."

Years afterwards, an excellent minister, Rev. Mr. Rodgers,

"Asked him whether he recollected the occurrence of the little boy who was so affected with his preaching as to let his lantern fall. Mr. Whitefield replied, 'O yes, I remember it well; and have often thought I would give almost any thing in my power, to know who that little boy was, and what had become of him.' Mr. Rodgers replied with a smile, 'I am that little boy.' Mr. Whitefield, with tears of joy, started from his seat, took him in his arms, and with strong emotion remarked, that he was the *fourteenth* person then in the ministry whom he had discovered in the course of that visit to America, in whose conversion he had, under God, been instrumental."

"From Philadelphia, Whitefield was invited to New York. Upon his arrival, the commissary of the bishop, he says, 'was full of anger and resentment, and denied me the use of his pulpit before I asked for it. He said they did not want my assistance. I replied, that if they preached the gospel, I wished them good luck: I will preach in the fields; for all places are alike to me.' The undaunted evangelist therefore preached in the fields; and on the evening of the same day, to a very thronged and attentive audience, in the Rev. Mr. Pemberton's meeting-house, in Wall street; and continued to do so twice or three times a day, with apparent success."

"As to the localities honored by Whitefield's preaching in and about the city of New York, we find many records of his discoursing in the open fields of the surrounding country; the old City Exchange, which stood at the foot of Broad street, near Water street, and which was built on large arches, was a favorite spot for itinerant preachers, and for Whitefield among the rest. During his various visits to New York, from 1745 to 1760, he generally preached in the Presbyterian church in Wall street, which was then the only church of that denomination in the city, and of which the Rev. Dr. Pemberton, from Boston, was the minister. Afterwards, a few years before his death, he was accustomed to preach in the Brick church in Beekman street; which was then familiarly called the 'Brick Meeting,' and in common parlance, said to be 'in the fields;' so little was the city extended at that period. So prosperous was his ministry in New York, that it was found necessary immediately to enlarge the Presbyterian church in Wall-street, by the erection of galleries; and a year or two afterwards it was again enlarged about one-third, in order to accommodate the stated worshippers."

In this city occurred the well-known illustration of his dramatic power, when, preaching to a large number of sailors, he introduced a description of a storm and shipwreck, carrying away their imaginations so irresistibly that in the climax of the catastrophe they sprang to their feet, exclaiming, "Take to the long boat!"

From New York Whitefield returned southwards to his destination in Georgia, preaching through New Jersey to great multitudes, among whom, as Edwards has already noted for us, a work of grace had recently been enjoyed under the labors of "young Mr. Frelinghuysen." Passing through Philadelphia, he found the churches closed against him, and preached in the fields.

"Societies for worship were commenced in different parts of the town; not a few began seriously to inquire after the way of salvation; many negroes came to the evangelist with the inquiry, 'Have I a soul?' and a church was formed, of which the distinguished Gilbert Tennent was the pastor. No less than one hundred and forty, who had undergone a previous strict examination as to their personal piety, were received as constituent members of this church, and large additions were from time to time made to their number.

"Mr. Jones, the Baptist minister of the city, told Whitefield of the change produced by his former preaching on the minds of two ministers; one of whom stated to his congregation that he had hitherto been deceiving both himself and them, and added, that he could not preach to them at present, but requested them to unite in prayer with him; and the other resigned his charge, to itinerate among the unenlightened villages of New Jersey and elsewhere. Another fact was, that an Indian trader became so impressed with the preaching of Whitefield, that he had given up his business, and was gone to teach the Indians with whom he used to trade.

"There had been a drinking club, which had attached to it a negro boy remarkable for his power of mimicry. This boy was directed by the gentlemen who composed the club to exercise his powers on Mr. Whitefield: he did so, but very reluctantly; at length he stood up and said, 'I speak the truth in Christ, I lie not; unless you repent, you will all be damned.' This unexpected speech had such an effect as to break up the club, which met no more."

He went on preaching to the South, encountered a determined persecution from ecclesiastical authorities in Charleston, laid the first brick in his orphan-house in Georgia, had a melting season of labor with the hearts of his young people there, and soon (April, 1740) returned northward, preaching all the way to immense numbers, in the same manner as before.

In September he arrived at Newport, on his first visit to New England. He was welcomed with great expectation in all the principal cities and towns, and remained about six weeks, preaching with powerful effect, to very large audiences; although it is observable that the rush to attend his preaching, as well as its immediate and visible influence upon his audiences, was by no means so remarkable as in England and in other parts of this country.

Again, he went on preaching to the South, through New York, New Jersey and Philadelphia; meeting and laboring with the Tennents and the celebrated evangelist, Davenport, and setting the country all in a flame of religious excitement. In January, 1741, he returned to England, where he found all men turned against him in consequence of sectarian controversies in which he had mingled to oppose, by letter, the narrower views of popular favorites who had held the field in his absence. He went on preaching the gospel, nevertheless, with all his peculiar disinterestedness, breadth and singleness of purpose, and with all his unmatched power; and in a few days the tide was turned, and his usefulness became more eminent than ever. In the following summer, for the first time, he went through Scotland, in which he made, in the whole, no less than fourteen preaching tours, from 1741 to 1768.

"Perhaps no man was ever more free from sectarianism than George Whitefield. It is true, that he was ordained a clergyman of the Church of England, and never manifested any degree of reluctance to officiate within its walls; but it is equally true, that the vast majority of his sermons were delivered in connection with other bodies of Christians.

When he was once preaching from the balcony of the court-house, Market street, Philadelphia, he delivered an impressive apostrophe: 'Father Abraham, who have you in heaven? any Episcopalians?' 'No.' 'Any Presbyterians?' 'No.' 'Any Baptists?' 'No.' 'Have you any Methodists, Seceders, or Independents there?' 'No, no!' 'Why who have you there?' 'We don't know those names here. All who are here are Christians, believers in Christ—men who have overcome by the blood of the Lamb, and the word of his testimony.' 'Oh, is that the case? then God help me, God help us all, to forget party names, and to become Christians, in deed and in truth.'"

The breadth of his mind was exhibited, as already remarked, in his constant refusal to permit any memorial to be left of him or of any peculiar views and plans of his own, in the shape of a sect or a party. There is inexpressible significance in such a stand on the part of such a man, in such a time. The men who founded schools and sects in that age of reformation, were great—some of them, certainly—but he who could see and feel with the foremost of them, and yet could refuse to found anything, and build solely on "the foundation that is laid," was greater. The secret of this lay in the wholeness of his devotion to Christ, and to that unity of His people which was the burden of the wondrous intercession left on record for us in the 17th chapter of John. But we have another instance of broad wisdom and rare purity of heart, in declining a species of power which is almost universally thought legitimate and desirable to the Christian laborer. During his stay in Scotland, in the year 1759, a young lady, Miss Hunter, who possessed a considerable fortune, made a full offer to him of her estate in money and lands. He promptly refused the offer; and upon his declining it for himself, she offered it to him for the benefit of his orphan-house. *This also he absolutely refused.*

Over three years passed before his next visit to America, during which his stated employment and object, what may be called the *thread* of his career, was still, as at all other times, the support of his charitable enterprise in Georgia. Upon this thread, however, was strung an immeasurable amount of evangelistic labor, always incidental as to its occasions, and without any general plan, yet so great and absorbing as to conceal this original purpose almost wholly from view. Many remarkable incidents occurred before his third voyage to his own 'parish' in Georgia, from which the following are selected:

During a visit to Bristol, Whitefield's ministry was owned of God in the conversion of Thomas Olivers, a young profligate Welshman. It is said, he had so studied profanity and cursing, that he would exemplify the richness of the Welsh language by compounding twenty or thirty words into one long and horrid blasphemy. He had often sung profane songs about Whitefield, and was now induced by curiosity to go to hear him. Being too late on the first occasion, he went on the following evening nearly three hours before the time. The text was, "Is not this a brand plucked out of the fire?"—Zech. iii. 2. His heart became broken with the sense of his sins, and he was soon enabled to trust in the mercy of Christ. He became a zealous and successful minister of Christ among the followers of Mr. Wesley, and was the author of the well-known hymn,

"The God of Abram praise," etc.

On one occasion, while preaching under the shade of a venerable tree, in a lovely meadow, a poor unhappy man, thinking to turn him into ridicule, placed himself on one of the overhanging boughs, immediately above the preacher's head, and with monkey-like dexterity mimicking his gestures, endeavored to raise a laugh in the audience. Guided by the looks of some of his hearers, Whitefield caught a glance of him, but, without seeming to have noticed him, continued his discourse. With the skill of a wise orator, he reserved the incident for the proper place and time. While forcibly speaking on the power and sovereignty of divine grace, with increasing earnestness he spoke of the unlikely objects it had often chosen, and the unlooked for triumphs it had achieved. As he rose to the climax of his inspiring theme, and when in the full sweep of his eloquence, he suddenly paused, and turning round, and pointing slowly to the poor creature above him, he exclaimed, in a tone of deep and thrilling pathos, "Even *he* may yet be the subject of that free and resistless grace." It was a shaft from the Almighty. Winged by the divine Spirit, it struck the scoffer to the heart, and realized in his conversion the glorious truth it contained.

When he was in Edinburgh a regiment of soldiers were stationed in the city, in which was a sergeant whose name was Forbes, a very abandoned man, who, everywhere he could do so, run in debt for liquor, with which he was almost at all times drunk. His wife washed for the regiment, and thus obtained a little money. She was a pious woman, but all her attempts to reclaim her husband were unsuccessful. During one of Mr. Whitefield's visits to the city, she offered her husband a sum of money, if he would for once go and hear the eloquent preacher. This was a strong inducement, and he engaged to go. The sermon was in a field, as no building could have contained the audience. The sergeant was rather early, and placed himself in the middle of the field, that he might file off when Mr. Whitefield ascended the pulpit; as he only wished to be able to say that he had seen him. The crowd, however, increased; and when the preacher appeared, they pressed forward, and the sergeant found it impossible to get away. The prayer produced some impression on his mind, but the sermon convinced him of his sinfulness and danger. He became a changed man, and showed the reality of his conversion by living for many years in a very penurious manner, till he had satisfied the claims of every one of his creditors.

"While he was at Plymouth, four well-dressed men came to the house of one of his particular friends, in a kind manner inquiring after him, and desiring to know where he lodged. Soon after, Mr. Whitefield received a letter informing him that the writer was a nephew of Mr. S——, an attorney in New York; that he had the pleasure of supping with Mr. Whitefield at his uncle's house, and requested his company to sup with him and a few friends at a tavern. Mr. Whitefield replied to him that he was not accustomed to sup abroad at such houses, but he should be glad of the gentleman's company to eat a morsel with him at his own lodging. The gentleman accordingly came and supped, but was observed frequently to look around him, and to be very absent. At length he took his leave, and returned to his companions in the tavern, and on being asked by them what he had done, he answered, that he had been treated with so much civility and kindness that he had not the heart to touch him. One of the company, a lieutenant of a man-of-war, laid a wager of ten guineas that he would do his business for him. His companions, however, had the precaution to take away his sword.

"It was now about midnight, and Mr. Whitefield having that day preached to a large congregation, and visited the French prisoners, had retired to rest, when he was awoke and told that a well-dressed gentleman earnestly wished to speak with him. Supposing that it was some person under conviction of sin, many such having previously called upon him, he desired him to be brought to his room. The lieutenant came, sat down by his bedside, congratulated him upon the success of his ministry, and expressed considerable regret that he had been prevented from hearing him. Soon after, however, he began to utter the most abusive language, and in a cruel and cowardly manner beat him in his bed. The landlady and her daughter, hearing the noise, rushed into the room and laid hold of the assailant; but disengaging himself from them, he renewed his attack on the unoffending preacher, who, supposing that he was about to be shot or stabbed, underwent all the feelings of a sudden and violent death. Soon after, a second person came into the house, and called from the bottom of the stairs, 'Take courage, I am ready to help you.' But by the repeated cries of murder the neighborhood had become so alarmed, that the villains were glad to make their escape. 'The next morning,' says Mr. Whitefield, 'I was to expound at a private house, and then to set out for Biddeford. Some urged me to stay and prosecute, but being better employed, I went on my intended journey, was greatly blessed in preaching the everlasting gospel; and, upon my return, was well paid for what I had suffered, curiosity having led perhaps two thousand more than ordinary to see and hear a man that had like to have been murdered in his bed. And I trust, in the five weeks that I waited for the convoy, hundreds were awakened and turned unto the Lord.'

"As Whitefield was one day preaching in Plymouth, a Mr. Henry Tanner, who was at work as a ship-builder at a distance, heard his voice, and resolved, with five or six of his companions, to go and drive him from the place where he stood; and for this purpose they filled their pockets with stones. When, however, Mr. Tanner drew near, and heard Mr. Whitefield earnestly inviting sinners to Christ, he was filled with astonishment, his resolution failed him, and he went home with his mind deeply impressed. On the following evening, he again attended, and heard Mr. Whitefield on the sin of those who crucified the Redeemer. After he had forcibly illustrated their guilt, he appeared to look intently on Mr. Tanner, as he exclaimed, with great energy, 'Thou art the man!' These words powerfully impressed Mr. Tanner; he felt his transgressions of the divine law to be awfully great, and in the agony of his soul he cried, 'God be merciful to me a sinner!' The preacher then proceeded to proclaim the free and abundant grace of the Lord Jesus, which he commanded to be preached among the very people who had murdered him; a gleam of hope entered the heart of the penitent, and he surrendered himself to Christ. Mr. Tanner afterwards entered the ministry, and labored with great success, for many years, at Exeter."

We now return to New England, and the events which ensued upon the first visit of Whitefield, and the preaching of Gilbert Tennent, who followed up his labors there with a power which was perhaps not much inferior, relatively to the character of the New England mind. Whitefield had spent a season of spiritual delight with Edwards and his church, at Northampton, in the fall of 1740. The revival had returned to this people already, in the spring, and continued in this and the following year. The preaching of the gospel was attended with the most wonderful power, in every part of New England, and revivals gave new life and multiplied numbers to the churches, in a larger number of towns than our space enables us to enumerate, throughout New England, and in the Middle States. This is the period which, by eminence, is called "the Great Awakening." As one example of the power of the gospel in those days, the celebrated sermon preached by Edwards at Enfield, July 8, 1741, must be mentioned:

"While the people of the neighboring towns," says Trumbull, "were in great distress about their souls, the inhabitants of Enfield were very secure, loose, and vain. A lecture had been appointed there, and the neighboring people were so affected at the thoughtlessness of the inhabitants, and had so much fear that God would, in his righteous judgment, pass them by, that many of them were prostrate before him a considerable part of the previous evening, supplicating the mercy of heaven in their behalf. And when the time appointed for the lecture came, a number of the surrounding ministers were present, as well as some from a distance—a proof of the prayerful interest felt on behalf of the town." Mr. Edwards chose for his text, the words, 'Their feet shall slide in due time.'—Deut. xxxii. 35. 'When they went into the meeting-house, the appearance of the assembly was thoughtless and vain; the people scarcely conducted themselves with common decency.' But as the sermon proceeded, the audience became so overwhelmed with distress and weeping, that the preacher was 'obliged to speak to the people and desire silence, that he might be heard.' The excitement soon became intense; and it is said that a minister who sat in the pulpit with Mr. Edwards, in the agitation of his feelings, caught the preacher by the skirt of his dress, and said, 'Mr. Edwards, Mr. Edwards, is not God a God of mercy?' Many of the hearers were seen unconsciously holding themselves up against the pillars, and the sides of the pews, as though they already felt themselves sliding into the pit. This fact has often been mentioned as a proof of the strong and scriptural character of President Edwards' peculiar eloquence—the eloquence of truth as attended by influence from heaven; for his sermons were read without gestures."

Probably a period of at least a quarter of a century ought to be regarded as covered by the "Great Awakening." It cannot be doubted that at least 50,000 souls were added to the churches of New England out of a population of about 250,000, as it is estimated; which makes the remarkable proportion of twenty per cent. of all the inhabitants—a fact sufficient to revolutionize, as indeed it did, the religious and moral character, and to determine the destinies, of the country. But this was not all. Perhaps as many converts were made within the churches as without them; and this, as every experienced Christian knows, is a change of double moment to the church, at once adding strength and removing the most depressing of all burdens. Not less than 150 new congregational churches were established in twenty years. The increase of Baptist churches in the last half of that century, was still more wonderful, rising from *nine* to upwards of *four hundred* in number, with a total of thirty thousand members. The increase of the Presbyterians and other denominations in the Middle States, appears to be less distinctly traced, but it is said that the ministers of the former denomination were more than doubled in number, within " a few years," while the churches had multiplied in a still larger proportion.

But all these numerical changes express very little of the profound revolution which took place in the religious life of the church and the country. We cannot enter into a thorough comparison of the state of religion before and after the revival, nor into a view of the important doctrinal and practical conflicts which it produced, and ultimately settled in a manner now universally felt to have been vital to the soundness and prosperity of religion. An illustration may set this subject in a strong light. The colossal EDWARDS, almost in the zenith of his reputation and influence, was dismissed from the pastoral office, by the church in Northampton of which he was little less than the spiritual father, with the advice of a council, as late as 1750, for having taken that side of the " regeneration " controversy which held that credible evidence may be communicated from man to man, of an inward experience of regeneration, and ought to be exacted as the condition of communion with the church. This shows what a gulf of latitudinarianism was closed by the new Reformation when Edwards and the Revivalists triumphed, and the great body of churches of every name, expressly or tacitly adopted the now prevailing test. The consequences escaped by this timely change, may be inferred from the fate of the churches which persisted in " the good old way," and became Unitarian or extinct. The Presbyterian church was rent by substantially the same controversy which in their case hinged more particularly on conversion as a necessary qualification for ministers of the Gospel, and on the liberty claimed by the Revivalists, of preaching in the parishes of unconverted ministers. " A large majority in the Presbyterian church, and many, if not most, in New England, held that the ministrations of unconverted men, if neither heretical in doctrine nor scandalous for immorality, were valid and their labors useful." In 1741, Tennent and his friends were in a minority in the Synod, and were excluded. In 1762, their majority in the Synod was about *forty-nine to fourteen.*

"This doctrine of the 'new birth,' as an ascertainable change, was not generally prevalent in any communion when the revival commenced; it was urged as of fundamental importance, by the leading promoters of the revival; it took strong hold of those whom the revival affected; it naturally led to such questions as the revival brought up and caused to be discussed; its perversions naturally grew into, or associated with, such errors as the revival promoted; it was adapted to provoke such opposition, and in such quarters, as the revival provoked; and its caricatures would furnish such pictures of the revival, as opposers drew."

With these mere examples and illustrations of the Reformation under Whitefield and Edwards, the Tennents, the Wesleys, and their illustrious host of co-laborers, we must relinquish our hasty sketchings. Whitefield, it is well known, swept on in his impetuous course with unchecked ardor and energy, over sea and land, for thirty-four years, to the last day of his life, which was the 30th of September, 1770. His last sermon was at Exeter, Mass. An eye-witness says: "It was usual for Mr. Whitefield to be attended by Mr. Smith, who preached when he was unable on account of sudden attacks of asthma. At the time referred to, after Mr. Smith had delivered a short discourse, Mr. Whitefield seemed desirous of speaking; but from the weak state in which he then was, it was thought almost impossible. He rose from the seat in the pulpit, and stood erect, and his appearance alone was a powerful sermon. The thinness of his visage, the paleness of his countenance, the evident struggling of the heavenly spark in a decayed body for utterance, were all deeply interesting; the spirit was willing, but the flesh was dying. In this situation he remained several minutes, unable to speak; he then said, 'I will wait for the gracious assistance of God, for he will, I am certain, assist me once more to speak in his name.' He then delivered perhaps one of his best sermons, for the light generally burns most splendidly when about to expire. Among these last words were the following: 'I go, I go to rest prepared; my sun has arisen, and by aid from heaven, given light to many; 'tis now about to set for—no, it cannot be! 'tis to rise to the zenith of immortal glory; I have outlived many on earth, but they cannot outlive me in heaven. Many shall live when this body is no more, but then—oh, thought divine!—I shall be in a world where time, age, pain, and sorrow are unknown. My body fails, my spirit expands; how willingly would I live forever to preach Christ! but I die to be with him. How brief, comparatively brief, has been my life, compared with the vast labors I see before me yet to be accomplished; but if I leave now, while so few care about heavenly things, the God of peace will surely visit you.' These and many other things he said, which, though simple, were rendered important by circumstances; for death had let fly his arrow, and the shaft was deeply enfixed when utterance was given to them; his countenance, his tremulous voice, his debilitated frame, all gave convincing evidence that the eye which saw him should shortly see him no more for ever."

We cannot resist quoting a passage from his last sermon in England, which, though very inadequately reported, is too full of pith and force to leave any doubt of the sterling solidity of his genius. His text was:

"'My sheep hear my voice, and I know them, and they follow me: and I give unto them eternal life; and they shall never perish, neither shall any man pluck them out of my hand.'

"These words, it will be recollected, were uttered by Christ at the feast of the dedication. This festival was of bare human invention, and yet I do not find that our Lord preached against it. And I believe that when we see things as we ought, we shall not entertain our auditories about rites and ceremonies, but about the grand thing. It is the glory of Methodists, that while they have been preaching forty years, there has not been, that I know of, one single pamphlet published by them about the non-essentials of religion.

"The Lord divides the world into sheep and goats. O sinners, you are come to hear a poor creature take his last farewell; but I want you to forget the creature and his preaching. I want to lead you further than the Tabernacle—even to Mount Calvary, to see with what expense of blood Jesus Christ purchased 'his own.' Now, before I go any further, will you be so good, before the world gets into your hearts, to inquire whether you belong to Christ or not. Surely the world did not get into your hearts before you rose from your beds. Many of you were up sooner than usual. [The sermon was preached at seven o'clock in the morning.] I hope the world does not get into your hearts before nine. Man, woman, sinner, put thy hand upon thy heart, and say, Didst thou ever hear Christ's voice so as to follow him?"

We have been permitted but to exemplify and illustrate a vast subject in part, within the restrictions of a few hours' leisure and a few pages of room; and much that is omitted may be equally worthy of notice with much that has been selected. One or two of these unused elements in the religious history of the eighteenth century, are of too eminent importance to be ignored with propriety, even in that which does not pretend to be properly so much as a historical sketch. The influence, vastly wider than their direct agency, of that remarkable missionary society, the United Brethren, or Moravian Church, must be taken into account by any one who would frame a proper conception of the religious movement of that day. But the great constructive and organizing mind, appointed doubtless by the Head of the church, to gather and embody the fruits of the new popular evangelism, can by no means be forgotten. As Evangelists, John and Charles Wesley, with their own peculiar associates, performed a very eminent part in the work of awakening and conversion; but in nourishing and guiding the multitude of humbler minds which this out-door evangelism gathered to Christ, and organizing them into a new spiritual estate, so to speak, of His realm, destined to an unparalleled growth, activity, and success—in this important office, John Wesley is rather alone than eminent. Without exalting systems unduly in comparison with the pure and simple vitality for *want* of which they exist in the world, and which seems only to be exhibited prophetically, "a sign and a wonder," in a Paul or a Whitefield; we must recognize their great importance in their place, and relatively to the necessities of that stage of progress which evolved them, and as employed in the hand of Him who hath done all things well. Among them the system of Methodism must be admitted, by every observer of ordinary information, to have been one of the most important products of this latter day, and a striking manifestation of God's wisdom and power in Providence. It has given an embodiment, a consciousness, and an impulse, as well as a luxuriant development, to the most energetic order, perhaps, of the Christian mind; an order before known to itself and the church only in a weak and dependent capacity. It is the greatest, aptest, single monument of the popular religious movement of the last century—the crystallization of that mighty fusion of the masses which everywhere attended the preaching of Whitefield and his friends. Evangelism swept down the indiscriminate harvest with its scythe: Methodism came after, binding it in bundles for the garner.

From this great epoch to the present day, the varying progress of the cause of Christ has been, on the whole, visibly onward. Less than one hundred years have passed; and the religious change in England and America is so great as to render the then state of things, both within and around the church, almost inconceivable to the modern mind, as so near to us in time. The rise of Missions, Sabbath-schools, Christian liberty and union, missions to outcasts, philanthropic movements and moral reforms, and above all, of the standard of life and activity in the churches, which we now witness as the fruit of that spring-time, strikes us with astonishment when we consider the brief period, not more than many an individual's pilgrimage on earth, in which all this has come to pass. In the latter half of this interval, revivals have come to be regarded in the light of an indispensable institution, and their frequent recurrence in every church is expected as the ordinary blessing of God upon ordinary fidelity and prayerfulness. Looking forward by the light of experience, and comparing our present starting-point with that from which we set out a century ago, we are admonished to pitch our conceptions and anticipations higher, and direct our enterprises and prayers toward developments more marvellous yet than hope can measure.

CONVERSION OF EMINENT PERSONS.

Martin Luther.

On attaining his eighteenth year, Luther was sent to the University of Erfurth, in 1501. His father required him to study the law. Full of confidence in his son's talents, he desired to see him cultivate them, and make them known in the world. At Erfurth, Luther outstripped his schoolfellows. Gifted with a retentive memory and a vivid imagination, all that he had heard or read remained fixed on his mind; it was as if he had seen it himself. But even at this early period the young man of eighteen did not study merely with a view of cultivating his understanding. There was within him a spirit of serious thoughtfulness. He felt that he depended entirely on God, and fervently invoked the divine blessing on his labors. Every morning he began the day with prayer; then he went to church; and afterwards commenced his studies, which he prosecuted all day without intermission. One would almost say of him that he lacked nothing.

When Luther had been two years at Erfurth, he saw a Bible for the first time. It was in the university library. On opening it he was filled with astonishment to find in it more than those fragments of the Gospels and Epistles which the church had selected to be read to the people in their places of worship. Till then he had thought that these were the whole word of God. With eagerness, and indescribable feelings, he turned over the leaves of this Latin Bible. He read and re-read, and then, in his surprise and joy, he went back to read again.

In this same year Luther was laid on a sick-bed. Death seemed at hand, and serious reflections filled his mind. All were interested in the young man. "It was a pity," they thought, "to see so many hopes so early extinguished." Nor were they extinguished. Luther recovered, and seemed to himself to have been called to a new vocation. But yet there was no settled purpose in his mind. He resumed his studies, and, in 1505, was made doctor in philosophy. Encouraged by the honors which were heaped upon him on this occasion, he prepared to apply himself entirely to the study of the law, agreeably to the wishes of his father. But God willed otherwise.

Whilst Luther was engaged in various studies and beginning to teach in the university, his conscience incessantly reminded him that religion was the one thing needful, and that his first care should be the salvation of his soul.

He had learned God's hatred of sin ; he remembered the penalties that his word denounces against the sinner ; and he asked himself, tremblingly, if he were sure that he possessed the favor of God. His conscience answered "No."

His character was prompt and decided : he resolved to do all that depended on himself to insure a well-grounded hope of immortality. Two events occurred, one after another, to rouse his soul and confirm his resolution. Among his college friends there was one named Alexis, with whom he was very intimate. One morning a report was spread that Alexis had been assassinated. Luther hurried to the spot, and ascertained the truth of the report. This sudden loss of his friend affected him, and the question which he asked himself, "What would become of me if I were thus suddenly called away ?" filled his mind with the liveliest apprehension.

During the summer of 1505, Luther visited the home of his childhood at Mandsfeldt, and on his return to the university, he was within a short distance of Erfurth, when he was overtaken by a violent storm. The thunder roared ; a thunderbolt sank into the ground at his side. Luther threw himself on his knees : his hour is perhaps come : death, judgment, eternity, are before him in all their terrors, and speak with a voice which he can no longer resist ; encompassed with the anguish and terror of death, as he himself says, he makes a vow, if God will deliver him from this danger, to forsake the world and devote himself entirely to his service. Risen from the earth, having still before his eyes that death which must one day overtake him, he examines himself seriously, and inquires what he must do. The thoughts that formerly troubled him return with redoubled power. He has endeavored, it is true, to fulfill all his duties ; but what is the state of his soul ? Can he with a polluted soul appear before the tribunal of so terrible a God ? He must become holy. He now thirsts after holiness as he had thirsted after knowledge ; but where shall he find it ? How is it to be attained ? The university has furnished him with the means of satisfying his thirst for knowledge. Who will assuage this anguish, this vehement desire that consumes him now ? To what school of holiness can he direct his steps ? He will go into a cloister ; the monastic life will insure his salvation. How often has he been told of its power to change the heart, to cleanse the sinner, to make men perfect ! He will enter into a monastic order. He will there become holy. He will thus insure his eternal salvation.

Such were the resolutions and hopes which filled the breast of Luther as he reëntered Erfurth. His resolution was unalterable. Still, it is with reluctance that he prepares to break ties that are so dear to him. One evening he invites his college friends to a cheerful and simple repast. Music once more enlivens their social meeting. It is Luther's farewell to the world. At the moment when the gaiety of his friend it at its height, the young man can no longer repress the serious thoughts that occupy his mind. He speaks. He declares his intention to his astonished friends. They endeavor to oppose it ; but in vain. And that very night Luther, perhaps dreading their importunity, quits his lodgings. Leaving behind his books and furniture, and taking with him only Virgil and Plautus (he had not yet a Bible), he goes alone in the darkness of the night, to the convent of the Hermits of St. Augustine. He asks admittance. The door opens and closes. And, not yet two-and-twenty years old, he is separated from his parents, his companions, and the world.

Luther imagines himself now with God and safe. His decision and renunciation of the world are commended by the monks and reprobated by his father and friends. As for himself, he is quite in earnest. The ring he received when made doctor of philosophy, he returns to the university, that nothing may remind him of the world he has renounced. Within his new home he performs the meanest offices. And then, when the young monk, who was at once porter, sexton, and servant of the cloister, had finished his work, "With your bag through the town !" cried the brothers ; and, loaded with his bread-bag, he was obliged to go through the streets of Erfurth, begging from house to house, and perhaps at the doors of those very persons who had been either his friends or his inferiors. But he bore it all. Inclined, from his natural disposition, to devote himself heartily to whatever he undertook, it was with his whole soul that he had become a monk. Besides, could he wish to spare the body ? to regard the satisfying of the flesh ? Not thus, he thought, could he acquire the humility, the holiness, that he had come to seek within the walls of a cloister.

The prior of the convent, upon the intercession of the university, freed Luther, ere long, from the mean offices which the monks had imposed upon him; and the young monk resumed his studies with fresh zeal. The works of the fathers, especially St. Augustine, attracted his attention. Nothing struck him so much as the opinions of this father upon the corruption of man's will, and upon the grace of God. He felt, in his own experience, the reality of that corruption, and the necessity for that grace. The words of Augustine found an echo in his heart. He loved above all to draw wisdom from the pure spring of the word of God. He found in the convent a Bible, fastened by a chain, and to this chained Bible he had constant recourse. He understood but little of the word; but still it was his most absorbing study.

Burning with a desire after that holiness which he had sought in the cloister, Luther gave himself up to all the rigor of an ascetic life. He endeavored to crucify the flesh by fastings, macerations, and watchings. Shut up in his cell as in a prison, he was continually struggling against the evil thoughts and inclinations of his heart. A little bread, a single herring, were often his only food; and for days together he would go without eating or drinking. Nothing was too great a sacrifice, at this period, for the sake of becoming holy to gain heaven. Never did a cloister witness efforts more sincere and unwearied to purchase eternal happiness. Had they lasted much longer, he would have become a martyr literally, he declared afterwards, through watchings, prayer, reading, and other labors.

Never did human soul obey this natural impulse to essay its own redemption, both from guilt and from sin, with more promptness and earnestness than did Luther's. In his agony of mind, he had recourse to all the practices of monkish holiness. When temptations assailed him, "I am a lost man," he said, and then resorted to a thousand methods to appease the reproaches of his heart. "I confessed every day. But all that was of no use. Then, overwhelmed with dejection, I distressed myself by the multitude of my thoughts. See, said I to myself, thou art envious, impatient, passionate; therefore, wretch that thou art, it is of no use to thee to have entered into this holy order." One day, overcome with sadness, he shut himself in his cell, and for several days and nights suffered no one to approach him. At last the door was broken open, and Luther was found stretched on the floor in unconsciousness and without any sign of life. And there, through mental suffering and bodily self-mortification, he would have perished, but for those who rescued him by a gentle violence.

The superior of the Augustinian order was a man of enlightened mind. The study of the Bible and of St. Augustine, the knowledge of himself, the war which he, like Luther, had to wage with the deceitfulness and lusts of his own heart, had led him to the Saviour. And he found, in faith in Christ, peace to his soul. This good man, John Staupitz, found Luther reduced by study, fasting, and watching, so that you might count his bones. He saw, in his countenance, the expression of a soul agitated with severe conflicts, but yet strong and capable of endurance. He approached him affectionately, and endeavored to overcome the timidity of the novice. The heart of Luther, which had remained closed under harsh treatment, at last opened and expanded to the sweet beams of love. He felt that the vicar-general understood him, and did not refuse to open to him the cause of his sadness.

"It is vain," said the dejected Luther, "that I make promises to God; sin is always too strong for me." "Oh, my friend," answered the vicar-general, "I have vowed to the holy God more than a thousand times that I would live a holy life, and never have I kept my vow. I now make no more vows; for I know well I shall not keep them. If God will not be merciful to me for Christ's sake, and grant me a happy death when I leave this world, I cannot with all my vows and good works, stand before him. I must perish." The young monk was terrified at the thought of divine justice. He confessed all his fears. The unspeakable holiness of God, his sovereign majesty, filled him with awe. "But why," said Staupitz, "do you distress yourself with these speculations and high thoughts?" Look to the wounds of Jesus Christ, to the blood which he has shed for you; it is there you will see the mercy of God. Instead of torturing yourself for your faults, cast yourself into the arms of your Redeemer. Trust in him, in the righteousness of his life, in the expiatory sacrifice of his death. Do not shrink from him; God is not against you; it is you who are estranged and averse from God."

But Luther could not find in himself the repentance which he thought necessary to his salvation; he answered, "How can I dare to believe in the favor of God, so long as there is in me no real conversion? I must be changed before he can receive me." His venerable guide endeavored to show him that there can be no real conversion so long as man fears God as a severe Judge. "What will you say, then," cried Luther, "to so many consciences, to whom are prescribed a thousand insupportable penances in order to gain heaven?" The answer to this question seemed to him a voice from heaven. "There is," said Staupitz, "no true repentance but that which begins in the love of God and of righteousness. That which some fancy to be the end of repentance is only its beginning. In order to be filled with the love of that which is good, you must first be filled with the love of God. If you wish to be really converted, do not follow these mortifications and penances. Love Him who has first loved you." These words penetrated the heart of Luther. Guided by this new light, he consulted the Scriptures. He looked to all the passages which speak of repentance and conversion—words which were no longer dreaded but became the sweetest refreshment. Those passages of Scripture which once alarmed him seemed now, he says, to run to him from all sides, to smile, to spring up, and play around him.

"Before," he exclaims, "though I carefully dissembled with God as to the state of my heart, and though I tried to express a love for him, which was only a constraint and a mere fiction, there was no word in the Scripture more bitter to me than *repentance.* But now there is not one more sweet and pleasant to me. Oh, how blessed are all God's precepts, when we read them, not in books alone, but in the precious words of the Saviour!"

This change, however, was not instantaneous, but gradual. "Oh! my sin! my sin! my sin!" he cried, one day, in the presence of the vicar-general, and in a tone of the bitterest grief. "Well, would you be only the *semblance* of a sinner," replied the latter, "and have only the *semblance* of a SAVIOUR? Know that Jesus Christ is the Saviour of those even who are *real* and *great* sinners, and deserving of utter condemnation." To the doubts of his conscience were added those of his reason. He wished to penetrate into the secret counsels of God—to unveil his mysteries, to see the invisible, and comprehend the incomprehensible. Staupitz checked him. He persuaded him not to attempt to fathom God, but to confine himself to what he has revealed of his character in Christ. "Look at the wounds of Christ," said he, "and you will there see shining clearly the purpose of God towards man. We cannot understand God out of Christ. 'In Christ you will see what I am and what I require,' hath the Lord said; 'you will not see it elsewhere, either in heaven or on earth.'"

The conscience of the young Augustinian did not, however, find solid repose without further conflict. His health at last sunk under the exertions and stretch of his mind. He was attacked with a malady which brought him to the gates of the grave. And all his anguish and terrors returned in the prospect of death. His own impurity and God's holiness again disturbed his mind. One day (it was now the second year of Luther's abode at the convent), when he was overwhelmed with despair, an old monk entered his cell, and spoke kindly to him. Luther opened his heart to him, and acquainted him with the fears which disquieted him. The old man uttered in simplicity this article of the Apostles' Creed:—"I believe in the forgiveness of sins." These simple words, ingenuously recited at a critical moment, shed sweet consolation in the mind of Luther.

"*I* believe," repeated he, to himself, on his bed of suffering, "I believe the remission of sins." "Ah," said the monk, "you must not only believe that David's or Peter's sins are forgiven: the devils believe that. The commandment of God is, that all men believe that sins are remitted to them."

"From that moment," says D'Aubigné, "the light shone into the heart of the young monk of Erfurth. The word of grace was pronounced, and he believed it. He renounced the thought of meriting salvation, and trusted himself with confidence to God's grace in Christ Jesus. He did not perceive the consequence of the principle he admitted; he was still sincerely attached to the church of Rome, and yet he was thenceforward independent of it; for he had received salvation from God himself, and Romish Catholicism was virtually extinct to him. From that hour, Luther went forward; he sought in the writings of the apostles and prophets, for all that might strengthen the hope which filled his heart. Every day he implored help from above, and every day new light was imparted to his soul."

Bishop Latimer.

The first character in which we know Hugh Latimer, is that of a genial, merry lad. He had followed the pursuits of a yeoman's life without stain of vice or dishonor. At the age of fourteen he was sent to the University of Cambridge, and took as much interest in the amusements as in the studies of the place. He was fond of pleasure and of cheerful conversation, and mingled frequently in the festivities of the youthful crowd around him. At what age the transition took place from light-heartedness to asceticism, we are not aware; but he was still young, and the circumstances have been recorded. When Latimer and a company of his fellow-students were dining together, one of the party exclaimed, in the Latin of the Vulgate translation of Eccl. iii. 12, "There is nothing better than to be merry and to do well." "A vengeance on that *do well!*" replied a monk of impudent mien; "I wish it were beyond the sea; it mars all the rest." Young Latimer was startled. "I understand it now," he said; "that will be a heavy *do well* to these monks when they have to render God an account of their lives." Forsaking pleasure, the yeoman's son threw himself, heart and soul, into the practices of superstition, and became distinguished for his asceticism and enthusiasm. He learned to attach the greatest importance to the merest trifles. As the missal directs that water should be mingled with the sacramental wine, often while saying mass he would be troubled in his conscience for fear he had not put sufficient water. And this fear never left him a moment's tranquillity during the service. He became notorious for his ardent fanaticism, and his zeal was rewarded by the appointment of cross-bearer to the university. And in this capacity he was conspicuous for seven years, amidst the chanting priests and splendid shows of every religious procession. A more religious man than he was, in his own way, there could not be ; not Saul of Tarsus, not Luther in the Augustinian monastery, not Ignatius Loyola.

At this time the University of Cambridge was greatly agitated by the publication of the Greek New Testament, with a Latin translation by Erasmus. And there was no one to whom the hopes of the enemies of this book looked so confidently as to the cross-bearer of the university. This young priest combined a biting humor with an impetuous disposition and indefatigable zeal. He followed the friends of the word of God into the colleges and houses where they used to meet, debated with them, and pressed them to abandon their faith. On occasion of receiving the degree of Bachelor of Divinity, he had to deliver a Latin discourse in the presence of the university, and chose for his subject "Philip Melanchthon and his doctrines." Latimer's discourse produced a great impression. "At last," said his hearers, "Cambridge will furnish a champion for the church that will confront the Wittenberg doctors and save the vessel of our Lord."

Among the cross-bearer's hearers on this occasion was Thomas Bilney, almost hidden through his small stature. Bilney easily detected Latimer's sophisms, but at the same time loved his person, and conceived the design of winning him to what he believed to be the truth. He reflected, prayed, and at last planned a strange plot. He went to the college where Latimer resided. "For the love of God," he said, "be pleased to hear my confession." The confessor expected to hear a recantation of Bilney's new doctrines. My discourse against Melanchthon has converted him, he thought. The pale face and wasted frame and humble look of his visitor seemed to indicate that he would still be one of the ascetics of Rome. And Latimer at once yielded to his request. Bilney, kneeling before his confessor, told him, with touching simplicity, the anguish he had once felt in his soul, the efforts he had made to remove it, their unprofitableness, and the peace he had felt when he believed that Jesus Christ is the Lamb of God that taketh away the sin of the world. He described to Latimer the Spirit of adoption he had received, and the happiness he experienced in being able to call God his Father. Latimer listened without mistrust. His heart was opened, and the voice of the pious Bilney penetrated it without obstacle. From time to time the confessor would have chased away the new thoughts which came crowding into his bosom ; but the penitent continued. His language, at once so simple and so lively, entered like a two-edged sword. At length the penitent rose up, but Latimer remained seated, absorbed in thought. Like Saul on the way to Damascus, he was conquered, and his conversion, like the apostle's, was instantaneous. He saw Jesus as the only Saviour given to man : he contemplated and adored him. His zeal for the superstitions of his fathers he now regarded as a war against God, and he wept bitterly. Bilney consoled him : "Brother, though your sins be as scarlet, they shall be white as snow." Latimer received the truth, and was henceforward a changed man. His energy was tempered by a divine unction, and he ceased to be superstitious. His conversion, as of old the miracles of the apostles, struck men's minds with astonishment. To the hour of his martyrdom he proclaimed Jesus Christ as him who, having tasted death for every man, has delivered his people from the penalty of sin. With this blessed doctrine Bilney and Latimer explored even the gloomy cells of the mad-house to bear the sweet voice of the gospel to the infuriate maniacs. They visited the miserable lazar-house without the town, in which several poor lepers were dwelling ; they carefully tended them, wrapped them in clean sheets, and wooed them to be converted to Christ. The gates of the jail at Cambridge were opened to them, and they announced to the poor prisoners that word which giveth liberty. Before princes and people they testified the gospel of the grace of God. And many years after they sealed their testimony with their blood.

The Founder of the Waldenses.

Peter Waldo was a rich merchant of Lyons, in the 12th century, and enjoyed his opulence without thoughts of a hereafter, till he was startled out of his pleasant dreams by an alarming providence. One evening, as he sat after supper with his friends, one of the party fell lifeless on the floor. This incident reminded him of his own mortality, and made so powerful an impression on his mind, that he resolved to abandon all other concerns and occupy himself wholly with the concerns of religion. Happily, his attention was drawn to the Holy Scriptures, and he resolved to know, from the original fountain itself, the way of life and salvation. He read the Vulgate for himself, and, in addition, employed learned men to translate the Gospels and other portions of the Bible into the Romance language. He thus acquired a correct idea of Christ's gospel, and found peace with God. Peter Waldo now distributed his wealth among the poor, and proposed to form a spiritual society of apostolicals—a society for the spread of evangelical truth among the neglected people in city and country. He employed for this purpose multiplied copies of his Romance version of the Scriptures, which, by degrees, was extended to the whole Bible. He and his companions labored with great zeal, and without any thought, at first, of separating themselves from the Roman communion, but simply aiming at a spiritual society, like many others, in the service of the church: with this difference—that, while other founders of such societies were animated with a zeal for the church, and its laws possessed for them all the force of truth drawn directly from the word of God, Peter Waldo, on the other hand, was influenced more by the truth derived immediately from the Scriptures. But an influential union of laymen, associated for the purpose of preaching to the people—a union which made the Sacred Scriptures themselves the source of religious doctrine—could not long escape opposition and persecution. The Archbishop of Lyons forbade Peter Waldo and his companions to expound the Scriptures and to preach. But they did not think they ought, in obedience to this magisterial decree, to desist from a calling which they were conscious was from God. They declared that they were bound to obey God rather than man, and persevered in the work which they had began. The anathema of the pope, however, soon drove Waldo from Lyons. His flock were scattered, and "went everywhere preaching the word." Many of them found an asylum in the valleys of Piedmont, where they took with them their new translation of the Bible. They there united with others of the same faith, and are known in history as the Waldenses, or Vaudois. Waldo himself, after many wanderings, carrying with him everywhere the glad tidings of salvation, settled at length in Bohemia, where the fruit of his labors was seen, "after many days," in the rapid extension throughout that country of the principles of the Reformation, and where, in the fourteenth century, as many as eighty thousand persons are said to have been put to death "for the word of God, and for the testimony which they held." That sudden death in the house and presence of the rich merchant of Lyons was indeed a fruitful providence—the occasion of spiritual benefits and moral changes which, in the course of centuries, became too widely spread to be traced or numbered.

John Newton.

The pious mother who had taught John Newton to bend his infant knee before the throne of the heavenly grace was taken from him before he was seven years old. At the age of fifteen he had religious convictions, which were soon dissipated, and he learned to curse and blaspheme. Upon his being thrown from a horse, near a dangerous hedge-row, his conscience suggested to him the dreadful consequences of appearing as he was before God, and he abandoned his profane practices for a time—but only for a time; and the consequence of such struggles between sin and conscience was that, on every relapse, he sank into still greater depths of wickedness.

In one of his reforming moods, Newton became a Pharisee. "I did everything (he says) that might be expected from a person entirely ignorant of God's righteousness, and desirous to establish his own. I spent the greatest part of every day in reading the

Scriptures, and in meditation and prayer. I fasted often ; I even abstained from all animal food for three months. I would hardly answer a question for fear of speaking an idle word."

From an ascetic, John Newton became an infidel.

The wickednesses in which he now indulged were as varied as his circumstances permitted. And his misery was complete.

After a series of sins and sufferings, we find him on the coast of Africa in the employ of a slave-dealer, reduced to wants which made him a literal representative of the prodigal son. He was a very outcast, ready to perish. But, unlike the prodigal in our Lord's parable, his distress did not at this time awaken him out of the stupor of sin to say, "I will arise and go to my Father."

Unexpectedly rescued from this life of degradation, it was only to encounter fresh disaster and peril at sea. He was regarded as a Jonah on board the ship which carried him from off the coast of Africa. Though not ordinarily addicted to drunkenness, he challenged four or five of his comrades one evening to try who could hold out longest in drinking rum. Dancing on the deck like a madman, his hat fell overboard, and, seeing the ship's boat by moonlight, he endeavored to throw himself into it to recover his hat. His sight, however, had deceived him : the boat was twenty feet from the ship's side. He was half overboard, and would in one moment have plunged into the water had not some one caught hold of him and pulled him back. The tide ran very strong at the time ; his companions were too much intoxicated to save him, and the rest of the ship's company were asleep ; and as for himself, he could not swim even had he been sober. An unseen Providence watched over a life that was yet to be made a blessing.

Among the few books that were on board his ship was "Thomas à Kempis." Newton took it up carelessly one day, as he had often done before ; but now the thought occurred to him, "What if these things should be true ?" He could not bear the force of the inference, and shut the book. He went to bed that night in his usual spiritual indifference, but was awaked from a sound sleep by a violent sea, which broke on the vessel and filled the cabin where he lay with water. The cry arose immediately that the ship was sinking. He essayed to go on deck, but was met upon the ladder by the captain, who desired him to bring a knife. On his return for the knife another person went up in his place, and was instantly washed overboard. For four weeks the vessel, an almost perfect wreck, was at the mercy of the winds and waves. While holding the helm at the solemn midnight hour, his former religious professions, his many warnings and deliverances, his licentiousness, his profane ridicule of Holy Scripture—all rose up before him, and his sins seemed too great to be forgiven. He waited with fear and impatience to receive his inevitable doom. But with the returning hope of safety there gleamed into his soul some hope towards God. He began to pray. "O God, save me, or I perish," was the cry of the returning prodigal. "The God of the Bible forgive me, for his Son's sake." "My mother's God, the God of mercy, have mercy on me." Before reaching port he felt he had satisfactory evidence of the truth of the gospel, and of its exact suitableness to his necessities. He saw that "God might declare not his mercy only, but his justice also, in the pardon of sin, on account of the obedience and sufferings of Jesus Christ." "Till then he was like the man possessed with the *legion.* No arguments, no persuasion, no views of interest, no remembrance of the past nor regard to the future, could restrain him within the bounds of common prudence; but now he was restored to his senses." He had yet much to learn, but he left that broken ship a new man. And after a few years he became a devoted minister of Jesus Christ, and one of the most useful men of his age. The storm was in this instance the minister of Providence to arrest a godless youth, and to give to Christ's church one of the holiest men that have ever ministered at her altar.

John Bunyan.

John Bunyan was brought up by his father in his own craft of brazier and tinker. As to his early character, he never was a drunkard, a libertine, or a lover of sanguinary sports: his special sins were profanity, Sabbath-breaking, and heart-atheism. "The thing which gave Bunyan any notoriety in the days of his ungodliness, and which made him afterwards appear to himself such a monster of iniquity, was the energy which he put into all his doings. He had a zeal for idle play and an enthusiasm in mischief which were the perverse manifestations of a forceful character." "Elstow," says his biographer, Dr. Hamilton, "is a quiet hamlet of some fifty houses sprinkled about in the picturesque confusion and with the easy amplitude of space which gives an old English village its look of leisure and longevity. And it is now verging to the close of a long summer's day. The daws are taking short excursions from the steeple, and tamer fowls have gone home from the darkening and dewy green. But old Bunyan's donkey is still browsing there, and yonder is old Bunyan's self—the brawny tramper dispread on the settle, retailing to the more clownish residents tap-room wit and roadside news. However, it is young Bunyan you wish to see. Yonder he is, the noisiest of the party, playing pitch-and-toss—that one with the shaggy eyebrows, whose entire soul is ascending in the twirling penny—grim enough to be the blacksmith's apprentice, but his singed garments hanging round him with a lank and idle freedom which scorns indentures; his energetic movements and authoritative vociferations at once bespeaking the ragamuffin ringleader. The penny has come down with the wrong side uppermost, and the loud execration at once bewrays young Badman. You have only to remember that it is Sabbath evening, and you witness a scene often enacted on Elstow Green two hundred years ago." "The only restraining influence of which he then felt the power was terror. His days were often gloomy through forebodings of the wrath to come; and his nights were scared with visions, which the boisterous diversions and adventures of his waking day could not always dispel. He would dream that the last day had come, and that the quaking earth was opening its mouth to let him down to hell; or he would find himself in the grasp of fiends who were dragging him powerless away."

These were the fears of childhood. As he grew older he grew harder. He experienced some remarkable escapes from death, but these providences neither startled nor melted him. He married very early, and his wife was the daughter of a godly man. Her whole property consisted of two small books, "The Plain Man's Pathway to Heaven," and the "Practice of Piety," which her father had left her on his death-bed. Young Bunyan read these books, and was often told by his wife what a good man her father had been. The consequence was that he felt some desire to reform his vicious life, and went to church twice a day, and said and sang as others did. He became at the same time so overrun with the spirit of superstition, that "had he but seen a priest, though never so sordid and debauched in his life, his spirit would fall under him, and he could have lain down at the feet of such and been trampled upon by them; their name, their garb and work, did so intoxicate and bewitch him." But whilst adoring the altar, and worshipping the surplice, and deifying the individual who wore it, Bunyan continued to curse and blaspheme and spend his Sabbaths in the same riot as before.

One day, however, he heard a sermon on the sin of Sabbath-breaking, and it haunted his conscience throughout the day. When in the midst of the excitement of that afternoon's diversions, a voice seemed to dart from heaven into his soul, "Wilt thou leave thy sins and go to heaven, or have thy sins and go to hell?" His arm, which was about to strike a ball, was arrested, and, looking up to heaven, it seemed as if the Lord Jesus was looking down upon him in remonstrance and deep displeasure, and at the same time the conviction flashed across him that he had sinned so long that repentance was now too late. "My state is surely miserable," he thought; "miserable if I leave my sins, and but miserable if I follow them. I can but be damned; and if I must be so, I had as good be damned for many sins as few." In the desperation of this awful conclusion he resumed the game; and so persuaded was he that heaven was forever forfeited, that for some time after he made it his deliberate policy to enjoy the pleasures of sin as rapidly and intensely as possible. "For a month or more he went on in resolute sinning, only grudging that he could not get such scope as the madness of despair solicited. When one day standing at a neighbor's window, cursing and swearing, and 'playing the madman after his wonted manner,' the woman of the house protested that he made her tremble, and that truly he was the ungodliest fellow for swearing that she ever heard in all her life, and quite enough to ruin the youth of the whole town. The woman was herself a notoriously worthless character; and so severe a reproof from so strange a quarter had a singular effect on Bunyan's mind. He was silenced in a moment. He blushed before the God of heaven; and as he there stood with hanging head, he wished with all his heart that he were a little child again, that his father might teach him to speak without profanity; for he thought his bad habit so inveterate now, that reformation was out of the question."

So it was, however, that from that instant onward Bunyan ceased to swear, and people wondered at the change. Immediately after this circumstance, interested by the conversation of a poor man who seemed religious, he betook himself to his Bible, and began to take pleasure in reading the historical parts of it. His outward life underwent much reformation. His own account of himself says: "I did set the commandments before me for my way to heaven; which commandments I also did strive to keep, and, as I thought, did keep them pretty well sometimes, and then I should have comfort; yet now and then should break one, and so afflict my conscience; but then I should repent, and say I was sorry for it, and promise God to do better next time, and there got help again; for then I thought I pleased God as well as any man in England. Thus I continued about a year; all which time our neighbors did take me to be a very godly man, a new and religious man, and did marvel much to see such great and famous alteration in my life and manners; and, indeed, so it was, though I knew not Christ, nor grace, nor faith, nor hope; for, as I have well since seen, had I then died, my state had been most fearful. But, I say, my neighbors were amazed at this my great conversion from prodigious profaneness to something like a moral life; and so they well might, for this my conversion was as great as for Tom of Bedlam to become a sober man. Now I was, as they said, become godly; now I was become a right honest man. But, oh! when I understood these were their words and opinions of me, it pleased me mighty well. For though, as yet, I was nothing but a poor painted hypocrite, yet I loved to be talked of as one that was truly godly."

He had gone to Bedford in prosecution of his calling; when, passing along the street, he noticed a few poor women sitting in a doorway and talking together. He listened to their conversation. It surprised him; for, though he had by this time become a great talker on sacred subjects, their themes were far beyond his reach. God's work in their souls, the views they had obtained of their natural misery and of God's love in Christ Jesus, what words and promises had particularly refreshed them and strengthened them against the temptations of Satan—it was of matters so personal and vital that they spoke to one another. They seemed to Bunyan as if they had found a new world. Their conversation made a deep impression on his mind. He saw that there was something in real religion into which he had not yet penetrated.

What John Bunyan heard in the society of these humble instructors suggested to him a sort of waking vision. "I saw as if they were on the sunny side of some high mountain, there refreshing themselves with the pleasant beams of the sun, while I was shivering and shrinking in the cold, afflicted with frost, snow, and dark clouds. Methought, also, betwixt me and them, I saw a wall that did compass about this mountain ; now, through this wall my soul did greatly desire to pass, concluding that, if I could, I would even go into the very midst of them, and there also comfort myself with the heat of their sun. About this wall I thought myself to go again and again, still prying as I went, to see if I could find some gap or passage to enter therein. But none could I find for some time. At the last I saw, as it were, a narrow gap, like a little doorway in the wall, through which I attempted to pass. Now, the passage being very straight and narrow, I made many offers to get in, but all in vain, even till I was well right beat out in striving to get in. At last, with great striving, methought I at first did get in my head, and after that, by a sideling striving, my shoulders and my whole body. Then I was exceeding glad ; went and sat down in the midst of them, and so was comforted with the light and heat of their sun. Now, this mountain and wall were thus made out to me. The mountain signified the church of the living God ; the sun that shone thereon, the comfortable shining of his merciful face on them that were therein ; the wall, I thought, was the world, that did make separation between the Christian and the world ; and the gap which was in the wall, I thought, was Jesus Christ, who is the way to God the Father. But forasmuch as the passage was wonderful narrow, even so narrow that I could not, but with great difficulty, enter in thereat, it showed me that none could enter into life but those who were in downright earnest, and unless they left that wicked world behind them; for here was only room for body and soul, but not for body and soul and sin."

But he now fell into a very common error. The object to which the eye of an inquiring sinner should be directed is CHRIST, the finished work, and the sufficient Saviour. But, in point of fact, many go in quest of that act of the mind which unites the soul to the Saviour and makes salvation personal; and it is only by studying faith that they come at last to an indirect and circuitous acquaintance with Christ. By some such misdirection Bunyan was misled. In quest of faith he went a long and joyless journey, and was wearied with the greatness of the way. There is scarcely a fear which can assail an inquiring spirit which did not at some stage of his progress arrest his mind. He was no longer a proud Pharisee, but a deeply humbled sinner. "My original and inward pollution—that was my plague and affliction. *That* I saw at a dreadful rate, always putting forth itself within me—*that* I had the guilt of to amazement; by reason of *that* I was more loathsome in my own eyes than a toad; and I thought I was so in God's eyes too."

Years of despondency passed over him before he came to the enjoyment of the peace of the gospel.

The light which first stole in upon his soul, and in which his darkness finally melted away, was a clear discovery of the person of Christ, more especially a distinct perception of the dispositions which he manifested while here on earth. And one thing greatly helped him: he alighted on a congenial mind, and an experience in many respects like his own. Providence threw in his way an old copy of Luther's Commentary on Galatians, "so old," he says, "that it was ready to fall piece from piece if I did but turn it over. When I had but a little way perused the book, I found my condition in his experience so largely and profoundly handled, as if his book had been written out of my heart." And such were the benefits he derived from this book, that he preferred it ever after before all the books he had ever seen, excepting the Holy Bible, "as most fit for a wounded conscience." His happiness was now as intense as his misery had been. He wished he were fourscore years old, that he might die quickly, that he might go to be with Him who had made his soul an offering for his sins. "I felt love to him as hot as fire; and now, as Job said, I thought I should die in my nest." But another period of fearful agony awaited him, and, like the last, it continued for a year. The trial which beset him was a truly diabolical one. "It was to sell Christ, to exchange him for the things of this life, for anything." And those words, "Sell him, sell him," would be impressed upon his thoughts an hundred times running, for hours together, and that during a succession of many weeks. It may well be supposed he prayed and strove against this temptation; at last he found nothing so much relieve him as answering the enemy in his own way, as fast as his temptations were repeated: "I will not, I will not, I will not! no, not thousands, thousands, thousands, thousands of worlds!" At length, after much striving, he felt the thought pass through his heart, as he expresses it, "*Let him go if he will;*" and he imagined also that, for the moment, it had his free consent. "Now," says our author, "was the battle won; and down fell I, as a bird shot from the top of a tree, into great guilt and fearful despair," and thus continued until he was relieved with that comfortable word, "The blood of Jesus Christ cleanseth us from all sin."

During this period the tempter, he tells us, would not let him eat his food in quiet; but "forsooth," says he, "when I was set at my table at my meat, I must go hence to pray; I must leave my food now, and just now; so counterfeit holy would this devil be! When I was thus tempted, I would say in myself, 'Now I am at my meat let me make an end.' 'No,' said he, 'you must do it now, or you will displease God, and despise Christ.'" And when he omitted to obey this temptation, his conscience smote him, as if he had refused to leave his meat for God. The supposition that he had committed the unpardonable sin, had such an effect on Bunyan, that it not only distressed his mind, but affected his very body for many days together; and produced such a stoppage and heat at his stomach, as greatly disordered him. Thus his mind continued for weeks, and months, and in the whole for years, "hanging" (so he expresses it) "as in a pair of scales; sometimes up and sometimes down: now in peace, and anon again in terror."

One day, as he was passing into the field, these words fell upon his soul, "Thy righteousness is in heaven." The eyes of his soul saw at the same time Jesus Christ at God's right hand, and there, he said, is my righteousness. "I saw, moreover, that it was not my good frame of heart that made my righteousness better, nor my bad frame that made my righteousness worse; for my righteousness was Jesus Christ himself, 'the same yesterday, to-day, and forever.'" Now was he loosed from his afflictions and his irons; his temptations also fled away, and he went home rejoicing for the grace and love of God. The words, "Thy righteousness is in heaven," were not to be found in the Bible, but then there were these: "He is made of God unto us wisdom, and righteousness, and sanctification, and redemption." This blessed truth was his peace with God. He was complete in Christ Jesus; and, though sometimes interrupted by disquieting thoughts and strong temptations, his subsequent career was one of growing comfort and prevailing peace.

Colonel Gardiner.

James Gardiner was born in the year of the English Revolution —1568. Such was his reckless daring that he had fought three duels before he attained to the stature of a man. In the first of his country's battles in which he was engaged, he was left among the wounded on the field of action, and his conduct in this melancholy position, shows how godless and hardened his heart was. He was now in the nineteenth year of his age. His life had already been steeped in licentiousness, but he had no thoughts of repentance; his one concern was how to secure the gold which he had about him. Expecting to be stripped by the enemy, he took a handful of clotted gore, placed his gold in the midst of it, shut his hand, and kept it in that position till the blood so dried and hardened that his hand would not easily fall open if any sudden surprise overtook him. The next morning he lay faint and exhausted, through loss of blood, and overheard one Frenchman say to another, "Do not kill that poor child." And when he was able to open his fevered lips, the first thing he did was to tell a deliberate falsehood, namely, that he was nephew to the governor of Huy, a neutral town in the neighborhood. His sufferings the following night were such that he begged those who were carrying him to Huy to kill him outright ; but still he had no thoughts of God. And when his recovery was perfected, and he was restored to his country, it was only to plunge into all manner of excesses. The most criminal intrigues formed the staple of his existence from this period till the thirtieth year of his age. By his military companions he was called "the happy rake." But he was not happy. On one occasion, while his profligate associates were congratulating him on his criminal successes, a dog happened to enter the room, and the young soldier (as he well remembered afterwards) could not forbear groaning inwardly, "Oh that I were that dog !"

Towards the middle of July, 1719, he spent an evening of folly with some of his gay associates. The company broke up about eleven, and at twelve he had made a criminal appointment. The intervening hour must be bridged over by some employment. A pious mother had, without his knowledge, slipped into his portmanteau, Watson's "Christian Soldier, or Heaven taken by Storm." The title attracted him, and he expected some amusement from its military phraseology. He took it and read, but it produced no seriousness nor reflection. While the book was yet in his hand, however, impressions were made on his mind, the fruit of which must be regarded as the best index to whence they came. Whether he was asleep or awake at the time, he felt it afterwards difficult to determine. But if asleep, so vividly was what he saw and heard impressed on his mind, that it seemed to be a waking reality. "He thought he saw an unusual blaze of light fall on the book while he was reading, which he at first imagined might happen by some accident in the candle. But, lifting up his eyes, he apprehended, to his extreme amazement, that there was before him, as it were, suspended in the air, a visible representation of the Lord Jesus Christ upon the cross, surrounded on all sides with a glory; and was impressed, as if a voice, or something equivalent to a voice, had come to him to this effect, 'O sinner! did I suffer this for thee? and are these the returns?'" Affected as were Daniel and John by the supernatural visions they saw, "there remained hardly any life" in Colonel Gardiner, and he continued, he knew not how long, insensible; but when he opened his eyes he saw nothing more than usual.

The dreamer arose from his seat, after a period of unconsciousness, and walked to and fro in his chamber under a tumult of emotions, till he was ready to drop down in unutterable astonishment and agony of heart, appearing to himself the vilest monster in the creation of God, who had all his lifetime been crucifying Christ afresh by his sins. With this was connected such a view, both of the majesty and goodness of God, as caused him to loathe and abhor himself, and to repent as in dust and ashes. He immediately gave judgment against himself, that he was most justly worthy of eternal damnation, and was astonished that he had not been immediately struck dead in the midst of his wickedness. For several months after, it was a settled point with him that the wisdom and justice of God almost necessarily required that such an enormous sinner should be made an example of everlasting vengeance, and he dared hardly ask for pardon. His mental sufferings were now extreme, but he often testified afterwards that they arose not so much from the fear of hell "as from a sense of that horrible ingratitude he had shown to the God of his life, and to that blessed Redeemer who had been in so affecting a manner set forth as crucified before him." Those licentious pleasures which had before been his heaven became now absolutely his aversion. "And, indeed," says his biographer, "when I consider how habitual all those criminal indulgences were grown to him, and that he was now in the prime of life, and all this while in high health too, I cannot but be astonished to reflect upon it, that he should be so wonderfully sanctified in body, as well as in soul and spirit, as that, for all the future years of his life, he, from that hour, should find so constant a disinclination to and abhorrence of those criminal sensualities to which he fancied he was before so invariably impelled by his very constitution, that he was used strangely to think and to say that Omnipotence itself could not reform him without destroying that body and giving him another."

At length, the heavy burden fell from off this weary pilgrim, as from others, when he saw the cross. His peace came by means of that memorable Scripture—"Whom God hath set forth to be a propitiation through faith in his blood, to declare his righteousness for the remission of sins; that he might be just, and the justifier of him which believeth in Jesus." Rom. iii. 25, 26. He had used to imagine that the justice of God required his eternal death. But now he saw that the divine justice might be vindicated, and even glorified, in saving him by the blood of Jesus Christ. "Then did he see and feel the riches of redeeming love and grace in such a manner as not only engaged him, with the utmost pleasure and confidence, to venture his soul upon it, but even swallowed up, as it were, his whole heart in the returns of love, which, from that blessed time, became the genuine and delightful principle of his obedience, and animated him with an enlarged heart to run in the way of God's commandments." The future life of Colonel Gardiner, from the hour of his conversion till he fell at Preston-Pans, in defence of the House of Hanover—a period of twenty-six years—was one of distinguished excellence. The "new man" was virtuous and pure and godly as the "old" had been licentious and profane.

The Experience of President Edwards.

"As the shining light, that shineth more and more unto the perfect day."

When I was a boy, some years before I went to college, at a time of remarkable awakening in my father's congregation, I was very much affected for many months, and concerned about the things of religion and my soul's salvation, and was abundant in religious duties. My affections were lively and easily moved, and I seemed to be in my element when engaged in religious duties. But in process of time my convictions and affections wore off, and I returned, like a dog to his vomit, and went on in the ways of sin. But God would not suffer me to go on with any quietness; I had great and violent inward struggles, till I was brought wholly to break off all former wicked ways, and all ways of known outward sin, and to apply myself to seek salvation. I was indeed brought to seek salvation in a manner that I never was before; I felt a spirit to part with all things in the world for an interest in Christ. My concern continued and prevailed, with many exercising thoughts and inward struggles; but yet it never seemed to be proper to express that concern by the name of terror.

From my childhood up, my mind had been full of objections against the doctrine of God's sovereignty. But I remember the time very well when I seemed to be convinced and fully satisfied as to this sovereignty ; yet I never could give an account how or by what means I was thus convinced, not in the least imagining at the time, nor a long time after, that there was any extraordinary influence of God's spirit in it ; only that now I saw further, and my reason apprehended the justice and reasonableness of it. But I have often, since that first conviction, had quite another kind of sense of it than I had then. I have often since had not only a conviction, but a delightful conviction. The doctrine has very often appeared exceedingly pleasant, bright and sweet ; but my first conviction was not so.

The first instance that I remember of that sort of inward, sweet delight in God and divine things that I have lived much in since, was on reading those words : "Now, unto the King eternal, immortal, invisible, the only wise God, be honor and glory for ever and ever. Amen." 1 Tim. i. 17. As I read the words there came into my soul, and was, as it were, diffused through it, a sense of the glory of the Divine Being—a new sense, quite different from anything I ever experienced before. Never any words of Scripture seemed to me as these words did. I thought within myself how excellent a Being that was, and how happy I should be if I might enjoy that God, and be wrapt up to him in heaven, and be, as it were, swallowed up in him for ever! I kept saying over these words of Scripture to myself, and went to pray to God that I might enjoy him, and prayed in a manner quite different from what I used to do, with a new sort of affection. But it never came into my thoughts that there was anything spiritual or of a saving nature in this.

From about that time I began to have a new kind of apprehension and idea of Christ, and the work of redemption and the glorious way of salvation by him. An inward, sweet sense of these things at times came into my heart, and my soul was led away in pleasant views and contemplations of them. This I know not how to express otherwise than by a calm, delightful abstraction of the soul from all the concerns of this world ; and sometimes a kind of vision, or fixed ideas and imaginations of being alone in the mountains or some solitary wilderness, far from all mankind, sweetly conversing with Christ, and wrapt and swallowed up in God. The sense I had of divine things would often of a sudden kindle up an ardor in my soul that I know not how to express. As I was walking, and looking up on the sky and clouds, there came into my mind a sweet sense of the glorious *majesty* and *grace* of God, that I know not how to express. I seemed to see them both in a sweet conjunction; majesty and meekness joined together; it was a sweet, and gentle, and holy majesty; and also a majestic meekness—a high, great and holy gentleness.

After this, my sense of divine things gradually increased, and became more and more lively, and had more of that inward sweetness. The appearance of everything was altered; there seemed to be, as it were, a calm, beautiful appearance of divine glory in almost everything. God's excellency, his wisdom, his purity and love seemed to appear in everything; in the sun, moon and stars; in the clouds and blue sky; in the grass, flowers and trees; in the water and all nature, which used greatly to fix my mind. Scarcely anything, among all the works of nature, was so delightful to me as thunder and lightning; formerly, nothing had been so terrible to me. Before, I used to be uncommonly terrified with thunder, and to be struck with terror when I saw a thunder-storm rising; but now, on the contrary, it rejoiced me.

I felt then great satisfaction as to my good state; but that did not content me. I had vehement longings of soul after God and Christ, and after more holiness, wherewith my heart seemed to be full, and ready to break, which often brought to my mind the words of the psalmist: "My soul breaketh for the longing it hath." Ps. cxix. 28. I spent most of my time in thinking of divine things. I was almost constantly in ejaculatory prayer wherever I was. Prayer seemed to be natural to me, as the breath by which the inward burnings of my heart had vent.

My sense of divine things seemed gradually to increase for about a year and a half, when I went to preach at New York, and while I was there, I felt them very sensibly in a much higher degree than before. My longings after God and holiness were much increased. I felt an ardent desire to be in everything a complete Christian, and conformed to the blessed image of Christ. *I now sought an increase of grace and holiness, and a holy life, with much more earnestness than ever I sought grace before I had it.* I used to be continually examining myself, and studying and contriving for likely ways and means how I should live holily, with far greater diligence and earnestness than ever I pursued anything in my life, but yet with too great a dependence on my own strength, which afterwards proved a great damage to me.

There was no part of creature holiness of which I had so great a sense of its loveliness as humility, brokenness of heart, and poverty of spirit, and there was nothing that I so earnestly longed for. My heart panted after this; to lie low before God, as in the dust; that I might be nothing, and that God might be ALL; that I might become as a little child. My heart was knit in affection to those in whom were appearances of true piety; and I could bear the thoughts of no other companions but such as were holy, and the disciples of the blessed Jesus. I had great longings for the advancement of Christ's kingdom in the world, and my secret prayer used to be, in great part, taken up in praying for it. If I heard the least hint of anything that happened, in any part of the world, that appeared in some respect or other, to have a favorable aspect on the interests of Christ's kingdom, my soul eagerly seized upon it, and it would much animate and refresh me. I used to be eager to read public newspapers, mainly for that end, to see if I could not find some news favorable to the interests of religion in the world.

I had then, and at other times, the greatest delight in the holy Scriptures of any book whatsoever. Oftentimes, in reading it, every word seemed to touch my heart. I felt a harmony between something in my heart and those sweet and powerful words. I seemed often to see so much light exhibited by every sentence, and such a refreshing food communicated, that I could not get along in reading; often dwelling long on one sentence, to see the wonders contained in it; and yet almost every sentence seemed to be full of wonders.

The holiness of God has always appeared to me the most lovely of all his attributes. The doctrines of God's sovereignty and free grace, in showing "mercy to whom he would show mercy," and man's absolute dependence on the operations of God's Holy Spirit, have very often appeared to me as sweet and glorious doctrines. These doctrines have been much my delight. God's sovereignty has ever appeared to me a great part of his glory. It has often been my delight to approach God, and adore him as a sovereign God, and ask sovereign mercy of him.

I have loved the doctrines of the Gospel; they have been to my soul like green pastures. The Gospel has seemed to me the richest treasure, the treasure that I have most desired, and longed that it might dwell richly in me. The way of salvation by Christ has appeared glorious and excellent, most pleasant and most beautiful. It has often seemed to me that it would in a great measure spoil heaven to receive it in any other way.

Conversion of Rev. John Summerfield.

It was in the year 1817 that he was brought to reflect seriously on his past life and on the conduct he was then pursuing. He saw clearly that he was the cause of the distress to which his father was reduced; and his own prospects in life appeared at the same time awfully gloomy: these reflections had a dreadful effect upon his mind, and he experienced lashings of conscience too terrible for endurance. Instead of seeking and finding relief in prayer, he felt himself a reprobate before God, and was more than once tempted to commit suicide. He found no resting-place amid the "mire and clay," into which Satan had brought his feet, and saw no escape from the "horrible pit" of his own despair.

In this state of mental agony, he was one day wandering about in the streets of Dublin, weeping bitterly, when he was noticed and accosted by a pious man, by trade an edge-tool maker, who, with the tact of a Methodist and the simplicity of a saint, ascertained his state and endeavored to comfort him; at the same time inviting him to his house, where he was about to hold a prayer-meeting. The party assembled consisted chiefly of soldiers from the barracks; prayer was offered by different persons in turn, and the case of the visitor was specially presented before Him with whom "the effectual fervent prayer of a righteous man availeth much;" and such was the fervor of the good leader and the soldiers, and so sincere the contrition and supplication of the penitent, that he that very night found peace to his soul.

Having found such a blessing among these poor soldiers, he became much attached to them, and resolved to make them some return of kindness for what they had done for him. On inquiry, he ascertained that their situation at the barracks was by no means comfortable, they being perpetually ridiculed and insulted by wicked men in the regiment. Hearing this, he was determined to relieve them if possible—for on his visits he found their comrades as bad as they had been described—utterers of profane sarcasms and revilers of all religion. He commenced his work of reformation by relating entertaining anecdotes, and endeavoring by every means to make his company agreeable to them. In this he succeeded ; and in time, as his visits became frequent and acceptable, he began to check their swearing and other improper language. He would even occasionally condescend to assist them in little matters, as pipe-claying their belts, etc. At length, he so far gained their respect and established his own influence, that no improper language was ever allowed or used in his presence ; and if anything wrong happened to be going on at the time of his visit, the moment that he entered the yard, some one would give the signal, "He's coming," and presently all became order and regularity. He next got them to attend to reading the Bible, held regular prayer-meetings among them, and exhorted them to seek the Lord. The number of serious persons among the soldiers increased daily, and his plan prospered more and more, until, to his great regret, the regiment was removed. He commenced preaching in 1818, and continued in most abundant and distinguished evangelical labors until 1825, when he was cut off in the morning of his promise, at the age of 27.

Conversion of Rev. C. H. Spurgeon.

I shall never forget the hour when I hope God's mercy first looked on me. It was in a place very different from this, among a despised people, in an insignificant little chapel, of a peculiar sect. I went there bowed down with guilt, laden with transgression. The minister walked up the pulpit stairs, opened his Bible, and read that precious text: "Look unto me, and be ye saved, all the ends of the earth; for I am God, and beside me there is none else;" and, as I thought, fixing his eyes on me, before he began to preach to others, he said: "Young man! look! look! look! You are one of the ends of the earth; you feel you are; you know your need of a Saviour; you are trembling because you think he will never save you. He says this morning, 'Look!'" O how my soul was shaken within me then! What! thought I, does that man know me, and all about me? He seemed as if he did. And it made me "look!" Well, I thought, lost or saved, I will try; sink or swim, I will run the risk of it; and in that moment I hope by his grace I looked upon Jesus, and though desponding, downcast, and ready to despair, and feeling that I could rather die than live as I had lived, at that very moment it seemed as if a young heaven had had its birth within my conscience. I went home, no more cast down; those about me, noticing the change, asked me why I was so glad, and I told them I had believed in Jesus, and that it was written, "There is therefore now no condemnation to them that are in Christ Jesus, who walk not after the flesh, but after the Spirit."

"Nelson on Infidelity."

The author of this striking work, which has been blessed in bringing scores of infidels to Christ, and of which not far from 100,000 copies have been circulated, was eminent as an intelligent infidel physician, and then as an able minister of Christ. He loved much, for he had much forgiven.

At twelve he thought himself converted, and soon entered Washington College, near his father's residence, at which he graduated at sixteen, when he proceeded to Danville, Kentucky, where his elder brother was then settled in the ministry, and entered on the study of medicine with the celebrated Dr. Ephraim McDowell.

In the pursuit of medical science, while infidelity swayed the higher circles, and the works of Volney, Voltaire, and Paine were in high repute, Dr. Nelson—like many who in early life obtained a false hope of their conversion—was led to believe that he had been self-deceived, and that all religion, and the Bible itself, was a delusion.

The wonderful processes of his mind in giving up this infidelity, by reluctantly detecting the dishonesty and unfairness of Voltaire and other infidel writers, and by a patient, intelligent examination of the whole subject in his own heart, in the lives and conduct of believers and unbelievers, in practical writings, and especially in the word of God, form perhaps the most interesting portion of his now celebrated work. It is hard for any reader to question his sincerity, the stern integrity, patience, and thoroughness of his investigation, or doubt that he was led by the Holy Spirit in the true and right way.

At the age of twenty-five he joined the Presbyterian church, of which his father was an elder, deploring his long rejection of the Saviour he now delighted to honor, and resolving to redeem the time by the unreserved consecration of all his powers to him. At first his diffidence scarcely allowed him to lead others in prayer; but his inventive mind, warm heart, and ceaseless energy found many means of usefulness, including the wide circulation of good books, while in his extensive medical practice. It is stated that a sermon he heard from the lamented Dr. Cornelius, who passed through Tennessee, fired his mind with the most enlarged missionary spirit, which expired only with his life.

At about the age of thirty-three he gave himself publicly to the ministry of reconciliation, assisted for a time in editing a religious periodical, and was soon installed in Danville, Kentucky, where he had imbibed his infidelity, as successor of his worthy deceased brother, who had done so much for the church and college there. He soon proved that he had indeed been called to the work of the ministry. He became "a burning and a shining light," not only to his own congregation, but far and wide throughout the state, where the rich effusions of the Spirit abundantly attended his labors; and it was those revivals which were the manifest precursors of the great revival of 1831, which extended throughout the land, and added to the churches more than one hundred thousand souls. He seemed to imbibe, in measure, the whole spirit of our Lord. In personal efforts for the salvation of individuals, he labored like Harlan

Page. In the pulpit, his tall, manly form and kindled eye, his frankness and generosity of spirit, the gushing love of his heart for souls, his bold, free, original eloquence, his powerful appeals to the heart and conscience, his full and clear exhibition of Christ and his salvation, attracted and fixed the attention of his hearers.

He wrote the Cause and Cure of Infidelity about 1836, in the first summer of his residence in Illinois, chiefly under the shade of four large oaks, drawing mainly from the resources of his own mind and memory. He also wrote another treatise entitled "Wealth and Honor," breathing a missionary spirit as expansive as the ruins of the fall, summoning the whole energies of the church of God for the world's redemption, and showing that *her wealth* and *her honor* were in rescuing lost souls, and adding them as gems to the Redeemer's crown. He carried this work to the east for publication, but it is now supposed to be irrecoverably lost.

In his declining health, and often in severe suffering, he mourned mainly that he could not preach the gospel and labor to win sinners to Christ ; but he murmured not against the divine will. When the hour of his departure drew nigh, he called to him his wife and so many of his eleven children as were near, saying, "My master calls. I am going home. Kiss me, my children, and take your last farewell, for I shall soon be in a state of insensibility, and shall not know you." He expressed his wishes in various respects, and then said, "It is well," and slumbered till the resurrection-morn.

Conversion of Hedley Vicars.

Hitherto, says his biographer, Hedley Vicars had been the subject only of the awakening work of the Spirit. In later days, when he looked back on that period of his life, he distinctly stated, "I was not then converted to God." He was seeking, but he had not found, "the grace of life."

It was in the month of November, 1851, that while awaiting the return of a brother officer to his room, he idly turned over the leaves of a Bible which lay on the table. The words caught his eye, "The blood of Jesus Christ his Son cleanseth us from all sin." Closing the book, he said, "If this be true for me, henceforth I will live, by the grace of God, as a man should live who has been washed in the blood of Jesus Christ."

That night he scarcely slept, pondering in his heart whether it were presumptuous or not to claim an interest in those words. During those wakeful hours, he was watched, we cannot doubt, with deep and loving interest, by One who *never* slumbereth nor sleepeth; and it was said of him in heaven, "Behold he prayeth."

In answer to those prayers, he was enabled to believe, as he arose in the morning, that the message of peace *was* "true for him"—"a faithful saying, and worthy of *all* acceptation." "The past," he said, "then, is blotted out. What I have to do is, to go forward. I cannot return to the sins from which my Saviour has cleansed me with His own blood."

On the morning which succeeded that memorable night, he bought a large Bible, and placed it open on the table in his sitting-room, determining that "an open Bible" for the future should be "his colors." "It was to speak for me," he said, "before I was strong enough to speak for myself." His friends came as usual to his rooms, and did not altogether fancy the new colors. One remarked that he had "turned Methodist," and, with a shrug, retreated. Another ventured on the bolder measure of warning him not to become a hypocrite: "Bad as you were, I never thought you would come to this, old fellow." So, for the most part, for a time his quarters were deserted by his late companions. During six or seven months he had to encounter no slight opposition at mess, "and had hard work," as he said, "to stand his ground." But the promise did not fail, "The righteous shall hold on his way, and *he that hath clean hands* shall wax stronger and stronger."

We learn, from a letter recently quoted, from Charles Cay, Esq., assistant-surgeon, Coldstream Guards, late of the 97th, that from this time his conversion grew daily more deeply spiritual, and that he lost no opportunity of attending every public service in Dr. Twining's church, and his Bible classes for officers, soldiers, and those in hospital. His rapid growth in knowledge and grace is mainly attributed to the instruction and profit gained at these classes, by a senior officer (Lieutenant-Colonel Ingram) in the 97th, whose friendship he deeply valued.

A heart so large and loving by nature as that of Hedley Vicars can scarcely accept the open invitation to come to Jesus for pardon, peace, and eternal life, without giving him an immediate response to the injunction, "Let him that heareth say, come." Accordingly, he began to teach in a Sunday-school, to visit the sick, and to take every opportunity of reading the Scriptures and praying with the men singly. Of three of these, whom he describes as "once great sinners, nearly as bad as myself," he could soon say confidently that they had followed him in turning to God. At the same time he was also the means of awakening some of his brother officers to make the earnest inquiry, "What must I do to be saved?"

"As he felt he had been much forgiven," writes the friend before alluded to, "so in proportion was the ever-burning and increasing love to Him whom he had so long grieved by his sins. The name of Jesus was ever on his lips and in his heart. Much grace was given him to confess Jesus boldly before others; and when he was adjutant, his example and his rebukes to the men for swearing carried great weight, and showed his zeal for the honor of God."

Rev. Samuel Pearce.

When about fifteen years old he was sent by his father to inquire after the welfare of a person in the neighborhood, in dying circumstances, who (though before his departure he was in a happy state of mind, yet) at that time was sinking into deep despair. While in the room of the dying man, he heard him cry out with inexpressible agony of spirit, "I am damned forever!" These awful words pierced his soul; and he felt a resolution at the time to serve the Lord; but the impression soon wore off, and he again returned to folly.

When about sixteen years of age, it pleased God effectually to turn him to himself. A sermon delivered by Mr. Birt, who was then co-pastor with Mr. Gibbs, of the Baptist church at Plymouth, was the first means of impressing his heart with a sense of his lost condition, and of directing him to the gospel remedy. The change in him appears to have been sudden, but effectual; and the recollection of his former vicious propensities, though a source of bitterness, yet furnished a strong evidence of its being the work of God. "I believe," he says, "few conversions were more joyful. The change produced in my views, feelings, and conduct, was so evident to myself, that I could no more doubt of its being from God, than of my existence. I had the witness in myself, and was filled with peace and joy unspeakable."

His feelings being naturally strong and receiving a new direction, he entered into religion with all his heart; but not having known the devices of Satan, his soul was entangled by its own ardor, and he was thrown into great perplexity. Having read Doddridge's *Rise and Progress of Religion in the Soul*, he determined formally to dedicate himself to the Lord, in a manner recommended in the seventeenth chapter of that work. The form of a covenant, as there drawn up, he also adopted as his own; and that he might bind himself in the most solemn and affecting manner, *signed it with his blood*. But afterwards failing in his engagements, he was plunged into dreadful perplexity, and almost into despair. On a review of his covenant, he seems to have accused himself of a pharisaical reliance upon the strength of his own resolutions; and therefore, taking the paper to the top of his father's house, he tore it into small pieces, and threw it from him to be scattered by the wind. He did not, however, consider his obligation to be the Lord's, as hereby nullified; but feeling more suspicion of himself, he depended upon the *blood of the cross*.

After this he was baptized, and became a member of the Baptist church at Plymouth, the ministers and members of which, in a few years, perceived in him talents for public work. Being solicited by both his pastors, he exercised as a probationer; and receiving a unanimous call from the church, entered on the work of the ministry in November, 1786. Soon after this he went to the academy at Bristol, then under the superintendence of Dr. Caleb Evans.

Rev. Andrew Fuller.

"I was, at times, the subject of such convictions and affections that I really thought myself converted, and lived under that delusion for a long time. The ground on which I rested that opinion, was as follows: One morning, I think about the year 1767, as I was walking alone, I began to think seriously what would become of my poor soul, and was deeply affected in thinking of my condition. I felt myself the slave of sin, and that it had such power over me, that it was in vain for me to think of extricating myself from its thralldom. I walked sorrowfully along, repeating these words: 'Iniquity will be my ruin! Iniquity will be my ruin!' While poring over my unhappy case, those words of the Apostle suddenly occurred to my mind, 'Sin shall not have dominion over you; for ye are not under the law, but under grace.' Now, the suggestion of a text of Scripture to the mind, especially if it came with power, was generally considered, by the religious people with whom I occasionally associated, as a promise coming immediately from God. I, therefore, so understood it, and thought that God had thus revealed to me that I was in a state of salvation, and that, therefore, iniquity should not, as I had feared, be my ruin. The effect was, I was overcome with joy and transport. I shed, I suppose, thousands of tears as I walked along, and seemed to feel myself, as it were, in a new world. It appeared to me that I hated my sins, and was resolved to forsake them. Thinking on my wicked courses, I remember using those words of Paul, 'Shall I continue in sin, that grace may abound? God forbid!' I felt, or seemed to feel, the strongest indignation at the thought. But, strange as it may appear, though my face was that morning, I believe, swollen with weeping, before night all was gone and forgotten, and I returned to my former vices with as eager a gust as ever. Nor do I remember, that, for more than half a year afterwards, I had any serious thoughts about the salvation of my soul. I lived entirely without prayer, and was wedded to my sins just the same as before, or, rather, was increasingly attached to them.

"Some time in the following year, I was again walking by myself, and began to reflect upon my course of life; particularly upon my former hopes and affections, and how I had since forgotten them all, and returned to all my wicked ways. Instead of sin having no more dominion over me, I perceived that its dominion had been increased. Yet, I still thought that must have been a promise of God to me, and that I must have been a converted person, but in a backsliding state. And this persuasion was confirmed by another sudden impression, which dispelled my dejection, in these words : 'I have blotted out as a thick cloud thy transgressions, and as a cloud thy sins.' This, like the former, overcame my mind with joy. I wept much at the thoughts of having backslidden so long, but yet considered myself now as restored and happy. But this also was mere transient affection. I have great reason to think that the great deep of my heart's depravity had not yet been broken up, and that all my religion was without any abiding principle. Amidst it all, I still continued in the neglect of prayer, and was never, that I recollect, induced to deny myself of any sin, when temptations were presented. I now thought, however, 'Surely I shall be better for the time to come.' But alas ! in a few days this also was forgotten, and I returned to my evil courses with as great an eagerness as ever.

"One morning, I think in November, 1769, I walked out by myself, with an unusual load of guilt upon my conscience. The remembrance of my sin, not only on the past evening, but for a long time back, the breach of my vows, and the shocking termination of my former hopes and affections, all uniting together, formed a burden which I knew not how to bear. The reproaches of a guilty conscience seemed like the gnawing worm of hell. I thought, 'Surely that must be an earnest of hell itself !' The fire and brimstone of the bottomless pit seemed to burn within my bosom. I do not write in the language of exaggeration. I now know that the sense which I then had of the evil of sin, and the wrath of God, was very far short of the truth ; but yet it seemed more than I was able to sustain. In reflecting upon my broken vows, I saw that there was no truth in me. I saw that God would be perfectly just in sending me to hell, and that to hell I must go, unless I were saved of mere grace, and as it were in spite of myself. I felt, that if God were to forgive me all my past sins, I should again destroy my soul, and that in less than a day's time. I never before knew what it was to feel myself an odious, lost sinner, standing in need of both pardon and purification. Yet, though I needed these blessings, it seemed presumption to hope for them, after what I had done. I was absolutely helpless, and seemed to have nothing about me that ought to excite the pity of God, or that I could reasonably expect should do so ;

but everything disgusting to him, and provoking to the eyes of his glory.

"I was not then aware that *any* poor sinner had a warrant to believe in Christ for the salvation of his soul; but supposed there must be some kind of qualification to entitle him to do it; yet I was aware that I had no qualifications. On review of my resolution at that time, it seems to resemble that of Esther, who went into the king's presence, *contrary to law*, and at the hazard of her life. Like her, I seemed reduced to extremities, impelled by dire necessity, to run all hazards, even though I should perish in the attempt. Yet it was not altogether from a dread of wrath that I fled to this refuge; for I well remember, that I felt something attracting in the Saviour. 'I must—I will—yes—I will trust my soul, my sinful, lost soul in his hands—if I perish, I perish!' However it was, I was determined to cast myself upon Christ, thinking, peradventure, he would save my soul; and if not, I could but be lost. In this way I continued above an hour, weeping and supplicating mercy for the Saviour's sake: (my soul hath it still in remembrance, and is humbled in me!) and as the eye of the mind was more and more fixed upon him, my guilt and fears were gradually and insensibly removed. I now found rest for my troubled soul."

Adoniram Judson.

Young Judson is described as possessed of an acute intellect, with great powers of acquisition and unflagging perseverance. His temper was amiable, but his natural love of preëminence was unduly encouraged and fostered by his father, who fondly but unwisely told him he expected him to become a great man. When about fourteen years of age, his studies were interrupted by a serious attack of illness, and for a year after he was unable to resume his wonted occupations. When the violence of the disease subsided, he spent many long days and nights in reflecting upon his future course. His plans were of the most extravagantly ambitious character. Now he was an orator, now a poet, now a statesman; but, whatever his character or profession, he was sure in his castle-building to attain to the highest eminence. After a time, one thought crept into his mind and embittered all his musings. Suppose he should attain to the highest pinnacle of which human nature is capable: what then? Could he hold his honor forever? What would it be to him, when a hundred years had gone by, that America had never known his equal? He did not wonder that Alexander wept when at the summit of his ambition; he felt very sure that he should have wept too. Then he would become alarmed at the extent of his own wicked soarings, and try to comfort himself with the idea that it was all the result of the fever in his brain.

One day, his mind reverted to religious pursuits. Yes, an eminent divine was very well: though he should of course prefer something more brilliant. Gradually, and without his being aware of his own train of thought, his mind instituted a comparison between the great worldly divine, toiling for the same perishable objects as his other favorites, and the humble minister of the gospel, laboring only to please God and benefit his fellow-men. There was (so he thought) a sort of sublimity about that, after all. Surely the world was all wrong, or such a self-abjuring man would be its hero? Ah! but the good man had a reputation more enduring. Yes, yes, his fame was sounded before him as he entered the other world; and that was the only fame worthy of the possession, because the only one that triumphed over the grave. Suddenly, in the midst of his self-gratulation, the words flashed across his mind, "Not unto us, not unto us, but unto thy name give glory." He was confounded. Not that he had actually made himself the representative of this last kind of greatness; it was not sufficiently to his taste for that: but he had ventured on dangerous ground, and he was startled by a a flood of feelings that had till now remained dormant. He had always said and thought, so far as he had thought anything about it, that he wished to become truly religious; but now religion seemed so entirely opposed to all his ambitious plans, that he was afraid to look into his heart, lest he should discover, what he did not like to confess, even to himself, that he did not want to become a Christian. He was fully awake to the vanity of worldly pursuits, and was, on the whole, prepared to yield the palm of excellence to religious ones; but his father had often said he would one day be great man, and a great man he had resolved to be.

The transition from this state of mind to infidelity was very easy. French infidelity was, at this period, sweeping over the land like a flood. At Providence College there was a young man, who was amiable, talented, witty, exceedingly agreeable in person and manners, but a confirmed deist. A very strong friendship sprang up between the two young men, founded on similar tastes and sympathies, and Judson soon became, at least professedly, as great an unbeliever as his friend.

During a part of his collegiate course, Judson was engaged in the instruction of a school, at Plymouth, and, on closing school, set out on a tour through the Northern States, and thence to New York.

After seeing what he wished of New York, he pursued his journey westward, and visited the home of an uncle, a Christian minister. The uncle was absent, and the conversation of the young man who occupied his place was characterized by a godly sincerity, a solemn but gentle earnestness, which addressed itself to the heart; and Judson went away deeply impressed. The next night he stopped at a country-inn. The landlord mentioned, as he lighted him to his room, that he had been obliged to place him next door to a young man who was exceedingly ill, probably in a dying state; but he hoped that it would occasion him no uneasiness. Judson assured him that, beyond pity for the sick man, he should have no feeling whatever. But it was nevertheless a very restless night. Sounds came from the sick chamber—sometimes the movements of the watchers, sometimes the groans of the sufferer; but it was not these which disturbed him. He thought of what the landlord had said: the stranger was probably in a dying state; and was he prepared? Alone, and in the dead of night, he felt a blush of shame steal over him at the question, for it proved the shallowness of his philosophy. What would his late companions say to his weakness? The clear-minded, intellectual, witty E——, what would he say to such consummate boyishness? But still his thoughts *would* revert to the sick man. Was he a Christian, calm and strong in the hope of a glorious immortality? or was he shuddering upon the brink of a dark, unknown future? Perhaps he was a "freethinker," educated by Christian parents and prayed over by a Christian mother. The landlord had described him as a *young* man; and, in imagination, he was forced to place himself upon the dying bed, though he strove with all his might against it. At last, morning came, and its light dispelled all his "superstitious illusions." As soon as he had risen, he went in search of the landlord and inquired for his fellow-lodger. "He is dead," was the reply. "Dead!" "Yes; he is gone, poor fellow! The doctor said he would probably not survive the night." "Do you know who he was?" "Oh, yes; it was a young man from Providence College—a very fine fellow: his name was E——." Judson was completely stunned. After hours had passed, he knew not how, he attempted to pursue his journey. But one single thought occupied his mind, and the words, Dead! lost! lost! were continually ringing in his ears. He knew the religion of the Bible to be true, he felt its truth, and he was in despair. In this state of mind he resolved to abandon his scheme of travelling, and at once turned his horse's head towards Plymouth.

Mr. Judson's moral nature was now thoroughly aroused, and he was deeply in earnest on the subject of religion. Light gradually dawned upon his mind, and he was enabled, a few months later, to surrender his whole soul to Christ as his atoning Saviour. The change in Mr. Judson's religious character was not attended by those external indications of moral excitement which are frequently observed. The reformation wrought in him was, however, deep and radical. With unusual simplicity of purpose, he yielded himself up once and forever to the will of God, and, without a shadow of misgiving, relied upon Christ as his all-sufficient Saviour. From the moment of his conversion, he seemed never, through life, to have been harassed by a doubt of his acceptance with God. The new creation was so manifest to his consciousness, that, in the most decided form, he had the witness in himself. His plans of life were, of course, entirely reversed. He banished forever those dreams of literary and political ambition in which he had formerly indulged, and simply asked himself, how shall I so order my future being as best to please God? That he was moved by no transient impulse nor fit of enthusiasm, but was made partaker of a new *life*—the divine life—is sufficiently attested by the devotion of six-and-thirty years of unwearied toil to the salvation of idolatrous Burmah.

Samuel Budgett.

"Samuel Budgett," says his biographer, "was early taught to worship, and obey, and seek the God from whose hand his young being had come. What Lamartine so beautifully says of his own mother, might be said equally of Budgett's: 'We could not remember the day when she *first* spoke to us about God.'" One of the friends of his after-life thus states one of those events which pass silently within the bosom of Christian families, but which reappear in the life of their members, in blessed and memorable fruit: "He was about nine years of age, when one day, in passing his mother's door, he heard her engaged in earnest prayer for her family, and for himself by name. He thought, 'My mother is more earnest that I should be saved than I am for my own salvation.' In that hour he became decided to serve God, and the impression then made was never effaced." In this providential manner began the Christian life of one of the most useful and honored of the sons of commerce, who, rising from poverty, acquired wealth, and devoted it with a liberal hand to the service of religion and humanity.

Rev. James Hervey.

In the parish of Weston Favel, where he was his father's curate, there resided a ploughman, who usually attended the ministry of Dr. Doddridge in the neighboring town of Northampton. Mr. Hervey very frequently accompanied the ploughman in his rural employment for the sake of his health. Understanding the ploughman to be a religious person, he said to him one day, "What do you think is the hardest thing in religion?" To which he replied, "I am a poor illiterate man, and you, sir, are a minister: I beg leave to return the question." Then said Mr. Hervey, "I think the hardest thing is to deny sinful self," grounding his opinion on that solemn admonition of our Lord, "If any man will come after me, let him deny himself." "I argued," says Mr. Hervey, "upon the import and extent of the duty, showing that merely to forbear the infamous action is little: we must deny admittance, deny entertainment, at least, to the evil imagination, and quench even the unkindling spark of irregular desire. In this way I shot my random bolt." The ploughman replied, "There is another kind of self-denial to which the injunction goes ; it is of great consequence, and the hardest thing in religion : and that is, to deny *righteous* self." He went on to say with what pleasure he and his family had for a long time enjoyed the ordinances of religion under the ministry of Dr. Doddridge, and added, "But to this moment I find it the hardest thing to deny righteous self ; I mean the renouncing of our own strength, and of our own righteousness :—not leaning on that for holiness, nor relying on this for justification." In repeating the story to a friend, Mr. Hervey observed, "I then hated the righteousness of Christ ; I looked at the man with astonishment and disdain, and thought him an old fool, and wondered at what I then fancied the motley mixture of piety and oddity in his notions. I have since clearly seen who was the fool—not the wise old Christian, but the proud James Hervey."

Several noted Infidels.

It is told of Lord Lyttleton and his friend Gilbert West that they agreed together to write something in support of their unbelief. The former chose the conversion of St. Paul as his theme, and the latter the resurrection of Jesus Christ. But the result of their studies was the reverse of their anticipations. Lyttleton found in the history of the conversion of St. Paul an irrefragable argument in support of the entire Christian scheme, and West found a like argument in the history of our Lord's resurrection. And to this circumstance we owe the valuable works of these authors on these special topics in defence of the Christian faith.

The infidelity of John Newton gave way amid the terrors of the storm. The infidelity of Richard Cecil gave way through the wretchedness of soul to which it reduced him. Soame Jenyns, who was member of Parliament for Cambridge, could find no rest for his spirit, and was thus impelled to examine the grounds of his unbelief. The result was, that he discovered his error, believed in the Saviour of mankind, and wrote a small treatise in defence of the gospel, entitled, "A View of the Internal Evidences of Christianity." General Dykern was a professed deist till he received his mortal wound at the battle of Bergen, in 1759. During his illness, however, a great change was wrought upon his mind, and he died in the full assurance of faith, glorying in the salvation of Jesus, and wondering at the happy change that had taken place in his soul.

Isabella Graham.

In Mrs. Isabella Graham we have a beautiful specimen of true religion, at once feminine and practical. And its origin was peaceful, imperceptible, and early, like that of Albert Bengel. Her childhood and youth were spent among all the traditional associations of Eldersley, once the habitation of the Scottish hero, Sir William Wallace. Of the period at which her heart first tasted that the Lord is gracious, her biographer tells us she had no precise recollection. As far back as she could remember, she took delight in pouring out her soul to God. In the words of Eldersley, she selected a bush to which she resorted in seasons of devotion ; and under this bush she was enabled to devote herself to God, through faith in her Redeemer, before she attained her tenth year. To this favorite and (to her) sacred spot she would repair when exposed to temptation or perplexed with youthful troubles. From thence she caused her prayers to ascend, and always found peace and consolation.

That this was more than mere girlish sentiment was proved by its growing and practical character. While only twenty-four years of age we find her married, and with her husband, a regimental surgeon, resident at Fort Niagara, on Lake Ontario. The want of religious ordinances was here, no doubt, the occasion of injury to the life of God in her soul. But a conscientious observance of the Sabbath was the means of her preservation. She wandered, on those sacred days, into the woods around Niagara, searched her Bible, communed with God and herself, and poured out her soul in prayer to her covenant Lord.

A few years after we find her returning from America, a sorrowful widow with three infants to care for. After a stormy and trying voyage, she arrived in safety at Belfast, and thence embarked for Scotland on board a packet on which, as she afterwards learned, there was not even a compass. There arose a great storm, and they were tossed to and fro for nine hours in imminent danger. The rudder and the masts were carried away ; everything on deck was thrown overboard ; and, at length, the vessel struck in the night upon a rock on the coast of Ayr. The greatest confusion pervaded the passengers and the crew. Of a number of young students going to the University of Edinburgh, some were swearing, some were praying, and all were in despair. The widow only remained composed. The faith which was implanted in her while in girlhood she rambled among the woods of Eldersley, was her support. With her babe in her arms, she hushed her weeping family, and told them that in a few moments they should all go to join their father in a better world. The passengers wrote their names in their pocket-books, that their bodies might be recognized. One young man came into the cabin, asking, "Is there any peace here?" He was surprised to find a female so tranquil, and a short conversation showed that religion was the source of comfort and hope to them both in this perilous hour.

That her early piety, though of a quiet, imperceptible growth, was not superficial, nor merely emotional, will appear likewise from the language in which she described it many years after. Writing from New York to a friend in Edinburgh, she said, "It is now, I think, thirty-five years since I simply but solemnly accepted of the Lord's Christ as God's gift to a lost world. I rolled my condemned, perishing, corrupted soul upon this Jesus, exhibited in the gospel as a Saviour from sin. My views then were dark compared with what they now are ; but this I remember, that, at the time, I felt a heart-satisfying trust in the mercy of God as the purchase of Christ, and, for a time, rejoiced with joy scarcely supportable, singing almost continually the 103d Psalm."

The Earl of Rochester.

The case of the Earl of Rochester is well known—"a great wit, a great scholar, a great poet, a great sinner, and a great penitent."

He had sunk and wallowed in the very slough of wickedness, but, when "he came to himself," he regarded himself as the greatest sinner the sun had ever shone upon, and wished he had been a crawling leper in a ditch, rather than have offended God as he had done. "One day, at an atheistical meeting in the house of a person of quality," he told a friend afterwards, "I undertook to manage the cause, and was the principal disputant against God and religion; and for my performances, received the applause of the whole company. Upon this my mind was terribly struck, and I immediately replied thus to myself: 'Good God! that a man who walks upright, who sees the wonderful works of God, and has the use of his senses and reason, should use them to the defying of his Creator!'" But there was no genuine conversion till the fifty-third chapter of Isaiah was read to him, together with some other parts of the Sacred Scriptures, "when it pleased God to fill his mind with such peace and joy in believing, that it was remarkable to all about him. 'Oh blessed God,' he would say, 'can such a horrid creature as I am be accepted by thee, who have denied thy being and condemned thy power? Can there be mercy and pardon for me? Shall the unspeakable joys of heaven be conferred on me? Oh, mighty Saviour, never but through thine infinite love and satisfaction! Oh, never but by the purchase of thy blood!' adding, that with all abhorrence he reflected upon his former life—that from his heart he repented of all that folly and madness of which he had been guilty."

Martin Boos.

Martin Boos entered on the duties of the priest's office in the Roman Catholic Church with an unspotted character. From his earliest years his conduct had been irreproachable; his application to his literary and theological studies had been close and successful, and he was habitually conscientious and devout.

Twenty years afterwards (1811), he wrote of the "immense pains" which he took to be a very pious man, in these terms: "For years together, even in winter, I lay on the cold floor. I scourged myself till I bled again. I fasted and gave my bread to the poor. I spent every hour I could spare in the church or the cemetery.

I confessed and took the sacrament almost every week; in short, I gained such a character for piety that I was appointed prefect of the congregation by the ex-Jesuits. But what a life I led! The prefect, with all his sanctity, became more and more absorbed in self, melancholy, anxious and formal. The saint was evermore exclaiming in his heart, 'Oh, wretched man that I am! who shall deliver me?' And no one replied, 'The grace of God through Jesus Christ our Lord.' No one gave the sick man that spiritual specific, 'The just shall live by faith;' and when I had obtained it, and found the benefit of it, the whole world, with all its learning and spiritual authority, would have persuaded me that I had swallowed poison, and was poisoning all around me; that I deserved to be hung, drowned, immured, banished or burned."

The history of the change which the young priest Boos underwent is very simple. "In 1788 or 1789," he says, "I visited a sick person who was respected for her deep humility and exemplary piety I said to her, 'You will die very peacefully and happily.' 'Why so?' she asked. 'Because you have led,' I replied, 'such a pious and holy life.' The good woman smiled at my words, and said, 'If I leave the world relying on my own piety I am sure I shall be lost. But relying on Jesus my Saviour, I can die in comfort. What a clergyman you are! What an admirable comforter! If I listened to you, what would become of me? How could I stand before the divine tribunal, where every one must give an account even of her idle words? Which of our actions and virtues would not be found wanting if laid in the divine balances? No; if Christ had not died for me, if he had not made satisfaction for me, I should have been lost for ever, notwithstanding all my good works and pious conduct. He is my hope, my salvation, and my eternal happiness.'"

Martin Boos found instruction where he sought it not. He entered the house of affliction to console, without knowing the true consolation. At first he was astounded and ashamed, that what he, after all his studies, was ignorant of, should be taught him by a simple-hearted woman on her death-bed. Happily for him, he was humble enough not to reject the truth when conveyed to him by so mean an instrument. It made an indelible impression on his mind and formed the foundation of his future faith and life.

Caroline Fry.

Before her conversion took place, Caroline Fry descended into the lowest depth of irreligion. At her relative's table, where she was residing, there was a frequent guest, of literary reputation, of venerable age, courtly and high-bred, whose " wit spared nothing human or divine ; friends, life, mortality, religion, nothing barred the jest." " As was most natural, Caroline attached herself entirely to this fascinating old man." If his insidious flattery "failed to make any impression on her delicacy, artlessness, and purity of thought and feeling, there was that in which the influence of his corrupt companionship did not fail ; she was too innocent for his immorality, she was just ready for his irreligion. Never, perhaps, at the early age of nineteen and twenty, in a heart of such simplicity and uncorruptness and real ignorance of evil, was the enmity of the fallen nature so developed. Here, in the bosom of a simple girl, brought up in all the virtuous regularity and real religious observance of a secluded country life—a stranger to all that is morally evil, to a degree that would not be credited if it were fully explained—with a mind solidly instructed, and unused to any manner of evil influence by books or company, hitherto a stranger to sorrows, wrongs and fears, that tend to harden the ungracious heart—in this unvitiated, unworldly bosom was manifested at that early age, clear and strong to her memory as if it was of yesterday, a living, active hatred to the very name of God. She persuaded herself there was no God, and thought she believed her own heart's lie ; but if she did, why did she hate him ? Why did she feel such renovated delight when his name was the subject of the profane old poet's wit ? 'No God' was probably with her as it probably is with every other infidel, the determination of the heart, and not of the judgment. Thus, while she thought herself above all religious doubts, she seized delightedly on every manifesta tion of infidelity in those around her, and laughed with the very utmost zest of gratified aversion at every profanation of the holy name."

At this period Caroline Fry was residing in a family where every thing was against the probability of her receiving religious impressions, "except the restless, unsatisfied, unhappy state of her own mind, displeased with everything around her and within her ; weary and disgusted with the present, and gloomy and hopeless of the future, without a single sorrow but the absence of all joy." Living in the utter neglect of prayer, there were times when not upon her knees, but on her bed, she would give mental expression to her feelings thus: "God, if thou art a God, I do not love thee, I do not want thee, I do not believe in any happiness in thee; but I am miserable as I am; give me what I do not seek, do not like, do not want, if thou canst make me happy; I am tired of this world: if there is anything better, give it me."

"In the destitution of her affections at this moment, Caroline fixed them with vehement partiality on the daughter of a clergyman in an adjoining parish." This young lady was beautiful and fascinating, but disappointments of a painful character had made her moody and melancholy. She denounced the world, she wished to leave it, she talked much of its vanity; she was, or thought she was, of a consumptive habit, and not likely to live many years; she talked much of death, and much of eternity, and much of God. "I do not remember," says Miss Fry, "that she ever spoke of Christ, of atoning merit, or redeeming love; I believe she knew them not. She talked of the world's emptiness, levity, and injustice. I do not remember that she ever spoke of her own sin. I believe her religion was purely sentimental."

To this friend Caroline never spoke of her unbelief, nor confessed the total absence of religious feeling in her bosom. But she continually bewailed her impetuosity and want of self-control, compared with the composure and philosophy manifested by her friend on all occasions. Friendship, however, looked through the cover of silence that slightly concealed Caroline's infidelity. And her friend addressed a letter to her, to tell her that religion was the source of all the advantage over her which Caroline had so often noticed and so often envied—all that she called philosophy. The bare truth, that religion was the one thing needful that she had not, struck conviction to Miss Fry's soul: it pierced to the very depths of her moral being. Her first emotion on perusal of the letter was a paroxysm of grief and indignation—grief that the idol of her affections should condemn her, and indignation that she should presume to teach her; the next was a determined resolution that her friend should not influence or persuade her. On three successive days she attempted to answer the letter, but could not. "Before the third night arrived, the struggle was over; the battle had been fought and won; the strong man armed was vanquished; the banner of Jesus waved peacefully over the subdued and prostrate spirit of the infidel despiser of his word, the conscious hater of his most precious name."

"'Lord, save me, or I perish,' has been, and is, from first to last, the sum of her religion, dated from that most wondrous night, the first in which she knelt before the cross; in which she prayed; in which she slept in Jesus."

"The most immediate result of this change of heart was, the happiness to which it had at once restored her: at peace with God, she made up her quarrel with all things. The zest of life returned; she no longer quarrelled with her destiny, or felt distaste of all her pursuits, or grew weary of her existence without any reason. The void was filled; she never after wanted something to do, or something to love, or something to look forward to; the less there was of earth, the more there was of heaven in her vision; whenever man failed her, Christ took her up. She had no more stagnant waters, long as her voyage was through troubled ones; she was, with all the leaven of the older nature that remained, essentially a new creature to herself."

This great revolution was as entire as it was sudden. It was no mere paroxysm or convulsion of soul. It was a change which brought with it new principles of life. And, what may seem most strange, these principles were very different from those of the friend who was the unconscious instrument of Miss Fry's conversion. It was not to a mere religiousness, earnest and pharasaic, that she emerged out of her heart-chosen infidelity; it was to a faith in our Lord Jesus Christ as the one Mediator and High-Priest, and to a simple-hearted trust in Him as all her salvation. The bare truth that religion is the one thing needful stung her to the quick; but the seeds of other truths were in her mind, though hated and disbelieved. And these sprang up, now that the fallow ground was broken, and produced those fruits of humble trust in the Saviour of sinners, devout love to His holy name, and an earnest zeal to consecrate to his praise a life that had been redeemed by his mercy.

Wilberforce's Conversion.—Mr. Wilberforce was in the 24th year of his age when he was elected member of parliament for Hull. He afterwards attended the county election, and such was the charm of his eloquence on that occasion, in the large castle area at York, that the people all cried, "We will have that little man for our member." He was then one of the gayest of the gay: not an openly vicious man, but peculiar for his wit, and his distinction in the fashionable circles. His wit became innocuous under Christian principles. He was said to be the "joy and crown of Doncaster races." He went to pay a visit to a relation at Nice, and was accompanied by the Rev. Isaac Milner, afterwards dean of Carlisle. Mention was made of a certain individual who moved in the same rank, an ecclesiastical gentleman, a man devoted to his duty. Mr. W. said, regarding him, "that he thought he carried things too far;" to which Mr. Milner said, he was inclined to think that Mr. W. would form a different estimate on the subject, were he carefully to peruse the whole of the New Testament. Mr. Wilberforce replied that he would take him at his word, and read it through with pleasure. They were both Greek scholars, and in their journey they perused the New Testament together. That single perusal was so blessed to Mr. Wilberforce, that he was revolutionized; he became a new man; and the witty songster, the joy and crown of Doncaster races, proved the Christian senator, and at length became the able advocate for abolishing the slave trade.

Conversion of Augustine.—In the spring of the year 372, a young man in the thirty-first year of his age, in evident distress of mind, entered into his garden near Milan. The sins of his youth—a youth spent in sensuality and impiety—weighed heavily on his soul. Lying under a fig-tree, moaning and pouring out abundant tears, he heard, from a neighboring house, a young voice saying, and repeating in rapid succession, "Tolle, lege, Tolle lege!" take and read, take and read. Receiving this as a divine admonition, he returned to the place where he left his friend Alypius to procure the roll of St. Paul's epistles, which he had, a short time before, left with him. "I seized the roll," says he, in describing this scene, "I opened it, and read in silence the chapter on which my eyes first alighted." It was the thirteenth of Romans. "Let us walk honestly, as in the day; not in rioting and drunkenness, not in chambering and wantonness, not in strife and envying. But put ye on the Lord Jesus Christ, and make not provision for the flesh, to fulfill the lusts thereof." All was decided by a word. "I did not want to read any more," said he; "nor was there any need; every doubt was banished." The morning star had risen in his heart. In the language of Gaussen: "Jesus had conquered; and the grand career of Augustine, the holiest of the fathers, then commenced.

REMARKABLE CONVERSIONS

AND

REVIVAL INCIDENTS.

The Child-Witness.—A little German girl, about twelve years of age, in the city of P——, U. S., had been led to enter a church, and while there, the Lord graciously met her, and converted her soul. Full of joy and wonder, she ran home to tell her father, who was a bigoted Catholic, what a Saviour she had found ; but to her surprise, he became very angry, beat her cruelly, and forbade the mention of the subject again in his house. She continued to attend church, and expressed a wish to join the people of God. He told her if she did, he would beat her to death. With this prospect, she determined to do her duty, putting her trust in Him who hath said, "I will never leave nor forsake thee." When she returned home and told her father what she had done, he beat her most unmercifully, and drove her from the house, telling her never to return, until she had given up her new-fangled religion. Thus forsaken of her father, the Lord took her up ; she was provided with a place in a pious family, at service, reserving to herself the first Monday in every month, which day she spent in distributing tracts to all the German families of her acquaintance, and whenever permitted, she prayed with them before she left, always taking her father's house in her way, though sure of being beaten and driven from it. Month after month she offered the hardened man a tract, at the same time entreating him to think of his poor soul, and offering to pray with him. Although uniformly driven away, with severe blows, she said, "I did not care for the blows, for, sir, my poor father's soul was all I thought of or cared for." In this course she persevered, how long do you think, indolent Christian? not one month, which many think too long to wait for an answer to prayer; but *eighteen months,* without seeing any fruit of her labor. Two months before I met her, she found, on visiting her father, that he was in tears over his work; he suffered her to read, converse, and pray without interruption, and at parting, bade her come again. The next month he was even more tender, and on the day I first saw her, she had seen him again, and she said, "*Oh, how changed was my poor father!* with tears he begged me to forgive him, and pray for him. I told him I had laid nothing up against him, and asked him to pray for himself. He knelt down by my side, but could only say, 'O Lord, forgive, forgive, O Lord, forgive;' and now, sir, I am sure the Lord will hear and convert my poor father."

The next evening, on entering the praying circle, I recognized the voice of the little German girl in the individual who was addressing the throne of grace. Her father was there, inquiring with trembling eagerness the way to the Saviour's feet. The father and daughter left the room together that night, rejoicing in the grace which had washed away their stains.

Conversion of a Moralist.—Miranda N., says a Christian minister, was about 18 years of age, much distinguished for personal beauty, but more for uncommon sweetness of disposition, and great amiableness of deportment. There was not, probably, among all the people of my charge, one whose case would have been more promptly cited, and perhaps none so effectively, to disprove the doctrine of the entire sinfulness of the unregenerate heart. She was deservedly a general favorite. She seemed to entertain the kindest affection towards all, and every one who knew her loved her. One evening at an inquiry meeting, held at my house, I noticed, in a full room, a female in great apparent distress. The disturbance she made by her loud sobs, and frequent and painful interruption of the silence of the room, induced me to pass by others and go to her at once. On coming to her seat, I was not a little surprised to find myself by the side of Miranda. The first inquiry I put to her was this: "What has brought you here M.?" With emphasis, she replied, "My sins, sir." With a view to test the reality and depth of her convictions, I then said, "But what have *you* done which makes either your heart or your life appear so heinously sinful?" At this second question she broke out in a voice that reached the extreme part of the room and thrilled through every heart, for she was known and loved by every person there,—"I HATE GOD, AND I KNOW IT. I HATE CHRISTIANS, AND I KNOW IT. I HATE MY OWN BEING. OH THAT I HAD NEVER BEEN BORN!" As she uttered this acknowledgment, she rose and left the room in irrepressible agony.

A few minutes after this, while walking the adjoining room in great distress, her eye lighted upon a copy of Village Hymns, which lay upon the sideboard. She eagerly caught it up, and read at the first page to which she opened, these words:

"There is a fountain filled with blood,
Drawn from Immanuel's veins;
And sinners plunged beneath that flood,
Lose all their guilty stains."

As she finished this verse she dropped the book and exclaimed, "I have found my Saviour. This is the Saviour I need. O precious Saviour!" and many other expression of the same kind. Her enmity to God was gone. Her burden was removed.

Whitefield's Brother Converted.—Mr. Whitefield, brother of the noted preacher, had fallen into a backslidden state. In conversation with the Countess of Huntingdon one day, he said, "My lady, I know what you say is true. The mercy of God is infinite: I see it clearly. But, ah! my lady, there is no mercy for me—I am a wretch, entirely lost." "I am glad to hear it, Mr. Whitefield," said Lady H. "I am glad at my heart that you are a lost man." He looked with great surprise. "What, my lady, glad! glad at your heart that I am a lost man?" "Yes, Mr. Whitefield, truly glad; for Jesus Christ came into the world to save the lost!" He laid down his cup of tea on the table. "Blessed be God for that," said he, "Glory to God for that word," he exclaimed. "Oh, what unusual power is this which I feel attending it! Jesus Christ came to save the lost! then I have a ray of hope," and so he went on. As he finished his last cup of tea, his hand trembled, and he complained of illness. He went out into the chapel court for the benefit of the air, but staggered to the wall, exclaiming, "I am very ill." Soon after he was brought into the house he expired.

The Bethel Rock.—A ship, says Rev. John Blain, was wrecked amongst the rocks near Cape Horn. While the winds fiercely blowed, and the foaming billows dashed the timbers in pieces, one seaman reached a lonely, barren rock. The day passed slowly away. He stretched his eye to the east and west, to the north and south, over the deep, dark, and ever restless waters—but no friendly sail appeared! The sun disappeared, and he sat down to pass in solitude the lonely night. His shipmates were cold and silent in their watery graves. The waves dashed against the rock, the winds passed swiftly onward, the lamps of night shed their dismal light on the bosom of the deep—but no human voice sounded in his ear, no brother's hand administered to his wants. Hunger and thirst made strong demands, but he had no means to relieve them. The bread and the water were entombed with his companions. Nor had he any consolation to draw from a future world. The Bible and the Redeemer had been neglected, and he was strangely indifferent. Another day came and passed, and another night. On the third night, as he lay on his back, gazing into the starry heavens, he began to think about *God* and *eternity*, his past life, and the interests of his soul. But all was dark. His skin was peeling from his face, his teeth all loose, his thirst almost intolerable, and death seemed to stand by his side. He had never prayed, nor did he know how to pray. A single commandment was all he remembered, and that commandment his dear mother taught him when a child. And how should he meet that mother and his God in a future world? His sins passed in review, and pressed on his guilty conscience, while bitter tears of repentance began to roll down his scalded cheeks. Without knowing what the Lord required of him, he rose, stood on his knees, lifted his feeble hands towards heaven, and there on that lonely rock, far, far away from home and friends, he submitted all to God, and most solemnly promised, if his life was spared, he would *learn* and do whatever God required. From that consecrated and blessed hour, peace flowed into his soul —Christ was his Saviour, and hope entered within the vail. The next day the life-boat from a passing ship took him from the Bethel rock. He landed in Boston, found the sailor's friend and the sailor's home, and listened to the gospel of peace. Father Taylor gave him a Bible, which he read with prayerful attention. He came to New York—visited different churches, searched for truth, remembered his solemn vow, and in February, 1843, while I was preaching in the Baptist Tabernacle, he offered himself to the church. On hearing his experience, every heart felt—every eye wept. Brother William W. Everts baptized him, welcomed him to the church, and *he went on his way rejoicing.*

Doctor Spring's Discouragement.—Dr. Spring, of New York, once related, that during the period of a revival of religion in that city, a young lady, the object of high hope, the centre of wide influence, capable of noble things, yet careering on the giddy steep of fashion and folly, created in him no small solicitude, as he would have to give an account for her soul, every avenue to which seemed most sedulously guarded. He delayed the visit of counsel and exhortation; and delayed, till, rebuked by conscience, he could do so no longer. As soon as he called, and was ushered into the saloon, the first and only person whom he saw was this young lady, bathed in tears, who immediately exclaimed, "My dear pastor, I rejoice to see you. I was fearful I was the only one who had escaped your friendly notice." What a rebuke to fear! What an encouragement to hope, and to action!

"It's too late now, Pa!"—During a series of religious meetings, held in the school-house of a small village, a very little girl became much interested for the salvation of her soul. Her father, a hater of holiness, who lived next door to the place of meeting, finding that his little daughter was much interested in the meetings, and had been forward to be prayed for, strictly forbade her again entering the "house of prayer." The poor little girl was much oppressed, and knew not what to do, but obeyed her father until the next meeting was nearly half through, then slipping out without his knowledge, and getting through a hole in the back yard fence, she hastily ran to the meeting. It was some time before her father missed her, but when he found her gone, he went immediately to the meeting, where she was on her knees, with others whom the people of God were praying for. So enraged was he, that he went directly forward, and took her in his arms, to carry her from the place. As he raised her from her knees, she looked up with a heavenly smile, and said, "It is too late now, pa; I have given my heart to the Saviour." This was too much for the hardened sinner: he too sunk on his knees, while he was prayed for; and very soon he found that Saviour he had in vain attempted to shut out from his daughter's heart.

A Singular Revival.—In the township of R., in the western part of New York, says a writer in the Christian Watchman, without any special or known cause, numbers of individuals were suddenly aroused to anxious inquiry and trembling respecting their souls. Some in different parts of the town, without any knowledge of the affections of others, were alarmed by the consideration of their sins. Two men, from different directions, came to a clergyman in the morning, asking, What shall we do? About nine o'clock in the same morning, one of the members of the church called upon the same clergyman, to go and visit several anxious individuals in his neighborhood; and before night it was ascertained, that almost the whole population of a considerable district, were solemnly, and with weeping, asking the prayers and instructions of the people of God.

Accompanied by the pastor, on that and the subsequent day, we visited from house to house; but wherever we went the Spirit had preceded us. The whole region was a Bochim. A solemn awe pervaded our soul, and we could not but feel that "God is in very deed in our midst."

Work of Grace in Ceylon.—During a remarkable effusion of the Holy Spirit upon the several stations on this island, the following scene occurred at Panditeripo:

On the 13th of February, 1824, while Mr. and Mrs. Scudder were absent, and after the boys of the boarding-school had gone to their room, and were about to lie down to sleep, Whelpley (a native member of the church), was induced to exhort them, most earnestly, to flee from the wrath to come. They were roused and could not sleep. By little companies, they went out into the garden to pray, and the voice of supplication was soon heard in every quarter, each one or each company praying and weeping as if entirely alone. More than thirty were thus engaged in a small garden. The cry was, "What shall I do to be saved?" and "Lord, send thy Spirit." In about an hour Dr. Scudder returned, and after waiting awhile, rang the bell for the boys to come in. They came, and with weeping proposed the inquiry, "What shall we do to be saved?" The next day they seemed unmindful of everything but the salvation of their souls. And soon, under the judicious instructions they received, more than twenty at this place gave encouraging evidence of conversion. This was a specimen of the displays of divine mercy witnessed at the several stations of the mission.

The "Hell-Fire Club."—This was the name of a society in Bristol, England, the members of which always endeavored to coin a new oath for each evening on which they met, the chairman deciding who had the preference. As one of them was walking towards the club in the evening, he was asking himself what sin he had not committed, resolving he would commit it before he went to bed. His attention was arrested by the lights of the chapel, and the voice of the preacher. After some hesitation, whether he should enter the chapel for sport now, or as he returned from the club, he determined on the former. He entered as the preacher was repeating his text, "All manner of sin and blasphemy shall be forgiven unto men; and whosoever speaketh a word against the Son of man, it shall be forgiven him: but whosoever speaketh against the Holy Ghost, it shall not be forgiven him, neither in this world, neither in the world to come." He described the nature of the sin; the reason why it was unpardonable; showed who had not committed it, and proved that their sins might be pardoned. The man went home, locked himself in his bedroom, fell on his knees, thanked God he was out of hell, and prayed for the pardon which he was delighted to know he might yet receive, though he had often wished to die, that he might know the worst of hell. He read, prayed, heard the gospel, looked by faith to Christ, and soon enjoyed a sense of pardon, and the privilege of friendship with God.

Mr. Whitefield and the Trumpeter.—On one occasion, during Whitefield's residence in America, a black trumpeter, belonging to an English regiment, resolved to interrupt him during a discourse which he was expected to deliver in the open air. At the hour appointed for the sermon, he repaired to the field where it was to be preached, carrying his trumpet with him on purpose to blow it with all his might about the middle of the sermon. He took his stand in front of the minister, and at no great distance. The concourse that attended became very great, and those who were towards the extremity of the crowd pressed forward, in order to hear more distinctly, which caused such a pressure at the place where the trumpeter stood, that he found it impossible to raise up the arm which held the trumpet at the time he intended to blow it. He attempted to extricate himself from the crowd, but found this equally impossible, so that he was kept within hearing of the gospel as securely as if he had been chained to the spot. In a short time, his attention was arrested, and he became so powerfully affected by what the preacher presented to his mind, that he was seized with an agony of despair, and was carried to a house in the neighborhood. When the service was over, he was visited by Mr. Whitefield, who tendered some seasonable counsels; and the poor trumpeter from that time became an altered man.

"Sir, who have you been talking with?"—It was the favored lot of a poor little girl in Vermont, about eight years of age, to fall into a family where daily prayers were offered up to Almighty God. Prayer she was unacquainted with. At home she never heard a prayer. An astonishment seized her, when she saw her master, night and morning, standing in one corner of the room, talking, as she termed it, with something that she could not see. An anxiety swelled in her little bosom to know who it could be.

One morning, after her master had been talking with the unknown being, she stepped up before him, and said, " Sir, who have you been talking with this morning !" " I have been trying to talk with God." " God !" said she, with astonishment, " where is he ? where does he live ?" etc. Many questions of a similar nature she put with much interest and feeling, to which her master gave her such answers as were calculated to awaken the liveliest feelings of her mind, in regard to Jehovah. After she had learned all her little mind could contain of divine things, she desired to go home and see her parents, with an earnestness that could not be resisted. Go she must ; leave was granted ; she went home to her father's cottage, a place where prayer was not wont to be made, with her little bosom beating with a high tone of pious feeling in view of the importance of prayer. She went to her father, and said, " Father, pray." She urged with warmth a compliance ; but he utterly refused. She then went to her mother and asked her to pray ; but with no better success. She could not endure it any longer ; her feelings must vent themselves in words. She said, " Let us pray." She knelt down and prayed. In answer to her prayer, both of her parents were brought under conviction, which terminated in hopeful conversion to God. And this was the beginning of an extensive revival of religion.

The Discouraged Father.—The Rev. A. D. Merrill states that there was once a pious father with seven children, who had maintained the worship of God in his family, until all his children had grown up to manhood, and womanhood, and not one of them had been as yet converted to God. At last the old man's faith began to fail, in relation to the promise ; and growing " weary and faint in his mind," he resolved to give up his family worship, and confine his devotions to the closet, and to leave his children to do as they pleased. But before he finally proceeded to do this, he concluded to call his children together once again, to pray with them, and explain to them his reasons for this course. Being assembled, and taking up the " old family Bible," from which he had so often read to them " the words of eternal life," he thus addressed them : " My children, you know that from your earliest recollection I have been accustomed to call you together around this altar, for family worship. I have endeavored to instruct you in the ways of the Lord, and to imbue your minds with the truth. But you have all grown up, and not one of you is converted to God. You are yet in your sins, and show no signs of penitence. I feel discouraged, and have concluded to make no further efforts for your salvation—to demolish my family altar—to confine my own devotions to my closet, and thus to endeavor still to work out my own salvation, while I leave you to yourselves." Upon his speaking thus, first one and then another fell upon their knees, until they were all bowed before God, and besought him that he would not do as he had resolved, but that he would still continue to pray for them, and that he would do it now; for they were now ready to give their hearts to God. He bowed with them. The Spirit descended according to the promise, and before they rose from their knees, they were all made happy in God. One of their number, who was married and away from home, upon returning on a visit, and hearing what great things the Lord had done for the rest of the family, likewise immediately submitted to God, and thus were they all saved, and the covenant promise fulfilled.

A Chain of Influence.—The 31st of January, 1841, when Mr. Jay, of Bath, England, completed fifty years of his ministry, it was observed by his people as a Jubilee. On that occasion, the Rev. Timothy East, of Birmingham, stated, that a sermon Mr. Jay preached in London in the early part of his ministry, was blessed to the conversion of a thoughtless and dissolute young man, who became a minister. A sermon preached by that minister thirty-nine years ago, was the arrow of the Almighty that brought Mr. East to repentance, just as he had determined to leave his native country forever. And a sermon preached by Mr. East twenty-seven years ago, in London, was the means of the conversion of a careless and dissipated young man, who was John Williams, the late missionary to the South Seas.

Dr. Beecher's Sermon to one Hearer.—Dr. Beecher once engaged to preach for a country minister on exchange, and the Sabbath proved to be one excessively stormy, cold, and uncomfortable. It was in mid-winter, and the snow was piled all along in the roads, so as to make the passage very difficult. Still the minister urged his horse through the drifts, put the animal into a shed, and went in. As yet there was no person in the house, and after looking about, the old gentleman—then young—took his seat in the pulpit. Soon the door opened, and a single individual walked up the aisle, looked about, and took a seat. The hour came for commencing service, but no more hearers.

Whether to preach to such an audience, was a question—and it was one that Lyman Beecher was not long deciding. He felt that he had a duty to perform, and he had no right to refuse to do it, because only one man could reap the benefit of it; and, accordingly, he went through all the services, praying, singing, preaching, and the benediction, with only *one* hearer. And when all was over, he hastened down from the desk to speak to his congregation, but he had departed.

A circumstance so rare was referred to occasionally, but twenty years after, it was brought to the doctor's mind quite strangely. Travelling somewhere in Ohio, the doctor alighted from the stage one day in a pleasant village, when a gentleman stepped up and spoke to him, familiarly calling him by name. "I do not remember you," said the doctor. "I suppose not," said the stranger; "but we once spent two hours together in a house alone in a storm." "I do not recall it, sir," added the old man; "pray, when was it?' "Do you remember preaching, twenty years ago, in such a place, to a single person?" "Yes, yes," said the doctor, grasping his hand, "I do, indeed, and if you are the man, I have been wishing to see you ever since." "I am the man, sir; and that sermon saved my soul, made a minister of me, and yonder is my church! The converts of that sermon, sir, are all over Ohio."

Guthrie and the Papist.—Mr. Guthrie, an eminent minister in Scotland, was one evening travelling home very late. Having lost his way on a moor, he laid the reins on the neck of his horse, and committed himself to the direction of Providence. After long travelling over ditches and fields, the horse brought him to a farmer's house, into which he went, and requested permission to sit by the fire till morning, which was granted. A popish priest was administering extreme unction to the mistress of the house, who was dying. Mr. Guthrie said nothing till the priest had retired: then he went forward to the dying woman, and asked her if she enjoyed peace in the prospect of death, in consequence of what the priest had said and done to her. She answered, that she did not; on which he spoke to her of salvation through the atoning blood of the Redeemer. The Lord taught her to understand, and enabled her to believe the message of mercy, and she died triumphing in Jesus Christ her Saviour. After witnessing this astonishing scene, Mr. Guthrie mounted his horse, and rode home. On his arrival, he told Mrs. Guthrie he had seen a great wonder during the night. "I came," said he, "to a farm-house, where I found a woman in a state of nature; I saw her in a state of grace; and left her in a state of glory."

Howe and his Enemy.—When the melancholy state of the times compelled this excellent man to quit the public charge of his beloved congregation at Torrington, in Devonshire, impressed with a sense of duty, he embraced every opportunity of preaching the word of life. He and Mr. Flavel used frequently to conduct their secret ministrations at midnight in different houses in the north of Devonshire. One of the principal of these was Hudscott, an ancient mansion belonging to the family of Rolle, between Torrington and Southmolton. Yet, even here, the observant eye of malevolence was upon them. Mr. Howe had been officiating there, in a dark and tempestuous wintry night, when an alarm was made that information had been given, and a warrant granted to apprehend him. It was judged prudent for him to quit the house; but in riding over a large common, he and his servant missed their way. After several fruitless efforts to recover it, the attendant went forward to seek for a habitation, where they might either find directions or a lodging. He soon discovered a mansion, and received a cheerful invitation to rest there for the night. But how great was Mr. Howe's surprise, to find, on his arrival, that the house belonged to his most inveterate enemy, a country magistrate, who had often breathed the most implacable vengeance against him, and, as he had reason to believe, was well acquainted with the occasion of his travelling at such an hour. However, he put the best face he could upon it, and even mentioned his name and residence to the gentleman, trusting to Providence for the result. His host ordered supper to be provided, and entered into a lengthened conversation with his guest; and was so delighted with his company, that it was a very late hour before he could permit him to retire to his chamber. In the morning, Mr. Howe expected to be accosted with a commitment, and sent to Exeter; but, on the contrary, he was received by the family at breakfast with a very hospitable welcome. After mutual civilities, he departed to his own abode, greatly wondering to himself at the kindness of a man from whom he had before dreaded so much.

Not long after, the gentleman sent for Mr. Howe, who found him confined to his bed by sickness, and still more deeply wounded with the sense of sin. He acknowledged that, when Mr. Howe came first to his door, he inwardly rejoiced that he had an opportunity of exercising his malice upon him, but that his conversation and his manner insensibly awed him into respect. He had long ruminated on the observations which had fallen from the man of God, and was become a penitent, earnestly anxious for the blessings of eternal life. From that sickness he recovered, became an eminent Christian, a friend to the conscientious, and an intimate companion of the man whom he had threatened with his vengeance.

Say your Prayers in Fair Weather.—A sea captain of a profligate character, who commanded a vessel trading between Liverpool and America, during the last war, once took on board a man as a common sailor, to serve during the voyage, just as he was leaving port. The new comer was soon found to be of a most quarrelsome, untractable disposition, a furious blasphemer, and, when an opportunity offered, a drunkard. Besides all these disqualifications, he was wholly ignorant of nautical affairs, or counterfeited ignorance to escape duty. In short, he was the bane and plague of the vessel, and refused obstinately to give any account of himself, or his family, or past life.

At length a violent storm arose, all hands were piped upon deck, and all, as the captain thought, were too few to save the ship.

When the men were mustered to their quarters, the sturdy blasphemer was missing, and my friend went below to seek for him ; great was his surprise at finding him on his knees, repeating the Lord's prayer with wonderful rapidity, over and over again, as if he had bound himself to countless reiterations. Vexed at what he deemed hypocrisy or cowardice, he shook him roughly by the collar, exclaiming, " *say your prayers in fair weather.*" The man rose up, observing, in a low voice, " God grant I may ever see fair weather to say them."

In a few hours the storm happily abated, a week more brought them to harbor, and an incident so trivial passed quickly away from the memory of the captain ; the more easily, as the man in question was paid off the day after landing, and appeared not again.

Four years more had elapsed, during which, though the captain had twice been shipwrecked, and was grievously hurt by the falling of a spar, he pursued without amendment a life of profligacy and contempt of God. At the end of this period, he arrived in the port of New York, after a very tedious and dangerous voyage from England.

It was on a Sabbath morning, and the streets were thronged with persons proceeding to the several houses of worship, with which that city abounds—but the captain was bent on far other occupation, designing to drown the recollection of perils and deliverances, in a celebrated tavern which he had too long, and too often, frequented.

As he walked leisurely towards this goal, he encountered a very dear friend, a quondam associate of many a thoughtless hour. Salutations over, the captain seized him by the arm, declaring that he should accompany him to the hotel. " I will do so," replied the other, with great calmness, " on condition that you come with me first for a single hour into this house (a church), and thank God for his mercies to you on the deep. The captain was ashamed to refuse, so the two friends entered the temple together. Already were all the seats occupied, and a dense crowd filled the aisle ; and by dint of personal exertion, they succeeded in reaching a position right in front of the pulpit, at about five yards distance. The preacher, one of the most popular of the day, riveted the attention of the entire congregation, including the captain himself, to whom his features and voice, though he could not assign any time or place of previous meeting, seemed not wholly unknown, particularly when he spoke with animation. At length the preacher's eye fell upon the spot where the two friends stood. He suddenly paused—still gazing upon the captain, as if to make himself sure that he labored under no optical delusion—and after a silence of more than a minute, pronounced with a voice that shook the building, "*say your prayers in fair weather.*"

The audience were lost in amazement, nor was it until a considerable time had elapsed, that the preacher recovered sufficient self-possession to recount the incident with which the reader is already acquainted, adding, with deep emotion, that the words which his captain uttered in the storm, had clung to him by day and by night after his landing, as if an angel had been charged with the duty of repeating them in his ears—that he felt the holy call as coming direct from above, to do the work of his crucified Master—that he had studied at college for the ministry, and was now, through grace, such as they saw and heard.

At the conclusion of this affecting address, he called on the audience to join in prayer with himself, that the same words might be blessed in turn to him who first had used them. But God had outrun their petitions—the captain was already His child, before his former shipmate had ceased to tell his story. The power of the Spirit had wrought effectually upon him, and subduced every lofty imagination. And so, when the people dispersed, he exchanged the hotel for the house of the preacher, with whom he tarried six weeks, and parted from him to pursue his profession, with-a heart devoted to the service of his Saviour, and with holy and happy assurances which advancing years hallowed, strengthened and sanctified.

The Dumb Sermon.—The Rev. William Tennent once took much pains to prepare a sermon, to convince a celebrated infidel of the truth of Christianity. But, in attempting to deliver this labored discourse, he was so confused, as to be compelled to stop, and close the service by prayer. This unexpected failure, in one who had so often astonished the unbeliever with the force of his eloquence, led the infidel to reflect that Mr. T. had been, at other times, aided by a Divine power. This reflection proved the means of his conversion. Thus God accomplished by silence what his servant wished to effect by persuasive preaching. Mr. Tennent used afterwards to say, his dumb sermon was one of the most profitable sermons that he had ever delivered.

The Mathematician Confounded.—A young man, who had graduated at one of the first colleges in America, and was celebrated for his literary attainments, particularly his knowledge of mathematics, settled in a village where a faithful minister of the gospel was stationed. It was not long before the clergyman met with him in one of his evening walks, and after some conversation, as they were about to part, addressed him as follows: "I have heard that you are celebrated for your mathematical skill; I have a problem which I wish you to solve." "What is it?" eagerly inquired the young man. The clergyman answered, with a solemn tone of voice, "What shall it profit a man, if he shall gain the whole world, and lose his own soul?" The youth returned home, and endeavored to shake off the impression fastened on him by the problem proposed to him, but in vain. In the giddy round of pleasure, in his business, and in his studies, the question still forcibly returned to him, "What shall it profit a man, if he shall gain the whole world, and lose his own soul?" It finally resulted in his conversion, and he became an able advocate and preacher of that gospel which he once rejected.

The Christian's Gloomy Death.—A pious parent had three sons, who, notwithstanding all his admonitions and instructions, mingled with many prayers and tears, grew up to manhood in skepticism and profligacy. The father lay dying; and, conceiving that it might perhaps produce a good impression on the minds of his abandoned children, to let them see how a Christian dies, the friends of the family introduced them to the bedside of their expiring parent. But, to their unspeakable grief, the good man died without any expressions of Christian confidence, and appeared destitute of those strong consolations which believers in Jesus usually experience in the closing scene. It was now apprehended that the effect of this melancholy circumstance on the young men would be to confirm them in their prejudice against religion, and afford them, in their opinion, a sufficient evidence that it is all a cunningly devised fable. However, it was not so: the ways of God are not as our ways, neither are his thoughts as our thoughts. A few days after the funeral, the younger brother entered the room in which the other two were; and observing that he had been weeping, they inquired the cause of his grief. "I have been thinking," said he, "of the death of our father." "Ah," said they, "a dismal death it was; what truth or reality can there be in religion, when such a man as he died in such a state of mind?" "It has not affected me in this way," replied the younger brother; "we all know what a holy life our father led, and what a gloomy death he died; now I have been thinking, how dreadful our death must be, who lead such a wicked life!" The observation was like an arrow to their consciences; and they began to be alarmed. They repaired to the ordinances of religion, which, in their father's life time they had neglected, and ultimately became as eminent for piety as their exemplary parent had been.

The Actress's Last Appearance.—An actress in one of the English provincial or country theatres, was one day passing through the streets of the town in which she then resided, when her attention was attracted by the sound of voices, which she heard in a poor cottage before her. Curiosity prompted her to look in at an open door, when she saw a few poor people sitting together, one of whom, at the moment of her observation, was giving out the following hymn, which the others joined in singing:

"Depth of mercy! can there be
Mercy still reserved for me?"

The tune was sweet and simple, but she heeded it not. The words had riveted her attention, and she stood motionless, until she was invited to enter, by the woman of the house, who had observed her standing at the door. She complied, and remained during a prayer which was offered up by one of the little company; and uncouth as the expressions sounded, perhaps, to her ears, they carried with them a conviction of sincerity on the part of the person then employed. She quitted the cottage, but the words of the hymn followed her. She could not banish them from her mind, and at last she resolved to procure the book which contained it. She did so, and the more she read it, the more decided her serious impressions became. She attended the ministry of the gospel, read her hitherto neglected and despised Bible, and bowed herself in humility and contrition of heart, before Him whose mercy she now felt she needed, whose sacrifices are those of a broken heart and a contrite spirit, and who has declared, that with such sacrifices he is well pleased.

Her profession she determined at once and forever to renounce ; and for some little time excused herself from appearing on the stage, without, however, disclosing her change of sentiments or making know her resolution finally to leave it.

The manager of the theatre called upon her one morning, and requested her to sustain the principal character in a new play which was to be performed the next week for his benefit. She had frequently performed this character to general admiration ; but she now, however, told him her resolution never to appear as an actress again, at the same time giving her reasons. At first he attempted to overcome her scruples by ridicule, but this was unavailing ; he then represented the loss he should incur by her refusal, and concluded his arguments by promising, that if, to oblige him, she would act on this occasion, it should be the last request of the kind he would ever make. Unable to resist his solicitations, she promised to appear, and on the appointed evening went to the theatre. The character she assumed required her, on her first entrance, to sing a song ; and when the curtain drew up, the orchestra immediately began the accompaniment. But she stood as if lost in thought, and as one forgetting all around her, and her own situation. The music ceased, but she did not sing ; and supposing her to be overcome by embarrassment, the band again commenced. A second time they paused for her to begin, and still she did not open her lips. A third time the air was played, and then, with clasped hands, and eyes suffused with tears, she sang, not the words of the song, but

"Depth of mercy! can there be
Mercy still reserved for me?"

It is almost needless to add, that the performance was suddenly ended ; many ridiculed, though some were induced from that memorable night to "consider their ways," and to reflect on the wonderful power of that religion which could so influence the heart, and change the life of one hitherto so vain, and so evidently pursuing the road which leadeth to destruction.

It will be satisfactory to the reader to know, that the change in Miss —— was as permanent as it was singular ; she walked consistently with her profession of religion for many years, and at length became the wife of a minister of the gospel of our Lord Jesus Christ.

Power of a Child's Prayer.—In the town of W——, Connecticut, there was a pious little girl belonging to the Sabbath School, whose father was an opposer of religion. One day he had several men to assist him in haying. They indulged in profanity and scoffing at religion; and their employer rather encouraged them in it. The little girl overheard them, and was so shocked and grieved at their conduct, that she went into the meadow and asked them if they did not know it was wicked to use such profane language? This drew forth their ridicule, and so exasperated her father that he gave her a severe rebuke, and sent her back into the house. She returned as commanded; but retired to her closet and prayed for those who had abused her. In the course of the day she overheard their profanity again, and resolved again to reprove them, whatever might be the results.

As she addressed them the second time, in her artless manner, her father became so angry, he told her: "My daughter, we don't want any of your religion here; if you say anything more upon that subject, you must quit my house. Now return and attend to your business." The little girl returned; but resolved rather to quit the paternal roof than to do violence to her conscience. She went back to her chamber, and having prayed to God, proceeded to tie up her clothes, and then put on her bonnet and went out, scarce knowing whither she went.

She went first to the field to bid her father farewell, and fell at his feet, saying, "Pa, I must leave you. I am going away, but I shall pray for you." She immediately left the field, and passing over the hill was soon out of sight. The unfeeling father now began to reflect on what he had done; and his torpid conscience began to awake. He could not work; and after some time he threw down the scythe and started in pursuit of his daughter. As he was hurrying on to overtake her, he came near to a grove, and as he listened he heard a voice in the adjacent field. He crept softly along to the stone wall and listened again. The woods were still, he heard it again. It was the voice of prayer—the voice of his little daughter praying for her father's salvation! The stubborn heart of the father was melted; he hastened over the wall to his daughter; and clasping her in his arms, asked her to pray for him, "for," said he, "I am a great sinner." Oh! it was an affecting scene, one that must have awakened the joy of angels! He carried his little daughter home in his arms, and ere long obtained forgiveness of his sins, and father and child were soon rejoicing together in the blessings of the Christian's hope.

Converted by His own Preaching.—When the Rev. G. Whitefield and J. Wesley commenced their zealous and successful labors, there was a very prevalent disposition to oppose and misrepresent them. Many of the public-houses became places where their doctrines and zeal were talked of and ridiculed. Mr. Thorpe, and several other young men in Yorkshire, undertook at one of these parties to mimic the preaching of these good men. The proposition met with applause; one after another stood on a table to perform his part, and it devolved on Mr. T. to close this very irreverent scene. Much elated, and confident of success, he exclaimed, as he ascended the table, "I shall beat you all." Who would have supposed that the mercy of God was now about to be extended to this transgressor of his law! The Bible was handed to him, and, by the guidance of unerring Providence, it opened at Luke xiii. 3. "Except ye repent, ye shall all likewise perish." The moment he read the text his mind was impressed in a most extraordinary manner; he saw clearly the nature and importance of the subject; and as he afterwards said, if he ever preached with the assistance of the Holy Spirit, it was at that time. His address produced a feeling of depression in his auditors ; and, when he had finished, he instantly retired to weep over his sins : he associated with the people of God, and became a useful minister of the New Testament, and died at Masborough, in 1776.

Burglars Arrested.—An eminently pious curate, in England, was accustomed, on account of the village in which he resided being at a great distance from the church, to preach on the Sabbath evening in his own house. On his return from his stated parochial duties, one Sabbath afternoon, he was warned by one of his neighbors to keep a strict look-out against two suspicious characters then lurking in the village, as there was some reason to apprehend that they intended that night to rob his house. They contrived, however by some means, to get within his premises while the people were assembling in considerable numbers for worship, and concealed themselves in a retired part of the house ; but not being far from the room where the worthy man was preaching, they could distinctly hear his voice. The sword of the Spirit pierced their hearts ; they were not only convinced of the wickedness of their meditated bur glary, but of the awful criminality of sin as committed against God, and left their dark retreat under the most pungent sense of guilt. From this time, an effectual change was wrought in their minds and conduct, and the pious clergyman, after several years, could bear testimony that by their unblamable lives, they adorned the gospel of Christ.

The Negro's Sermon.—A worthy and excellent bishop of the Episcopal Church was in early life an immoral and dissipated man. Dining one evening with a party of gentlemen, they sat late over their wine, and with a view to promote merriment, this young man sent for one of his slaves, who was in the habit of preaching to his companions in slavery, and ordered him to preach a sermon to the company. The good man hesitated for a time, but at length began to address them. Instead of the mirth, however which they anticipated from the ignorance and simplicity of the poor man, the piety and fervor of his discourse produced a contrary effect. The solemn truths he delivered sank deeply into the hearts of some of the company, and, through the Divine blessing, carried conviction to the heart of his master, who now seriously inquired after the way of salvation ; which having learned, he began from a sense of duty to publish the grace of Christ, and became an ornament to the Christian ministry.

Conversion of Madan.—The Rev. Mr. Madan was educated for the bar. His conversion to God arose from the following circumstances. Some of his companions, when assembled one evening at a coffee-house, requested him to go and hear the Rev. John Wesley, who, they were informed, was to preach in the neighborhood, and then to return and exhibit his manner and discourse for their entertainment. With that intention he went to the house of God. Just as he entered the place, Mr. Wesley read as his text, "Prepare to meet thy God," Amos iv. 12, with a solemnity of accent which excited his attention, and produced a seriousness which increased as the good man proceeded in exhorting his hearers to repentance. Mr. Madan returned to the coffee-room, and was asked by his companions if he had taken off the old Methodist. He replied, "No, gentlemen, but he has taken me off ;" and from that time forsook their company, associated with true Christians, and became an eminently good man.

The Three Scoffers.—In a sea-port town on the west coast of England, notice was once given of a sermon to be preached there one Saturday evening. The preacher was a man of great celebrity; and that circumstance, together with the object of the discourse, being to enforce the duty of strict observance of the Sabbath, attracted an overflowing audience. After the usual prayers and praises, the preacher read his text, and was about to proceed with his sermon, when he suddenly paused, leaning his head on the pulpit, and remained silent for a few moments. It was imagined that he had become indisposed ; but he soon recovered himself, and, addressing the congregation, said, that before entering upon his discourse, he begged to narrate to them a short anecdote. "It is now exactly fifteen years," said he, "since I was last within this place of worship, and the occasion was, as many here may probably remember the very same as that which has now brought us together. Amongst those who came here that evening were three dissolute young men, who came not only with the intention of insulting and mocking the venerable pastor, but even with stones in their pockets to throw at him as he stood in the pulpit. Accordingly, they had not attended long to the discourse, when one of them said impatiently, 'Why need we listen any longer to the blockhead?—throw!' But the second stopped him, saying, 'Let us first see what he makes of this point.' The curiosity of the latter was no sooner satisfied, than he, too, said, 'Ay, confound him, it is only as I expected—throw now!' But here the third interposed, and said, 'It would be better altogether to give up the design which has brought us here.' At this remark his two associates took offence, and left the place, while he himself remained to the end. Now mark, my brethren," continued the preacher, with much emotion, "what were afterwards the several fates of these young men? The first was hanged, many years ago, at Tyburn, for the crime of forgery; the second is now lying under the sentence of death, for murder, in the jail of this city. The third, my brethren"—and the speaker's agitation here became excessive, while he paused, and wiped the large drops from his brow—"the third, my brethren, is he who is now about to address you!—listen to him."

The Infidel's Sermon to the Pirates.—A native of Sweden, residing in the south of France, had occasion to go from one port to another in the Baltic Sea. When he came to the place whence he expected to sail, the vessel was gone. On inquiring, he found a fishing-boat going the same way, in which he embarked. After being for some time out to sea, the men observed that he had several trunks and chests on board, concluded he must be very rich, and therefore agreed among themselves to throw him overboard. This he heard them express, which gave him great uneasiness. However, he took occasion to open one of his trunks which contained some books. Observing this, they remarked among themselves that it was not worth while to throw him into the sea, as they did not want any books, which they supposed was all the trunks contained. They asked him if he were a priest. Hardly knowing what reply to make, he told them he was ; at which they seemed much pleased, and said they would have a sermon on the next day, as it was the Sabbath.

This increased the anxiety and distress of his mind, for he knew himself to be as incapable of such an undertaking as it was possible for any one to be, as he knew very little of the Scriptures ; neither did he believe in the inspiration of the Bible.

At length they came to a small rocky island, perhaps a quarter of a mile in circumference, where was a company of pirates, who had chosen this little sequestered spot to deposit their treasures. He was taken to a cave, and introduced to an old woman, to whom they remarked that they were to have a sermon preached the next day. She said she was very glad of it, for she had not heard the word of God for a great while. His was a trying case, for preach he must, still he knew nothing about preaching. If he refused, or undertook to preach and did not please, he expected it would be his death. With these thoughts he passed a sleepless night. In the morning his mind was not settled upon anything. To call upon God, whom he believed to be inaccessible, was altogether vain. He could devise no way whereby he might be saved. He walked to and fro, still shut up in darkness, striving to collect something to say to them, but could not think of even a single sentence.

When the appointed time for the evening arrived, he entered the cave, where he found the men assembled. There was a seat prepared for him, and a table with a Bible on it. They sat for the space of half an hour in profound silence ; and even then, the anguish of his soul was as great as human nature was capable of enduring. At length these words came to his mind—" Verily, there is a reward for the righteous : verily, there is a God that judgeth in the earth." He arose, and delivered them ; then other words presented themselves, and so on till his understanding became opened—his heart enlarged, in a manner astonishing to himself. He spoke upon subjects suited to their condition ; the rewards of the righteous—the judgments of the wicked—the necessity of repentance, and the importance of a change of life. The matchless love of God to the children of men had such a powerful effect upon the minds of these wretched beings, that they were melted into tears. Nor was he less astonished at the unbounded goodness of Almighty God, in thus interposing to save his spiritual as well as his natural life, and well might he exclaim—"This is the Lord's doings, and marvellous in our eyes." Under a deep sense of God's goodness, his heart became filled with such thankfulness that it was out of his power to express. What marvellous change was thus suddenly brought about by divine interposition! He who a little before disbelieved in communion with God and the soul, became as humble as a little child; and they who were so lately meditating on his death, now are filled with love and good will towards each other, particularly towards him; manifesting affectionate kindness, and willing to render him all the assistance in their power.

The next morning they fitted out one of their vessels, and conveyed him where he desired. From that time he became a changed man. From sentiments of infidelity he became a sincere believer in the power and efficacy of the truth as it is in Jesus.

An Affecting Meeting.—At the foot of a lofty hill, writes a correspondent of an American periodical, crowned to the summit with the richest verdure, a miserable mud cabin peeped out from among encircling bushwood and straggling elms. A stillness seemed to lie around the spot, and I felt an indescribable sensation creep over me as I drew near the house of mourning. I paused at the entrance. A low murmuring kind of sound stole upon my ear, and again all was hushed. I gently opened the door, and bent myself forward, as if to ascertain, unnoticed, what was passing within. I saw at the first glance that death had been there. The apartment, on the threshold of which I now stood, was of the meanest construction; it was without a single piece of furniture that deserved the name. In one corner of it a dead body lay stretched out, very slightly covered with a tattered coat, and a cold kind of horrible feeling ran through my very soul; and it would probably have shrunk away from any further investigation, if I had not been suddenly arrested by a soft sweet voice, mingled with a low groan, somewhat like a death-rattle, that seemed to issue from the same apartment. I turned my head around, and beheld a sight that chained me, as if by magic, to the ground. Oh, it was heart-thrilling to behold! On a bundle of straw, a woman, somewhat in years, lay apparently in the agonies of death. Near her head hung, reclining in deep sorrow, a beautiful, little half-naked child. On one side, a lovely girl, about thirteen years of age knelt; a Bible clasped in her thin slender hands, with which she was endeavoring to comfort her dying mother. I instantly recognized two of my Sabbath-school children. The meeting was affecting. They had been without food for some days. The mother died next day, in the triumph of that faith which her little daughter taught her out of the Bible. The girls grew up to be respectable members of society, and one of them has been a teacher in a Sabbath school for several years.

My Son is my Spiritual Father.—At a Wesleyan class meeting, a man rose and addressed the leader thus:—"I am very thankful to God, and to you, for your Sunday school. My son, who now sits beside me, is my spiritual father. He heard me cursing, while in a state of drunkenness, and said to me, 'O father! my teacher said to-day, at the Sunday school, that neither drunkards nor swearers could enter into heaven.' This so affected my mind, that from that time I was enabled, by the grace of God, to leave off those wicked practices; and both myself and my son are now members of your society." He then laid his hand on his son's head, and repeated, "my son is my spiritual father."

A Pious Boy's Fidelity.—In New York city a little boy lived, who appeared to take little or no interest in learning, so that he was pronounced by his teachers a very dull scholar. He learned to read but very slowly, and finally neglected the school, thinking he should never succeed. There was a Bible class organized, which he was induced to attend. And here he soon began to manifest an interest in the study of the Scriptures. He learned to read well, which much astonished his father, who was a very wicked man. One Sabbath, his father took some nails and a hammer to nail up a fence, when he was reproved by his little son, who spoke about working on the Sabbath day, and invited him to attend public worship. The enraged father drove him from his presence, and threatened to punish him if he ever talked in that way again. The child went away sorrowful. Not long after this, as the little boy returned from public worship, he went and looked over his father's shoulder, and observed that he was reading Hume's History of England. He went into the middle of the room, and said, "Father, where do you expect to go when you die?" Such a question from such a child could not be borne. "Away," said he, "from my presence, immediately, or I will whip you." The child retired; but the father was troubled. He went out to walk, but still a load was pressing on his agonizing soul. He thought of attending public worship, for nothing else seemed so likely to soothe his troubled feelings. He entered while the minister was at prayer, and that day was the beginning of better days to him. He sought from God the forgiveness of his sins, and soon obtained the hope of eternal life.

A few years passed away, and the old man was on his dying bed. His son attended him, constantly ministering to his spiritual wants. To a Christian minister, the father said, "I am dying, but I am going to heaven; and my son has been the instrument of saving my soul." Soon his spirit was released to be welcomed, as we have no reason to doubt, into the mansions of glory. Happy child! to be the instrument of saving his father from death. Happy parent! to be bleseed with such a child.

Conversion under Hydrophobia.—A little boy, about eleven years of age, a Sunday scholar in Camberwell, was bitten by a mad dog; the part was cut out, and caustic applied, but the fatal poison could not be arrested in its progress, and nine weeks after the accident, decided symptoms of hydrophobia were manifested. It appears that the poor boy depended chiefly, if not entirely, on Sunday school teaching for all his religious instruction, and now the great advantage of correct information on scriptural subjects was evinced. He was aware of the nature of his disease, took patiently the medicines recommended to him, and bade farewell to a playmate, saying, he should never see him again. But frightful paroxysms of pain came on; sometimes he was lifted suddenly upright in the bed, while the agony of speaking was so great that he could only utter words at intervals, and then in reply to necessary questions. But in the midst of judgment God remembered mercy,—an interval of comparative composure, a fact almost unprecedented in this disease, was granted the sufferer; and then was felt the sweet influence of that religion which he had been taught, and which gives divine wisdom to the meanest capacity. He knelt on the bed, and prayed—prayed to Jesus, and besought the salvation of his soul. He needed comfort; but he had not, as is too frequently the case, to seek it amid the pains and confusions of a dying hour, and, in the darkness of nature, mistake broken reeds for substantial supports; no, the way of peace and life had again and again been pointed out to him; he believed, and who can doubt that he was saved? He repeated and sung most of the hymns he had been taught; joy beamed on the countenance which had been so lately distorted with agony; he called on those around to attend to the things of religion, and prayed that their hearts might be turned from stone to flesh. "Come to Jesus, come with me," said the little sufferer, as he quietly passed to glory.

The Blind Man and his Wife.—A pious man came into western New York, from one of the New England States. He was then perfectly blind. He had a near relative in this country, who advised him to leave or sell his farm, and come and reside with him, to be taken care of. He then had a wife of a similar religious character (since dead). They accepted the proposal of their relative and came; and, coming from society highly refined and moral, they were not prepared to encounter the disadvantages, and real evils which attended a society the reverse of this. Their first Sabbath in "York State," he declared would never be forgotten. No sooner was its sacred dawn ushered in, than shooting and other recreations commenced in the immediate vicinity of his relative, while the latter, being a merchant, dealt out the whisky to all who applied. Consequently the day was trampled on, and its hallowed hours spent in dissipation. Before breakfast, which was delayed to receive a party of visitors from another town, this devoted pair resolved to seek some retreat from the noise and profaneness, fled into an adjacent wood, the wife taking the Bible and leading her blind husband. Here, in the deep solitude of the forest, they spent the first Sabbath in fasting and prayer, and reading the Word of

God. After the Sabbath was past, they informed their relative they could not live with him if such were the manner of spending the Sabbath, in amusements and dissipation. They must have a house of their own. He replied that it would avail nothing, for people would visit him on the Sabbath. Mr. D—— said firmly, that he would risk their visits to him. Accordingly a house was provided. The first Sabbath in their new residence, two of their neighbors called to see them, one of whom was a magistrate. His wife was reading the Bible. After passing the usual compliments, and providing seats, she went on reading aloud. Before the chapter was finished, one of the visitors left, and before the close of the second, the other left. But he was not troubled with visitors. He commenced visiting some of his ungodly neighbors, and conversing with them on the subject of religion, his wife leading him. Soon they began to hold meetings on the Sabbath, and many attended. The wife read sermons, and the husband prayed and exhorted. One wicked man, whose shop was opposite the meeting, set open his door, and worked in order to disturb it. The next Sabbath, this same man came into the meeting, fell on his knees, confessing his sins and asking forgiveness. The Lord came down by his Spirit on that wicked neighborhood, and forty became the members of a church, afterwards formed in that place, as the fruits of that revival. There was no regular preaching in the place previously, and it was evidently through the instrumentality of this blind man and his wife. That church, the writer is acquainted with. It is quite flourishing. They have built a handsome house of worship, and settled a minister to break unto them the bread of life.

The Little Babe's Prayer.—I can state, says Mr. Wilderspin, that a man discontinued drunkenness from the simple prattle of his infant. He was in the habit of frequently getting drunk; there were two or three children under seven years of age, and they all slept in the same room, though not in the same bed. The man came home one night drunk; his wife remonstrated with him, when he struck her. The woman cried very much, and continued to cry after she got into bed; but a little creature, two or three years old, got up, and said, "Pray, father, do not beat poor mother;" the father ordered it to get into bed again: the little creature got up again, and knelt down by the side of the bed, and repeated the Lord's prayer, and then concluded in this simple language: "Pray, God, bless dear father and mother, and make father a good father. Amen!" This went to the heart of the drunkard; the man told me he covered his face over with the bed-clothes, and that the first thoughts he awoke with in the morning, were thoughts of regret, that he should stand in need of such a remonstrance from such a young child, and it produced in him self-examination and amendment of life. The family became united to a Methodist chapel, in that neighborhood, and I have learned that they are useful and valuable members of that society.

Happy Results of one School.—In a certain school in New England, in 1832, *sixty-one* out of fifteen classes of 160 pupils, under 16 years of age, became hopefully pious. In six classes, embracing 71 young persons over 16 years of age, *sixty* indulged hope that they had passed from death unto life, making in all ONE HUNDRED AND TWENTY-ONE who became hopefully pious in a school of 231 scholars.

Revivals in Ten Schools.—In a County Sabbath-school Society, in Mass., embracing ten parishes, and the same number of schools, the Lord smiled upon this institution, in 1834–5, and shed down upon it the influence of his Holy Spirit. Six schools were blessed with powerful revivals of religion. THREE HUNDRED scholars from these ten schools made a profession during the year. It is supposed the whole number that passed from death unto life is over FOUR HUNDRED! "This is the Lord's doing, and it is marvellous in our eyes."

One Hundred Scholars Converted.—In ——, Mass., efforts were made in the early part of the year 1835, to excite a more general and deeper interest in the Sabbath-school concert. The influence of these efforts was to increase the number of the school and the fidelity of the teachers. "This general interest," says the pastor, "increased through the summer till September, when more manifest signs appeared—though two or three conversions had before taken place—of the presence of the Holy Spirit. In a few weeks the attention had become general throughout the school. The work of God was very solemn, as well as animating, still and deep. ONE HUNDRED OR MORE MEMBERS OF THE SCHOOL, we hope, HAVE BEEN CONVERTED.

What a Teacher can do.—About the first of September, 1833, a deep and solemn interest upon the subject of religion began to be visible in the Presbyterian church and congregation of Washingtonville, New York, and particularly in the Sabbath school. Here commenced that revival flame which subsequently spread through the county, and brought salvation to a multitude of souls.

One *Sabbath school teacher*, feeling deeply the responsibility resting upon her, and the worth of immortal souls, before the school was dismissed on the Lord's day, affectionately requested her class, consisting of little girls about twelve or thirteen years of age, to remain after the rest of the school had retired. She then began, with an aching heart and with flowing tears, to reason and plead with them upon the subject of personal religion. They were deeply affected, and "wept bitterly" in view of their lost condition. They then all knelt together before the Lord, and the teacher prayed for their salvation; and immediately the scholar next to her commenced praying for herself, and then the next, and so on, until the *whole class*, with ardent supplications, begged for the forgiveness of their sins and the salvation of their souls. It would take long to tell the history of this class, and relate particular instances of conversions, and the happy changes which took place in the families to which they belonged, and show the family altars which were established. These scholars, with their teacher, *and their fathers and mothers, brothers and sisters*, were ere long seen commemorating a Saviour's dying love together. The revival extended itself to other towns, and the great day can alone unfold the astonishing results.

The Child's Last Prayer.—A pious little boy, who attended the Sabbath school, a few hours before his death broke out into singing, and sung so loud, as to cause his mother to inquire what he was doing. "I am singing my sister's favorite hymn, mother." "But why, my dear, so loud?" "Why," said he, with peculiar emphasis, "because I am so happy." Just before his death, with uplifted hands, he exclaimed, "Father! Father! take me, Father." His father went to lift him up, when, with a smile, he said, "I did not call you, father; but I was calling to my heavenly Father to take me; I shall soon be with him:" and then expired.

"I have given myself to my Saviour."—S. A. E. (writes the wife of a pastor in Massachusetts) was constant in her attendance on the Sabbath school, punctual and very correct in her lessons, and amiable in her deportment. But it was not until the age of 16 that the precious treasure of divine truth, stored up in her memory, was made instrumental of awakening her conscience, and leading her to the "Fountain opened for sin." The moment will never be forgotten when, in a circle of weeping associates, who had assembled to inquire of their pastor "What shall I do to be saved?" S. A. E. arose, and with her characteristic decision exclaimed, "I have given myself to my Saviour!" Nor will those who had assembled at that hour to *pray* for their beloved children, forget the thrill of joy which pervaded the room as the pastor announced the fact, that this child of many prayers and tears, had, it was believed, accepted the offers of mercy. Five years, until her death, she adorned her profession; and the rich fruits of gentleness, meekness, submission under severe trials, and filial piety, hung thickly on this youthful plant.

Becoming a Man-of-War's-Man.—I know a man, said Rev. Mr. Lord, seaman's chaplain at Boston, who is now a member of the church, and who was hopefully converted four years ago by reading "*Little Henry and his Bearer.*" He went home; but on reflection, made up his mind to go on board a man-of-war, *for the purpose of doing good.* He shipped at Charlestown, furnishing himself with tracts, Bibles, and the Society's volumes. The crew were so wicked, that, at the end of nine months, the chaplain was compelled to leave the ship. But this man and one or two other pious men remained. At last God blessed him. One of the men was sent up to the foretopsail as a punishment. He asked this man to lend him a book, which he did. He was a wicked man, and had been accustomed to read Tom Paine and similar works. But now he came down serious, and inquired what he should do to be saved. God opened the windows of heaven, and in three weeks there were between twenty and thirty inquirers, and fifteen or twenty entertaining hope. There was great and continued opposition from the officers. But at the end of three years and a half the vessel arrived, and *eleven men,* who had endured this fiery persecution all this time, *sat down to commemorate the dying love of Jesus.*

The Little School-boy's Prayer Meeting.—A little lad in one of the villages of Connecticut was converted to God. He attended school at this time; and he began to study how he might benefit his playmates, and win their hearts to Christ. He was not satisfied with merely living like a Christian before them, watching carefully over his words and actions, and bearing with patience all their persecutions and ridicule on account of his piety; but he determined to use some active means for their salvation. With this in view, he gave notice that there would be a prayer meeting in the school-house during the intermission.

Drawn by curiosity, and to enjoy the sport they wickedly expected, the scholars assembled. But who was to conduct the meeting? Our little friend, strengthened by the Saviour, gives out his hymn, sings and prays, and then simply, affectionately, and faithfully, exhorts his companions. Some, during the exercises, behave with propriety, others jeer, laugh, and attempt to break up the little service.

Unmoved by these persecutions, and his apparent ill success, the little hero continues the meeting on succeeding days.

The master attended, to see if everything was properly conducted, and was astonished, undoubtedly (for he was an unconverted man), at the confidence and calmness of the lad. He severely reprimanded those who were only present to disturb the devotions, and saved the young Christian from further persecution. Soon some of the lads became anxious, penitent, and were hopefully converted. Their parents witnessing the change, were induced to come with them at their hour of devotion, and ere long several of these were seeking for mercy among the little flock of pious, praying lambs. The ministers of the place, hearing this wonderful intelligence, were aroused, and eventually came in and took charge of the services. Other meetings were appointed, and the result was, that about sixty obtained the salvation of their souls. The whole work, the importance and value of which eternity alone can show, originated, and was in a large sense carried on by this pious, faithful, and courageous little lad! O! how much good young Christians may accomplish!

The Elder's Twelve Prayers.—Elder S—— was a distiller, carried on the business largely, and supplied his neighbors with the good creature. At length one and another, and another, became drunkards, squandered away their property, and reduced their families to beggary and wretchedness. Nevertheless, the Elder continued to supply them, "for the public good," and being a sober man, did it very regularly. By and by one of his customers came to settle with him, and on settlement owed him twenty dollars; and yet had nothing to pay, and nothing with which to supply his family with a rag of clothing or a morsel of bread. He and they were literally destitute. And the Elder inquired of himself, "What has made this man a drunkard, and brought his family to poverty and wretchedness?" Conscience answered, "Your whisky." "And who must answer in the day of judgment?" said the Elder. Conscience replied, "You;" and spoke with a voice which the Elder could not but hear. He went away heavy-hearted; and sorely pressed, as conscience continued to echo, "You must answer at the day of judgment for making that man a drunkard." He retired to bed, but not to rest, or to sleep. He got up, kneeled down and prayed, and went again to bed, but obtained no relief. He got up, and kneeled down and prayed again, and retired, and so again and again, till he got up, prayed, confessed his sins, implored mercy, prayed for the man and his family whom he had ruined, and laid down no less than *eleven* times. And his distress grew greater and greater. Not only this man, but one, and another, and another, great numbers whom he had made drunkards, and for whose ruin he must answer at the day of judgment, rose up to his view, and he was well-nigh overwhelmed with the conviction of his guilt. He rose and kneeled down the *twelfth* time before God, and not only confessed his sins, but now, for the first time, resolved without delay to forsake them. He promised, before the Lord, that no portion of his time, or property, should ever again be employed in making that which tends to destroy the bodies and souls of men. And he meant what he said. He then laid down and slept till morning. Next morning he rose, cleared out his distillery, and said that no whisky should ever be made there again. He made known his determination to his children and his neighbors. One of them thought he had become too superstitious, and offered him for the use of his distillery five hundred dollars a year. But he utterly refused, saying that none of his property should ever again be employed by anybody in that way. He held to his resolution till his death, and tried to induce all to follow his example. With his children he was successful, and numbers of them before his death were hopefully made partakers of divine grace and heirs of the kingdom of God. The elder appeared to live the life and die the death of a penitent, and went to give up his account to the Judge of the quick and dead. There he expected to meet with many whom his business had ruined, but as, during the time of divine forbearance, he trusted that he had confessed his sins, he died, hoping for pardon, through the boundless mercy of God in the Redeemer.

The Unanswerable Argument.—R——, the blacksmith was an infidel and scoffer, was a man of extensive reading, and master of all the ablest infidel writers. He possessed a ready wit, and when he could not talk his opponent down, he would laugh him down The pastor had often approached him, and had as often been repulsed. As a last resort, he had requested his able and skillful neighbor, a lawyer of piety and talents, to visit Mr. R——, and endeavor to convince him. But it was like attempting to reason with the tempest, or soothe the volcano.

The following was the manner of his conversion, as related by himself in a prayer meeting :

"I stand," said Mr. R——, "to tell you the story of my conversion." His lips trembled slightly as he spoke, and his bosom heaved with suppressed emotion. "I am as a brand plucked out of the burning. The change in me is an astonishment to myself; and all brought about by the grace of God, and that *unanswerable argument*. It was a cold morning in January, and I had just begun my labor at the anvil in my shop, when I looked out and saw Mr. B—— approaching. He dismounted quickly, and entered. As he drew near, I saw he was agitated. His look was full of earnestness. His eyes were bedimmed with tears. He took me by the hand. His breast heaved with emotion, and with indescribable tenderness he said, 'Mr. R——, I am greatly concerned for your salvation—greatly concerned for your salvation,' and he burst into tears. He stood with my hand grasped in his. He struggled to regain self-possession. He often essayed to speak, but not a word could he utter; and finding that he could say no more, he turned, went out of the shop, got on his horse, and rode slowly away.

"'Greatly concerned for my salvation!' said I, audibly, and I stood and forgot to bring my hammer down. There I stood with it upraised—'*greatly concerned for my salvation!*'

"I went to my house. My poor, pious wife, whom I had always ridiculed for her religion, exclaimed, 'Why, Mr. R——, what is the matter with you?' 'Matter enough,' said I, filled with agony and overwhelmed with a sense of sin. 'Old Mr. B—— has ridden two miles this cold morning to tell me he was greatly concerned for my salvation. What shall I do; what shall I do?'

"'I do not know what you can do,' said my astonished wife; 'I do not know what better you can do than to get on your horse, and go and see him. He can give you better counsel than I, and tell you what you must do to be saved.'

"I mounted my horse, and pursued after him. I found him alone in that same little room, where he had spent the night in prayer for my poor soul, where he had shed many tears over such a reprobate as I, and had besought God to have mercy upon me.

"'I am come,' said I to him, 'to tell you that I am greatly concerned for my own salvation.'

"'Praised be God!' said the aged man. 'It is a faithful saying, and worthy of all acceptation, that Jesus Christ came into the world to save sinners, even the chief,' and he began at that same scripture, and preached to me Jesus. On that same floor we knelt, and together we prayed—and we did not separate that day till God spoke peace to my soul.

"I have often been requested to look at the evidence of the truth of religion, but, blessed be God, I have evidence for its truth *here*," laying his hand upon his heart, "which nothing can gainsay or resist. I have often been led to look at this and that argument for the truth of Christianity; but I could overturn, and, as I thought, completely demolish and annihilate them all. But I stand here to-night, thankful to acknowledge that God sent *an argument* to my conscience and heart, which could not be answered or resisted, when a weeping Christian came to tell me how greatly concerned he was for my salvation. God taught him that *argument*, when he spent the night before him in prayer for my soul."

The Norwegian Apostle.—Many years ago, a Norwegian farmer was, at the age of twenty-five, in the habit of making excursions from his father's dwelling, for the purpose of distributing religious tracts, which he had caused to be printed at his own expense, and which he sold or gave away. The effects of his labors were perfectly astonishing; not less than 50,000 peasants dating the period of their conversion to sound and vital Christianity, at the time when they first became known to that remarkable individual. To the sufferings which he had undergone, it is most distressing to advert; he endured eleven several imprisonments, one of which lasted for a period of ten years. There is a passage towards the close of his journal, dated in the year 1814, from which it appears that a fine of a thousand rix-dollars was imposed upon him, and that all which he possessed on earth was sold for the liquidation of that debt: he might have escaped it, could he have prevailed on himself to petition the king, saying that he was unable to pay the amount; but such was his love of truth, that no consideration under heaven could induce him to declare a falsehood; and, in consequence, he suffered himself to be reduced to the lowest degree of poverty: he allowed everything which he possessed, down to the meanest utensil, to be sold, rather than declare that which he knew to be false.

A Colporteur in Norway.—When there was great spiritual darkness on the continent of Europe, and everything seemed to threaten that the light of the gospel would be completely removed from Norway, God, in his providence, raised up a poor peasant, who lived near Indenckihill, on the confines of Sweden. He had received nothing but a common education, but the Lord made him acquainted with the truth, and filled him with zeal to communicate that truth to his countrymen, who were perishing for lack of knowledge. This good man, with his knapsack on his back, set out on the road, went through the length and breadth of Norway, proclaiming the gospel in that wild and romantic country, to thousands and tens of thousands ; and the Lord gave testimony to the word spoken in a most remarkable manner ; for hundreds were, in a short time, by his instrumentality, made to see and embrace the truth. It may be easily conceived, that he was not allowed to go on in peace : the unenlightened clergy would not endure him : they stirred up the magistrates against him, and he was cast into prison ; as soon, however, as he got out, he was again at his work ; but, at length, having come to Christiana, the capital, a most bigoted place in regard to religion, he was apprehended, and cast into a dungeon, and kept eleven years, from 1800 to 1811. But he was not idle there ; for, like Bunyan, he was writing treatises, and sending them forth into every part of the country ; contriving, in the space of a very short time, to have one hundred and twenty-two tracts published at Cassel. The effect of this peasant's labors is, that at this day there not fewer than ten thousand followers of the Lord Jesus in that country.

"Helping in" the House-breaker.—A very devoted minister was converted under the following circumstances :

He was long a most abandoned, dissipated character. One night he was found trying to get into a neighbor's house at a late hour. The family were aroused by the noise, got up, helped him in, and made him comfortable till morning, and then put a small tract in the crown of his hat, and sent him home.

When he discovered the tract, he wondered how it should have come there. He read it again and again, still wondering where such a message should have come from. He was finally brought under deep conviction for sin, and fled to the Saviour ; was drawn to the ministry, and is now a very successful preacher of the gospel.

The Man of Decision.—It was immediately after the great fire of 1835, in New York, that I was at Boston, in company with a Christian friend. We put up at the Tremont Hotel. On the succeeding Sabbath we were walking in the parlor, conversing on the afflictive providence with which our city had been visited ; in the course of which reference was made to the power and sovereignty of God. There was but one other person in the room, and he was seated silently near the fire. As the above remark was uttered, he stepped up to us, and inquired whether he had the happiness to address those who loved the Lord Jesus Christ. With some surprise at the sudden and *uncommon* inquiry, we replied with pleasure that we trusted it was so. He then apologized, with much courtesy and in a gentlemanly manner, for the intrusion upon our conversation ; remarking that he was a stranger in Boston, where he had come a short time previous, having business with eminent merchants there. He further stated that he had, as he hoped, been led to taste the wonders of redeeming love, and to rejoice in that liberty wherewith the Lord makes his people free.

We had become by this time greatly interested in his remarks, and encouraged him to give us a history of the hope that was in him, to which he readily assented.

During the year in which we met with him, he was providentially led to the city of New Orleans, where he had large transactions in business. Here the Holy Spirit led him, while walking the streets one Sabbath morning, to enter a church, in which the Rev. Mr. P—— was then preaching. His attention was so led to a consideration of the holiness of the Lord's day, and the sin of desecrating it, that immediately after service, with a frankness and promptitude which appeared to be characteristic of the man, he went to the counting-room of a French merchant with whom he had engaged to dine that day at his country-seat, and told him that he must be excused from dining with him. Upon being asked the reason, he unhesitatingly replied, that at church that day he had heard what had convinced him that it was wrong so to do, and although the invitation was again urged with great importunity, he steadily refused. The transaction, however, did not appear to make any lasting or saving impression on his mind.

Shortly after this he went to New York, and from thence to Boston. While there, walking one evening past where a number of persons were at the moment leaving a prayer-meeting, a lady handed to him a tract, and politely requested him to peruse it. He took it to his room, and read it. The title was, "*Quench not the Spirit.*" Its perusal made him solemn, awakened in him emotions to which he had hitherto been a stranger, and led him to commune thus with himself: "R——, how foolish and inconsistent has been your conduct. You have provided yourself with whatever is conducive to your comfort and convenience while travelling. You have around you all the appliances needful for the body. But what of the immortal soul? What have you done for its happiness and welfare? Nothing; nothing! You have not even a Bible in your trunk, to direct your soul to its Author and Preserver." Without delay he went to the nearest book-store and purchased a copy of the word of God, and at once set about its perusal. The truths, the warnings, the invitations there found, only fastened the arrow of conviction more deeply in his wounded heart, and the effect was not lessened by a reperusal of the tract.

On the morning of the next, or the succeeding, Sabbath, in deep agony of spirit, he wandered from his hotel without any settled purpose. He came in front of a church into which many people were flocking, and he entered with them. The Rev. Mr. S——, of the Methodist Church, addressed the audience from the words, "Quench not the Spirit," and powerfully unfolded the sin and danger of so doing. The words pierced the very soul of the stranger, and taught him more and more the total depravity of his heart, and his need of an all-sufficient Saviour to satisfy that holy law which he had fearfully broken. He returned to his room, and again engaged in earnest prayer, in reading the Scriptures, and in self-examination. I think he stated that it was on the succeeding Thursday evening when, having obtained no relief, he took the word of God, laid the sacred volume open upon a chair, and upon it the tract, and kneeling down, prayed for divine mercy with an earnestness which could not take a denial. Thus engaged, he continued upon his knees until nearly the dawn of day, when it pleased HIM, with whom is boundless compassion, to speak peace to his soul, and enable him to rejoice in Jesus Christ our Lord.

It was a fitting sequel to this interesting event, upon visiting the tract depository in New York, a few weeks after, to purchase some copies of the above tract, that we heard the respected depositary observe that his stock of this tract had been lately greatly reduced, as one gentleman had purchased no less than six hundred copies for distribution in the West Indies ; and upon inquiry we found that he was the warm-hearted brother whose story is here narrated.

Example of a Christian Life.—The small farm-house which we found at the end of the lane, was plain and neat. We were received by Miss —— with great cordiality. Her dress was simple and appropriate; her manner ingenuous and unaffected; and her conversation was unconstrained and highly spiritual—though betraying sufficient defects in early education to excite our wonder at her present attainments in divine knowledge.

During our conversation, I expressed a desire to know something of the manner of her conversion. "What was it," I inquired, "that led you to the cross?" "Sin!" she replied. "Our house used to be a very wicked place. The young people from —— were in the habit of coming out here to dance and play cards. I was a very wild girl. One night in February, eleven years ago, a gay, noisy party were here, and there was music and dancing. They became very boisterous, began throwing the plates about in their frolic, and behaved very badly. In the midst of the noise and confusion I sat down by my sister, and said, 'Sister, what do you think of all this?' 'I am tired of it; a'n't you?' she replied. 'Yes; and I mean to live a different life.' I thought of the sad prospect before me if I should die that night; and I determined to seek the Lord, and perish, if perish I must, at the foot of the cross."

"But had you no previous religious impressions?" I inquired.

"Yes; three years before that ball, when at the West, I was under conviction for sin, and there was much prayer for me in a revival of religion. I began then to study the Bible; but I returned home soon after, and our house was such a wild place that I could not read except on the Sabbath. I had nearly read the Bible through, when the Spirit of the Lord met me at the ball I spoke of. The pastor of the church at —— soon heard what was passing in our family, and came to see us; but I feared it was nothing but excitement, and knew that I must repent before the Lord for myself; so I refused to see him. Five members of our family were rejoicing in the hope of pardoning mercy within two months of that period; but I was the last of the five to yield to the claims of God and take refuge in Christ Jesus."

"Why were you the last to give your heart to the Saviour?" I asked.

"Oh, I was so jealous of myself," she replied, "I did not dare to hope."

"Were your convictions deep?"

"They were overwhelming. I saw that I was a great sinner—all vileness and pollution. My heart seemed a fountain of corruption."

"Have you enjoyed constant peace since you began to hope?"

"Yes; although I have had occasional doubts, my peace has been like a river. I have not known what it was to be free from bodily suffering for years; yet I have not lacked divine support, and I don't see how I could have lived through my trials but for the grace of God and the hopes of the gospel."

"I love the word of God!" she exclaimed in this connection; and her features lit up with a smile that was full of spiritual joy, as the conversation turned upon the Bible. In reply to the question as to the frequency and manner of reading it, she informed us that she had "*read the Bible through several times on her knees before God.*" "I have *meditated* the Scriptures through three times," said she, "with the exception, for the third time, of the last eight chapters of the book of Revelation."

"Do you mean, Miss ——, by '*meditating*' the Bible through, that you have read distinct passages, and meditated on them at the time of reading?"

"No," she replied: "it has become so familiar that I don't need to do that. I recall the historical, biographical, or prophetical portions of God's book, in the order they stand, and bring all the incidents to mind, and then trace out the connections of the scene or event before me with other and parallel passages in the word of God. I take Genesis, and think of all that is recorded there; then Exodus, etc. One book of the Pentateuch will last me two or three months in subjects for meditation. What a beautiful book Deuteronomy is! Then I take the Psalms and the prophets, etc.; and in this way I meditate through the Bible. I do not generally attempt to commit the words, but try to make the scenes, characters, incidents, and events all my own. Ezekiel is delightful. Sometimes, when meditating some of the visions, types, or seals, I seem half taken to heaven. I think the last nine chapters of Ezekiel are the most difficult to understand in all God's book." Turning to her friend, she inquired with affectionate interest, "You meditate in this way, do you not, Mrs. —— ? You'll be a growing Christian if you do. and there is no lost time; one can be thinking of the exodus, or of the offering of Isaac, or of the captivity, when about household duties."

"Let me inquire, Miss ——, if you read a commentary with the prophetical writings?"

"Not now," she replied; "I have read the Comprehensive Commentary until I have learned the views of the different writers. I find so many opinions expressed, that it is rather confusing. So I confine my reading now chiefly to Scott, or meditate on the prophecies till I understand them, with what light I have received from the helps I have enjoyed, and from above."

"But do you not find the New Testament most profitable and delightful of all?"

"Yes; the Old Testament, however, explains the New, and makes it clear. The types and prophecies relating to the Saviour are so striking, and their fulfillment so complete, that you cannot understand the New Testament fully without them. I love the whole of the word of God. Matthew and John are my favorite evangelists—though you can find all of Matthew, with the exception of thirty-eight verses, in the other gospels. Then there is so much in Luke! It is a beautiful gospel to meditate upon. All of the Bible is beautiful."

We were impressed with the facility and artlessness with which a personal, practical inquiry was thrown out, now and then, as the conversation advanced. Thus, when speaking of "meditation, self-examination and prayer, as three of the most important Christian duties," and explaining the value of meditation, among other things, as an aid to self-examination, she turned to Mrs. ——, and said, with great tenderness, "You examine yourself every night, of course, Mrs. —— ; *every Christian does that.*"

In answer to a direct inquiry on the subject of prayer, she said, "I have been in the habit of retiring to my room for the study of the Scriptures and prayer soon after family devotions in the morning ; then at noon, and at sundown. *Of course,* I commend myself to God before I go to bed at night, and when I get up in the morning. All Christians do that, don't they ?"

"Do you find any occasion for ejaculatory prayer ?" I inquired.

"O yes ; I go to God with everything. When I am about the house, or baking, or washing, or when a troublesome neighbor is here, or anything goes wrong in the family, or I am suffering pain, I can lift my heart to God, and he hears me just as well as in the closet. When I am in church, and the minister is preaching, I can fix my mind on some impenitent sinner, and entreat God to bless his word to that soul ; and yet I can hear all he says, and profit by preaching all the more."

The next day was stormy and unpleasant ; but I could not deny myself the satisfaction of another interview with Miss ——. An hour's familiar conversation concerning the precious gospel, the experience of its power on her own heart, and the means she employed for imparting it to others, only increased my interest in her history, and my gratitude for the grace of God displayed in it. When I expressed a desire that she would remember in her prayers one who was ready to sink under the weight of public responsibilities and private bereavements, she replied, "I have prayed for you ever since the day you were here." It was but the previous afternoon—frequent prayer made it seem longer. "I pray for all my friends. When I think of the ——— family on my knees, they seem to be right before me. O, how I love them !"

For several years after her conversion, her health allowed little more than the cultivation of her own graces, and occasional efforts for the salvation of others. About three years since, however, she was so far restored as to be able to commence more systematic and efficient plans for the spiritual benefit of her neighbors. The population around her was very wicked. The Sabbath was a holiday; profanity and intemperance abounded. No Sabbath-school gathered the children from the streets ; no church called the people from their houses.

She called on two families, and invited the children to come to her Sabbath-school. The kitchen was arranged for the purpose, and has since been the scene of her patient toil. By denying herself the morning service at church, she gains the quiet hours when the family are away. One by one the families around sent their children, until the number increased from twenty-seven the first year, to forty-eight at the time of our visit. From one family, residing on the hill three miles distant, five children, the youngest but five years old, walked to the school. With the exception of such aid as was rendered by two of the oldest of her pupils, in teaching the younger children to read, she was the only instructor. Sometimes, from illness, she has been under the necessity of laying her head upon her pillow, while carrying forward the instruction of nearly fifty pupils. The arrangement of her school-room must be done chiefly by her own hands. The government of her untutored charge all devolved on her. But with these disadvantages she has persevered, until that humble school has become the centre of religious light to all that district.

The results of such an attempt to do good under difficulties, with the divine blessing, are suited to encourage the humblest of Christ's disciples to like efforts. The Sabbath is now honored where it was profaned ; religious books, which she constantly loaned to families through the children, furnished a substitute for preaching, and did much to promote Sabbath observance, temperance and piety ; the children were gaining a knowledge of the Scriptures, and were often in tears while the gospel was unfolded to them ; and although there were as yet no marked instances of conversion among her scholars, it was no source of discouragement to her. She lived in daily expectation of a visitation from on high, which should quicken the seed she was sowing in hope. The harvest-time is coming.

On Sabbath morning, my friends from the mansion accompanied me to the Sunday-school of the farmer's daughter. Perhaps one-half of the more distant pupils were prevented from attending, by the rain. In the small, neat kitchen were gathered about twenty children and youths, between the ages of four and eighteen, including three or four little black boys. A few older persons had also come to enjoy her instructions. The order of the school was perfect. Though a little embarrassed by the presence of strangers, she proceeded calmly with the lesson, which related to the character of Judas, and the betrayal of the Son of God. She gave a clear exposition of the passage, and added remarks of a practical nature adapted to the comprehension of her youngest hearer. After this exercise, she requested the scholars, in order, to repeat the Commandments. A young woman, perhaps seventeen years of age, repeated the command, "Thou shalt have no other gods before me." The teacher addressed her in the most solemn and direct manner, "Sarah ——, you have broken this commandment of the Lord. You have an idol in your heart which keeps you from the love of God. What is it? Is it dress? Is it pleasure? You know. It will ruin your soul if it is not renounced. Will you give it up?` To-day? Now?" This was said in a tone of affection, and yet with a solemnity that was dreadful. Sarah's conscience was roused; she covered her face with her book, but, for many minutes, the tears trickling down her cheeks, and the heaving of her breast, betrayed the emotion which these simple words awakened. This must serve as a sample of her manner.

After the commandments were repeated and commented upon, she began a review of her "lists," as she termed them, or a series of questions in manuscript, which she had prepared, embracing the principal events in biblical history, and the more prominent doctrines of the word of God. These were answered with great promptness, in turn, even by the youngest scholars. A class of the smallest children was then examined in the "Scripture Catechism." In such ways were these young minds familiarized with the word of God, and with such a living exemplification of its spirit and power before them, as to impress every truth on the mind and heart.

Within a few months after this, Miss —— commenced visiting

the parents of these children, and other neglected families in her vicinity, distributing tracts and books, conversing on personal religion, and endeavoring to bring all under the influence of the gospel. Besides being a Sabbath-school teacher, she became, in this sense, a colporteur. She also sustained a school for colored people, embracing several adults, after the service on each Sabbath afternoon.

Such are some of the ways in which piety in the heart works out in the life. This feeble, suffering female laid the foundations of pure morals and vital religion in that ignorant, destitute neighborhood; and became as truly a missionary as was Harriet Newell or Harriet Winslow. Her efforts were appreciated, and her religious character respected by all around her. She was "a light shining in a dark place," and the judgment-day may reveal many an heir of glory led to the cross by the consistent example and self-denying labors of the farmer's daughter.

About "Election," etc.—I had been reading Baxter's Saints' Rest. I had studied that part of it that describes the condition of those who lose that rest. My soul burned within me. I had an indescribable desire to do something to save the impenitent from that condition. I felt my commission from the Most High renewed; that my commission as a messenger from God to sinners was as good as any angel's. I visited the house of two ladies who had for a long time supported themselves with their needles. The elder one was a professor, but the younger had no hope. "If you should die as you are," said I, "do you think you should go to dwell with Christ in Heaven?" "I suppose I should not," replied the younger. "How then can you rest until you have made your peace with God? If you were doomed to hell only for twenty-four hours, and tears and cries could rescue you, you would weep day and night until the pardon came." Then turning to the older sister, I said, "I will pray with you, if you have no objections." "None, none," said she; "I desire it." I took from my pocket my Bible, and after reading, I commended them to God, praying for the younger especially. As I arose, I saw that she turned away her face, as if to conceal her tears.

At my second visit she wished to get me upon some puzzling doctrine. "How do you understand *election*?" she said. "In this way," said I: "if you ever are so happy as to get to heaven, you will give all the glory to God. But if you go to despair, you will bear the blame for ever." A solemn pause ensued. "Well, I do not see," she continued, "that *I* can do anything." "There is one thing," said I, "you can do. You can go on in sin, as you have done; grieve the Holy Spirit; put off the matter until death overtakes you. Then, if you perish, will God be to blame?" A pause again. "I have tried a great many times," she said, "to find what you recommend, but I have come to the conclusion that all my efforts are an abomination in the sight of God." "Well," said I, "if your prayers are offensive to God, how do you think the rest of your life appears in his sight?" She wept, and her sister wept. Then I took her Bible from the stand, and read the parable of the prodigal son, applying every point of it to her as I went on. I went to prayer. Both of them fell on their knees. After prayer they said, "Call again." The next Sabbath they walked a long way to find our meeting. As I reasoned of sin and of righteousness, the older one prayed and the other trembled.

"I saw you last evening at the prayer-meeting. I was glad to see you: and now, Nancy," said I, "have you given that hard heart to Christ?" "I fear not," she said, and covered her face in her handkerchief. Then her sister spoke, and said, "She thinks she has done all she can. I have told her everything that I can think of, but she has remained right there. She has said over and over again, how I wish Mr. —— would come." "Yes," said I, "and as soon as ever I knocked, she asked me in: but my Saviour may knock at her door all day and all night, 'until his head is filled with the dew, and his locks with the drops of the night,' but she keeps her door locked against him." I took my hat and went out to a solitary place, and there that poor sinner was by no means forgotten. But she thought then that she was lost—that I despaired of such a wretch as she was. In a few hours I went in again. Every tear was dried. She looked despair itself. She wanted to know if I had given her up. I told her, "No. But there is a work between you and God that I cannot do. I have prayed for you, and shall continue so to do." "But can I give my heart to God now?" she asked. "Why not?" said I. "It is my hard heart: I know I am a hardened sinner," she said. "But," said I, "you are a greater sinner than you are aware. If you should see *all* your heart in the light of God's law, you could not live. You would sink. But Christ is as great a Saviour as you are a sinner." I prayed and left them.

"Well, Nancy I have come once more to see if that hard heart relents. Do you keep up your rebellion against God?" "I fear I do. I have done everything I can. It all does no good. I fear I am given over for ever." "This acknowledgment turned into a prayer would be a good one," said I. "Go and say, O Lord, I am a desperate sinner. I have gone this way and that, and am only in the dark. My feet are in 'the horrible pit and miry clay,' and every struggle only sinks me the deeper. I am sinking. *Lord save; I perish.* Other sinners," said I, "are one after another coming in, and here you are fighting against God. He is more willing to pardon you, than you are to repent. Why not repent, and believe in Christ?"

I knocked. Nancy was at the door. She took me by the hand. Tears stood in her eyes; but a partial smile shone through them, like the sun after a shower, shining through the last rain-drops. "How is your mind this morning?" To describe her mind, she gave me the hymn, "Rock of ages, cleft for *me*." "Can you accept the first line?" said I. "I think I can." "Does the Saviour seem near and precious?" "O, 'the chiefest among ten thousand;' but I have not as much light as I could wish." "Hav'n't you as much as you *deserve*?" said I. "O yes; more." "Walk softly, then," said I, "and rejoice with trembling."

At the communion she was present and looked on. She looked at the bread and wine. She thought on Calvary, and on the resurrection. She had loved her money; but now she was ready for the contribution. She wanted to do something for the missionaries; and every time there was an opportunity to help the

Tract Society, she did it. Now she is on missionary ground, where her tender sympathy and her benevolence have room for action. When her sister was pining on her death-bed, it seemed hard for them to part; but after *she* had gone home, Nancy had nothing more to give up. She bade farewell to friends, and the dear church she had joined, for a home among strangers.

Taught of God.—During a revival of religion in one of our New England villages, a son of the clergyman returned home for a brief visit. The lad was a deaf mute, and had spent his first term in the asylum just then commencing its history. His parents having no knowledge of the language of signs, and the boy being an imperfect writer, it was almost impossible to interchange with him any but the most familiar ideas. He, therefore, heard nothing of the revival.

But before he had been many days at home he began to manifest signs of anxiety, and at length wrote with much labor upon his slate, "*Father, what must I do to be saved?*" His father wrote in reply, "My son, you must repent of sin, and believe in the Lord Jesus Christ." "How must I do this?" asked the boy again upon the slate. The father explained to him as well as he could, but the poor untaught boy could not understand. He became more than ever distressed: he would leave the house in the morning for some retired place, and be seen no more until the father went in search of him. One evening, at sunset, the boy was found upon the top of the hay, under the roof of the barn, on his knees, his hands uplifted, and praying to God in the signs of the mutes. The distress of the parents became intense. They sent for one of the teachers of the asylum, and then for another, but it seemed that the boy could not be guided to the Saviour of sinners. There were enough to care for his soul, but there were none to instruct him.

Days passed—days of parental fear and agony. One afternoon, the father was on his way to fulfill an engagement in a neighboring town, and as he drove leisurely over the hills, the poor, inquiring, and hopeless son was continually in his thoughts. In the midst of his supplications, his heart became calm, and the long distracted spirit was serene in the one thought that God is able to do his own work. The speechless boy at length began to tell how he loved his Saviour, and stated that he first found peace on the very afternoon when the spirit of his agonized father on the mountains was calmed and supported by the thought, that what God had promised he was able to perform.

The converted mute became an instructor of others, and every Sabbath-day found him in one of our large cities, with a gathered congregation of fellow-mutes, breaking to them the bread of life, and guiding their attentive souls to that God who has power to do his own work.

The Bird in the Church.—The town of E—— is embowered in trees. Its ancient and spacious church, with its chiming clock, and towering steeple, of beautiful proportions, although in the centre of the town, is yet in the centre of forest-trees, which nearly conceal it from view; and, what is more, it is the centre and home of the affections of a people whose ancestors, for nearly two hundred years, have there worshipped God in spirit and in truth.

On a Sabbath of a year of unusual interest, in the late spring, that church was crowded with multitudes anxious about their souls, and hanging upon the lips of their beloved pastor, who, with earnestness and tears, was expounding to them the way of reconciliation with God. The doors of the church were open, and the windows were all closed. During the progress of the service, a bird entered by the door, and flew up to the vaulted roof, and, alarmed by the voices which it heard, gave every evidence of anxiety to make its escape. There sat in one of the pews a female under deep conviction for sin, and who for months had been seeking without finding peace for her soul. Her eye soon lit upon the fluttering bird, and followed him from window to window, in his vain efforts to escape. It sought an exit at every window, and almost at every pane of glass; and, as it fluttered from one window to another, this female would say in her heart, "O foolish bird, why strive to get out there; is not the door wide open?" It would now rise to the ceiling—now renew its vain attempts at the windows; while she repeated to herself, "O foolish bird, why strive to get out there; is not the door wide open?" And when its wings were weary, and when all hope of escape seemed to be abandoned, and, as if unable to sustain itself longer, it lowered itself into the body of the church, it caught a view of the door, and was out in a moment, singing a song of triumph over its release, amid the branches of the trees.

When the bird was gone, the thoughts of the convicted person reverted to her own state and doings. The voice of the preacher was unheard amid the conflict of her own thoughts. "I have been acting," said she, "like that foolish bird. I have been seeking peace in ways in which it is not to be found, and to go out from the bondage of sin through doors that are closed against me. Christ is the door; through him there is escape from the dominion of sin. I have acted like that foolish bird long enough. What the door was to it, Christ is to me. As it escaped through the door, so may I through Christ." And she found peace in believing. And almost as soon as the bird commenced its melody in the trees, rejoicing over its escape, she commenced making melody in her heart unto the Lord.

An Indian's Gift to Christ.—In a portion of the southern territory from which the red man has now been driven, I once attended a large protracted meeting, held in the wild forest. The theme on which the preacher dwelt, and which he illustrated with surpassing beauty and grandeur, was "Christ and him crucified." He spoke of the good Shepherd who came into the world to seek and to save the lost. He told how this Saviour met the rude buffetings of the heartless soldiers. He drew a picture of Gethsemane, and the unbefriended Stranger who wept there. He pointed to him as he hung bleeding upon the cross.

The congregation wept. Soon there was a slight movement in the assembly, and a tall son of the forest, with tears on his red cheeks, approached the pulpit, and said, "Did Jesus die for me—die for poor Indian? Me have no lands to give to Jesus, the white man take them away; me give him my dog, and my rifle." The minister told him Jesus could not accept those gifts. "Me give Jesus my dog, my rifle, and my blanket; poor Indian, he got no more to give—he give Jesus all." The minister replied that Christ could not accept them. The poor, ignorant, but generous child of the forest bent his head in sorrow, and meditated. He raised his noble brow once more, and fixed his eye on the preacher, while he sobbed out, "*Here is poor Indian, will Jesus have him?*" A thrill of unutterable joy ran through the souls of minister and people as this fierce son of the wilderness now sat, in his right mind, at the feet of Jesus. The Spirit had done his work, and he who had been so poor, received the earnest of an inheritance which will not fade when the diadems of earth shall have mouldered for ever.

"Do let me Alone."—T. S——, says a minister in the State of New York, was a man who suffered no one to approach him on the interests of his soul; nor would he allow any of his family to converse with him on the subject. He would say to them, "If you wish peace in the family, if you wish unmolestedly to enjoy the privileges of your religion, you must be quiet towards me, and let me and my belief alone." I thought him a troubled man, by no means at ease in his spirit; but whenever I entered his house, he was sure to leave before I could converse with him.

At one of my Wednesday evening meetings, some one of the family informed me that he was to start the next morning for a short journey. I had before arranged to go that morning into his neighborhood for pastoral visitation; and as I came in sight of his house, which was about forty rods from the road, knowing that he had not seen me, I dropped at his gate the tract, "Danger of Delay," and passed on, still unobserved, when I felt inclined to pause and see how he would treat the little message I had laid in his way. When he came to the gate, he took it up, looked about him, and seating himself upon a rock, commenced reading. I soon observed him wipe his eyes; and when he had read it through, he held his handkerchief to his face for some time, and then arose, returned to his house, and relinquished his journey.

The scene took such hold on my feelings that, after making a few visits, I returned and called at his house. On inquiring for him, I learned from his weeping wife that the tract had so alarmed him, that he dared not go on his journey; and that he had fastened himself in his stable, and refused admittance to any one. I went to the stable; but in agony, and with an emphasis which I can never forget, he begged me, if I did not wish to increase his misery in hell, not to talk to him on religion, or even pray for him ; "for," said he, "I am sure of damnation ; for me, who have so long rebelled, and who have so willfully slighted such infinite mercy, there can be no hope." I tried to convince him that God was willing to be gracious even to him, however great were his sins. But his constant and agonizing cry was, "Do let me alone ; there is no hope for me." I left him, and returned to the family, whom I found all engaged in prayer for their distressed husband and father. After uniting with them in a season of prayer, I returned home ; calling on one of my deacons, and requesting his family to spend the evening in joining their prayers with those of the family of Mr. S—— and mine, for that poor awakened man.

On Friday afternoon I called again, and found him still in his stable, and in as deep agony as when I left him the day before. He still begged me not to talk with him, or even to pray for him, lest it increase his condemnation in the coming world. After praying with the family, I again returned home, but never felt a heavier burden on my heart. On Saturday morning I again called, and still found him in his stable, having utterly refused to converse with his family, or to receive any food.

I went to the stable, and said to him, "Mr. ——, are you determined to increase the long catalogue of your sins by self-murder?" He replied, "Mr. B——, how can you think that of me? No, no, I will not add that sin to the dark catalogue." "But," said I, "you are doing it as surely as though you were to cut your throat ; for you can no more live without food, than you can without blood. The best thing that you can do is to come out of your concealment, and act like a rational man."

He finally came out, and after taking some refreshment, seemed more calm. I conversed with him ; and after praying with him, I told him that it would be better to attend meeting the following day, than to stay away, even were he finally lost ; for then the sin of turning away from the sanctuary and the means of grace would not rest upon his soul. He promised me that if able he would attend ; and he did. And as he entered our large school-house, every Christian seemed to drop the head, as though in silent prayer.

On that morning I preached from the words, "Come unto me, all ye that labor and are heavy laden, and I will give you rest." Near the close I proposed the inquiry, "Who of you will come to Christ? *He* is *ready*, he *waits*, he *calls*, yes, he *urges you*, poor *sinking*, *burdened*, and *dying* sinner, to come to him and find *rest*, and *peace*, and *joy*, and eternal salvation. Will you come; and come now?" Persons who sat by him afterwards informed me that they heard him distinctly say, "Yes, I will come; and I will come now."

He soon after made a public profession of religion; and in relating his experience, he remarked that when he felt the resolve in his heart to yield to Christ, the removal of his burden was so sudden, and his joy was so great, that he could hardly refrain from shouting, "Glory to God," for so wonderful a display of the riches of grace. A deeper sense of guilt, or a more exalted view of the power and grace of God, than he expressed, I never witnessed. His family altar burned morning and evening, he was punctual at the prayer-meeting, and was one of our most consistent, active, energetic, and devoted Christians. Thus he continued to live for many years, when he died in the triumphs of faith, and went to join the church triumphant in the song of redeeming grace and dying love.

Believing in God.—In the year 18—, a young man from the South entered a New England college. He was the child of infidel parents. The influences of home had all been adverse to the religion of Christ. He went to college quite young, and was a frivolous, inconsiderate youth. He had no religious or moral principle to guide him, and to seek his own present pleasure was his object in life. He was quick and passionate in his disposition, easily taking offence, and not hesitating to resort to a challenge to mortal combat, as the proper method of settling the difficulties of a ball-room.

In becoming a member of a "puritanic" New England college, he found himself in a new world. He attended prayers regularly, because it was required by the laws of college; but when he stood up in that consecrated chapel, and heard the venerable president address an invisible Being, he said to himself, "What folly! There is no God to listen to this prayer." He said in his heart, "There is no God."

As one looked over that assembly, no one among those hundreds of young men seemed in so hopeless a case as that young infidel. But God had said of him, "He is a chosen vessel unto me, to bear my name before the Gentiles, and kings, and children of Israel." He was affected by the Christian influences about him. The Spirit of God touched and softened his heart. He began to ask himself, "Am I mistaken? Is it possible that there is a God?" The president of the college took much interest in him, and gave him, in private, such instruction as he thought would benefit him.

One evening the president talked with him very earnestly and affectionately. He talked long and faithfully, and when —— left him, he said to him, "When you return to your room, you will find it occupied by gay young men; and if you go in and joim them in their amusements, all these impressions will be effaced from your mind: but do not go there; go away alone, and pray earnestly that God will enlighten and teach you." He left the president and went to his room; but did he enter it? No. He heard the loud laugh of his companions, and he remembered the words of the president. He went away alone, and, perhaps for the first time in his life, he communed with his Maker.

He told me that he distinctly remembered the moment when the truth of the existence of a God was first impressed upon his mind. He was in the chapel at college-prayers, and when the president rose to pray, his old disbelief passed away, and he felt that there was a God. He could truly say, "Lord, I believe; help thou mine unbelief." He could hardly restrain his emotions during the service, and as soon as the prayer was closed, he seized the arm of a pious young man, saying, "Do you believe in a God?" He wondered that, if the Christian young men about him did believe, they did not manifest the excitement and deep feeling which he experienced at that moment. A light had suddenly shined into his soul from heaven, and like Paul, he trembled and was astonished.

During the last two years of his college life, he associated but little with his former companions. He roomed alone, and spent a portion of each day in the study of the Bible and prayer. He was greatly changed in his external character.

When he left college, the Holy Spirit accompanied him. He

placed himself under the influence of a Christian minister and Christian friends, and he made his Bible his constant study. He became a pupil, and afterwards a teacher in the Sabbath-school. At length he ventured to hope that he had been brought out of nature's darkness into God's marvellous light. And now this young man is a Missionary of the Cross (the Rev. E. J. P——) in a dark and benighted corner of the world.

The Proud Husband and Praying Wife.—During a work of grace in C——, N. Y., Mrs. —— became deeply impressed upon the subject of personal religion, and the duty of yielding her heart to God, and securing an interest in the "great salvation." With a decision of mind characteristic of the lady, she cast away the weapons of her warfare, made an unconditional surrender of herself to the Lord, and speedily found "peace in believing," and "joy in the Holy Ghost."

With some apprehension of a refusal, Mrs. —— informed her husband that she felt it to be her duty to serve God and to unite with the church, and wished his consent to her so doing. He heard her request in silence, his countenance indicating a severe mental conflict, and at length, with an effort at composure, said, "I have no objections. I do not wish to act the part of a tyrant over you; unite with the church, if you feel it to be your duty, but I cannot go with you." Grateful to God that he had put it into the heart of her husband to give his consent to her uniting with the church, she hastened with joyful steps to the temple of God, where the saints kept "holy day." Upon her return from the meeting, in the evening, she found that her companion had retired for the night. She entered the chamber softly, supposing him to be asleep, and bowing by the bedside, poured out her soul to God in prayer on the behalf of her much-loved but unconverted husband.

When the time had arrived for those who proposed uniting with the church, "to give a reason for the hope within them," Mrs. —— was one of the many who presented themselves as candidates for membership; but her husband was not there; he had voluntarily remained at home, "to keep the children."

During the introductory exercises of the morning, to the wonder and surprise of all, Mr. ——, the husband, entered the house, and with a calm and cheerful countenance went forward and took a seat by the side of his wife, near the pulpit. At a proper time, he rose and said as follows: "Christian friends, I have come to tell you what God has done for my soul. I remained without any interest concerning my soul up to the time when my dear wife asked my permission to unite with the church. Her request fell upon my ears like a thunderclap, and went to my heart like a dagger. I felt that the peace of my family was destroyed, and my proud and rebellious heart rose up in opposition, and had I followed my own inclination, I should have forbidden her to make a profession of religion. But I feared public sentiment; I did not wish to be called a tyrant, and I gave reluctant consent. I was very unhappy; I knew I ought to be a Christian, but was too proud to confess it, and I resolved that I would not confess to any one how I felt upon the subject of religion, but would privately seek God and have religion, and none should know it. I resorted to secret prayer; but the more I prayed the worse I felt, and yet I could not forego prayer. I assumed a cheerful aspect, but there was a crushing weight upon my heart. On the occasion of my wife's praying for me by my bedside, on her return from meeting, I was not asleep, but lay like a guilty culprit, trembling with fear, while she pleaded with God on my behalf. A more wretched being did not exist than I felt myself to be, but I was not humble enough to own it to my companion: I slept but little during that night. The next evening I was induced to attend the house of God, while she remained at home: upon my return, and entering the house, I found that she had retired to her chamber; but there lay the Bible open upon the stand where she had been reading, and there stood the chair by which I felt assured she had knelt and prayed for my guilty soul. I trembled with emotion. What must I do? was the language of my throbbing heart. I read the book of God. I bowed my knees where my wife had bowed before me, and with tears I sought the mercy of God; but no relief could I find, because I was not satisfied to take salvation without any conditions. I spent another restless night. This morning, after my wife had left me to come to this place, my anguish increased; I felt that I could not live, I must yield or die. I could not find relief in my business, I could not take comfort in my little children; I was of all men most miserable. I felt a drawing to the house of God, and after asking God to direct me, I resolved to come to his temple. I went out among my neighbors, and left my little children in their care, and with eager steps I pressed my way to this place, sighing and groaning, like Bunyan's pilgrim, beneath my burden, until, as I was ascending the hill upon which this house stands, my mind was led to Calvary, to Christ and his finished work, and I was enabled to believe on him with all my heart; my burden was loosed and rolled away, and my soul is filled with the love of Jesus. And now, as a brand plucked from the burning, I wish to unite with my dear companion in serving God, and when the proper time shall come, to unite with the Church as one who has obtained mercy of the Lord as the chief of sinners."

The Faithful Wife.—God had revived his work in many churches in the city of B——; multitudes of weary sinners had sought and found rest in Him who is exalted to give repentance and forgiveness of sins. J—— H—— was a skeptic and scoffer, but one evening was led by his affectionate, pious wife to hear the gospel. On their return home, he solemnly asserted his intention to go no more. "Why not, my dear husband?" said the alarmed lady. "I was both provoked and insulted," said he; "that entire sermon on infidelity was preached at me, and scarcely one in the house but knew it. I have forever done with church-going and preaching."

Weeks elapsed; the wife prayed and friends prayed for this deluded man—and God heard their cry. Said the deeply concerned Mrs. H—— one evening, "Dear, will you grant me one little request?" Being unwilling to promise till he knew its purport, she continued, "Go with me to-night to meeting." "I will go to the door, but no further," said he. "That will do," said this amiable Christian. They went together, parted at the entrance; her heart absorbed as she took her seat in fervent prayer for her beloved partner. Some minutes elapsed, and service had commenced, when suddenly the door opened, a heavy step advanced, and, to her unspeakable joy, her husband calmly seated himself near her.

That night Mr. H—— was interested and affected. Hope beat high among his friends. The next evening, after tea, as Mr. and Mrs. H—— sat conversing at their pleasant fireside, he rose, and while a tear dropped from his cheeks, "Wife," said he, "*is it not time to go to church?*" She sprung from her chair, and though it was early by an hour and a half, she feared delay; and, taking hat and cloak, they went. That was the happiest night of her life, for Mr. H—— presented himself, a humble inquirer for the way of salvation, and numbered many years in his Redeemer's service. All who knew him believe that, under God, he owed what he is to the sweet influences of a loving, patient, meek, Christian wife: "For what knowest thou, O wife, whether thou shalt save thy husband?" 1 Cor. vii. 16.

The Lost Bank-Note.—Mr. A—— was an irreligious man, nearly sixty years of age. He had long neglected the house of God, and indulged in the use of profane language. One day he lost a bank-note in his barn. He sought for it several times, but did not find it. At length he said to himself, "That note is in the barn, and *I will search for it till I find it.*" Accordingly, he went to the barn, and carefully moved straw and hay, hour after hour, till he found the note.

He had told me, two months before, that he knew that his soul was not right with God, and he intended to live a better life, and seek salvation. His anxiety increased. A few weeks after he lost the note, he sat by the fire musing on the state of his soul, when he turned to his wife and asked, "What must one do to become a Christian?" "You must seek for it," she replied, "as you sought for the bank-note." She said no more. It was "a word fitly spoken." He tried to follow the direction, and through the grace and mercy of Christ, he found the "pearl of great price," and rejoiced in hope of the glory of God.

Influence of a Wife.—Among the early settlers in L——, Green county, New York, on the Catskill mountains, religion hardly had a name. But there were two females who met weekly for prayer. The Lord heard their cry; a small church was gathered, which was soon visited with a revival of religion, and several of the most respectable families were brought into its communion.

Among those added to the church was Mrs. T. P——, who earnestly sought the blessing of God on her unconverted husband and children; but he became decidedly opposed to all religion, and persecuted his wife in various ways. She was not permitted to pray with her children in the house, but used daily to retire to the barn, and there worship that Saviour whose birth-place was a manger. She was decided in every Christian duty, but yielded, as far as she could conscientiously, to the wishes of her husband.

Mr. P—— was a man of high spirit. He became excessively fond of company, and used to spend his Saturdays at a public-house, where he indulged in drinking freely, and by his associates was called "Old Head."

In the early part of May, more than forty years since, one Saturday evening Mr. P—— returned from his associates, and found his pious wife, who had commended her family to God for the night, engaged in reading.

"What book have you there?" said he.

"I have the Connecticut Evangelical Magazine."

"Where did you get it?"

"It was left for me by my friend B——, who called to see me this afternoon."

"This Mr. B—— has determined to ruin the peace and happiness of my family. You shall not read the book. Put it up, and go to your rest."

Mrs. P—— replied, "I will lay by the book because my husband requires it, though it is a great sacrifice, as I am much interested in it. The blessed Bible teaches me submission to the will of my husband."

They retired to rest—the bosom of the one full of holy peace and anxious solicitude for her wandering husband; the bosom of the other full of dark and fiend-like passions, cursing God, and persecuting his people.

Soon Mr. P—— arose, saying, "I cannot sleep with one so religious and saint-like as you are." She proposed to retire to another room, but this he would not allow. The night was spent in silent but ardent prayer by Mrs. P——, and in anxious tossings and bitter revilings by her husband.

In the morning, the children, as usual, were assembled in the barn, and commended to God by the pious, heart-broken mother, and in due time were all neatly clad for the house of God, when Mrs. P—— gently asked her husband if he would not accompany them. With an oath, he replied, "No; I do not believe in the stuff taught there for religion." With deep solicitude she bent her steps to the sanctuary, where, with his people, she could cast her burden on that Arm pledged to sustain her.

Mr. P—— was now left alone, and to the most bitter reflections. The amiable, decided, and conscientious deportment of his wife; her patient sufferings from his irascible temper; her firmness in every religious duty, shone with such lustre, that the contrast led him to see that there was a difference between the righteous and the wicked here, and must be hereafter. For a moment, he thought he would follow his wife to the house of God; and then, with his razor in his hand, he was about to take his own life; but God was near, and he put away the instrument of death.

When the time of the afternoon service arrived, his wife again invited him to accompany her; but his spirit was unyielding, and he promptly said he would not. After she had gone, however, he determined that for once he would go.

He went, with a heart rankling with hatred to God and his people; but he soon became awed at the presence of Jehovah in his sanctuary. His soul was deeply agitated until the close of the last prayer, when, with wonder and astonishment, he beheld by faith "the Lamb of God, who taketh away the sin of the world." His proud heart was humbled; God was exalted; his people loved; and to use his own words, every spear of grass seemed to praise its Maker.

He returned home, begged his wife's forgiveness, acknowledged his sin against God and her, and expressed his hope of pardon through the merits of the Lord Jesus Christ.

The grateful joy of Mrs. P—— cannot be described. Her persecuting husband was now a man of prayer; the unnatural father was now the pious and devoted leader of his household at the throne of grace

On sitting down at his first meal, his reflections were most bitter. "From deep poverty," said he, "I have been raised to a comfortable living; God has provided for me; but I have been rebellious against him." He asked God's blessing, and forgiveness for past ingratitude. At evening he called his family around him, confessed his sins to his children, prayed for and with them; and for more than thirty years was a consistent, devoted Christian, and a deacon of the church at L——.

"My Mother's Prayers haunt me."—A mother with several children was left a widow. Feeling her responsibility as a parent, she gave diligence to train her household for Christ. That her instructions might be blessed and her children converted, she was unceasing in her supplications at the throne of mercy. She would arise at midnight, and in the chamber where her little ones were sleeping, would kneel and pray for them with wrestling importunity.

Her eldest son becoming restless under religious restraints, abandoned his mother and the home of his childhood. He bent his steps to a seaport, and enlisted as a sailor. He was absent several years, made a number of voyages, and under the influence of wicked companions became profligate.

At length he was induced to visit the place of his nativity. His mother, who had heard nothing of him from the time of his departure, was dead, and the residue of her family scattered. Of her death the sailor felt an interest to learn some particulars, and whether any members of the family were still living, or remained in the vicinity of his birth. But how was he to obtain the desired information! "A man's heart deviseth his way, but the Lord directeth his steps." It was a time of religious revival in the congregation where his mother had been accustomed to worship. He was told of a prayer-meeting in the neighborhood; and knowing that his devout parent used to attend such meetings, he directed his course thither, thinking that he might there meet some of her old acquaintances.

When the sailor arrived at the place of worship, he found the meeting in progress. He entered and took a seat in an obscure corner, intending, at the close of service, to ask for the information he was seeking. The assembly was one of great stillness and solemnity, such as a genuine revival of religion usually produces. The mariner would not have been dismayed at the thunder of the storm upon the heaving ocean, but he could not brave the silent power of the prayer-meeting and religious conference. He could hear nothing, save the voice of one and another relating what God had done for their souls, or the suppressed sigh and stifled sob, which arose from different parts of the congregation. The "still small voice" of the Holy Spirit, who had conducted him thither, was speaking to his conscience. Unable to quench the fire within, or longer conceal his anguish, he exclaimed vehemently, "*My mother's prayers haunt me like a ghost!*"

Those who well remembered the praying mother, and had a slight recollection of the wayward boy, now became deeply interested in the distressed man. Such counsel was imparted as the circumstances and state of his feelings seemed to demand; but he writhed with keen conviction for several weeks. At length he found peace in hopeful reconciliation to God and faith in the Lord Jesus Christ; and in due time became an exemplary and useful member of the same church with which his mother had been connected.

"Don't Put it Off."—We were delayed in our journey, and Saturday evening came upon us. As Providence ordered, we were welcomed by a pious father and mother, whose children had all left them and settled in the world, except their youngest son, aged nineteen, who remained as the staff of their old age, and for whose salvation the mother continually offered her agonizing prayer. He knew his duty, but urged that he should have a more "convenient season."

In family prayer his case was laid at the footstool of sovereign mercy. In the morning, when leaving for public worship, I felt an inexpressible desire to give the young man a tract from a basket with which I was supplied; and the first that appeared was the two-leaved tract, "Don't put it off." He read aloud the title, and was evidently moved. An arrow had pierced through "the joints of the harness;" and as he afterwards said, his old *refuge* from that moment failed him. He attended meeting, and returned to peruse the tract, every word of which went to his soul. With new interest he looked into his Bible, in which he laid the precious leaf which had proved to him such a messenger of mercy, requesting that it might always remain there. Great was his agony lest he had "put it off" too long; but a reperusal of the tract made him urge his plea the stronger, and while reading those encouraging words, "him that cometh to me I will in no wise cast out," light from on high broke upon his mind. His mother felt that indeed salvation had come to her house, that her son who was dead now began to live. He gave the most decided evidence that he was born of the Spirit. "Don't put it off," was his faithful admonition to those who were without Christ. When I some time afterwards called on the family, I found the weeping mother bereaved of her son. She showed me the tract, and blessed God that our visit had been instrumental in bringing her child to a saving knowledge of Christ.

The Word by the Mouth of a Child.—About thirty years ago, visiting H——, in the wilderness of northeastern Ohio, in company with the Rev. Luther Humphrey, and examining candidates with a view to organize a church, I was struck with the narrative given of herself by Mrs. M——.

Living about two miles from her father's in Massachusetts, she one day took her little son, five years old, to visit her parents; and a thunder-storm arising, they were obliged to tarry for the night.

"In the evening," she said, "my father, as his custom was, called his family together, read from his large Bible, and commended all to God in prayer. In the morning, the family were also assembled, when he again read the Bible and prayed; and I returned home with my little boy.

"I soon noticed that the little fellow seemed pensive and very sober, and asked him, 'What is the matter?' After a little hesitation, he said, 'Why doesn't pa do as grandpa does?' I said to him, 'Poh, go away to your play.' My little boy looked disappointed at my answer, but ran to his play. He was gone, however, but a short time, before he came running to me, and with more earnestness, again said, 'Ma, ma, why doesn't pa do as grandpa does?" I frowned upon him, and bade him the second time go away to his play. He semed grieved, but went away. Soon he came running back to me a third time, and still more earnestly cried out 'Ma, ma, why doesn't pa do as grandpa does?" To pacify him, I asked him, 'How does grandpa do?' 'Why, ma, he gets his great Bible and reads, and then goes to prayer.' 'Well, ask pa when he comes home.'

"My husband was abroad on business, and was not expected home till evening. The boy seemed to wait impatiently for his father to come. When evening came, I said, 'My little boy, it is now time for you to go to bed.' 'No, ma, I must sit up till pa comes.' I soon tried again to influence his little mind to think it best for him to go to bed. But no, he must sit up, contrary to his usage, and see his pa. So he waited till between eight and nine, when his father returned. As soon as he stepped his foot within the door, the little boy ran to meet him, saying, 'Pa, pa, why don't you do as grandpa does?' 'Away, away; what are you up at this time of night for. Off to bed.'

"Nothing more was heard from our little boy until morning. He lay in bed later than usual, even till we had breakfasted. When he got up, I placed his breakfast before him, and drew him up to the table. But he did not eat anything. He sat very demure, looking at his food. I said, 'Why don't you eat?' He said nothing, but still sat almost motionless. I asked him again, "Why don't you eat your breakfast?" 'I am waiting to ask a blessing, for I don't see that anybody will, if I don't.'

"My feelings were overcome; I could contain myself no longer, and immediately retired into another room, where I might weep and pray undiscovered. I informed my husband. He was deeply affected. Without delay, we sought an interest in the Redeemer. Our own family altar was erected; and soon, as we hope, we found, to our unspeakable joy, HIM of whom Moses in the law and the prophets did write."

The father was elected deacon of the church, in which office he served acceptably to the day of his death. And the little boy, grown into the meridian of life, became an ornament to the Christian name and cause.

Prayer Answered "without Hand."—A work of divine grace in H—— county, Va., in 1850, was characterized by deep solemnity in the public assembly, and by an unusual spirit of prayer. A daily morning concert was held at six o'clock, and many who were made subjects of special prayer at these seasons, found Christ to be precious.

Among these was a young lady at a boarding-school, who, having experienced a change of heart, became much concerned for the salvation of her aged father, who lived about twenty miles distant. She endeavored to send for him by a special messenger, but did not succeed in procuring one. She then addressed him by letter, informing him what "the Lord had done for her soul," and urging him to come up to the meetings; but fearing that such a communication might offend the skeptical mind of her father, she did not send it. There was one resort, to her covenant God and Redeemer. She not only offered her fervent petitions, but went from one Christian to another, and engaged them to pray for her father at the six o'clock concert. This was on Saturday. On the morrow, many hearts unitedly cried to God, and through that holy day unceasing prayer ascended to the mercy-seat in his behalf. It was a Sabbath full of blessings to that people, and our young friend evidently felt, in common with the people of God, that the place was a Bethel, one of the heavenly places in Christ Jesus.

On Monday morning, we were again convened in the sanctuary; and just as the minister announced his text, "And yet there is room," an aged man, a stranger, entered the church and got the only vacant seat, near the door, the house being crowded. He gave unbroken attention to the discourse, and was much moved; at times the unbidden tear ran down his cheeks. At the conclusion of the service some one remarked, "There is Mr. ——, for whom we have been praying." I looked in the direction indicated, and behold, it was the stranger just alluded to.

I made my way towards him, but before I could reach him he was with his daughter. There she sat, smiling and weeping for joy; and yet, like the incredulous disciples, when they heard that "Peter stood at the gate," she could scarcely believe that she saw and heard her own father, while he stood over her, saying to her, "My child, I have been an unfaithful, wicked father to you ; I have taught you both by precept and example to neglect religion, and live for the present world ; and now I see the folly, the guilt, and the peril of it, and have come here to-day to advise you to seek true religion as your portion for this world and the next.

"My father," said she, "that portion I hope I have found in Jesus, and if you will be a Christian too, dear father, my cup of happiness will overflow."

"I am too great a sinner," he replied ; "but you are young, you can be a Christian, and I rejoice in it."

"My father," said she, "you can be a Christian too, the precious blood of Jesus 'cleanses from all sin.'"

The father had been a skeptic, and had lived in the neglect of the public and private means of grace until the last Sabbath morning, when, from a motive unknown to himself, he went to —— church, distant about ten miles, where there was only occasional preaching, and not knowing certainly that there was service there that day. But the Lord directed his steps ; for then and there he heard a most faithful sermon from the late Rev. S. T——, who was on a visit to that church. He returned to his home deeply impressed. "The multitude of his thoughts troubled him." He found no rest by day, and sleep forsook his eyelids. In the Bible of his deceased wife he read, to his own conviction and condemnation. And yet he read, and thought, and paced his chamber, and read, and thought again, the livelong night, until the burden of his sins brought the proud, stout-hearted skeptic to his knees. He then thought of his daughter, whose spiritual interests he had neglected, and he resolved to visit her in the morning. He accordingly rode to the school, a distance of nearly twenty miles ; and there learning that the family were at church, he hastened on and got there just as the preacher was announcing his text.

On the morrow, he returned again to the church, we trust, a changed man, rejoicing in our redeeming God and Saviour.

Poor Zeke and His Prayers.—In a wild, sequestered place, quite away from the bounds of my congregation, there lived a very wicked family—a father, mother, two brothers, and three sisters. None of them attended any meeting. One of the brothers was wanting in common sense. His name was Ezekiel. As he was not supposed to have mind enough to be put to any work, he used to stroll away, and be gone sometimes several days.

One day, as I was preaching on the pity Jesus has for poor sinners, I observed "poor Zeke" looking me in the face, and every time I said Jesus pitied poor sinners, the tears would start from his eyes. As there was more than usual attention to religion, we had meetings often; and whether it was a lecture, or a prayer meeting, or an inquiry-meeting, "poor Zeke" was sure to be there.

At length I asked him if he loved Jesus, and he answered, "Yes." "Why do you love Jesus?" said I. "O, 'cause he love poor wicked Zeke so." "Have you been wicked?" "Yes, I *full, full* of wicked." "Do you pray?" said I. "O, yes." "What do you say when you pray?" "I say, O my Jesus, pity poor Zeke. O take all my wicked away."

After a while he went home. His appearance was changed. He had lost his seeming vacancy of look and thought. But he dare not pray in the house, for all were full of fun and noise. So he went to the barn, and there he fell on his knees and uttered his broken prayer to Him who "hath chosen the weak things of this world to confound the mighty." His brother, going into the barn, heard him crying to God so fervently that it alarmed him. He went in and told his father, with an oath, that Zeke was in the barn praying. At this, his father ran to the barn and listened, and found the boy indeed at prayer. He went in and spoke to him; but he "cried so much the more a great deal." "Stop your noise, Zeke," said his angry father; but he kept on. So they took hold of him and got him into the house, in hopes of quieting him.

They asked him where he had been, and how he came to feel so. He told them a very rational story about it. But the more he talked, the more his father scolded. Poor Zeke found he could say no more, and then fell down on his knees again. His father tried to silence him; but his mother loved her poor boy, and begged them to let him pray.

When he had risen from prayer, his mother said, "It is high time we all prayed. Ezekiel, will you pray for your mother?" "O yes," he said; and down again he went upon his knees, and his mother with him. Not many days after, she too was full of joy at the thought of Jesus' dying pity. By this time, the brother who first heard him pray was sobbing out, "What shall I do?" Poor Zeke said, "Go to Jesus." Then he and his mother prayed for him, and he, too, found his distress giving way for unspeakable joy. Then there were three to pray for a hardened husband and an unfeeling father. He fought and ridiculed until their three daughters were added to the Lord. This made five who had now joined Ezekiel and embraced his religion.

At last his father saw himself alone. His heart broke; he wept like a child. He went to his son and confessed his sin in opposing him, and asked him to pray for him. His burden was removed; he rejoiced in God. He erected the family altar, and it was a solemn sight to see seven persons who had a few weeks before been profane and careless, now all brought over from the service of Satan to the service of the Lord. And it was a joyful day when poor Zeke, with his father and mother, his brother and sisters, united with God's people, and came together to the communion.

Jesus Christ's Residence.—Let us strive to get hold of the kernel, let us hold on to that and throw the husk away. It is related of the Rev. Dr. Nettleton, that when he was preaching in the State of ——, where revivals of religion attended him, he took an early walk one morning, and passing a family of much pretension, he called. The lady of the house came to the door. "Good morning, madam," said he; "does Jesus Christ live here?" The lady, thrown off her guard replied, "No, sir; he does not." "Ah," said he, "then I was mistaken; I thought he might. Good morning, madam," and walked immediately on. This put the lady on a course of thinking which resulted in her conversion. She pulled off the husk and got at the kernel.

The Thirty Years' Prayer.—At the weekly prayer-meeting in ——, an aged, wealthy and influential man entered, who, during a long life, had been seemingly indifferent to his spiritual welfare; and, to the surprise of all present, he rose, under deep emotion, and asked the prayers of God's people for his own conversion. The next week he was again among them, apparently a penitent at the foot of the cross.

As the intelligence of his hopeful conversion spread next day in the congregation, it reached an infirm and aged Christian, who had for years been confined to his house, and was daily waiting his summons to depart. On hearing it, he insisted on being carried to see the wealthy man, and would intrust his message to no one. After a long interview, he returned home rejoicing.

The cause of the infirm man's interest in this visit was perhaps known only to himself and his venerable pastor. Thirty years ago, as he was burning coal on the mountain-side, two of his neighbors visited his little shanty, found him engaged in reading his Bible and in prayer, and joined him in his devotions. Ere they separated, they agreed to meet again the next week on the mountain to pray, as did the Saviour ; and from week to week they met in this quiet retreat, which proved indeed a Bethel. One evening they spoke of their wealthy neighbor, mourning that he was living for this world only, when he was so much needed in the church of Christ ; and they at last entered into a written secret covenant with each other, before God, not to cease praying for his conversion until he should be brought in or die, or they should all be called to their final account.

Years of prayer passed on, during which their faith failed not ; one of the suppliants was at length called home, then another ; and the old coal-burner, though left alone, yet persevered. Thirty years had passed when the above news reached him ; his visit was made, and he came out of the house of his wealthy neighbor, saying, "Now, Lord, lettest thou thy servant depart in peace ; for mine eyes have seen thy salvation."

An Angry Controversy Settled.—In the year 1831, in one of the Southern States, there existed a legal controversy between two neighbors, who had, up to this time, been intimate friends, and soon it engendered a bitter personal animosity between them, and alienated their respective friends. Their families belonged to the same congregation, and their wives were members of the same church, and were held in high esteem for their intelligence and piety. Considering the family relations of the parties, it is not surprising that the church and the community should be seriously agitated by this quarrel; and that it proved a source of annoyance and grief not only to Christians, but to all their right-minded neighbors.

They were men of strong nerve, of great physical power, and distinguished in a high degree by what the world calls courage. Urged on by pride, ambition, or revenge, the contest waxed hotter and hotter, so that all acquainted with the circumstances were in constant fear of a bloody, if not of a deadly rencontre.

One of the parties had prepared and intended to file a bill in chancery within the next ten days, which he knew would greatly irritate his antagonist, and provoke him to a personal assault, when the case would probably have been settled by the death of one or both of them. On all public occasions they carried deadly weapons.

In this state of things, the Lord poured out his Spirit upon that community; hundreds of minds became impressed with religious truth, and it is believed many souls were truly converted to God. The third Sabbath in June is a day to be held in everlasting remembrance by that congregation. On that day more than one hundred and fifty persons presented themselves as inquirers after the way of salvation, some of whom then and there sought and found hope in Christ. These two litigants were present, and were smitten and wounded by the sword of the Spirit. "The strong men" bowed themselves, and at the close of the services went away overwhelmed with a sense of their guilt and ruin, though entirely ignorant of the state of each other's minds.

On the morrow, they again repaired to the house of the Lord; and previous to the commencement of public worship, the two belligerents providentially met face to face, while walking in a beautiful grove near the church. Mr. —— first spoke, and said, "Captain ——, I have a proposition to submit to you." The "captain," supposing he had reference to the suit that was to be tried in a few days, replied, with as much coldness and hauteur in his manner as he could command, "I am ready to hear you, sir; what is it?" Mr. ——, unable any longer to restrain his feelings, answered with the deepest emotion, "It is, sir, that we cast behind us our follies and sins, and live together from this day as neighbors and Christians."

The captain was subdued and unmanned; in a moment they were locked in each other's arms, weeping like little children, and vying with each other in making acknowledgments and concessions. They were friends. The pious rejoiced, and were greatly encouraged in the work of the Lord, and the impenitent received a most impressive illustration of the power and value of the Christian religion, and many more sought and found it in the "pearl of great price." The lawsuit was settled without a trial, the loaded pistols were uncharged and put away; and henceforth they lived as neighbors on terms of amity.

The Stone rolled away.—In 1842, an unusual seriousness prevailed in one of our New England colleges; meetings for prayer were held in different rooms, and there was less rudeness and levity in the halls and about the college grounds.

In one of the prayer-meetings held by the pious students of the Senior class, it was determined to make a direct personal appeal to each of their unconverted class-mates. It fell to my lot to converse with one who had been a master-spirit among the ungodly, who ridiculed everything serious, and in fact made a mock of all religion. The duty was declined, as I felt that I was altogether inadequate to the task. I was diffident, slow of speech, and could not think of approaching one whose tongue was ever ready with biting sarcasm and brutal infidel wit. But my brethren would not excuse me. With a trembling heart I consented, though with little faith as to any good result flowing from the interview.

At the close of the meeting I retired to my room, and falling on my knees, prayed for courage and arguments. I determined to go at once to the room of the irreligious student: on approaching his door, my fear returned and almost drove me away, but summoning resolution, I knocked, and entered. Once, in I would gladly have been out again, but suddenly the thought arose, this is but a man, and he has a soul of unspeakable value: you have associated with him for nearly four years, and have never introduced the subject of personal religion ; soon you are to separate, do not lose this opportunity of doing him good.

With a silent prayer, the object of my visit was introduced. "I am come, Mr. V——, to confess to you my unfaithfulness, to make known to you my interest in your spiritual welfare, and to urge you to give immediate attention to the concerns of the soul." Imagine my surprise when the individual from whom I expected only abuse, took me by the hand, and with a voice broken by deep emotion, exclaimed, "Mr. W——, I am glad to see you. I have been a great sinner—will you pray for me ?" Both sobbed aloud. What had God wrought ? "The stone was rolled away"—"Saul was among the prophets." That interview of an hour was a precious one. I discovered that V—— had been serious for some time ; in fact, that he was studying his Bible when I sought admittance, and had been wishing that some one of his pious class-mates would speak to him on religion, though his heart was too proud to allow him to seek an interview. For the remainder of his college life, V—— was a changed man.

A happy Mistake.—The heart of Miss Y——, who was afflicted with deafness, had been deeply moved to a sense of the danger of the unconverted. Receiving a call from a young lady, an impenitent friend of hers, and acting according to her quickened sense of duty and her yearnings for the safety of her friend, she urged her to yield herself to God, and accept the great atonement. Miss E—— listened politely for a time; but the subject was irksome to her, and seeing a piano in the room, she thought to change the conversation by saying abruptly to Miss Y——, "Will you play for me ?" Miss Y——, from her defective hearing, supposed her friend had asked her to *pray* for her, as Miss E—— made the request soon after having been asked to pray for herself. With glad surprise Miss Y—— knelt beside her, but had scarcely begun a prayer before a conviction of her mistake flashed across her mind. Instantly there followed the thought, "*This is from God ;*" and recovering from her embarrassment, she pleaded for the descent of the Spirit upon the heart of her friend.

At the close of her prayer, Miss E—— seemed in much distress of mind, and soon after left the house. The next morning, before nine o'clock, Miss Y—— discovered Miss E—— approaching the gate. It was a bleak, chilly morning early in March, and the snow was still quite deep. Miss E—— entered with a heart so burdened with a sense of sin, as not to allow her to say anything except, "Oh, I am *so unhappy!*" Then followed an interview of the deepest interest. Her distress continued two or three days, and then she trusted in a forgiving Saviour. From that hour, Miss Y——'s affliction has seemed to her to possess more of the brightness of a blessing, and she rejoices in the dealings of that infinite wisdom which "doeth all things well."

An aged Sinner.—Mrs. F—— had started on an errand of mercy, when she met an aged female groping her way. She was a wretched-looking object, bent with age, and clothed with tattered garments. Mrs. F—— had passed her, but conscience whispered that she might be losing an opportunity of doing good and relieving suffering, and she retraced her steps.

"My friend," she said to her kindly, "you seem very aged and infirm." "If I see the seventeenth of next month, I shall be ninety-two." "That is a great age," said Mrs. F——. "And is your soul at peace with God?" "Who asks about my soul?" she exclaimed. "You are the first person that ever spoke to me about it. I cannot see you well, for I am so blind, but go with me and talk." Mrs. F—— determined not to defer the opportunity, and accompanied the old woman to her miserable home. She found her the inmate of a low, wretched family, who boarded her for the rent of the hovel they occupied, which belonged to her son in an adjacent city. From the family the old woman suffered the most unkind treatment. So long had the voice of kindness been a stranger to her ear, that she was deeply affected by it, and seemed not only willing but anxious to hear, while Mrs. F—— talked to her of Jesus, and his love for ruined man. She had wonderfully retained her mind for one of her years, and was not so ignorant as she was hardened in vice, for in childhood she had been instructed in her Bible, and its blessed precepts were not wholly forgotten. What encouragement to parents to sow the seed.

Mrs. F——, upon inquiry, learned much of her history. A wayward youth and ungovernable temper, that had driven husband and children from her ; a life of infamy for twenty-five years, followed by wretchedness and poverty ; discarded by the respectable friends and family to whom she belonged, and disowned by her son, she was reaping the bitter wages of sin when met by our good Samaritan Mrs. F——, whose first efforts were to relieve her bodily wants, while she did not neglect her still greater spiritual need.

Daily did Mrs. F—— visit the aged sinner, reading and praying with her, though the family who professed to take care of her often insulted Mrs. F—— with coarse language, and even interrupted her while she knelt to pray ; but she heeded them not, for she was engaged about a great work, under god, "saving a soul from death." Christian friends, too, remonstrated with her upon expending so much effort upon such a hopeless case, and the impropriety of visiting so bad a character. She only replied, "The more wicked she is, the more faith and effort she requires." Amidst all the discouragements in her labor of love, she persevered, until God saw fit to bless her by sending the Holy Spirit to enlighten her darkened mind, and break the bondage of sin which had so long bound her. The work seemed a gradual one, but not the less sure. She was permitted to live long enough to manifest the wonder-working power of God.

A year from the day Mrs. F—— first met her, she was called to stand by her death-bed, and hear her rejoice in the love of Jesus. Her last words were, "I am a great, great sinner, but Jesus is a great, great Saviour ; glory be to his name." What a reward for a short year of prayer and effort was this ! Fellow Christian, go thou and do likewise ; be not discouraged. Remember, with God all things are possible."

Answer to United Prayer.—On the 20th of October, 1799, twenty-four persons joined a church in New England, of whom four youths were intimate friends. One of them married a worthy young man, and another a virtuous young woman, and the other two had each a father—none of whom were pious ; and they agreed on a concert of prayer for each other, and for their relatives.

They knew what they wanted; it was the life of the soul for which their united and earnest cries continued to ascend. But it was not in a day, or a week, or a month, or a year, that they obtained what they greatly longed for. To cheer them when almost ready to faint, a letter from one of the four announced to two at a distance, that his wife was rejoicing in hope of the glory of God. This news called forth joyful thanksgivings. Some few years passed on, and the young man that had been the subject of these united intercessions, gave signs of spiritual life, which again thrilled their hearts with holy gratitude and joy.

But the case of the two aged fathers was more trying. Increasing hardness made faith stagger; and often did the fear arise that their day was past. About twelve years thus rolled on; one was more than fifty, and the other more than sixty years of age. Suddenly, at length a friend wrote to the son at a distance, that his aged father had apparently awaked from the long slumber of a state of sin, and given evidence of conversion. This was as "life from the dead;" this was a rebuke to unbelief. More earnestly did the friends ply the throne of grace; and what was their joy, when, about twenty years from the time that the concert commenced, the other aged father, more than threescore and ten, was baptized into the name of the Father, and of the Son, and of the Holy Ghost.

Mission of a Tear.—A faithful and devoted teacher had a large class of young ladies committed to her care, in the Sabbath-school connected with one of the churches in the city of Philadelphia. For a long time, Sabbath after Sabbath, she earnestly labored with them, seeking to instill into their minds the saving truths of God's word. The class were, for the most part, respectfull and attentive, and evidently much attached to their teacher; but her instructions and her earnest entreaties seemed to make no lasting impression on their minds. They were thoughtless, inconsiderate young people, in love with the pleasures of the world, and charmed with the scenes of gaiety by which they were surrounded. As they advanced in years, they manifested less interest in the exercises of the class, and were at times disposed to turn away from the warm and affectionate pleadings of their faithful friend and teacher.

By degrees her heart became discouraged ; she felt that her labors were in vain, and that perhaps the instructions of some other person might be more appreciated by the class, and result in their conversion to God. On one occasion, when the class had been more inattentive than usual to the instruction imparted, Miss S—— resolved that at the close of the session, she would give up her class-book to the superintendent, and request him to appoint another teacher in her place. As she came to this conclusion, sorrow filled her heart, and tears dimmed her eyes : it was no small sacrifice she was about to make ; she loved her class, the affections of her heart were entwined around her pupils, and the thought that these ties must now be sundered, filled her with distress.

As was her usual practice, she addressed a few words to each one of the young ladies, before dismissing them. She had nearly gone through the class, when, as she was speaking to one on the duty to yield her heart to God, and no longer resist the invitations of the gospel, she saw, with gratitude and joy, the quivering lip, and a tear glistening in the eye. The influence of that tear was electrical; hope at once sprang up in the heart of the desponding teacher, and silently her heart was lifted to God in prayer, that he would deepen the impression which had been made. The exercises closed with a deeper seriousness upon the minds of all, than had ever been noticed before; and nothing was said about resigning the class.

When next they came together, it was evident that the Spirit of God was moving on the hearts of several of the members of that class, and the teacher labored with new zeal, animated by the remembrance of the tear she had seen in the eye of her pupil.

In a few weeks, she in whose eye the pearl-drop shone, stood before the church to give a reason of the hope she cherished that she was a child of God. She began her relation by referring to the impressions made upon her mind on that Sabbath, when her beloved teacher addressed her so tenderly and solemnly on the duty of serving God. It proved to be a "word in season." Led by the Spirit of God, she earnestly sought the pardon of her sins through the atoning sacrifice of the Crucified, and God, in his rich mercy, had spoken peace to her troubled soul, and filled her with joy unspeakable.

The conversion of this dear young lady, and her consecration to God in baptism, were the means of the awakening of many others, and the commencement of a gracious work in the church; and, in the course of a few months, thirteen of that Bible-class were hopefully converted and added to the church, several of whom became faithful and devoted Sabbath-school teachers.

Converted by his own Sermon.—Mr. Thomas Tregross, of Exeter, dated his conversion, after he had been some time in the minstry, and a sufferer for nonconformity too! And it is a circumstance which deserves remark, that he considered a sermon composed and preached by himself, on Luke xii. 47, as the means of his conversion.

Why he Wept.—A godly minister of the gospel, occasionally visiting a gay person, was introduced into a room near to that wherein she dressed. After waiting some hours, the lady came in, and found him in tears. She inquired the reason of his weeping. He replied, "Madam, I weep on reflecting that you can spend so many hours before your glass, and in adorning your person, while I spend so few hours before my God, in adorning my soul." The rebuke struck her conscience. She lived and died a monument of grace.

The Unwelcome Snow-Storm.—In February, of 1820, the writer, then living at Saratoga Springs, a young man, looking forward to the ministry, went to Malta, ten miles from the Springs, to enjoy the further luxury of being with his friend, Dr. Nettleton, then engaged in a precious revival in that region.

We spent a happy day at the house of Mr. P——, who had been a Universalist, but was then a humble convert; and while there I was much interested in the serious appearance and conversation of Mrs. C——, an intelligent relative of Mr. P——, from Nassau, though she seemed not to have deep convictions of sin.

This lady appeared to be anxious to converse with Dr. Nettleton, upon the subject of her salvation. She had heard him preach several times, but he had not said a word to her. He evidently avoided doing what Mrs. C—— expected and desired him to do. I discovered this, and asked him why he did not talk with the lady. His reply was, "O, she is expecting it so much." That night there was to be a prayer-meeting at the house of Mr. P——, where many of the young converts and many anxious sinners were expected to attend. A little before night, Dr. Nettleton proposed to me to ride with him to a Mr. D——'s, about a mile distant. After we had spent a short time with Mr. D—— and his family, Dr. Nettleton said to me, "I shall not return with you to Mr. P——'s to-night. Do you go back and conduct the meeting as well as you can. I give it up to you. Go." It was in vain that I entreated him to return and take charge of the meeting. He positively declined, and I left him with a trembling heart. The people would expect Dr. Nettleton to be there, and how great would be their disappointment. What should I do?

However, just at night, the heavens gathered blackness, the wind blew violently, and the result was one of the most furious snow-storms that I ever witnessed. Not a soul came to the meeting. We were all sadly disappointed, though I felt relieved of a great responsibility.

Supper being ended, and finding no one present except the family, I conversed with Mrs. C—— as to her prospects for eternity. I soon found that she was self-righteous, trusting in her daily prayers, and her amiable, irreproachable life. I endeavored to show her that her prayers were dead, her heart unrenewed, and her precious soul under the condemnation of God's holy law. The smile which had been playing upon her lips instantly passed away; she raised and fixed her eyes upon me, and sat in silence. New thoughts were passing in her mind. She saw that she was lost. She burst into tears, arose, and went to her room, and did not return for some time.

There was sitting in the room, Miss J——, a daughter of Mr. P——, who had passed thus far through the revival without sharing its benefits. I immediately turned to her, and began to talk with her about her soul. She listened very attentively a few minutes, became agitated, burst into tears, and left the room. After a while, both of these ladies returned to the sitting-room bathed in tears, and writhing under the deepest convictions. I pointed them to the blessed Redeemer; we prayed with and for them again and again, and in this way we spent a great part of the night—a night never to be forgotten. At length morning came, but no light dawned upon those benighted souls. To them, all seemed as dark as Egypt. We prayed for them, and wept over them; but God alone could relieve them.

Perhaps about eleven o'clock, I said to Mrs. C——, "Will not your heart yet yield to God?" Putting her hand to her breast, and fixing her streaming eyes upon me, she exclaimed, "My heart will kill me"

Soon after this, the storm without having passed away, I stepped into a sleigh and rode over to Mr. D——'s to inform Dr. Nettleton of what God was doing. In relating the solemn transactions of the night and the morning, I mentioned to Dr. Nettleton the striking expression of Mrs. C——, "My heart will kill me." Instantly he replied, "That woman is near the kingdom of heaven. I will go back with you."

We returned, and, as we entered the house, Mrs. C—— and Miss P—— both came rushing from their room, with countenances beaming with holy, heavenly joy. The moral storm was over. All was calm. Mrs. C—— ran to Dr. Nettleton, seized his hand, and stood for some moments overwhelmned with emotion. As she stood weeping for joy, Dr. Nettleton asked her, "Have you submitted your heart to God?" Her answer was spontaneous and singular: "O yes, sir—but no thanks to you." Dr. Nettleton was almost convulsed with laughter, which was *very* unusual with him.

That afternoon Mrs. C——, while her heart was almost bursting with joy, wrote a letter to one of her friends in Nassau, which she read to me. That simple letter, giving an account of her own convictions of sin and hopeful conversion, was the means, in God's hands, of awakening several impenitent sinners.

When Mrs. C—— returned to Nassau, she found some deep seriousness, and immediately wrote to Dr. Nettleton, begging him to repair to the place as soon as possible. He went, and the glorious results are well known to all who are acquainted with the life and labors of that extraordinary man.

Sent for by the Spirit.—Dr. Staunton was called the searching preacher. Preaching once at Warborough, near Oxford, a man was so much affected with his first prayer, that he ran home, and desired his wife to get ready and come to church, for there was one in the pulpit who prayed like an angel. The woman hastened away, and heard the sermon which, under the Divine blessing, was the means of her conversion, and she afterwards proved an eminent Christian.

"Thou knowest not which shall prosper."—Lady H—— once spoke to a workman who was repairing a garden wall, and pressed him to take some thought concerning eternity and the state of his soul. Some years afterwards she was speaking to another on the same subject, and said to him, "Thomas, I fear you never pray, nor look to Christ for salvation." "Your ladyship is mistaken," answered the man: "I heard what passed between you and James at such a time, and the word you designed for him took effect on me." "How did you hear it?" "I heard it on the other side of the garden, through a hole in the wall, and shall never forget the impression I received."

The Bullet's Text.—When Oliver Cromwell entered upon the command of the Parliament's army against Charles I., he ordered all the soldiers to carry a Bible in their pockets (the same which is now called Field's). Among the rest there was a wild, wicked, young fellow, who ran away from his apprenticeship in London for the sake of plunder and dissipation. This fellow was obliged to be in the fashion. Being one day ordered out upon a skirmishing party, or to attack some fortress, he returned to his quarters in the evening without hurt. When he was going to bed, pulling the Bible out of his pocket, he observed a hole in it. His curiosity led him to trace the depth of this hole into his Bible; he found a bullet was gone as far as the 11th chapter of Ecclesiastes, 9th verse. He read the verse. "Rejoice, O young man, in thy youth, and let thy heart cheer thee in the days of thy youth, and walk in the ways of thy heart, and in the sight of thine eyes; but know thou that for all these things God will bring thee into judgment." The words were set home upon his heart by the Divine Spirit, so that he became a very serious and sound believer in the Lord Jesus Christ, and lived in London many years after the civil wars were over. He used pleasantly to observe, to Dr. Evans, author of the "Christian Temper," that the Bible was the means of saving his soul and body too.

A very impressive Genealogy.—A certain libertine, of a most abandoned character, happened one day to stroll into a church, where he heard the fifth chapter of Genesis read; importing that so long lived such and such persons, and yet the conclusion was, "they died." Enos lived 905 years, and he died. Seth 912, and he died. Methusalem 969, *and he died.* The frequent repetition of the words, *he died,* notwithstanding the great length of years they had lived, struck him so deeply with the thought of death and eternity, that through divine grace he became a most exemplary Christian.

Flavel on keeping the Heart.—Mr. Flavel being in London in 1673, his old bookseller, Mr. Boulter, gave him the following relation, viz.: That some time before, there came into his shop a sparkish gentleman, to inquire for some play-books. Mr. Boulter told him he had none; but showed him Mr. Flavel's little treatise of "Keeping the Heart," entreated him to read it, and assured him it would do him more good than play-books. The gentleman read the title; and, glancing upon several pages here and there, broke out into these and such other expressions: "What a fanatic was he who made this book!" Mr. Boulter begged of him to buy and read it, and told him, "he had no cause to censure it so bitterly." At last he bought it, but told him he would not read it. "What will you do with it, then?" said Mr. Boulter. "I will tear and burn it," said he, "and send it to the devil." Mr. Boulter told him, "then he should not have it." Upon this the gentleman promised to read it; and Mr. Boulter told him, "If he disliked it upon reading, he would return him his money." About a month after, the gentleman came to the shop again in a very modest habit, and with a serious countenance addressed Mr. Boulter thus: "Sir, I most heartily thank you for putting this book into my hands—I bless God that moved you to do it ; it hath saved my soul. Blessed be God that ever I came into your shop." And then he bought a hundred more of those books of him, and told him, "he would give them to the poor, who could not buy them."

A Bold Personal Appeal.—A godly faithful minister, of the seventeenth century, having finished prayer, and looking around upon the congregation, observed a young gentleman just shut into one of the pews, who discovered much uneasiness in that situation, and seemed to wish to get out again. The minister feeling a peculiar desire to detain him, hit upon the following singular expedient. Turning towards one of the members of his church, who sat in the gallery, he asked him this question aloud : "Brother, do you repent of your coming to Christ !" "No, sir," he replied, "I never was happy till then. I only repent that I did not come to him sooner." The minister then turned towards the opposite gallery, and addressed himself to an aged member in the same manner—"Brother, do you repent that you came to Christ ?" "No, sir ; I have known the Lord from my youth up." He then looked down upon the young man, whose attention was fully engaged, and fixing his eyes upon him, said, "Young man, *are you* willing to come to Christ !" This unexpected address from the pulpit, exciting the observation of all the people, so affected him that he sat down and hid his face. The person who sat next him encouraged him to rise, and answer the question. The minister repeated it, "Young man, are you willing to come to Christ ?" With a tremulous voice, he replied, "Yes, sir." "But *when*, sir ?" added the minister, in a most solemn and loud tone of voice. He mildly answered, "Now, sir." "Then stay," said he, "and hear the word of God, which you will find in 2 Cor. vi. 2 : 'Behold *now* is the accepted time, behold *now* is the day of salvation.'" By this sermon he was greatly affected. He came into the vestry, after service, dissolved in tears. That unwillingness to stay, which he had discovered, was occasioned by the strict injunction of his father, who threatened that, if ever he went to hear the fanatics, he would turn him out of doors. Having now heard, and unable to conceal the feelings of his mind, he was afraid to meet his father. The minister sat down and wrote an affectionate letter to him, which had so good an effect, that both father and mother came to hear for themselves. They were both brought to the knowledge of the truth ; and father, mother and son were together received with universal joy into that church.

A Terrible Reason for it.—A married woman became an exemplary Christian, but her husband was a lover of pleasure and of sin. When spending an evening, as usual, with his jovial companions, at a tavern, the conversation happening to turn on the excellences and faults of their wives, the husband just mentioned gave the highest encomiums of his wife, saying she was all that was excellent, only she was a d——d Methodist. "Notwithstanding which," said he, "such is her command of her temper, that were I to take you gentlemen home with me at midnight, and order her to rise and get you a supper, she would be all submission and cheerfulness." The company, looking upon this merely as a brag, dared him to make the experiment by a considerable wager. The bargain was made, and about midnight the company adjourned, as proposed. Being admitted, "Where is your mistress ?" said the husband to the maid-servant who sat up for him. "She is gone to bed, sir." "Call her up," said he. "Tell her I have brought some friends home with me, and desire she would get up, and prepare them a supper." The good woman obeyed the unreasonable summons, dressed, came down, and received the company with perfect civility; told them she happened to have some chickens ready for the spit, and that supper should be got as soon as possible. The supper was accordingly served up ; when she performed the honors of the table with as much cheerfulness as if she had expected company at a proper season.

After supper, the guests could not refrain from expressing their astonishment. One of them particularly, more sober than the rest, thus addressed himself to the lady : "Madam," said he, "your civility fills us all with surprise. Our unreasonable visit is in consequence of a wager, which we have certainly lost. As you are a very religious person, and cannot approve of our conduct, give me leave to ask, what can possibly induce you to behave with so much kindness to us ?" "Sir," replied she, "when I married, my husband and myself were both in a carnal state. It has pleased God to call me out of that dangerous condition. My husband continues in it. I tremble for his future state. Were he to die as he is, he must be miserable for ever ; I think it therefore my duty to render his present existence as comfortable as possible."

This wise and faithful reply affected the whole company. It left an impression of great use on the husband's mind. "Do you, my dear," said he, "really think I should be eternally miserable ? I thank you for the warning. By the grace of God, I will change my conduct." From that time he became another man, a serious Christian, and consequently a good husband.

Ananda Rayer's Conversion.—The account of Ananda Rayer's conversion is given by the Rev. Dr. John, the aged missionary at Tranquebar, in a letter to Mr. Desgranges. This Brahmin applied (as many Brahmins and Hindoos constantly do) to an older Brahmin, of some fame for sanctity, to know "what he should do that he might be saved ?" The old Brahmin told him that "he must repeat a certain prayer four lack of times—that is, four hundred thousand times. This he performed in a pagoda, in six months, and added many painful ceremonies, but finding no comfort or peace from these external rites, he went to a Romish priest and asked him if he knew what was the true religion ? The priest gave him some Christian books in the Telinga language ; and, after a long investition of Christianity, the inquiring Hindoo had no doubt remaining on his mind, that "Christ was the Saviour of the world." But he was not satisfied with the Romish worship in many points ; he disliked the adoration of images and other superstitions ; and having heard from the priests themselves, that the Protestant Christians at Tanjore and Tranquebar professed to have a pure faith, and had got the Bible translated, and worshipped no images, he visited Dr. John, and the other missionaries at Tranquebar, where he remained four months, conversing, says Dr. John, "almost every day with me," and examining the Holy Scriptures. He soon acquired the Tamul language (which has an affinity with the Telinga), that he might read the Tamul translation ; and he finally became a member of the Protestant church. The missionaries at Vizagapatam being in want of a learned Telinga scholar, to assist them in a translation of the Scriptures into the Telinga language, Dr. John recommended Ananda Rayer; "for he was averse," says he, "to undertake any worldly employment, and had a great desire to be useful to his brethren of the Telinga nation."

God Opened his Ears.—When the Rev. Mr. —— went to his living in the country, a very great audience collected from the neighboring towns and villages, in one of which lived an old inn-keeper, who, having made free with his own tap, had well carbuncled his nose and face, which bore visible marks of his profession. He heard the report of the concourse at this church, as many went from his own town; but he always stoutly swore he would never be found among the fools who were running there: on hearing, however, of the particularly pleasing mode of singing at the church, his curiosity was a little excited, and he said he did not know but he might go and hear the singing; but, with some imprecation, that he would never hear a word of the sermon.

He was a corpulent man, and, as it was a hot summer's day, he came in all of a perspiration, and having with difficulty found admission into a narrow open pew with a lid, as soon as the hymn before sermon was sung, which he heard with great attention, he leaned forward, and fixing his elbows on the lid, secured both ears against the sermon with his fore-fingers. He had not been in this position many minutes before the prayer finished, and the sermon commenced with an awful appeal to the consciences of the hearers, of the necessity of attending to the things which were made for their everlasting peace; and the minister addressing them solemnly, "He that hath ears to hear let him hear." Just the moment before these words were pronounced, a fly had fastened on the carbuncled nose of the inn-keeper, and, stinging him sharply, he drew one of his fingers from his ear, and struck off the painful visitant: at that very moment, the words "He that hath ears to hear, let him hear," pronounced with great solemnity, entered the ear that was opened as a clap of thunder; it struck him with irresistible force: he kept his hand from returning to his ear, and, feeling an impression he had never known before, he presently withdrew the other finger, and hearkened with deep attention to the discourse which followed.

That day was the beginning of days to him ; a change was produced upon him, which could not but be noticed by all his former companions. He never from that day returned to any of his former practices, nor ever afterwards was he seen in liquor or heard to swear. He became truly serious, and for many years went, in all weathers, six miles to the church where he first received the knowledge of Divine things. After about eighteen years' faithful and close walk with God, he died rejoicing in the hope of that glory he now enjoys.

A Sermon in a Leaf.—In the village of H——, a laborious pastor was standing in his place on a beautiful Sabbath of October, and with aching heart was delivering his message to a people that *seemed* indifferent to all his utterances. Behind the pulpit was a window, through which could be seen a tree whose foliage had been changed by autumnal frost. A young man in a remote pew, while gazing listlessly in the direction of the pulpit, saw a leaf separate from a twig of the tree, and with slow vibrations descend to the ground. Instantly, he said, as if the leaf had a tongue and spoke to him, the reflection arose, "*I am like that leaf.* My hold on life is just so slender. I may soon be detached and fall like that sere leaf. Then where shall I be ?" One consideration started another, and thought piled on thought, until his mind was stirred to its lowest depths, and he was in an agony of solicitude respecting his prospects for eternity. God's still small voice in the leaf spoke louder to him than thunder.

The Thoughtless Swearer.—As Mr. Romaine was one day walking in the street with another gentleman, he heard a poor man call upon God to damn him. Mr. R. stopped, took out half a crown, and, presenting it, said, "My friend, I will give you this if you will do that again." The man started : "What ! sir," said he, "do you think I would damn my soul for half a crown ?" Mr. R. answered, "As you did it just now for nothing, I could not suppose you would refuse to do it for a reward !" The poor creature, struck with his reproof, as Mr. R. intended he should be, replied,

"God bless and reward you, sir, whoever you are. I believe you have saved my soul; I hope I shall never swear again while I live."

When ye Stand Praying, Forgive.—1. During a protracted meeting held in G——, a pleasant summer retreat, in one of our Southern States, an address was made to those who were professedly the people of God. Amongst other things, they were exhorted to cherish a spirit of brotherly love, and if they had had any quarrel with another, to forgive. They were affectionately urged to pass an act of forgiveness without delay, and to seize the very first opportunity to extend the hand, and to do it cordially. In about twenty minutes after, while the services were yet going on, an elderly lady rose up, passed by me, and gave her hand to another lady. I certainly did not expect the exhortation to operate so soon, or at least in this way, but verily I was not displeased—no one was displeased. On the contrary, a wave of delicious feeling passed over the whole assembly. Many eyes were filled with tears, and methinks in that moment the God of love looked propitious down. Mark the sequel! The lady at that time had two sons and a daughter, all grown, and all yet unconverted. Before the protracted meeting closed, she had the unspeakable satisfaction of seeing all three rejoicing in the hope of glory! What is this but the broad seal of heaven's approbation? "Beloved," says John, "let us love one another, for love is of God, and every one that loveth is born of God, and knoweth God. He that loveth not, knoweth not God, for God is love."

2. I recollect another case which occurred in Virginia. Whilst addressing professors of religion, I, as my custom was, urged the great duty of forgiveness, and in order to give greater effect to my exhortations, I stated the case already mentioned, as one pleasing to God and worthy of all commendation, and then made a remark of this kind: "If there are any present in similar circumstances, let them go and do likewise." Whilst I was yet speaking, an elder of the church reached out his hand over the benches to one who sat at some distance, and with much feeling said, "Neighbor, here is my hand." Another elder also arose, a man of silvery locks, and hurry

ing to another part of the house, gave his hand to an individual, who grasped it, and said aloud, "This is the very thing I have long wished for." Need I say that a revival followed! Of a truth we had blessed times.

Ask and ye shall Receive.—In a certain town in Georgia, lived Mrs. M——, a pious widow lady. She had two sons in a distant State, whom she had not seen for many years. They were thoughtless young men, and avowedly infidel in their sentiments. She received a letter from her sons promising an early visit. The young men came; remained several days, and then said they must return. They fixed on Friday night, when they must go without fail, in the stage. Having ascertained that the stage would not go until nine or ten o'clock, she entreated her sons to go to church, and there remain until the sounding of the stage horn should summon them away. "Come, my sons, go with me to church this evening, and hear what you can." They yielded. They went; and that night God answered the mother's prayers. Both were brought under powerful conviction. Near the closing of the services of the sanctuary, the sounding of the stage horn was heard. According to arrangement they hurried away to the office—but, behold! the stage was full! They were obliged to remain until Monday following. On the Sabbath we had a most solemn time. When the anxious were invited to come forward, or kneel at their seat, if they desired the prayers of God's people, (according to the custom of that place,) several immediately knelt at their seats. Two young men came forward and kneeled near the desk—and only two. I saw an elderly lady at some distance, rise, and leaning forward, she fastened her tearful eyes upon them. It was the mother, and these young men were her sons! Many eyes were fixed upon her, but nobody said, Madam, sit down.—No! It was a sacred sight. That day both of these young men obtained a joyful hope. Verily, it would have touched a heart of rock to have seen the sons, both of them throwing their arms around the neck of their beloved mother—now a thousand times dearer than ever—and telling her that the Lord had heard her prayers, and blessed them, as they hoped, with his forgiving love!

I saw the happy mother. She grasped my hand. She wept tears of joy. For a few moments she was silent. When she spoke she blessed God, and said, in the very words of Mary, "My soul doth magnify the Lord, and my spirit hath rejoiced in God my Saviour, for he hath regarded the low estate of his handmaiden."

The effectual Prayer.—Whilst a meeting of much interest was going on in a certain country town in Virginia, Mr. K——, a pious young man, selected a young lawyer who was a noted scorner, and made him the subject of special prayer. About two days afterwards the young lawyer came to the house where the pastor was. I myself was in the same house at the time, but being particularly engaged, I requested the pastor to speak to him. "O," says he, "he is not serious." Yes I replied, he must be, or he would not come here. "I know him better than you do," said the pastor, "he is a scorner. There is no hope of him." The young lawyer was permitted to depart, I believe, without a single religious remark having been made to him. My conjectures were true. He was then under awakening influences.

Perhaps two weeks after that, this young lawyer, now rejoicing in Christ, was riding along the road on his way to a protracted meeting, about to be held in an adjacent county. Before he reached the place, he fell in with another young man, Mr. P.——, going to the same meeting. Religious conversation was introduced, and the awakened lawyer spoke freely of the change of views and feelings which he had experienced, and ascribed them, under God, to the prayers of his friend, Mr. K——, who had selected him as the subject of special prayer. "Ah!" said Mr. P——, "I had friends once who used to pray for me; but I have been so careless, so wicked, they do not think it worth while to pray for me now. They have all given me up. There is not an individual I suppose on earth who remembers me in prayer." "O yes," replied the young lawyer, "there is one, I know." "Who is it?" quickly asked Mr. P——, "The very same who prayed for me has made you the subject of special prayer." "Is it possible!" said Mr. P——, and throwing himself back, he had well-nigh fallen from the horse upon which he was riding. From that moment he waked up to the claims of his undying soul. A few days after, with great joy, he was telling to those around what a dear Saviour he had found. Blessed be God, the effectual fervent prayer of a righteous man availeth much. Take another case.

Where Sin abounded, Grace did much more abound.—Some time ago, a meeting of several days' continuance was held in G——, South Carolina. Awakening influences went abroad upon the people almost from its very commencement. To increase the solemnity, the providence of God concurred with the preaching of the word. A young lawyer was cut down in the midst of his years! All classes of persons now seemed to be aroused to a concern for their undying souls. There was one young man, however, the only son of his mother, and she a widow, who took his stand openly on the side of opposition. He was an avowed infidel. He threatened to lay the hand of violence upon the ministers, and once made this remark: "When I die, I will go to hell, and make a row there, and drive the Almighty from his throne!" That evening he went to church, and, as usual, endeavored to make sport of what was said from the pulpit. It pleased God, however, to send a word like an arrow to his heart. His sins flashed upon his view. He literally trembled upon his seat, and after the benediction was pronounced he came up to me, grasped my hand, and with great anxiety asked what he must do to be saved? It was but another case of the Philippian jailer, and I could do no better than reply in the words of the apostle, "Believe in the Lord Jesus Christ, and thou shalt be saved." Two days after this I saw him, all joy and peace in believing. O, it would have done any one good to have seen his dear mother throwing her arms around him, and saying, in the joy of her heart, "This my son was dead and is alive again, was lost and is found!" Subsequently this young man went to the North, to prepare to preach "the glorious gospel of the blessed God."

The Irresistible Spirit.—A few weeks after the meeting just mentioned, one of a similar kind was held at ——, about fifty miles distant. The first sermon was preached on Tuesday night, and by Thursday afternoon the waters were troubled, and a goodly number had stepped into the pool. There was one man, however, who had no good opinion of such "*carryings on.*" He was a very irreligious man, and although he heard perhaps every sermon, he liked none of them, but generally returned from church in a rage. On Thursday evening I was invited to take tea at the house where he lodged. When he heard it he was angry. When he saw me coming, he, as I have been told, swore terribly. On entering the house I was introduced by a friend, who immediately retired. Left alone with this man, I confess I felt very awkwardly fixed, and scarcely knowing what to say, I made a remark of this kind: "Well, sir, I think we have had a very interesting meeting this afternoon." Immediately he burst into tears, crying aloud, "Mercy! mercy! Lord have mercy upon me!" "Shall I pray for you, my dear sir?" said I. "Most willingly, most willingly," replied he. When I finished praying, he seemed so bowed down he could scarcely rise from his knees. That night there was no rest for him. The next day he was found amongst the anxious—a few days after, amongst the people of God! and is now, it seems, a valuable member of the church.

An Apostate Minister Converted in his Bed.—The case of Dr. B., brought in at the eleventh hour, is remarkable. Licensed by the Presbytery of ——, in the year 1793, he preached a few sermons (he entered the ministry purely, it seems, to please his parents), then abandoned the ministry, and became a deist. In the year 1797 he declared himself an atheist. From that period, and for many a long year afterwards, even until his locks became hoary with age, he waged open war with the God of the Bible. At a protracted meeting held at M——, Dr. B. was present. He was awakened—was brought under deep and pungent conviction. At prayer-meeting he requested permission to make a remark. He arose, with much emotion, and said, "My friends, I have been a most flagitious sinner." He went on in this strain for about ten minutes, and then sat down in great distress of mind. It was a most affecting sight. That day he was brought to the very borders of despair. "There is no hope," said he; "Saul of Tarsus cannot be compared with me—I must be damned!" "O no," said I, "the blessed Jesus is both able and willing to save you." "No, sir," replied he, with great emotion, "there is no possibility of my salvation—I must be damned." About ten o'clock he was conducted into his chamber. I slept in the same room; but there was no sleep for Dr. B. He felt that he was a lost sinner. Tossing himself about in the bed, he sighed, and groaned, and wept. All was dark and cheerless to his soul until about one o'clock, when he spoke aloud, and calling me by name, said, "Mr. B., are you awake?" When informed—"O, sir," exclaimed he, "I feel a change! I can accept of the Saviour now! If Jesus Christ does not save me, I am damned for ever! I am happy! I am happy! I would not part with my present feelings for ten thousand worlds." "Well," said I, "Dr. B., I suppose you can say, 'O to grace, how great a debtor.'" Clapping his hands together, he exclaimed, with great emphasis, "The very thing, sir, the very thing!" As he said this, he arose and began to dress himself. No sun had yet lighted up the eastern horizon, but what was better still, the Star of Hope had risen upon his soul!

"Brightest star that ever rose,
Sweetest star that ever shone!"

The next day, in the presence of the great congregation, he presented himself as a miracle of grace, and told what the Lord had done for his soul. I suspect, that moment angels in heaven struck a note loud and long, rich and sweet. Some ten years after this, I mentioned this case to a certain lady in conversation. "O, sir," said she, "Dr. B. is my brother-in-law." "Indeed!" said I. "Well, is he still alive?" "Yes," said she, "he is still alive." "And, madam," continued I, "how does he hold on?" "O, very well,' said she, "very well; he is a member of the church, and a useful member, too." Surely, grace is triumphant, and reigns like a conqueror.

The Soldier's Mother.—Some few years since, when in Texas, I unexpectedly lighted upon a military post. The soldiers, so far as their spiritual interests were concerned, had been sadly neglected. No one had preached to them, nor had any one, it seems, given them a single Bible or tract—no man cared for their souls. Having obtained permission of the commander, I preached several times to them. On one occasion, in the midst of my discourse, I observed—"Soldiers! most of you, I suppose, are from the United States, and are perhaps entirely regardless of the interests of your souls; but I wonder if some of you have not pious mothers at home, who have loved you, and prayed for you, aye, and have wept on your account." Having made these, or very similar remarks, I cast my eyes rapidly over the faces of those before me, and observed one who was exceedingly wrought upon. Every muscle of his face seemed to be moved, and the tears began to trickle down his cheeks. Then addressing him particularly—"Soldier!" said I, "come here, I want to talk with you." Sure enough, he immediately followed me, and when we had gone a little way off, "Tell me," said I, "have not you a pious mother?" Bursting into a flood of tears, "Yes, sir," said he, "I have a very pious mother, a member of the Methodist Church in Pennsylvania." Here he wept aloud; so loud that he might have been heard a very considerable distance. After pointing out the way of salvation to him, through a crucified Saviour, as clearly as I could, I left him. Some two or three days after I called again, and found him rejoicing in the hope of glory. He had found his mother's Saviour and his mother's God! Heaven bless mothers, *pious* mothers, all the world over! and let all the angels of God say Amen. Thank God, I too had a pious mother.

Forgiveness Received.—Mr. Innis, a great Scotch minister, once visited an infidel who was dying. When he came to him the first time, he said, "Mr. Innis, I am relying on the mercy of God; God is merciful, and he will never damn a man forever." When he got worse and was nearer death, Mr. Innis went to him again, and he said, "O! Mr. Innis, my hope is gone; for I have been thinking, if God be merciful, God is just too; and what if, instead of being merciful to me, he should be just to me? What would then become of me? I must give up my hope in the mere mercy of God; tell me how to be saved!" Mr. Innis told him that Christ had died in the stead of all believers; that God could be just, and yet the justifier through the death of Christ. "Ah !" said he, "Mr. Innis, there is something solid in that ; I can rest on that ; I cannot rest on anything else ;" and it is a remarkable fact that none of us ever met with a man who thought he had his sins forgiven unless it was through the blood of Christ. Meet a Mussulman ; he never had his sins forgiven ; he does not say so. Meet an infidel ; he never knows that his sins are forgiven. Meet a legalist ; he says, "I hope they will be forgiven ;" but he does not pretend they are. No one ever gets even a fancied hope apart from this, that Christ, and Christ alone, must save by the shedding of his blood.

"A Lost Man."—Mr. Whitefield had a brother, who had been a professor of religion, but he had backslidden ; he went far from the ways of godliness ; and one afternoon, after he had been recovered from his backsliding, he was sitting in a room in a chapel-house. He had heard his brother preach the day before, and his poor conscience had been cut to the very quick. Said Whitefield's brother, when he was at tea, "I am a lost man," and he groaned and cried, and could neither eat nor drink. Said Lady Huntingdon, who sat opposite, "What did you say Mr. Whitefield ?" "Madam," said he, "I said I am a lost man." "I'm glad of it," said she ; "I'm glad of it." "Your ladyship, how can you say so ?" "I repeat it, sir," said she ; "I am heartily glad of it." He looked at her, more and more astonished." "I am glad of it," said she, "because it is written, 'The Son of man came to seek and to save that which was lost.'" With the tears rolling down his cheeks, he said, "What a precious Scripture ; and how is it that it comes with such force to me ? O ! madam," said he, "madam, I bless God for that ; then he will save me ; I trust my soul in his hands ; he has forgiven me." He went outside the house, felt ill, fell npon the ground, and no long time after expired.

Outcast Converted.—Mr. Spurgeon tells a story of what once happened to Mr. Vanderkist, a city missionary in London. There had been a drunken broil in the street ; he stepped between the men to part them, and said something to a woman who stood there concerning how dreadful a thing it was that men should thus be intemperate. She walked with him a little way, and he with her, and she began to tell him such a tale of woe and sin too, how she had been lured away from her parents' home in Somersetshire, and had been brought up here to her soul's eternal hurt. He took her home with him, and taught her the fear and love of Christ; and when she returned to the paths of godliness, and found Christ to be the sinner's Saviour, she said, "Now I must go home to my friends." Her friends were written to; they came to meet her at the station at Bristol, and you can hardly conceive what a happy meeting it was. The father and mother had lost their daughter; they had never heard from her; and there she was, brought back and restored to the bosom of her family.

The Last Chance—"Here goes!"—Says a late writer, when appealing to sinners: "On a part of the British coast, where beetling cliffs, from three to five hundred feet in height, overhang the ocean, some individuals during a certain season of the year, obtain a solitary livelihood by collecting the eggs of rock-birds, and gathering samphire. The way in which they pursue this hazardous calling, is as follows: The man drives an iron crow-bar securely into the ground, about a yard from the edge of the precipice. To that crow-bar he makes fast a rope, of which he then lays hold. He next slides gently over the cliff, and lowers himself till he reaches the ledges and crags, where he expects to find the object of his pursuit. To gain these places is sometimes a difficult task; and when they fall within the perpendicular, the only method of accomplishing it is for the adventurer to swing in the air, till, by dexterous management, he can so balance himself as to reach the spot on which he wishes to descend. A basket, made for the purpose, and strapped between the shoulders, contains the fruit of his labor; and when he has filled the basket, or failed in the attempt, he ascends, hand over hand, to the summit. On one occasion, a man who was thus employed, in gaining a narrow ledge of rock, which was overhung by a higher portion of the cliff, secured his footing, but let go the rope. He at once perceived his peril. No one could come to his rescue, or even hear his cries. The fearful alternative immediately flashed on his mind: it was, being starved to death, or dashed to pieces four hundred feet below! On turning round, he saw the rope he had quitted, but it was far away. As it swung backwards and forwards, its long vibrations testified the mighty efforts by which he had reached the deplorable predicament in which he stood. He looked at the rope in agony. He had gazed but a little while, when he noticed that every movement was shorter than the one preceding, so that each time it came the nearest, as it was gradually subsiding to a point of rest, it was a little further off than it had been the time before. He briefly reasoned thus: 'That rope is my only chance of life; in a little while it will be forever beyond my reach; it is nearer now than it ever will be again; I can but die; here goes!' So saying, he sprang from the cliff, as the rope was next approaching, caught it in his grasp, and went home rejoicing." Sinner, you tremble at this incident; believe me, yours is greater peril! Beneath you yawns the lake, that burneth with fire and brimstone; stand where you are you cannot; time will force you thence. Salvation is set before you; it is as near, perhaps nearer now, than ever it will be again; lay hold of it; cling to it with the firmness of a death grasp. This is your only chance of safety; and it is not a chance alone; it is a certainty—a glorious certainty; and the only danger is, that, refusing to embrace it, you will defer escape until it becomes impossible. Then, make that plunge at once; beneath you are the everlasting arms; believe, and feel his purifying power.

Refusing a Revival.—A minister of my acquaintance, says the Rev. James Caughey, visited an American town some years ago. He had only preached a few sermons, when many sinners were awakened, and about twenty found salvation. But a few persons of importance were of opinion that the ordinary services were sufficient, and discouraged the active brethren, who, rather than cause any unpleasant feelings in certain quarters, held back. The Spirit of God was grieved, and the revival stopped. The man of God was disheartened, and went to another town, where ministers and people made him welcome, commenced hostilities against the ranks of sin, and the result was an extensive revival—hundreds of sinners were converted. News of these displays of the power of

God reached the former town, and caused great searchings of heart. They saw their error, humbled themselves, and invited him to return. In the mean time, to show how sincere were their desires for a revival, they began special services of their own accord. The minister returned, and found them holding their meetings in a large lecture-room. He proposed that they should open at once their spacious and beautiful chapel, have it lighted brilliantly every night, and comfortably warmed, for it was winter-time, and thus let the public know that they intended to accomplish something, by the help of the Most High, and upon a large scale. They did so. During the first and second weeks, sinners were very hard, although they had preaching twice a day, and little was done. At length, after their past unbelief and indifference had been well chastised, and their faith tried to the utmost, the Lord came down amongst them in glorious power, and sinners were converted on every hand.

Having seen their error in the former instance, they resolved now to improve this victory to the utmost. Opposers of the first effort entered fully into the work, and the revival efforts were continued several months, and the saved of the Lord were very many.

Getting the Smoke without the Fire.—In the Memoirs of the late Mr. William Dawson, is found the following anecdote :

Mr. Dawson, it seems, was one day accosted by an individual who said he had been present at a certain meeting ; that he liked the preaching very well indeed, but was much dissatisfied with the prayer-meeting, adding, that he usually lost all the good he had received during the sermon, by remaining in these noisy meetings. Mr. D. replied, that he should have united with the people of God in the prayer-meeting, if he desired to retain or obtain good. "Oh !" said the gentleman, "I went into the gallery, where I leaned over the front, and saw the whole. But I could get no good ; I lost, indeed, all the benefit I had received during the sermon."

"It is easy to account for that," rejoined Mr. Dawson.

"How so ?" inquired the other.

"You mounted to the top of the house, and, on looking down your neighbor's chimney to see what kind of a fire he kept, you got your eyes filled with smoke. Had you entered by the door, gone into the room, and mingled with the family around the household hearth, you would have enjoyed the benefit of the fire, as well as they. Sir, you have got the smoke in your eyes!

Conversion of Mr. George Inglis.—Very early in life he began to drink in iniquity like water, discovered strong prejudices against serious persons and serious things; associated with the gay, libertine, and dissipated; never read the Scriptures except so much of them as enabled him to construe his Greek lessons, whilst in college. His propensities to sinful indulgences increased with his years, and he became more and more confirmed in the habits of sin, until at length he was given up to almost every species of iniquity. Thus he continued, till some years afterwards, being in the town of Manchester, Virginia, without any natural (known) cause to produce the effect, he was smitten by the hand of God, whilst in the possession of good health, with the total loss of sight within a few days. In this situation his mind was all distraction. His cry was to man only for help; but to God his Maker, who giveth songs in the night to the afflicted and oppressed, he had not learned to cry. This lesson, however, he was taught not long afterwards. Mrs. Snowden, who was the instrument of his conversion, relates that she found him a man of strong passions, impatient of restraint and affliction, bitterly opposed to religion, and determined to destroy his own life if his eyesight should not be restored. She persuaded him to listen to the reading of the Scriptures. "It appeared to me," she continues, "that he waited impatiently for the arrival of the appointed hour, for, no sooner did the time come, than he sent for me. Beginning with the first chapter of Genesis, before we had gone through the chapter, he stopped me to express his admiration of the language. 'It was sublime beyond anything he had ever read.' While I was reading, he was all attention; and when the time arrived when I was under the necessity of leaving off, it was with regret that he observed that I had finished; putting me in mind, at the same time, of my promise to attend to him, on the next day. I think it was on the second day of my reading to him, that he cried out, 'What a wretch am I to have spoken against such a book! a book that I knew nothing of, having never given it an attentive perusal.' I went on for a few days, reading to him according to the plan laid down, which was one hour every day, when the distress of his mind greatly increased." It pleased God, by these means to bring him to very serious and deep impressions of his moral character, and to constrain him, after some time, to attempt to pray. "This change," says the Rev. Wm. Tennent, "was effected in the gentleness, kindness, and tenderness of infinite mercy, and without those horrors which often precede the conversion of high-handed and daring sinners. In his case, all was mercy, without extraordinary terror. He was embraced in the arms of redeeming love, and delivered from the fiery pit without beholding its awful flames. In his first attempt to supplicate the Deity, he was principally affected with a sense of the baseness of his conduct, and vile ingratitude for the mercies bestowed, and this exercise was accompanied with an involuntary flow of tears, and a desire to call God his Father, and afterwards to mention the blessed name of Jesus, the Saviour. Probably, this was the beginning of his new birth, and the hour of his conversion; which was not long afterwards confirmed by a remarkable vision of two books, with a glorious light shining in the midst of them, as he was lying in his bed; which he apprehended to be the Old and New Testaments of the living God, presented to, and impressing on his mind this sacred declaration, but without a voice, 'THIS IS THE WAY,' and filling his soul at the same time with inexpressible joy."

Soul and Body healed by Christ.—Says the Rev. Dr. Alexander: "A young gentleman of fortune and liberal education, had been for some months thinking seriously about his soul's salvation; but the work had not come to any maturity, when by making too great an exertion of his bodily strength, he ruptured a large blood-vessel in the lungs, and was brought to death's door; not being able to speak above a low whisper. Having been a pupil of mine, I was permitted to see him, and upon asking the state of his mind, he whispered in my ear, that he was overwhelmed with the most awful darkness and terror—not one ray of light dawned upon his miserable soul. I prayed with him and presented to him a few gospel invitations and promises, and left him, never expecting to see him alive. Next day I called, the physician coming out of his room, informed me, that while they were waiting for his last breath a favorable change seemed unexpectedly to have taken place, and he had revived a little. When I approached his bed, he looked joyfully in my face, pressed my hand, and said, 'All is well—I have found peace. This morning, about the dawn, I had the most delightful view of Christ, and of his ability and willingness to save me.' And upon inquiry, I found that that was the moment when the favorable change took place in his symptoms. Faith and joy accomplished what no medicine could, and acted as a reviving cordial to his dying body. He so far recovered as to live a number of years afterwards, though his lungs were never sound; and his consistent walk and conversation attested the reality of his change."

The Gentleness of Grace.—While spending a summer in Germantown, near Philadelphia, I was sent for to visit a young man whom I had often seen. He did not belong to my charge, but two pious ladies who did, were his friends, and had come out of the city to nurse him. He had a hemorrhage of the lungs, which left little room to hope for recovery. As he was a mild and moral man, I did not know but that he might be a professor of religion; but upon asking him a question respecting his hope, he frankly told me that he had been skeptical for many years, and had no belief that the gospel was divine. I never felt more at a loss. The man was too weak to attend to argument, and if I could, by reasoning, convince him of his error, it would not be a saving faith, and he must die before this process could be gone through. I found that his infidelity afforded him no comfort in a dying hour, and that he wished he could believe in Christ. It occurred to me that the word of God contained light and energy in itself, and that if he could not attend to the external evidences, the beams of truth might shine in upon his soul, and thus generate a saving faith by the efficient aid of the Spirit. After pointing out the probable sources of his skepticism, I requested the ladies who were attending on him, to read certain portions of the gospel to him, as he could bear it—for he was very low. This was done; and the next day, when I came to see him, he declared that his doubts were all scattered, and that he had hope in Christ. Afterwards, he was never able to converse ; but, as far as is known, died in hope.

Remarkable Interposition of the Spirit.—The following is the religious experience of G—— A—— S——, an Episcopal Clergyman in H——, communicated to the Rev. Dr. Alexander.

"I had become much involved in the spirit of infidelity, together with several others. One evening, in particular, I trembled at the thoughts of our conversation : in the darkness of our minds, we had denied all. A few days afterwards, one of my companions, noted for his brightness of intellect, called at my room, and said, I have been reading Alexander's 'Evidences of the Christian Religion,' and it almost persuaded me to be a Christian. I well remember with what great delight I received the communication, resolving to get the book, and 'see if those things were so ;' not, however, with any view or desire of becoming a Christian at PRESENT. In due time, the book was procured, I retired to my room, my heart as hard as the mill-stone. I opened to the introduction, the most blind of unbelievers. I began to read, I had proceeded half way through the introduction, *and was suddenly impressed that the religion of Christ was of God.* I did not doubt its truth more than I did my life : yet I was entirely without argument. At that time I could have given no reason, yet I did not doubt. I felt *a perfect belief* that an Omnipotent Spirit did it. Before, I hardly believed there was a God : now I felt it as by a two-edged sword. It was a most awfully sublime moment ; yet I had *not the least fear. I did not even think of sin.* The next impression was, that I was undergoing a conversion. This, I *would* not *then :* the thought was very pleasant, that now I knew Christ died for the world ; and that at some future time, I would go further in his love. I was happy, sublime ; no terror ; a thought did not enter my mind of the consequences of delay. To avoid the progress of conversion, I threw down the book perfectly satisfied, for I had attained to one of the most splendid pieces of consciousness imaginable ; a sight beyond the veil, within eternity, worth thousands of worlds to me. I turned to think of something else. And oh ! the horrors of hell, how they came flooding in upon my soul. I felt that an Omnipotent hand was guiding them there. Commensurate with my agony, was my awful sense of sinfulness ; a conviction of sin, righteousness, and judgment to come, rose before my eyes in immense reality. I felt no anguish, no fear, no sin, *until I resolved not to attend to these things at present.* My anguish of soul became insupportable, it thickened and darkened, I could not endure it longer. And *with the sole view* of escaping my present misery, I resolved to yield to the will of that Mighty Being who was rending my soul. I instantly caught up the book, and offered a prayer for mercy. The intensity of my anguish began immediately to subside. The wrath of God seemed to mitigate ; in a few moments, I settled down into a state of deep and solemn conviction of sin ; a state more tolerable than the former ; but still one of gloom so thick that it could be felt. A mountain weight pressed upon my soul ; how to remove it I knew not, for the spirit still held me bound. I did not know but this was to continue through life. I endeavored to lose my feelings, and feel at ease, but I could not. I knew nothing of the way of salvation ; I had no spiritual guide ; but in order to keep my present sorrow as light as possible, I continued to read and pray for mercy. Thus I continued in the wilderness for about a week : when, sitting by my fireside, dwelling upon my despair, a sudden light came down from heaven ; I saw the open gate—' the *way*, the *truth*, and the *life*'—a new song was put into my mouth, and I rejoiced with joy unspeakable, and full of glory !"

Sudden Conversion of an Officer in the U. S. Army.—"I was in the act of throwing myself on the settee, when I carelessly took up the Bible, which happened to be lying near me. The first chapter I opened at, was the 1st general Epistle of Peter, chapter 1st. But how shall I describe my feelings, the moment I cast my eyes upon its pages ! My heart was melted into deep contrition. I felt the love of God shed abroad in my whole being. I was convinced that I had the Holy Spirit at work within me. I was affected to tears at his goodness. *I wept like a child.* I felt that I had been a sinner. My ingratitude came like a flood upon me. I was overcome with gratitude for *his* mercy. It completely filled my whole being. I rejoiced in the thought, that though I had been a wanderer from *him*, yet *he* was a good and kind Saviour, and was ready to forgive me all the injuries I had done *him*. I could indeed say, with deep conviction, as I read the passage which presented himself to me : 'Blessed be the God and Father of our Lord Jesus Christ, which, according to his abundant mercy, hath begotten us again unto a lively hope, by the resurrection of Jesus Christ from the dead.' Indeed, this whole chapter seemed to be perfectly adapted to my state. I recollect, in particular, the eighth verse was singularly pleasing to me. 'Whom having not seen, ye love ; in whom though now ye see him not, yet believing, ye rejoice with joy unspeakable, and full of glory.'

"Another remarkable circumstance connected with this display of divine goodness, was, the wonderful acuteness of intellect I felt myself to have, in reading the word of God. And not only could I perceive things in the gospel that I never saw before, but I felt my whole character changed. I felt not only a strong love to God, but to everybody around me. I could have wept upon the bosom of my bitterest enemy. Oh ! the joys of that moment ! But, alas ! how vain and impotent are the attempts of man, unless the Holy Spirit of God remains with him. I recollect very well, that I thought I would go and see the minister, and tell him what had passed. But not acting up to the suggestion immediately, I neglected it, and soon again, sad to say, I had relapsed into my former forgetfulness of the Lord. The fear of the ridicule of the world had been too strong for my faith, and I felt, too, that I could not yet give up the world, and declare myself on the Lord's side. But still *he* would not let me go. He would not give me up. I was removed shortly afterwards to another station, and here I can see the all gracious design of Providence in this change. I was by this means thrown into the society of several pious officers. One in particular, whom I valued very highly, and who, the very evening he conversed with me upon the goodness of God, in twice leading him back from signal relapses into sin, was seized with the fever, that in five days carried him to his grave, was in particular of great service to me, under the divine blessing, in confirming me in my resolves to renounce the world, and cleave unto the Lord ; and so, indeed, were all the others. Suffice it to say, that not many months after I came among them, I openly proclaimed myself on the Lord's side, and sealed the covenant by partaking of the emblems of *his* body and blood. And it is an additional source of happiness for me to state, that it was not long after, that the partner of my bosom also renounced the world, and joined me in the race set before us in the gospel."

A Wanderer Restored.—There have been very remarkable instances (says Mr. Spurgeon, in one of his sermons) of God delivering his people out of the snare of the fowler, as the following illustration will show :

"A young lady, who belonged to a church in the city of New York, married a young man who was not a Christian. He was a merchant, engaged in a lucrative business, and the golden stream of wealth flowed in upon him till he had amassed a large fortune. He accordingly retired from business, and went into the country. He purchased a splendid residence ; fine trees waved their luxuriant foliage around it ; here was a lake filled with fish, and there a garden full of rare shrubbery and flowers. Their house was fashionably and expensively furnished ; and they seemed to possess all of earth that mortal could desire. Thus prospered, and plied with an interchange of civilities among her gay and fashionable neighbors, the piety of the lady declined, and her heart became wedded to the world. And it is not to be wondered at, that her three children, as they grew up, imbibed her spirit and copied her example. 'A severe disease,' it is said, 'demands a severe remedy ;' and that God soon applied. One morning intelligence came that her little son had fallen into the fish-lake, and was drowned. The mother's heart was pierced with the affliction, and she wept and murmured against the providence of God. Soon afterwards, her only daughter, a blooming girl of sixteen, was taken sick of a fever and died. It seemed then as if the mother's heart would have broken. But this new stroke of the rod of a chastening Father seemed but to increase her displeasure against his will. The only remaining child, her eldest son, who had come home from college to attend his sister's funeral, went out into the fields soon afterwards, for the purpose of hunting. In getting over a fence, he put his gun over first to assist himself in springing to the ground, when it accidentally discharged itself and killed him! What then were that mother's feelings? In the extravagance of her grief, she fell down, tore her hair, and raved like a maniac against the providence of God. The father, whose grief was already almost insupportable, when he looked upon the shocking spectacle, and heard her frenzied ravings, could endure his misery no longer. The iron entered into his soul and he fell a speedy victim to his accumulated afflictions. From the wife and mother, her husband and all her children were now taken away. Reason returned, and she was led to reflection. She saw her dreadful backslidings, her pride, her rebellion; and she wept with the tears of a deep repentance. Peace was restored to her soul. Then could she lift up her hands to heaven, exclaiming, 'I thank thee, O Father!—the Lord hath given, the Lord hath taken away, and blessed be the name of the Lord.' Thus did her afflictions yield the peaceable fruit of righteousness, and her heavenly Father chasten her, 'not for his pleasure, but for her profit, that she might become partaker of his holiness.'"

Revival in Montreal.—I remember a revival, which occurred in the city of Montreal, Canada, in the winter of 1835; but its commencement showed a difference of administration by the same Spirit. I had not the privilege of being present during the hour in which was displayed this manifestation of the power of God over mind. Those who witnessed it informed me that it was a scene of overpowering interest. During more than one week they had preaching every night. On the evening in question, the discourse was more than usually pointed and solemn. A death-like stillness pervaded the large assembly. At the close of the sermon, an unexpected influence came down upon the people. But, instead of two or three persons manifesting a desire for salvation, the entire congregation seemed to be moved at once, like a forest bending beneath a heavy gale. There was very little noise; no shouting or screaming; but many tears and sighs among the multitudes; and strong men bowing themselves, in penitential sorrow, before the

Lord God of hosts, with earnest prayer; but evidently restraining the deep emotions which agitated their souls. When an invitation was given to penitents, and they were exhorted to come forward for the prayers of God's people, the aisles were speedily filled, all crowding toward the communion-rails; rich and poor were seen mingling together. I cannot enter into all the particulars; but it was supposed that, within the short space of four weeks, four hundred sinners were converted to God.

A Terrible Death-Scene.—A very short time ago, says the Rev. James Caughey, God took away an infidel in the still hour of night, in the town of ——, while the inhabitants were wrapt in profound slumber. An infidel felt his final hour approaching; his infidelity vanished before the upraidings of his guilty, awakened conscience. "Go," said the dying man, "to such a local preacher, and beg him to come and give me some advice about my soul." The messenger hastened away, and, though the preacher had been laid up with a bad arm, he dressed himself, and paced his way through the silent streets, and by the aid of the lamp that gleamed on his path, soon found his way to the door of the poor dying infidel. As he entered the room, the eyes of the dying man turned towards him, lit up with an unearthly lustre;—his very soul seemed gleaming in his eyes; he cried, "O, sir, save me, save me, do save me!"

"My friend, I cannot save you; God alone can save you,—cry to him for salvation."

"O, sir, do you save me!"

Said the preacher, "God sometimes makes man the instrument of enlightening a dark mind like yours, but he alone can save your soul." The preacher knelt down and pleaded with God that he would save the man,—pleaded with unusual liberty; pleaded, read, and exhorted him for two hours. The expiring man listened with the deepest attention, and appeared to drink in every word that fell from the lips of the man of God. At length, the devil seemed to make his last effort, and, we are grieved to add, we fear a successful one. When the preacher expected symptoms of penitence, he roused himself up, as though a fiend had taken possession of him;

he began to swear in a most horrible manner, and to blaspheme the name of God. He turned his eyes upon the preacher, and said, "Out, out of my room! If I could reach, I would dash your brains out!" The preacher said, "I knew he was too weak to leave his bed to reach me. I felt resolved, however, not to give up the contest; I therefore knelt down again, and pleaded with God for his salvation. As death approached,—as the dimness of the grave began to gather over him,—as the room was growing dark to his fading sight,—he became more and more furious. The tones of agonizing prayer and the horrible ravings of the infidel blended in wild confusion, and, doubtless, presented to *heaven* and *hell* a scene of fearful conflict, of intense interest. The closing scene was evidently fast approaching,—the struggle was reaching its climax. The moment that was to fix him in heaven or hell was just at hand. The scene was intensely exciting. The quiet that reigned without in the street, the solemn hour of midnight, added to the solemnity of the scene. Nothing was heard now but the two voices,—that of prayer and swearing vying with each other in energy. The fatal moment now arrived,—the whole frame of the infidel was convulsed in the agonies of death. He fixed his two elbows on the pillow, raised himself up in the bed, and, with a wild and frightful scream, cried, '*O God, this moment damn my soul!*'"—*he fell back upon the pillow, and expired.* The scene on earth closed, and the eyes of another world looked upon the sequel.

A Singular Conversion.—In a certain part of America, surrounded with woods, a minister of Jesus was preaching the gospel to a listening crowd. A stranger, on horseback, proceeding through the forest, hearing the sound of a human voice, paused; and then, through curiosity, approached sufficiently near to hear the truth delivered by the earnest preacher, but did not alight. What he heard, it seems, made no impression upon his mind at the time, and he continued his journey. As he rode along, he began to reflect upon the importance of the truth he had just been hearing. The Spirit of God accompanied his meditations in so forcible a manner to his conscience, that he fell from his horse, as one dead. How long he lay upon the ground, he could not tell; but upon coming to his senses, he perceived that a surprising change had taken place in his mind. Love, peace, and sweet communion with God, had taken possession of his heart; he was a new creature in Christ Jesus. Upon looking round for his horse, it was gone, and had carried off his portmanteau, in which was all his money, etc. Returning upon his track, he found the animal entangled by the bridle in a brake, and all his property safe. He remounted, and proceeded on his way rejoicing. When he arrived at a certain town (a place, by the way, notorious for wickedness), he began to proclaim what great things God had done for his soul. The people were astounded, and considered the man *insane*, and were about to confine him. He told them, with heaven beaming in his countenance, that he had never been in the right exercise of his reason till a few hours before; but that now he was in his right mind, and very happy in God, and that they need not give themselves any uneasiness about him. He then related the circumstances of his conversion, and exhorted them to flee from the wrath to come. The power of God attended his exhortations, and many gave heed to the things spoken by the stranger; a revival began from that day, and a great number of people were the saved of the Lord.

The Romish Penitent.—Among the Roman Catholics in Wiggensbach, of which Martin Boos was curate for a time, were many persons who, failing to find comfort, either by attending the confessional or by receiving absolution from the priests, retired into convents, where they hoped to obtain relief for their spiritual wants. Of this class was a female, who, having been disgusted with the world, formed the design of entering a nunnery, imagining that in such a retreat she would lead a holy and happy life. Accordingly, she withdrew to a nunnery, with a feeling of ecstasy, as if entering heaven itself. But she found there no spiritual life—no Saint Theresa—and told her associates that they were no nuns, but mere hood-wearers. She soon left them, and then tried what pilgrimages could do for her. She travelled twice to Maria Einsiedel, in Switzerland, but the second time came back more uneasy and dissatisfied than before. She entreated her parish priest to tell her some other method of appeasing the inexpressible longings of her heart; but to no purpose. He only taxed her with pride and folly, and asked her whether she was not learned enough, or whether she wanted to be wiser than himself. At last she consulted Boos, and found what her soul had been seeking: he led her to Christ, and in him she found the rest and comfort which he offers to the weary and heavy laden. From that time she felt no delight in her rosary, and other formal devotions. This disturbed her, and she almost suspected herself of heresy. She laid the matter before Boos. He asked her what so occupied her time and thoughts, that she could no longer use her rosary. "I do nothing and think of nothing," she replied, "but to love Jesus because he is in me and with me." "You can do nothing better than that," said Boos: "it is no heresy to love Jesus and think of him. To do everything out of love to him is of more worth than many rosaries." This satisfied her for a while; but soon after the thought struck her, "This clergyman makes so little account of rosaries, perhaps he is not of much worth himself." she went and told him, with fear and trembling, what had passed through her mind. Boos laughed heartily, and said, "Yes, you are in the right; in myself I am of no worth, but what I have taught you is of worth, for it was taught by Jesus Christ and his apostles; that remains true: continue then in the faith; do good and shun evil."

Not long after, a feast of indulgences was held in her neighborhood; but instead of attending it she went to Boos, fifteen miles off On his asking her the reason, she said, "Jesus is my absolution, since he died for me. His blood, simply and alone, is the absolution for all my sins." "But who teaches you this?" said Boos. "No one," she replied; "the thought comes of itself into my mind: Jesus takes away my sins, and those things, too, on which I have depended so much, but have found them to afford neither rest nor peace. I am now convinced that all is of no avail, unless Jesus takes away our sin and dwells in our hearts."

Bunyan's Pastor, Gifford.—Southey states that he had been a major in the king's army, and continuing true to the cause after the ruin of his party, engaged in the insurrection of his loyal countrymen (the Kentish men), for which he and eleven others were condemned to the gallows. On the night before the intended execution, his sister came to visit him ; she found the sentinels who kept the door, asleep, and she urged him to take the opportunity of escaping—which he alone of the prisoners was able to attempt, for his companions had stupefied themselves with drink. Gifford passed safely through the sleeping guard, got into the field, lay there some three days in a ditch, till the great search for him was over, then, by help of his friends, was conveyed in disguise to London, and afterwards into Bedfordshire, where, as long as the danger continued, he was harbored by certain royalists of rank in that county. When concealment was no longer necessary, he came as a stranger to Bedford, and there practised physic. Gifford was at that time leading a profligate and reckless life, like many of his fellow-sufferers, whose fortunes had been wrecked in the general calamity. He was a great drinker, a gambler, and oaths came from his lips with habitual profaneness. Some of his actions, indeed, are said to have evinced as much extravagance of mind as wickedness of heart ; and he hated the Puritans so heartily for the misery which they had brought upon the nation, and upon himself in particular, that he often thought of killing a certain Anthony Harrison, for no other provocation than because he was a leading man amongst persons of that description in Bedford. For a heart and mind so distressed there is but one cure, and that cure was vouchsafed at a moment when his bane seemed before him. He had lost one night about fifteen pounds in gambling—a large sum for one so circumstanced. The loss made him furious, and "many desperate thoughts against God" arose in him, when, looking into the books of Robert Bolton, what he read startled him into a sense of his own condition. He continued some weeks under the weight of that feeling ; and when it passed away, it left him in so exalted, and yet so happy a state of mind, that from that time till within a few days of his death, he declared "he lost not the light of God's countenance—no, not for an hour." And now he inquired after the meetings of the persons he had formerly most despised, and, "being naturally bold, would thrust himself again into their company, both together and apart. They at first regarded him with jealousy ; nor when they were persuaded that he was sincere, did they readily encourage him in his desire to preach ; nor after he had made himself acceptable as a preacher, both in private and public trials, were they forward to form themselves into a distinct congregation under his care. At length eleven persons, of whom Anthony Harrison was one, came to that determination, and chose him for their pastor; the principle upon which they entered into this fellowship one with another, and afterwards admitted those who should desire to join with them, being faith in Christ, and holiness of life, without respect to any difference in outward or circumstantial things." Bunyan afterwards united with this church by profession of his faith.

Influence of a Pure Conscience.—In the summer of 1746, Samuel Walker became curate of the gay little capital of Western Cornwall. He was clever and accomplished—had learned from books the leading doctrines of Christianity, and, whilst mainly anxious to be a popular preacher, had a distinct desire to do good—but did none. The master of the grammar-school was a man of splendid scholarship, but much hated for his piety. One day Mr. Walker received from him a note, with a sum of money, requesting him to pay it to the Custom-House. For his health, Mr. Conon had been advised to drink some French wine, but on that smuggling coast could procure none on which duty had been paid. Wondering whether this tenderness of conscience pervaded all his character, Mr. Walker sought Mr. Conon's acquaintance, and was soon as compgletely enchained by the sweetness of his disposition as he was awed and astonished by the purity and elevation of his conduct. It was from the good treasure of this good man's heart that Mr. Walker received the gospel. Having learned it, he proclaimed it. Truro was in an uproar. To hear their general depravity, and to have urged on them repentance and the need of a new nature by one who had so lately mingled in all their gaieties and been the soul of genteel amusement, was first startling and then offensive. But soon faithful preaching began to tell. And in a few years upwards of eight hundred parishioners had called on him to ask what they must do for their souls' salvation; and his time was mainly occupied in instructing large classes of his hearers who wished to live godly, righteously, and soberly, in this evil world. One November, a body of troops arrived in his parish for winter quarters. He immediately commenced an afternoon sermon for their special benefit. He found them grossly ignorant. But when they came under the sound of his tender but energetic voice the effect was instantaneous. With few exceptions, tears burst from every eye, and confessions of sin from almost every mouth. In less than nine weeks no fewer than two hundred and fifty had sought his private instructions; and though at first the officers were alarmed at such an outbreak of "Methodism" among their men, so evident was the improvement which took place, so rare had punishments become, and so promptly were commands obeyed, that the officers waited on Mr. Walker in a body, to thank him for the reformation he had effected in their ranks. On the morning of their march, many of these brave fellows were heard praising God for having brought them under the sound of the gospel, and, as they caught the last glimpses of the town, exclaimed, "God bless Truro."

The Cannibal's Experience.—When Christianity was introduced into the island of Rarotonga, two-and-thirty years ago, there was a native priest, a savage cannibal, who was so enraged at the success of the gospel, that, with seventy men of like character, he vowed a vow to die rather than submit to the new faith. This man assisted in burning down the first chapels and school-houses on the island, and for fifteen years was a determined, violent, and constant enemy to the truth. By some means he was induced to attend the preaching of the gospel, became convinced of his sins, and understood something of Christian truth, but only enough to make him unhappy. When, five years afterwards, he was admitted into the fellowship of the Christian church, he spoke to this effect: "Brethren, am *I* here? I who have been so wild a savage? Ah! *brethren* is a new name to us—we knew not what that meant in our heathenism." Pointing to the old men, he said, "You know me." To one of them he said, "You and I killed so and so in yonder mountain, and, with others, revelled in a cannibal feast on his body." He then mentioned three persons by name whom he and they had murdered and eaten. "But you, young men," he said, "know me too; I burned down the chapel and schools: but you do not know all. These hands have murdered eleven persons in yonder mountains, and I have partaken of more than twice that number of feasts of human bodies. Am *I* here? I who have done these deeds? Some of you have been expecting me to come and make profession of my faith in Jesus long before now. But whenever I have thought of doing so, the sin and guilt of my cannibalism have prevented me. This has been the barrier, until the other day I heard the missionary preach from that text in Isaiah, 'I have blotted out, as a thick cloud, thy transgressions, and, as a cloud, thy sins.' That was the gospel to me. Among the sins making up that cloud, the sin of cannibalism was noticed, and all its enormity described; but it was shown that even that could be blotted out by the blood of Jesus. My burden was that moment removed. My heart found peace. I had conversation with the missionary, and now, as the result of the love and death of Jesus, it is true that I, even I, am here." And this man, from whom the demon of sin and savageism was expelled by the cross of Christ, is now one of the most intelligent and consistent elders in the Rarotongan church.

In the course of five-and-thirty years, five-and-thirty islands in these Southern seas have wholly cast away their idols as the fruit of the labors of one society. And other societies have been equally successful, so that there are now in these regions 240,000 persons who profess the faith of the Bible, and of these 46,000 are in actual membership as communicants at the table of our Lord.

A Bible, instead of a Sword.—Dr. Cæsar Malan received the following narrative from the subject of it. A young man, the son of French Protestant parents, was turned aside from the paths of religion and virtue during his attendance at the University of Paris. In the pursuit of sinful pleasure, instead of enjoying satisfaction, he was a terror to himself. "When I reached the age of twenty-six (he said) I was in the sight of God as a madman, or like the horse which spurns the bridle, rushes furiously into the battle, and falls, being wounded suddenly from every quarter. . . . . I had taken my degree, and entered on the duties of my profession (as a barrister), when, in one of my fits of ungovernable passion, I had a quarrel, which ended in a challenge to a duel with one whom I thoroughly hated, as I regarded him as a rival. Our combat (why not call it our mutual purpose of assassination?) was to take place in secret. I spent a whole day and night in preparing for it, and still I could not look forward to it without horror. Not that I dreaded either being wounded or killed, for I was unfeeling, and my heart was hardened. But, sir, my Bible frightened me. I had laid it aside in a closet, and to this closet I went to seek the sword with which I intended to meet my opponent. I opened the closet: it was nearly midnight. I climbed a chair, and reached to the highest shelf, feeling for my sword, when I laid my hand on my Bible. A sudden chill ran through my veins, and, without any time for deliberation, I took the book, opened it, and, still standing on the chair, I read the tenth Psalm, which was the first passage on which my eyes rested. Thus, sir, the voice of the Lord once more resounded through the dark recesses of my soul. I read with breathless eagerness, and still I went on reading, though my uneasiness increased, till I came to this verse: 'Wherefore doth the wicked contemn God? He hath said in his heart, Thou wilt not require it.'

"I felt confounded, and throwing myself prostrate on the floor of my room, I sobbed aloud and groaned, praying for pardon from God for the sake of Jesus. I dared not rise; I was afraid even to look up. I felt that the eye of God was upon me, and my sorrow is not to be described. The tortured criminal does not suffer what I then felt; and about an hour passed away, at the end of which time I felt somewhat more calm, and sat down, still holding my Bible in my hand. God had thus rescued me. The prayers of my poor mother were heard, and my sinful soul was restored to the narrow way of life, which, indeed, I had never totally forgotten, though I had in so great a degree trodden under foot the truths I had learned, seeking to crush them as I should a serpent.

"What followed? My duel was a painful subject, and I resolved to give it up. But this was not all; I was filled with sympathy for him whom I had regarded as my adversary, and I longed to make this known to him, and also to those who were to have been the witnesses of our crime. The day began to dawn, and the hour for our meeting arrived. My companions came to seek me; but I had gone on first, and hastened to the wood which had been the place chosen for the duel. I reached it first, and felt that the Lord was graciously present with me. My adversary, accompanied by his second and mine, arrived there, and, perceiving me, he cried out, 'Here I am; make ready!' I answered, seriously, but with much feeling, 'I am ready, in the presence of God, to ask pardon of you, if I have offended you, and to forgive you any wrong you may have done to me.' 'Coward! scoundrel!' he exclaimed; 'this is your meanness!' 'You need not insult me,' I ad ded; 'I speak in the presence of God who sees us both. He has humbled me and touched my heart, and I repent, and acknowledge my folly before Him, and entreat you also to fear Him, and no longer reject His mercy.'

"Thus, sir," said the narrator to Dr. Malan, "God prevailed. The contest was dropped, and I returned to the town, urging my companions no longer to live in rebellion against God. I know not if they yielded to my entreaties, for I left the town shortly afterwards, and had no further intercourse with them. But I cannot describe the joy of my pious mother, when she saw me to be such as she desired, and felt that the infinite love and mercy of the Lord had been manifested towards me."

The Infidel Convinced by a Child.—The coach stopped at the bottom of a steep ascent. It was a frosty morning, and a few flakes of snow had fallen. While we waited to rest the horses, the door of a cottage by the roadside opened, and three children came out. The oldest was a girl about twelve years old, another girl between six and seven, and a smiling, chubby-faced boy about four, followed her.

The eldest held a long hazel wand, at the end of which was fixed a nosegay of winter flowers, neatly tied up, to the window of the coach.

I was pleased with this little mark of industry, and putting sixpence into a cleft at the end of the wand, I took the nosegay.

"A happy New-Year to the gentleman," cried the children. "Well," said I, "I suppose I must give you something for your good wishes," and I threw them another sixpence.

The children exclaimed, "A happy New-Year, sir; may you live many happy years."

"How many?" said I. "Oh, a great many, sir: as many as you can."

"Thank you, my dear; but how many years do you suppose I shall live in this world?"

"Ah, sir, how can *I* tell!" said the girl. "Who *can* tell?" asked I.

This question appeared to puzzle her; our conversation attracted the attention of my fellow-travellers, even of the infidel; while the driver and the guard also seemed to listen; but no one replied.

I repeated, "Who can tell how many years longer I shall live?"

The two sisters said nothing, but the little boy, clasping his hands together, looked up at me, and said, "Sir, nobody but GOD knows that."

We continued silent for some time; at length he, who the day before had laughed at the Bible, and had dared to deny that there was a God, said, in a humble tone of voice, "Sir, last night you told the colonel, that you would read to him some passages from the Bible; these gentlemen and I would be glad to hear you."

The colonel looked at me with pleasure, the tears stood in his eyes; I could not restrain my emotion, but said, "Is it possible that God should have caused you to listen to his voice, from the mouth of that little child?" "What the child said certainly made a singular impression on me," replied he. "I will confess that, during the last hour, I have felt differently upon this subject from what I have ever done before; but, sir, I do not wish to recall what passed yesterday evening; I entreat that you also will try to forget it."

The colonel turned towards him, and took his hand, saying, "We deeply rejoice to hear what you have just said. It is of God, and it is, I trust, the beginning of the work of the Holy Spirit in your heart." "Read to us, sir," added he, addressing himself to me, "read to us the word of life; and may God bless it to all our hearts."

The morning was spent in this pleasant employment, and we were much gratified by the earnest inquiries of our companion. Several times he appeared struck to the heart, by that word which the Holy Spirit has compared to "a two-edged sword." (Heb. iv. 12.) At other times he brought forward objections, which were easily removed by the word of truth. I need not attempt to express how much we rejoiced at having reason to hope that God had touched that heart, which but a few hours before was in open rebellion against him.

At the inn where we stopped, our companion listened with attention, and more than once referred to what had passed in the boat and in the coach, and especially to the children of the cottage. This gave the colonel and myself an opportunity to observe that God hath chosen the weak things of the world to confound the things which are mighty.

"It is true," said our companion. "Yes. I feel that it is true: for I must confess, that when you asked the girl that question, I guessed the answer which you wished her to give, and I resolved to ridicule it; but when she did not reply, and after a long pause, the little boy so simply declared the name of God, it struck me to the heart, and I had not a word to say; I could almost suppose that his eyes were upon me; I shall never forget that moment; I was struck dumb."

He then rose from the table, and left the room; but soon returned with the two volumes which he had offered to read while we were in the boat.

"Here, sir," said he, "are the vile books, which for several years past have strengthened me in unbelief and blasphemy. May God, who now beholds me, and in whose presence I now stand, consume the evils they have nourished within my heart, as this fire consumes their wretched pages, and the blasphemies they contain."

He cast the volumes into the fire, and looked on in silence till they were burnt to ashes. "Now," said he, "I am relieved of part of my burden; those volumes can do no more harm; and may my right hand be cut off, rather than I be permitted again to open others like them. May God," added he, pointing to my Bible, "May God teach me and write upon my heart the truths contained in that precious book, which has this day shed a ray of light into my soul."

Little Hannah's Prayer Heard, and Overheard.— One Sabbath evening, John Price, after drinking and gambling all day, and having lost the earnings of the week, turned from his companions, and scarcely knowing what he did, took the road homewards. One of them called on him to return; entreated him to have one more game, and added, "You will be sure to win it all back, you know."

He stopped—"Why, if I could get it back," said he to himself. "Come, come," said his companion, "one more game, only one."

"No," said Price, "I've lost all my money, and so I can't, if I would." But at that moment it occurred to him that his quarter's rent, except what was to be made up out of his last week's work, had been put up in a cupboard in the kitchen at home; and if he could get that, he should be sure to win back all he had lost. The money was to be paid the next day; and hardened as he was, he trembled at what he was going to do, and was terrified lest his wife and children should see him.

He approached the house, then ventured to look in at the window, and perceiving no one, he entered the kitchen, and went hastily to the cupboard. It was locked: and he felt a momentary relief in the thought that he could not get the money. But again he said to himself, "I shall be sure to win;" and hastened softly up stairs to look for the key, thinking he knew where his wife had put it. As he passed the room in which his children slept, he thought he heard a slight noise; and listening, he heard sobs, and then a voice. It was poor little Hannah, praying that her father might see the error of his ways; that God would change his heart, and make him a comfort to her mother, and to them all. Her sighs and tears seemed almost to impede her utterance; and when he heard her call him her dear father, and felt how ill he had deserved such a name, he could scarcely forbear groaning aloud, in the anguish of his feelings. He forgot the key, crept to his bedroom, and fell on his knees. He uttered not one word, but the language of the heart is audible in the ears of mercy; and that evening, for the first time, it might have been said of him, "Behold, he prayeth."

After some time he went down stairs, where Hannah was rocking her little sister to sleep. She started with astonishment. For many months, and even for years, she did not remember seeing her father at home on a Sabbath evening. He went to the children and kissed them both. This was a mark of affection they did not often receive, and Hannah was as much pleased as she was surprised.

"Dear father," she said, "mother will be so glad to see you at home, and we shall be so comfortable. You will not go out again to-night, will you, father?"

"No, dear," he replied. And as she went to lay the babe on the bed, he heard her say to herself, "Father called me dear."

The return of his wife and boys from public worship, Price had been dreading. He knew not how to endure their looks of amazement: but it was soon over. The children at first looked fearfully at each other, as though their usual Sabbath evening's pleasure was over; for they always sat up later, and told their mother all that had happened at the Sabbath-school, and what they could remember of the sermons they had heard during the day. Hannah had prepared supper, and there was a nice fire and a clean hearth. Price felt at that moment, that if his own character were what it ought to be, he should indeed be happy.

"Father," said Hannah, as she entered the room, "here is a nice new-laid egg. It is my own, and you shall have it, father."

Price could not speak, but he kissed his child, and he saw the tears in her eyes. He thought it was the nicest egg he had ever tasted. When supper was over, Hannah said, "Father, you have not heard me read for a long time."

"Well," said he, "will you read something to me out of your reward book at the Sabbath-school?" He knew that this was the Bible, but had not courage to say so.

Hannah was almost perplexed. She looked first at her father, and then at her mother. Two hours ago, the sight of a Bible in her hands would have insured oaths which she shuddered to hear.

"Come, dear," said her father, "why don't you fetch it?"

Hannah obeyed, though not without trembling. She read the 51st Psalm. Price hid his face and wept. The first part seemed made on purpose for him. He restrained his feelings sufficiently to say, "Thank you, dear, you are very much improved. Read something else."

She turned to the 103d Psalm. "Surely God made her choose those two," thought Price. His wife beheld with astonishment the conduct of her husband, and the emotions which appeared to agitate him.

"Hannah, my dear," said she, "you had better be taking the boys to bed." Their mother kissed them, and told them they had been good boys; and then they turned to Hannah, as if to ask if they should go to their father. "Come, dears," said she, "wish father good-night." He kissed them, and they left the room.

"You'll have some additional refreshment, John?" said his wife. "You've had no beer to-night."

"Oh," said he, "I hope I shall never taste beer again."

With unutterable joy she started from her seat, and throwing her arms around his neck, burst into tears. For some minutes they wept together. Price tried to speak, but could not. At length recovering some degree of composure, he seated himself beside her, and hiding his face, told her all the occurrences of the evening.

"Can you ever forgive such a wretch?" said he: "Oh, Hannah, can you?"

"Forgive you! my dear husband," she replied; "I never loved you half so well, nor ever was half so happy before. Don't ask me to forgive you; ask God to forgive you, and he will." And then she talked to him of the infinite mercy of God, through Jesus Christ, and again begged him not to ask pardon of her, but of Him.

"I have, I have," said he; "but till I heard what our dear child read, I did not think he could ever forgive such a wicked sinner as I am."

"It is a faithful saying, and worthy of all acceptation, that Jesus Christ came into the world to save sinners, even the *chief*," said his wife.

"Does the Bible say *all* that? Does it say the *chief*?" he asked. "Indeed it does," she answered. "Then that must mean *me*," said he.

"Let us kneel down together, my dear John," said his wife, "and ask God to fulfill his promise to you." "I cannot pray," said he.

She took his hand, and made him kneel down beside her; and in the language of faith and affection, she commended him to the mercy of that God who had long been her Father and Friend.

After thus engaging in prayer, the mind of her husband became more composed ; and he expressed the hope that he should never lose the remembrance of *this evening*.

The change was as permanent as it had been remarkable. From this time his old companions were forsaken, and the ale-house abandoned. To the former he only spoke, to entreat them to turn from their wickedness ; and the latter he never entered but once, and then it was with his wife, to pay the landlord a debt he had contracted, for some windows broken in an affray with one of his depraved associates in a state of intoxication.

Influence of Tracts upon the Profane.—At the time of a revival of religion in a village in Vermont, a young man had become so profane that he would spend the silence of the night to invent blasphemies more horrid than he had heard or before conceived, and committing them to memory, would repeat them next the day in the presence of those who were laboring under the weight of conscious guilt. His father, one day addressing his son, said, "Here are some Tracts for you ; I wish you would read them." The son replied, with an oath too shocking to repeat, "you may read them yourself." But passing the table on which they were placed, the title "*Swearer's Prayer*" caught his eye, and thinking it would help him to be still more profane, he read it, and addressing his mother, said, "Mother, do you believe that tract to be true ?" "No doubt that he who wrote it, had reason to believe every word of it true," was the reply. "Then," said he, "I shall never swear again." He has since been received to the bosom of the church, as is believed, a humble and penitent Christian.

Tract blessed to a fashionable Lady.—The following circumstance occurred in the city of New York, under the immediate observation of the writer. A lady who shared in all the enjoyments which wealth and fashionable life can afford, but who neglected the "one thing needful," and seldom or never attended a place of worship, had a pious servant. This poor girl commiserated the condition of her mistress, though surrounded with elegance and splendor, and one evening deposited on her dressing-table the Tract entitled "*The End of Time.*" The lover of pleasure retired to array herself for the theatre—the Tract arrested her attention—she read, and conviction visited her heart. She immediately renounced the gay world, and now consecrates her wealth, talents, and influence, to the cause of God. She has for several years devoted regular portions of her time to visiting the families of her district and distributing Tracts, and has often been heard to declare, that one day, thus spent, is productive of more true enjoyment than a whole life of fashionable pleasure.

One Thousand Tracts.—An Agent in New York says, a young man in L——, being about to remove to Alleghany county, called at the Depository in Utica, and obtained about one thousand Tracts. These he caused to be faithfully distributed in the town where he had fixed his abode. Their distribution was soon followed by a general revival of religion. Between fifty and sixty professed converts to Jesus Christ were the fruits of this revival; and *nearly thirty of them traced their first serious impressions to the Tracts which had been put into their hands.*

A Bigot Converted without Argument.—Anthony Rollo was a young half-bred Indian, employed at the Baptist mission at Cary, Michigan, but in consequence of his jealous attachment to the religion in which he had been brought up, was not interfered with on religious subjects. But at a season of religious interest, he informed one of the missionaries that he was in great distress. He said he knew his soul would be lost. He was asked how he knew it? He replied, he was confident that he could not be saved out of the Catholic church. In this place there was no priest. He had lost his goodness, and he could not recover it without the aid of a priest. He was directed to apply for the forgiveness of his sins to the Lord Jesus Christ, and exhorted to read the Bible. He replied that he was forbidden by his religious instructors to read the Bible, and if this were not the case, our Bible was not the same as theirs, and he was averse to reading it.

On the same day, he seated himself beside another of the missionaries, who was at his writing-table, exhibiting signs of great distress, and the same strong attachment to his Catholic superstitions. He saw, he said, others happy in the enjoyment of their religion, while he could find no satisfaction in his, though he *knew* his was right. He had been good, but he had lost it all, and knew that, should he die, he would go to destruction. Formerly, at times, he had been troubled about these things, and he always found relief by praying ; but now his prayers afforded him no relief. "But," added he, "I have determined that I *never* will change my religion—*no change shall ever take place with me.*" He wept freely, and appeared almost distracted. He was evidently anxious to hear religious conversation, yet listened with fear lest he should hear something that would disclose an error, in what he termed "his religion."

In the latter part of December, he was induced to read a little in the Bible, being told, that if he found anything therein which would satisfy him that he ought not to read it, to lay it by. He commenced by reading a few verses at a time ; in doing which, he sometimes fancied he added sin to sin. Yet he could not forbear. In a short time he was constrained to admit that he found nothing which he ought not to read.

About the 1st of January, 1825, he had, by his proficiency in school, merited a book. A New Testament was offered him, which he accepted with apparent pleasure. And about this time he became a constant reader of the Scriptures. He often expressed a great desire to see a Catholic priest, that he might inquire of him why they forbade the people to read the Scriptures. He said he had himself been taught to believe, that if he read the Bible, it would certainly ruin his soul. His Bible now became not only his school-book, but his constant companion.

His distress of mind did not abate. He refused to be comforted. He said everything condemned him—our Bible condemned him, and he knew he would be lost—he had no hope. Said he, "I am in greater trouble than any one knows of beside myself. Sleep has, in a manner, left me. Some nights I sleep none, and when I do sleep, I often awake in terror not to be described."

But on the evening of the 16th of January, Anthony desired an interview with some of the missionaries, and gave them reason to believe that he exercised genuine faith in the Lord Jesus Christ

On the 1st of April following, he came before the church and congregation, and gave a satisfactory account of a work of grace upon his heart, and was unanimously received as a candidate for baptism. To one of the missionaries he said, "Christ is precious, and the Bible is the best of books. Oh, that every person had it, and would read it!" On his expressing a great desire, one day, to see a priest, he was asked if he thought a priest could help him? "No, no," was his reply, "if Christ does not help me, none else can. But I should like to ask a priest why he forbade me to read the Bible, that book, in the reading of which I find so much pleasure?"

Summary Method with an Infidel.—A Christian lady (a Baptist pastor relates) lay apparently dying. Her friends were weeping, and I addressed to one of them, a sister, some words of comfort concerning the blessed state and prospects of her who was about to leave them.

With some effort she repressed her sobs, and said, "I know that M—— (her sister's name) is safe; but I was thinking of my brother. Oh, he does not believe the Bible!"

"Not believe the Bible!" said I, looking him full in the face; "is that so?" He seemed disconcerted, and said, "This is no place to talk of that." But, moving my chair so as to place myself directly in front of him, I said, "This is, of all others, the very place. Your sister is now dying, and she is reposing her hopes for Eternity upon the truth of that blessed book"—pointing to a Bible which was lying upon a table near. "Surely we can talk as we ought under such solemn circumstances, and now, if ever, the subject will be interesting to *you*." He looked at me, and then, reaching out his hand, he took up the holy volume, and fixing his eyes steadily upon me, said, "How can I believe a book with so many contradictions in it as this?" For a moment I hesitated, but raising my heart in prayer, I asked the Lord to guide me, and following the impulse of the moment, I put out my hand, and somewhat hastily drew it from him, saying as I did so, "What have you to do with that book? or what right have you to pass judgment upon it?"

"Why," said he, "is it not given to all men to read and judge for themselves?" "Sir," said I, "it is given to God's people to be their chart while travelling through this wilderness, and to teach them what to say to such men as you." A meaning smile appeared upon his features as he replied—

"Oh, this is the first I have heard of it." "Well," said I, "treasure it in your memory, for it is very important. Too many presume to pass judgment upon what they do not understand; but let me speak with you about something which you do understand. I charge you here, and now, under these sad and impressive circumstances, with being a sinner against a good and holy Being who has created you, and kept you alive, in the midst of your wicked rebellion, for many years, and who is still exercising towards you the most amazing mercy!" He gazed intently upon my face. I saw by the serious aspect his countenance was assuming that his conscience was at work. At last, in a solemn and subdued tone, he said, "I do not deny the charge." I went on: "But I charge you with doing all this against light and knowledge, whatever may be your view of the Bible. You know that your course is wrong, and yet, with this knowledge, and in open violation of your own conscience, you persist in doing what you know that Being who has made you, and who has ever been merciful to you, condemns." Again he said, in deepening tones, "I do not deny it." "Do you," said I, "acknowledge yourself to be a sinner against this good Being, in open violation of light and knowledge which he has imparted to your own soul?" "I do," said he. "Here, then," said I, "take this book; it speaks to just such persons as you have acknowledged yourself to be, and if you will find me anything in it *affecting these points*, which is inconsistent with what you know to be true, or which, even in your own judgment, will warrant you in continuing in your present course, I will consent to your rejecting it. But let this one all-important matter be settled first; after that we may look at the contradictions of which you complain."

We parted. His sister did not die. He visited me in my study several times, and I met him at his own house, and conversed about the great question. He removed from the city, and was absent for more than a year; but during all that time we corresponded, and some two years after the events above related I baptized him. He is now a member of my church, and gives evidence of having indeed passed from death unto life.

Thomas Hamitah Patoo.—Patoo, a native of the Marquesas Islands, had reached the age of about fourteen, when, attracted by ships which occasionally touched at his native islands, he resolved to visit America; and, to secure his purpose, jumped on board a ship with her sails spread, just in time to see his afflicted father reluctantly wave his handkerchief as a signal of farewell. He arrived at Boston, and after a varied life of two or three years, and many sufferings occasioned by his own folly, was taken under the charge of Mr. D. H., a benevolent gentleman, who, in May, 1822, placed him in a pious family in Coventry, commending him to "the prayers and Christian kindness of the pastor and the whole church."

"At *a prayer-meeting at sunrise*, in the autumn of 1822," says the narrative of Harlan Page, "it was observed that Thomas was much affected and wept bitterly. He was made a subject of special prayer, and his conversation, at the close of the meeting, evidently showed that he was under the strivings of the Holy Spirit." These impressions were deepened by the clear exhibition of truth at successive meetings, and its faithful personal application to himself in private conversation. His distress was such one day, that he left home in the rain, first to find his Christian friend, and then to visit his pastor to obtain some relief. Truth presented took hold of his mind, but he rebelled against God, murmured at the conversion of a young acquaintance, and returned to spend a sleepless night in view of his hopeless condition. On the day following, his anxiety continued unabated; his distress was such that he could not attend to the business assigned him; most of the day was spent in agonizing prayer; till at length the Saviour appeared for him, his burdened conscience was relieved, and he found peace in believing. His own narrative of the way in which he was led, expressed in his broken idiom, is a delightful exemplification of the power and excellency of true religion.

"*Question.* Thomas, what was the state of your mind after the commencement of the revival in Coventry?

"*Answer*. Christians talk to me a great deal about my bad heart. Me think my heart good enough.

"*Q*. Did you then endeavor to pray?

"*A*. Mrs. T. teach me to say Lord's prayer. I think me got no mother, no father, no sister, no brother, here; and Mrs. T. good to me, so I do as she tell me. Then I kneel down before I go to bed, and say prayer.

"*Q*. Did you occasionally omit this duty?

"*A*. Sometimes. Then Deacon T. say you must say your prayers, Thomas, every night. Then me go pray, mad.

"*Q*. Had you any different feelings at the morning prayer-meeting at which you wept?

"*A*. Then me feel heavy; feel afraid to die; feel sorry for my sin. Me try to pray 'Our Father.' Me go home, think what minister say, then I pray. Next day forget it all—then feel light.

"*Q*. When you went to the inquiry-meetings how did you feel?

"*A*. I feel good some; then I feel heavy again. When minister say all about poor sinner, then I feel sorry.

"*Q*. What were your feelings at the meeting for inquiry on Sabbath evening?

"*A*. Heart feel hard. Somebody tell me J. B. got a new heart. I feel angry.

"*Q*. How did you spend the Tuesday following?

"*A*. Me want to see minister. I set out—go part way, feel so bad can go no further; then kneel down by a great rock and pray. Me say, O Lord have mercy on poor Thomas, poor heathen; give him new heart—take away old heart—Oh, give him new heart now. Then I go on. Go in minister's barn—'fraid to go in house; then I pray again. Then look round and say, God make this hay, this grain, all these things—why can't God make me new heart? Me wipe tears off my cheeks, but they come again. Then go in house. Mrs. C. say, What the matter, Thomas; you hurt you? I so 'shamed, me say, Oh, it rains out doors. Want to have her think it rain on my face.

"*Q*. What did you say to the minister?

"*A*. Me say me got that bad heart yet.

"*Q*. Did you feel glad when told that J. B. had a new heart?

"*A.* No, sir; me feel bad—me feel very heavy; me want to come first, before anybody get in. When me go away, hope me come to be like J. B.

"*Q.* How did you feel that night and the day following?

"*A.* That night me feel heavy—heavy all over. Eyes all tears—could no sleep. Next day, feel so all time. Afternoon go work in barn with W.; could no work. Feel me want to pray. Tell W. we kneel down. Then me say, O Lord, have mercy on poor Thomas, poor W.; give us new hearts. Then me think about Jesus Christ, and about Christian folks. Me never feel so before. Heavy all gone. Then me love to pray, and say, Our Father, and thank great God he give J. B. a new heart. Then me think me feel to love Christ; me go up on hay to find him—pray to him. Then me think Christ everywhere. Then come down.

"*Q.* What were your feelings during the meeting in the evening?

"*A.* Me want to shake hands with the minister, then feel to love all Christians.

"*Q.* How do you think you know a Christian from an impenitent sinner?

"*A.* Christian shake hand hard—his hand feel warm—sinner no shake hand.

"*Q.* What do you mean by a new heart?

"*A.* A heart that feel to love good thought.

"*Q.* How do you know your heart to be soft now?

"*A.* Why, me no feel mad to anybody; if man strike me, no want to strike him back again."

He had a great desire to unite with the church at the approaching communion, and when the pastor informed him, that at the suggestion of his distant friend, it was thought best that his admission be deferred, he replied with great feeling, "If, sir, you think best, then me wait; but may be me die soon—then me never own Christ before men."

He adorned the Christian character, loved the Bible, prayed much, especially for his own relatives and countrymen, for the heathen, and the impenitent in Christian lands; and, like the friend who made him the object of his Christian love and more than paternal regard, and wrote his history, he *put forth his most ardent efforts to bring sinners to Christ.*

"After our friend Thomas indulged a hope, I endeavored," says a young lady, "to avoid him as much as possible; but one day, after conversing with my sister, and expressing much joy because she had got a new heart, he turned to me and said, 'N., why you no give up that bad heart? Why you no come with C. and be a Christian? Me want you be a Christian too!' In order to evade what he said, and prevent his saying more, I replied, 'Thomas, why did you never speak to me about these things before? Perhaps, had you been as faithful in talking to me as you have been to my sister, I too should have had a new heart.' With an expression of deep regret, he replied, 'N., me very sorry me no talk to you before. Me *pray* for you before, and *now* me talk to you.' After this, he embraced every opportunity of affectionately urging upon me immediate submission to Christ.

"In the height of the revival, when a number of Christian friends were spending the day at our house, feeling no disposition to be with them, I retired to another room, and there stayed meditating on my hopeless condition. It was not long before some one rapped at the door, and who was it but Thomas. He immediately began in the most feeling manner, to entreat me to submit to Christ without delay. 'Christ ready to receive you—all the good Christians want you to come—angel in heaven ready to rejoice over you; why you no come?' After conversing in this manner for some minutes, he was silent. At length, looking at me most expressively, he said, 'Me sorry me no talk to you before. Me pray for you; me want to pray *with* you.' We knelt, and Thomas poured forth the feelings of his heart in language like this: 'O mercy, Father, have mercy on us sinners. Have mercy on this friend. Pray this friend may now give up that bad heart to Christ, and not go to hell,' etc. It was the burden of his prayer, that I might then submit to Christ. I will leave others to judge what were my feelings, to have this heathen, who had just learned there was a God, on his knees pleading for mercy on me, a stubborn sinner, hardened under the meridian light of the gospel."

One, *now a minister of the gospel,* states:

"The first time I saw Thomas after he thought he had been born again, was on Sabbath, December 8, 1822. I was then groaning under convictions of sin—I felt myself lost. It seemed that there was but a step between me and hell. I longed to converse with some one, but I was too proud to tell any one how I felt.

"Thus situated, Thomas approached me, and began to question me about my spiritual condition. I told him I felt that there was no hope for me: I had sinned against so much light, and so many strivings of the Spirit.

"He proceeded to urge me to immediate submission. 'Why you no give up that bad heart? It will do you no good to keep it. It will destroy you forever. Give it up *now* to Christ. Christ ready to give you a new, a good heart. Me hope me have given my bad heart to him. Me hope me have a new one. Oh, sir, do give up your bad heart.'

"I told him I wished I could, but it was so hard I could not: something was in the way, I did not know what.

"This excuse did not satisfy him. It only led him to press home with more earnestness the duty of immediately giving up my *bad heart* to Christ.

"I felt so distressed, I begged him to pray for me. This was the first time in my life that I ever had made such a request, and the very asking him to pray for me deepened my impressions. It came to my mind immediately, 'What, must you, a gospel-hardened rebel, call in to your help the prayers of a poor Marquesan, who has but just been converted from the worship of idols? He has just now heard of Christ, and received him as his Saviour; you have heard of him for years, and have been slighting his salvation, despising his offers of mercy, trampling on his blood, and grieving his Spirit.' These reflections were like daggers to my soul.

"Thomas promised to pray for me, but left me saying, '*Oh, sir, give up that bad heart* NOW.' This sentence was the most powerful sermon I ever heard; it contained the eloquence of the Spirit; and coming in the way it did, with an expression of the most tender pity and concern, left an impression on my mind which, I trust, will never be effaced. I have always considered his earnest exhortation to me at that time, as *the principal means in the hand of God of my conversion.*"

On the 30th of March he thus wrote to Mr. Page:

"MY DEAR CHRISTIAN FRIEND—I have received your very kind letter, and am now happy to answer it. One of my brothers writes for me, because I can't write well enough yet. I tell him what to write, so the word be some like Thomas. I very glad the great God in heaven make the Coventry people pray for poor heathen where there is no Saviour. I think they pray for me too, that I be prepared to tell the heathen all about the great God, and our Saviour Jesus Christ. I rejoice a great deal to hear about sinner come to Christ and get a new heart. I hope the good work continue always among you, so I rejoice always. The people here have no revival—no pray enough. I sorry; I hope we pray enough by and by. We have good many meetings, but no feel.

"I hope I go home by and by, and have sinner come to God in my country. Yes, my dear Mr. Page, *I go, if I live to be ready.* We have some scholars no love the Saviour. I tell them they must be born again or go to hell. I talk to some sinner all about they no come to Christ. I tell them I come away from heathen land, and find a good Saviour: they been here so long, and no come to Christ. You must pray a great deal for poor sinners in Cornwall school. May be we have a revival here.

"I must close now. I think I pray every day for you and all my friends. The great God bless you and make you do good while you live; and when you and I die, may we meet and *shake hand in heaven*, and stay always with our Saviour and all who love him.

"Your true friend,

"PATOO."

Rev. Joseph Smith.—He was a laborious and faithful pastor; was particularly diligent in seeking out those who were neglecting the ordinances of religion. The tide of emigration, especially from Virginia, poured around him considerable numbers of the profane and openly irreligious. He was skillful in devising methods of access to persons whom few would have thought it worth while to approach. On one occasion he was at the house of one of his elders over night, and rising early in the morning, he observed a house half a mile distant, and inquired of his elder who lived there. On being told that it was a person who had resided there but a few months, Mr. Smith asked if he came to church. The elder said he did not, but his wife and children came sometimes. Mr. Smith said that he would go and see him ; and telling the elder not to delay breakfast for him, immediately set off. Arrived at the house, he found the man and his family at home. He introduced himself as the minister who preached at Buffalo, and as such had called to see them. The man said he knew him, though he had not been to church, but added that his wife and children sometimes went. Mr. Smith called the family together, and talked with them on the subject of religion ; and, after some time, asked the man if he had had family worship that morning. He replied that he had not. "I suppose," said Mr. S., "that you pray in your family, of course." He admitted that he did not. "Then," said Mr. S., "you ought to do it ; and the sooner you begin the better. You must begin immediately." He then asked for a Bible, and read a passage, accompanying it with suitable comments, and immediately asked the man to pray ; and without giving him time to express either his assent or dissent, he knelt down forthwith. A long silence followed. Mr. Smith then turned to the man and urged him to pray. His importunate visitor again repeated his request. Under this process, his mind being deeply agitated, he cried out at length, in agony, "O Lord, teach me to pray, for I know not how to pray." "That will do," said Mr. Smith, as he rose from his knees ; "you have made a good beginning, and I trust you will soon be able to extend your petitions." The result was such as Mr. S. predicted. The tradition is, that from that time forth he became a man of prayer, and he and his family were soon consistent and active members of the church.

A New Test of Conversion.—An excellent pastor of Massachusetts writes to us (says the Evangelist) : Talking the other day with a brother minister who is enjoying a rich outpouring of reviving grace, he observed, that an influential man in his congregation had recently asked him to exchange pulpits with a neighboring pastor, towards whom this hearer had been wont to express great dislike as a preacher.

"Why," said my friend to him, "this is a strange request from you; you used to stay away from church when brother P. came here to preach."

"I know it," replied the parishioner; "but I hope I have lately become a Christian, and I thought if I could see Mr. P. going up our pulpit stairs without getting angry, I should have pretty good evidence that I am really converted."

"The Child's Call."—A dear little babe was in its tiny coffin, flowers were on its bosom, and a smile on its pale, cold cheek. The father and mother sat beside the coffin with their remaining children; friends came in; the venerable pastor also came to offer prayer and console these mourning parents. He had known the bitterness of parting with a loved infant, and tender were the words of condolence offered; he spoke of the little one who had been the joy of the household, now gone to the better land, and that it was calling to the father and mother to come—"Father, are you ready? Mother, are you ready?" The precious babe was laid in the cold earth; but the heart of the young father was touched with the Spirit of God, and he could not rid himself of the "child's call"—"Father, are you ready to die?"

A fortnight passed, and in a little village prayer-meeting was this father, a penitent, hoping for pardon through the blood of Jesus. He who for years had neglected the word of God, who had been in scenes of merriment and gaiety, who had profaned the name of his Maker, and had not thought of the value of the souls of his household, now came humbly confessing sin, and entreating others to prepare to die. Thus God in his wise providence takes away the prattling one to lead the parent to think of the better world, and to make preparations to enter therein.

The "Upper Chamber."—Some years ago, a young man from New England came to New York, and was employed as a clerk in a large dry-goods house down town. Shortly after his engagement, he came to his employer with the statement that some of the clerks were seriously interested in the subject of personal piety, and requested that a small upper room in the building might be set apart and furnished, to be used exclusively as a place of retirement, to which the various individuals connected with the establishment might resort for religious conversation, reading of the Scriptures, and prayer. This request was immediately granted, and the room was used for years for this only purpose, resulting in the conversion of a large number of the persons who, during that time, came in and went out of the employ of the establishment.

A Word in Season.—In Shropshire, England, some years ago, a number of acquaintances and friends had assembled to spend a social evening together. In the course of the evening they resolved to have a dance, and prevailed on Michael Onions, at whose house they were, to go out a distance of two miles to procure a fiddler for them. On his way he met a stranger, who, having missed his road, requested Michael to direct him to Madeley. Michael readily consented to do this, and walked about half a mile with him for this purpose. The stranger ascertained the errand on which Onions was going, and began to talk with him about his soul, showing him the unsuitableness of such follies to a dying man, his need of salvation and a personal interest in Christ, and his awful danger as an unsaved sinner. When the stranger left Michael, the conversation had so impressed him, that he dared not proceed on his errand, but returned to his home. When he opened the door, his friends inquired :

"Have you brought the fiddler ?"

He answered, "No."

"Is he not at home ?"

"Have you been at Brosely ?"

"No."

"Why, what is the matter ? You look ill, and are all of a tremble."

Michael then told them that he had met somebody, but whether a man or angel he could not tell ; he never before heard such a man. He repeated what had been said to him on spiritual subjects, and added, "I dare not go to Brosely ; I would not for the world."

The party was broken up. The next Sabbath, Michael and some of his friends attended Madeley church, and there, in Rev. John

Fletcher, the new vicar, he recognized the stranger who had conversed with him. The impression wrought on Michael was lasting in its character, and, under the influence of the Holy Spirit, led to his conversion. He became a zealous, devoted, and useful Christian. "A word spoken in due season, how good it is."

The Play-house a House of Prayer.—At the first prayer-meeting in Burton's old theatre, Rev. T. L. Cuyler said:

At the request of a Committee of the Young Men's Christian Association, I have come to conduct the service to-day. At last we may congratulate the defenders of the stage that a theatre has become a school of virtue and not a school of vice—a house of prayer, and not a haunt of profanity—a spot for the real tears of penitence, and not the scene of fictitious grief over fictitious sorrows! Let us give God the glory! This is not the first time that a theatre in New York has been used for a daily prayer-meeting. In 1831, the old Chatham street theatre—a haunt of obscenity and vice—was purchased by a committee for purposes of worship. It was during the height of the great religious revival of 1831, that two gentlemen called on the lessee of the theatre and proposed to buy his lease. "What for?" said he. "For a church." "A what?" "For a church," replied the gentlemen. The astonished man broke into tears and exclaimed, "You may have it, and I will give $1000 towards it!" The arrangement was completed. It was announced to the actors that there would be preaching on that stage every night! The first prayer-meeting in the theatre was attended by eight hundred persons. Among those who offered prayer were the late Rev. Heman Norton and Zachariah Lewis, one of the early proprietors of the New York Commercial Advertiser. On the 6th of May, the house was consecrated to the service of God, under the title of the "Chatham street Chapel." Rev. Mr. Finney preached from the text, "Who is on the Lord's side?" The bar-room was changed into a prayer-room! The first man who knelt there poured forth these striking words: "O Lord, forgive my sins! The last time I was here, thou knowest that I was a wicked actor on this stage. O Lord, have mercy on me!" To-day, for the second time in the history of New York, we set apart a disused play-house for a temporary house of worship. Oh, what fearful soul-tragedies may have been enacted in this very building! From yonder "pit" how many a ruined young man may have gone down to the pit of endless despair! Let our services here be as solemn as eternity. May no false fire be kindled on God's altar! May the Holy Spirit be here, and may this former habitation of the Tempter be the very habitation of Immanuel—the house of God—the gate of heaven to souls seeking after Jesus!

A Widow's Son.—A minister from England being, some years since, at Edinburgh, was accosted very civilly by a young man in the street, with an apology for the liberty he was taking: "I think, sir," said he, "I have heard you at Spafields chapel." "You probably may, sir; for I have sometimes ministered there." "Do you remember," said he, "a note put up by an afflicted widow, begging the prayers of the congregation for the conversion of an ungodly son?" "I do very well remember such a circumstance." "Sir," said he, "I am the very person; and, wonderful to tell, the prayer was effectual. Going on a frolic with some other abandoned young men, one Sunday, through the Spafields, and passing by the chapel, I was struck with its appearance, and, hearing it was a Methodist chapel, we agreed to mingle with the crowd, and stop for a few minutes to laugh and mock at the preacher and the people. We had only just entered the chapel when you, sir, read the note requesting the prayers of the congregation for an afflicted widow's son. I heard it with a sensation I cannot express. I was struck to the heart; and, though I had no idea that I was the very individual meant, I felt that it expressed the bitterness of a widow's heart who had a child as wicked as I knew myself to be. My mind was instantly solemnized. I could not laugh; my attention was riveted on the preacher. I heard his prayer and sermon with an impression very different from that which had carried me into the chapel.

"From that moment the truths of the gospel reached my heart; I joined the congregation, cried to God in Christ for mercy, and found peace in believing; became my mother's comfort, as I had long been her heavy cross, and, through grace, trust I have still been enabled to consecrate myself to the service of God. An opening having lately been made for an advantageous settlement in my own country, I came hither with my excellent mother, and, for some time past, have endeavored to dry up the widow's tears which I had so often caused to flow, and to be the comfort and support of her old age, as I had formerly been her torment and affliction. We live together in the enjoyment of every mercy, happy and thankful; and every day I acknowledge the kind hand of the Lord that led me to the Spafields chapel."

The Power of Meekness.—"A man of my acquaintance," says Dr. Dwight, "who was of a vehement and rigid temper, had, many years since, a dispute with a friend of his, a professor of religion, and had been injured by him. With strong feelings of resentment, he made him a visit for the avowed purpose of quarrelling with him. He accordingly stated the nature and extent of the injury, and was preparing, as he afterwards confessed, to load him with a train of severe reproaches, when his friend cut him short by acknowledging, with the utmost readiness and frankness, the injustice of which he had been guilty, expressing his own regret for the wrong which he had done, requesting his forgiveness, and proffering him ample compensation.

"As he was walking homeward, he said to himself, to this effect: There must be something more in religion than I have hitherto suspected. There is something in this man's disposition which is not in mine. There is something in the religion which he professes, and which I am forced to believe he feels.

"From this incident, a train of thoughts and emotions commenced in the mind of this man, which terminated in his profession of the Christian religion, his relinquishment of the business in which he was engaged, and his consecration of himself to the ministry of the gospel."

An Attentive Little Girl.—Several years ago, D—— was blessed with a revival of religion. One evening, Mrs. —— and her little daughter attended a meeting, and, while the preacher was speaking of the neglect of family duties, of reading the Scriptures, and of family prayer, the little daughter, who listened attentively, and perceived that the preacher was describing a neglect that she had witnessed herself, whispered to her mother, "Ma, is Mr. —— talking to you?" This was powerful preaching to the mother; she was immediately brought under deep convictions of sin, which resulted in her hopeful conversion to God.

Profanity Made a Means of Grace.—A poor wretched female, religiously educated, but afterwards abandoned to sin, misery and want, was struck with horror at hearing her own child repeat, as soon as she could well speak, some of the profane language which she had learned of herself. She trembled at the thought that she was not only going to hell herself, but leading her child thither. She instantly resolved that with the first sixpence she could procure she would purchase Dr. Watts' Divine Songs, of which she had some recollection, to teach her infant daughter. She did so, and on opening the book her eye caught the following striking verse:

> "Just as the tree cut down that fell
> To north or southward, there it lies;
> So man departs to heaven or hell,
> Fixed in the state wherein he dies."

She read on; the event was blessed to her conversion, and she lived and died a consistent professor of religion.

An Innkeeper's Family.—The late Rev. John Ryland, of Northampton, England, being on a journey, was overtaken by a violent storm, and compelled to take shelter in the first inn he came to. The people of the house treated him with great kindness and hospitality. They would fain have showed him into the parlor, but being very wet and cold, he begged permission rather to take a seat by the fireside with the family. The good old man was friendly, cheerful, and well stored with entertaining anecdotes, and the family did their utmost to make him comfortable; they all supped together, and both the residents and the guest seemed mutually pleased with each other.

At length, when the house was cleared and the hour of rest

approached, the stranger appeared uneasy, and looked up every time a door opened, as if expecting the appearance of something essential to his comfort. His host informed him that his chamber was prepared whenever he chose to retire. "But," said he, "you have not had your family together." "Had my family together; for what purpose? I don't know what you mean," said the landlord. "To read the Scriptures, and to pray with them," replied the guest; "Surely, you do not retire to rest in the omission of so necessary a duty." The landlord confessed that he had never thought of doing such a thing. "Then, sir," said Mr. Ryland, "I must beg you to order my horse immediately." The landlord and family entreated him not to expose himself to the inclemency of the weather at that late hour of the night, observing that the storm was as violent as when he first came in. "May be so," replied Mr. Ryland, "but I had rather brave the storm than venture to sleep in a house where there is no prayer. Who can tell what may befall us us before morning? No, sir; I dare not stay."

The landlord still remonstrated, and expressing great regret that he should offend so agreeable a gentleman, at last said he should have no objection to "call his family together," but he should not know what to do when they came. Mr. Ryland then proposed to conduct family worship, to which all readily consented. The family was immediately assembled, and then Mr. Ryland called for a Bible; but no such book could be produced. However, he was enabled to supply the deficiency, as he always carried a small Bible or Testament in his pocket. He read a portion of Scripture, and then prayed with much fervor and solemnity, especially acknowledging the preserving goodness of God that none had been struck dead by the storm, and imploring protection through the night. He earnestly prayed that the attention of all might be awakened to the things belonging to their everlasting peace, and that the family might never again meet in the morning, or separate at night, without prayer. When he rose from his knees, almost every individual present was bathed in tears, and the inquiry was awakened in several hearts, "Sir, what must we do to be saved?" Much interesting and profitable conversation ensued. The following morning Mr Ryland again conducted family worship, and obtained from the land lord a promise that, however feebly performed, it should not in future be omitted. This day was indeed the beginning of days to that family; most, if not all of them, became decided and devoted followers of the Lord Jesus Christ, and were the means of diffusing a knowledge of the gospel in a neighborhood which had before been proverbially dark and destitute.

A Persecutor in Danger.—The excellent Isaac Ambrose, in his "Treatise on Angels," gives an account of a profane persecutor who was brought to seek the mercy of God in a remarkable manner. He was out on a journey with his pious wife, when they were overtaken with a storm of thunder and lightning. He was seized with great terror, and his wife inquired into its cause. "Why," asked he, "are not *you* afraid?" She replied, "No; for I know it is the voice of my heavenly Father; and shall a child be afraid of a kind father's voice?" The man began to reflect that Christians must have within them a divine principle of which the world is ignorant, or they could not enjoy such calmness when the rest of the world were filled with horror. He went to Mr. Bolton, an eminent minister to whom he had been opposed, acknowledged and lamented his sins, and furnished good evidence of a change of heart.

Tract Visitation.—"Last evening," writes the devoted Harlan Page, "I closed up our efforts in the tract distribution for this month, and gave in my report. A few hours before the meeting, I found that a district of seventy-eight families had not been supplied; and to complete the distribution for the ward, undertook to supply it myself. I found several whose minds were very tender, and on whom the truth seemed to make a deep impression. A *young man and his wife* listened with fixed and trembling attention, as I conversed with them on the subject of their own personal salvation. Two pious females residing in the house soon joined the little circle, and we all knelt and endeavored to commit their case to Him who is able and willing to save. It was a solemn season, and our divine Redeemer seem to manifest his special presence.

"This morning I *called on them again.* I found both of them apparently trusting in the Saviour. They hoped they had surrendered themselves to him on the preceding evening. They had opened to each other freely the feelings of their hearts ; and had that morning erected the family altar, and were now determined to live together as fellow-heirs of the grace of life."

A Brand Plucked from the Fire.—A clergyman concluding a sermon to youth, took occasion to press upon parents the duty of parental faith, and illustrated its power in the following manner :

About two and twenty years ago a little circle were met around the couch of an apparently dying infant ; the man of God who led their devotions seemed to forget the sickness of the child in his prayer for his future usefulness. He prayed for the child, who had been consecrated to God at his birth, as a man, a Christian, and a minister of the word. The parents prayed with him. The child recovered, grew towards manhood, and ran far in the ways of folly and sin. One after another of that little circle ascended to heaven ; but two, at least, and one of them the mother, lived to hear him proclaim the everlasting gospel. "It is," said the preacher, "no fiction ; that child, that prodigal youth, that preacher, is he who now addresses you."

Religion Recommended by its Absence.—A young lady, the child of pious parents, had arrived at years of maturity apparently without having any salutary impressions made on her mind either by the instructions she had received, or the examples she had witnessed. In this state of mind she received the addresses of a gentleman destitute of religion, and who, probably, had not possessed her early advantages. He was moral, respectable, and honorable in social life, and had no idea that anything more was necessary. In due time they were married.

The worth of any blessing is often best taught by its loss. The very first day of her residence in the house of her husband, the young lady was struck with horror and distress at the omission of family prayers ; and that the family separated at night, and met in the morning, and no Bible was called for, no expressions of gratitude offered for protection and refreshment through the night, no supplication for provision, direction, and support through the day. She felt desolate and uncomfortable ; and that which she had so long disregarded in the house of her father, seemed now absolutely essential to her comfort. The deficiency was the means of awakening in her mind deep and serious convictions of her sin, in having failed to improve the privileges with which she had so long been favored. She was led to tremble at her awful state of guilt and danger as a sinner before God ; she humbly and earnestly sought mercy through the blood of the cross, and found joy and peace in believing. Now the instructions and admonitions of her pious parents, which had so long seemed to be like good seed rotting beneath the clod, began to spring up and yield fruit. She said, "The God of my parents shall be my God ;" and she gave herself up to him in a covenant never to be forgotten. She could not now be insensible to the best interests of her husband and family ; these became matter of deep solicitude and fervent prayer. Her pious endeavors were blessed : her husband was awakened to discern the things that belonged to his everlasting peace, and was made a partaker of the grace of God in truth. Their household was soon numbered among those in whose tabernacles is heard the voice of rejoicing and salvation. They became eminently pious, exemplary, and useful, and trained up their children in the nurture and admonition of the Lord.

Sent for by Providence.—A gentleman residing in the western part of the State of New York, a few years since, had sent two of his daughters to Litchfield, Conn., to be educated. While they were there, God was pleased to bless the place with a revival of religion. The news of it reached the ears of their father. He was much troubled for his daughters, "apprehensive," to use his own words, "lest their minds should be affected, and they should be frightened into religion."

Alive, as he thought, to their happiness, and determined to allay their fears and quiet their distresses, he sent a friend to Litchfield with positive orders to bring them immediately home, that they might not be lost to all happiness and hope, and consigned to gloom and despondency.

The messenger departed on this errand; but they had already chosen Christ for their portion, and had resolved that, whatever others might do, they would serve the Lord. They looked at both sides of the great question: they looked at the world and the pleasures of the world, and they thought of God and the glories of immortality; and with an eye full fixed upon heaven, they determined to live for eternity.

They returned to their father's not overwhelmed, as he expected, with gloom and despondency, but with hearts glowing with gratitude to God, and countenances beaming with serenity and hope. Indeed, they rejoiced in the Saviour.

Soon after their return home they were anxious to establish family worship. They affectionately requested their father to commence that duty. He replied that he saw no use in it. He had lived very well more than fifty years without prayer, and he could not be burdened with it now. They then asked permission to pray with the family themselves. Not thinking they would have confidence to do it, he assented to the proposition.

The duties of the day being ended, and the hour for retiring to rest having arrived, the sisters drew forward the stand, placed on it the Bible; one read a chapter—they both kneeled—the other offered prayer. The father stood, and while the humble, fervent prayer of his daughter was ascending to heaven his knees began to tremble; he also kneeled, and then became prostrate on the floor. God heard their prayer, and directed their father's weeping eyes, which had never shed tears of penitence before, to the Lamb of God, who taketh away the sin of the world.

Faithfulness of Harlan Page.—An estimable and pious young lady, Miss B., has informed the writer, that on becoming acquainted with Mr. Page, in 1827, he soon inquired if she was "a professor of religion;" and again, if she "had an interest in Christ;" if she "thought it desirable;" if she had sought to obtain it;" if she "had renounced the world, and resolved to live for the glory of God;" could she "give him the reason why she had not?" The impressions made on her mind by repeated conversations were such, that she could not rest till she found rest in Christ. "This result," she says,

"I cannot but view as in answer to fervent prayer, and in fulfillment of the promise, 'Them that honor me, I will honor.' His life was a living epistle. Often, to this day, has the solemn question, 'Are you a professor of religion?' warned me of danger, and summoned me to duty."

A Universalist converted on his Deathbed.—Says Harlan Page, in one of his letters, "I have just passed through a most affecting scene. On last Sabbath evening I went alone to the house where I had attended a prayer-meeting a week previous; but found there was no meeting, and that, under the same roof, a man was very sick. His wife, who is pious, appeared grateful for my call, gave me an account of their circumstances, and informed me that her husband had been a professed Universalist; but of late she thought his confidence in that error was shaken, though he would frequently argue the subject with her and others, even on his sick, and she feared, his dying bed. She informed him I was present, and asked if he wished prayer. He said he did. I told him I would comply—remarking that, as he seemed near to death, he must probably soon meet the eternal God, and asking if he felt prepared. He intimated that he did.

"'Do you think you have experienced that change of heart which is spoken of in the word of God as essential to salvation?'

"'Have I repented of my sins,' said he to himself, 'and believed on the Lord Jesus Christ?'

"'Do you love Christ?' said I. 'Is he the one altogether lovely?'

"'Yes, he is lovely to me. I hope to be saved by him.'

"'Do you believe all will be saved by Christ?'

"'Yes, I think so.'

"'What do you think of the passage, These shall go away into everlasting punishment?'

"'I cannot tell what it means.'

"'We read also, The wicked shall be turned into hell, and all the nations that forget God.'

"'Then,' said he, 'I must go there.'

"He seemed somewhat exhausted, and I was about to close my interview, when he again asked me to pray with him.

"'What petition shall I offer?' said I. 'Shall I ask that your heart may be changed?'

"'Yes,' said he, 'and that I may be purified.'

"Neighbors in the house were called in, and prayer was made in his behalf, amidst sobs and tears. His wife begged me to call again, which I did, with Mr. D., a young clergyman. He was evidently declining, but gave us no more satisfaction respecting his state.

"After we left him, he had much conversation with the Rev. Mr. J., and expressed his conviction of his ruin by sin, his renunciation of all the former grounds of his hope, his reliance solely upon Christ, and his peace and joy in him. He died the following day. His wife had long prayed earnestly for his conversion; and at last, when she had almost given him up as lost, had the satisfaction of seeing him give such evidence as he could in his last hours, that he fell asleep in Jesus."

Great Revival in New York, 1831.—Says Harlan Page, under date of January 24, 1831: "The Lord appears now to be coming down on all parts of this great city, to arouse his children and to awaken sinners. Thousands of Christians here are, I think, praying as they never prayed before. Public general meetings commenced yesterday afternoon, and are to be continued through the week. Conversions are occurring in all parts of the city. Churches are daily crowded to overflowing, and a most fixed and solemn attention is given to the dispensation of the truth."

This was then said to be by far the most signal revival of religion ever enjoyed in New York. As the fruits of which, there was an accession to evangelical churches of about two thousand souls.

No Hope.—At a meeting of his Sabbath-school teachers, Harlan Page called on each to know whether he thought he had a well-grounded hope in Christ or not, and recorded their several replies. Among them was an amiable young merchant, A. E., whom he highly respected, and who seemed not far from the kingdom of God.

"Have you a hope?" he tenderly inquired.

"No sir," was the reply.

"Then I'm to put down your name as having no hope?"

"Yes sir."

"Well, I write down your name as having no hope."

The young man pondered on this decision and record of his spiritual state, was troubled, and soon came to our brother, saying, "I told you to put me down as having no hope, but I can't say that." He is now a member of the church, and a decided supporter of all her institutions.

The Tract-house Revival.—Among the letters of Harlan Page, in 1827, occurs the following passage: "In the tract and Bible houses we have lately had a season of uncommon interest. A work of grace commenced a few weeks since among the young women employed in the two houses in folding and stitching Bibles and tracts, as the fruits of which we now number about sixteen hopeful conversions. It has been a most interesting and wonderful display of God's power and grace. On one day seven of them hope that they were brought from nature's darkness into the light and liberty of the gospel. That was one of the most interesting days of my life. Twice or thrice I was sent for to pray with them, and to take the hand of those who had just been brought to bow at the Saviour's feet, while with tears streaming from their eyes, they expressed the hope that they had surrendered themselves entirely to Him. Two of these had thought that I talked too severely, and discouraged them; they now wished to thank me for the very efforts in their behalf, of which they had before complained. To see those who were brought to hope in Christ clinging around their former companions in sin, and with tears beseeching them to come at once to the Saviour they had found so precious, was enough to move a heart of stone."

In a subsequent communication, he states that more than one hundred young women were then employed in the tract and Bible houses, and that of these God had brought "between fifty and sixty hopefully into his kingdom. One of them was convicted by means of the truths which caught her eye while folding the tract, 'Day of Judgment.'" "Many sheets of the word of God and tracts," he says, "as they have been folded and stitched, have been moistened with the tears of the convicted sinner and the broken-hearted penitent, and thence gone out on errands of mercy to a perishing world. Every day at twelve o'clock, the females of each of the two houses devote a part of their recess, in their retired rooms, to prayer and praise ; and on every Thursday evening we have a general meeting for prayer and conference, conducted by three or four brethren, the binder and printer of the two societies cordially taking part in the same."

The Reward Gained.—An ancient burgomaster, travelling to Germany, stopped at an inn on the borders of that country and Holland. He observed that the young woman who laid the cloth and made other preparations for his supper performed these offices neatly and with much alacrity, and he commended her, saying, "I trust that while you show yourself so careful in the performance of the common duties of your station, you are not less diligent in observing the duties and privileges of a Christian." The girl, who was quite ignorant of religion, replied by asking what he meant ; upon which he entered more particularly into an explanation of his meaning, dwelling especially on the importance of prayer, as he found that she lived in entire neglect of it. Her countenance and manner indicated a strict adherence to truth, and he told her that if when he again passed through the place she could assure him that she had knelt down every night and morning and uttered a short prayer, he would give her a ten-guilder piece—a gold coin, value four dollars. After some hesitation the girl agreed, and asked what the prayer was, the repetition of which was to procure her a larger sum than she had ever before possessed at one time. The burgomaster told her, "Lord Jesus, convert my soul." At first the girl hesitated, and thought that she might sometimes omit the repetition of these words, the full meaning of which she did not understand. A better feeling, however, induced her to continue, and also to inquire the meaning of these words.

About six months afterwards the old gentleman returned ; he went to the same inn ; another girl laid his supper-cloth ; he inquired for her predecessor in vain. He then asked for the landlord, who told him that five months back the girl alluded to had been seized with such a praying fit that he found she could no longer live in his family, and that she was then living with a private family in the neighborhood. In the morning the old gentleman sought her out, and said he was come to fulfill his promise. She immediately recognized him, but decidedly refused his offered money, saying, "I have found a reward much richer than any sum of gold."

John Dickson and his Babe.—John Dickson was a farmer near Edinburgh, and was for a long time negligent and irreligious. It pleased God to take away his wife, and it became necessary for him to have a nurse in the house, who happily was a pious woman. When his infant daughter was about twenty months old, she was in the room with her father and several of his profane companions. Most unexpectedly the child repeated, in its infantine tones, "Oh, the grace of God!" an exclamation she had often heard from her nurse. The attention of the father was thus excited, the Holy Spirit led him to deep and serious reflection, and thus was his conversion to God effected.

Anecdote of Harlan Page.—A letter from a young clergyman says: "The name of Harlan Page will ever be associated in my mind with all that is worthy of imitation in the Christian character. By the persuasions of an acquaintance, I was induced to engage as teacher in his Sabbath-school, and though I was then destitute of faith, he welcomed me and won my confidence and love. Very soon he began to address me with the utmost apparent tenderness and anxiety in reference to my own salvation. His words sunk deep into my heart. They were strange words, for though I had lived among professors of religion, he was *the first who for nine or ten years had taken me by the hand and kindly asked*, '*Are you a Christian?*' 'Do you *intend* to be a Christian?' 'Why not *now?*' Each succeeding Sabbath brought him to me with anxious inquiries after my soul's health. On the third or fourth Sabbath he gave me the tract, 'Way to be Saved,' which deepened my impressions. At his request, I also attended a teacher's prayer-meeting conducted by him, where my soul was bowed down and groaned under the load of my guilt. At the close of the meeting Mr. Page took my arm as we proceeded on our way to our respective homes, and urged upon me the duty and privilege of an immediate surrender of my heart to Christ. As we were about to part he held my hand, and at the corner of the street, in a wintry night, stood pleading with me to repent of sin and submit to God. I returned to my home, and for the first time in many years bowed my knees in my chamber before God, and entered into a solemn covenant to serve him henceforth in and through the gospel of his Son."

The Dying Father's Request.—A few years since a gentleman died who had for twenty years held on his course as a consistent, exemplary Christian. His only son possessed the exterior embellishments which attract and please—a noble form and elegant manners, and all the accomplishments which grace the convivial circle, the ballroom, and other places of fashionable resort; but he was an infidel in principle, a libertine in practice, and held the religion of the Bible in utter contempt. The amiable parent sickened and drew nigh to the gates of death, and the votary of dissipation was called to witness the last struggle. Grasping the hand of the young man, and with his eye fixed steadily upon him, the departing saint urged him to weigh well the scene before him, to anticipate his own dissolution, and to be assured that the same foundation which his dying father had built upon, and the same hope which he had so long cherished, could alone render death tolerable and eternity happy.

The parent died and was buried, and the surviving son having an increase of property, with proportioned avidity rushed on to destruction. A note penned by his departed parent a few weeks prior to his decease, containing a solemn injunction that he would on some suitable occasion retire to the room in which his father died and read the fifteenth chapter of St. Luke, fell into his hands. This was soon forgotten; but at length, after a year had elapsed, on a gloomy Sabbath morning in November, he carelessly sauntered into the chamber to look at his late parent's portrait, and kill the time until he should join a gay party at a hotel. There parental affection seemed still to smile in the well-depicted features of his deceased father; there was the bed on which "the pains, the groans, and dying strife" were exchanged for the anthems and praises of the heavenly world; and there, too, was the chair and the table on which stood the valuable family Bible, over the contents of which the sainted relative had so often prayed. Here he sat down. A host of overpowering recollections rushed upon his mind; a pale procession of past sins appeared before him, and like spectres whispered in his ear, "Judgment." The note referred to came to mind, and was read. The chapter spoken of was read too, and that proclaimed "mercy." The dinner-party were left to their festivity without his presence. The conviction flashed upon his mind for the first time, that his departed parent had died cheered by hopes that were now about to be realized. He groaned, he wept, he prayed. For some weeks he applied diligently to the study of the Scriptures, and afterwards adorned domestic life by discharging its duties, and honored a Christian profession by a course of useful and devoted service to his Maker.

The Hour Alone with God.—A pious and venerable father had a vain and profligate son; often had he reasoned and expostulated with him, mingling tenderness with advice and tears with remonstrance, but all was ineffectual. Bad company and vicious habits rendered the unhappy youth deaf to instructions. At last a fatal disorder seized his aged parent, who, calling his son to him, entreated him with his dying breath that he would grant him one small favor, the promise of which would alleviate the pangs of dissolving nature. It was this: that his son would retire to his chamber half an hour every day for some months after his decease. He prescribed no particular subject to employ his thoughts, but left that to himself.

A request so simple and easy, urged by parental affection from the couch of death, was not to be denied. The youth pledged his honor for the fulfillment of his promise, and when he became an orphan punctually performed it. At first he was not disposed to improve the minutes of solitude, but in time various reflections arose in his mind; the world was withdrawn; his conscience awoke; it reproved him for having slighted a parent who had done so much for his welfare; it renewed the impression of his dying scene; it gradually pointed him to a supreme cause, a future judgment, and a solemn eternity. God was pleased to sanctify these solitary moments, and to strengthen his convictions. Retirement effected what advice could not do, and a real and permanent change took place. He quitted his companions, and reformed his conduct; virtue and piety filled up the rest of his days, and stamped sincerity on his repentance. To say all in a word, he lived and died a Christian.

Admiral Williams.—The late Admiral Williams, when a young man, was gay, and so addicted to expensive pleasures, that no remonstrances could reclaim him. When his father died, he met with the rest of the family to hear the will read. His name did not occur among the other children, and he supposed the omission was a mark of his father's resentment against him. At the close of it, however, he found that he was mentioned as residuary legatee, in these words: "All the rest of my estate and effects I leave to my son Peere Williams, knowing that he will spend it all."

On hearing this he burst into tears. "My father," said he, "has touched the right string, and his reproach shall not be thrown away." His conduct from that time was altered, and he became an honor to the Christian profession.

Rev. Richard Cecil.—"My first convictions on the subject of religion," says the late Rev. Richard Cecil, "were confirmed by observing that really religious persons had some solid happiness among them which I felt the vanities of the world could not give. I shall never forget standing by the bedside of my sick mother. 'Are you not afraid to die?' I asked. 'No.' 'No! Why does the uncertainty of another state give you no concern?' 'Because God has said, "Fear not: when thou passest through the waters, I will be with thee; and through the rivers, they shall not overflow thee.'" 'Let me die the death of the righteous.'"

The Power of Consistency.—Mr. Innes, in his work on Domestic Religion, mentions a fact strikingly illustrative of the power of consistent conduct. A young man, when about to be ordained as a Christian minister, stated that at one period of his life he had been nearly betrayed into the principles of infidelity ; "but," he added, "there was one argument in favor of Christianity which I could never refute—the consistent conduct of my own father."

A Minister's Son.—A Christian minister in Somersetshire, a few years ago stated, that on the evening when the first permanent impressions were made on his mind, his pious mother was detained at home. She spent the time devoted to public worship in secret prayer for the salvation of her son ; and so fervent did she become in these intercessions, that she fell on her face and remained in fervent supplication till the service had nearly closed. Her son, brought under the deepest impressions by the sermon of his father, went into a field after the service, and there prayed fervently for himself. When he came home, his mother looked at her son with a manifest concern, anxious to discover whether her prayers had been heard, and whether her son had commenced the all-important inquiry, "What shall I do to be saved ?" In a few days the son gave evidence that he was the subject of religious impressions—impressions which lay the foundation of all excellence of character here, and of all blessedness hereafter.

The Mutilated Bible.—A father residing not far from Columbia, was about sending his son to the South Carolina college. But as he knew the influence to which he would be exposed, he was not without a deep and anxious solicitude for the spiritual and eternal welfare of his favorite child. Fearing lest the principles of the Christian faith which he had endeavored to instill into his mind would be rudely assailed, but trusting in the efficacy of that word which is quick and powerful, and sharper than any two-edged sword, he purchased, unknown to his son, an elegant copy of the Bible, and deposited it at the bottom of his trunk. The young man entered upon his college career. The restraints of a pious education were soon broken off, and he proceeded from speculation to doubts, and from doubts to a denial of the reality of religion.

After having become, in his own estimation, wiser than his father, he discovered one day while examining his trunk, with great surprise and indignation, the sacred deposit. He took it out, and while deliberating on the manner in which he should treat it, he determined that he would use it as waste-paper, on which to wipe his razor when shaving. Accordingly, every time he went to shave he tore out a leaf or two of the holy book, and thus used it till nearly half the volume was destroyed. But while he was committing the outrage upon the sacred book, a text now and then met his eye, and was carried like a barbed arrow to his heart. At length he heard a sermon which discovered to him his own character and his exposure to the wrath of God, and riveted upon his mind the impression which he had received from the last torn leaf of the blessed, yet insulted volume. Had thousands been at his disposal, he would freely have given them all, could they have availed in enabling him to undo what he had done. At length he found forgiveness at the foot of the cross. The torn leaves of that sacred volume brought healing to his soul, for they led him to repose on the mercy of God, which is sufficient for the chief of sinners.

A Profligate Son passed by.—Mr. Nathan Davies, the eldest son of a respectable Christian minister in Wales, was a youth of wild and dissolute conduct, and thereby occasioned much grief to his pious parents. Neither the mild nor the severe methods used to reclaim him had the desired effect. At length a period arrived when the aged and venerable father must die, and, like Jacob, he desired that his children should be called to his bedside to receive his dying admonitions. Having addressed them all one by one, except the profligate son, in a very affectionate and solemn manner, he concluded by warning them to shun the bad example and wicked ways of their eldest brother, and advised them to act towards him with caution and forbearance ; adding, that he feared they would experience from him nothing but sorrow and trouble. He then dismissed them, and soon after died.

The circumstance of the father's silence made a deeper impression on the mind of Nathan than all the reproofs and exhortations he had before received, and, to use his own expression, he thought at the time that his heart would have burst. He was then about twenty-seven years of age, and through the divine blessing a great change became visible in him ; he abandoned his former ways and companions, became a serious hearer of the word, and in a short time a member of the church over which his late father had been pastor. A few years afterwards he was called to the ministry, succeeded his father in the pastoral office, and was blessed in it with eminent success until the day of his death, which took place in the year 1726.

Sufficiency of the Bible.—The following narrative is from the Rev. Samuel Marsden, an excellent clergyman in New South Wales :

" Some time ago I was called to visit a young woman about twenty years of age, who was extremely ill, and who much wished to see me before she died. On my arrival at her father's house, I found her heavily afflicted ; and death appeared to be at no great distance. I sat by her bedside with the Bible in my hand, expecting to find her, as I have too often found others in similar circumstances, ignorant of the first principles of religion. I read a portion of this sacred book to her, and was most agreeably surprised to find that she understood not only the letter, but the spirit of the Scriptures. I asked her father how she became so well acquainted with the word of God. He said he did not know ; she was always reading her Bible at every opportunity, and sometimes sat up all night for that purpose. He observed she was a very dutiful daughter ; he had a large family, and she being the eldest, and very industrious, was of great service to her mother and the younger branches of the family ; the only indulgence she required was to be allowed to read the Bible when her work was done. But he could not account for her attachment to it ; and it seemed very strange to him that she should attend to it so much. I asked him if she was in the habit of going to church, as I did not personally know her. He said she went sometimes, but was generally prevented, from the distance and the large family she had to attend to.

" This young woman may be said to have obtained her religion wholly from the Bible. None of the family knew anything of the Scriptures but herself. I visited her during the whole of her illness, from the time she sent for me until she fell asleep in Jesus. Her faith was simple, her view of the way of salvation clear. She gave me many proofs of this in the various conversations which I had with her during her sickness. The Bible was more precious to her than gold ; she had found it, under the influences of the divine Spirit, her counsellor and her guide ; and by it she had been brought to a knowledge of the only true God, and Jesus Christ whom he hath sent ; and hereby was she filled with a hope full of immortality. Previously to her last illness she had enjoyed good health ; it was in the prime of youth and vigor she had read her Bible and loved it, so that she had not to seek God for the first time in this trying moment, but found him a present help in sickness and at the approach of death. The Bible had testified of Christ to her ; she had found eternal life in it, and the divine promises were both great and precious to her soul."

Sergeant Forbes and Whitefield.—Many years ago, in a regiment of soldiers stationed at Edinburgh, there was a sergeant named Forbes, a very abandoned man, who got in debt for liquor wherever he could. His wife washed for the regiment, and thus obtained a little money. She was a pious woman, but all her attempts to reclaim him were long unsuccessful. During one of Mr. Whitefield's visits to that city, she offered her husband a sum of money if he would for once go and hear him. This was a strong inducement, and he engaged to go. The sermon was in a field, as no building could have contained the audience. The sergeant was rather early, and placed himself in the middle of the field, that he might file off when Mr. Whitefield ascended the pulpit, as he only wished to be able to say that he had seen him. The crowd however increased, and when Mr. Whitefield appeared they pressed forward, and he found it impossible to get away. The prayer produced some impression on his mind, but the sermon most deeply convinced him of his sinfulness and danger. He became an altered man, and proved the reality of his conversion by living for many years with the strictest economy, in order to liquidate the claims of every one of his creditors.

A Sailor's Narrative.—A few years ago, on a voyage to the northwest coast, a young man sauntering on deck, observing one of the sailors more sedate than his companions, stepped up to him and abruptly asked him, "George, are you not a Christian?" His countenance brightened up as he replied, "I trust that I am; I think I can testify to the goodness of God in giving his Son to die for me." The manner in which he uttered this sentence interested his companion, who requested to know his history. His reply in substance was as follows:

"I have always been a sailor. My father was a sailor before me. My mother was a pious woman, and whenever I went on shore to see her she used to say a great many things to me about my soul. I paid no attention to them, but lived as though I had no soul. I was a fool, as I said in my heart, 'There is no God.' Boldly did I profane the name of Him who says, 'The Lord will not hold him guiltless that taketh his name in vain.' My frame trembles when I look back upon those days of sin and daring. In the midst of storms at sea, when the thunders and lightnings were abroad, faint emblems of the wrath of God, and when high upon the mast, or out on the yards, in imminent peril of being plunged into the deep, I have called upon God to curse my soul.

"Thus I went on from year to year, till I entered a ship commanded by a pious captain. He was a good man, and did much for the good of his crew. He read the Scriptures to us, and prayed with us. After some time, however, I began to tremble. The word of God convinced me of sin, and of righteousness, and of judgment to come. I saw my danger, and felt it too. My sins came up before me, and appeared as mountains that must forever separate me from peace and happiness. I was a miserable man, and thought I must always be so. At last I opened my heart to the captain. He felt for me, and told me of the mercy of God in Christ Jesus. With tears in his eyes, he directed me to 'behold the Lamb of God, which taketh away the sin of the world. My heart broke, tears of penitence ran down my cheeks; my faith took hold on the Son of God. He poured the oil of joy and peace into my broken heart, and bound up my bleeding wounds. I felt that I was a new creature. With the cup of salvation in my hand, I called on the name of the Lord. Oh, that all would come to the waters and drink from these wells of salvation."

At this time the young man who had elicited this narrative was not truly religious. The narrative of the sailor, given with simplicity and deep emotion, went to his heart and brought him to the feet of his Saviour. He soon after publicly professed his faith in Christ.

A Missionary Convert.—"Do you remember," said an Indian convert to a missionary, "that a few years ago a party of warriors came to the vicinity of the tribe to whom you preach, and pretending friendship, invited the chief of the tribe to hold a talk with them?"

"Yes," replied the missionary, "I remember it very well."

"Do you remember," continued the Indian, "that the chief, fearing treachery, instead of going himself, sent one of his warriors to hold the talk?"

"Yes," was the reply.

"And do you remember," proceeded the Indian, "that warrior never returned, but that he was murdered by those who, with promises of friendship, had led him into their snare?"

"I remember it all very well," replied the missionary.

"Well," the Indian continued, weeping with emotion, "I was one of that band of warriors. As soon as our victim was in the midst of us, we fell upon him with our tomahawks and cut him to pieces."

This man became one of the most influential members of the Christian church, and reflected with horror upon these scenes in which he formerly exulted. He gave his influence and his prayers, that there might be glory to God in the highest, peace on earth and good will among men.

Getting Respectability.—Some years ago a sailor in London, on going to a pawnbroker's shop to pledge some articles, saw a Bible lying on the counter, and inquired, with apparent interest, "What book is that?" To which he was answered, "That book is a Bible." "A Bible?" said the sailor; "why, I should very much like to have a Bible." At this remark, the curiosity of the shopman was somewhat excited, and he consequently inquired, "But can you read the Bible if you have it?" "Read?

oh no," said he, " I cannot read, but then you know it would be very respectable to have a Bible in the house." Accordingly, having inquired the price of it, he proceeded to deposit a number of other articles, and to the surprise of the pawnbroker, purchased the book, and walked off, delighted with the idea that by the possession of a Bible he should add very materially to his respectability.

Not doubting but his wife would feel as much interest in the book as he himself had done, he presented it to her, as soon as he reached home, with evident marks of satisfaction ; but he was surprised and chagrined to find that she was exceedingly angry, and called him a fool for buying the book when neither of them were able to read a chapter or a verse. Soon after this, two gentlemen connected with a Bible association called and wished to know of the woman whether she would subscribe to the association, or whether she wanted a Bible. The very mention of the word Bible was enough, and the preceding occurrence being brought fresh to her recollection, she expressed her anger most bitterly because her husband had bought a Bible, when neither of them could read. Its value and the importance of being able to read it were suggested, and she was advised to attend an adult school, which she accordingly did, and in a short time was able to read a chapter without difficulty. Delighted at the progress which his wife made, the sailor was also induced to attend the school, and it was not long before he also was able to peruse the sacred pages for himself. But what is more important still, there is reason to hope that the Bible was not purchased in vain, and that the sailor was at length led to see that the value of the inspired volume is to be estimated by a better standard than by the respectability which, according to his idea, was attached to the mere circumstance of having it in his possession.

Captivity.—It is related in Abbott's Religious Magazine, that as Dr. Cornelius was riding through the wilderness of the west, he met a party of Indian warriors just returning from one of their excursions of fire and blood. One of these warriors, of fierce and fiend-like aspect, led a child five years of age whom they had taken captive.

"Where are the parents of this child?" said Dr. Cornelius.

"Here they are," replied the savage warrior, as with one hand he exhibited the bloody scalps of a man and a woman, and with the other brandished his tomahawk in all the exultation of gratified revenge.

That same warrior became a disciple of Jesus Christ, a humble man of piety and of prayer. His tomahawk was laid aside, and was never again crimsoned with the blood of his fellow-men. His wife became a member of the same church with himself, and their united prayers ascended morning and evening from the family altar. Their daughters were amiable and humble, and devoted followers of the blessed Redeemer, trained up under the influence of a father's and a mother's prayers, for the society of angels and saints.

Dr. Hinde's Conversion.—Dr. Hinde, the family physician of General Wolfe, who brought him to America, had been educated in the principles of Christianity, but afterwards became a deist. His sentiments, however, at length underwent a radical change. His wife and daughter had been converted to Christianity, and attached themselves to a Christian church. For this act his daughter was banished from his house, and his wife was placed under medical treatment for what he considered, or affected to consider, insanity. His remedy was a blistering plaster to the whole length of the back, which he left on for several days. By this measure of violence he hoped to deter her from further attendance on places of public worship. But as he used to say, God placed a "huge blister" upon his own heart. The Christian fortitude and meekness with which his wife bore the protracted anguish which his cruelty inflicted on her, excited his sympathy and filled his soul with remorse. A feeling of respect was awakened towards that religion whose votaries could endure such persecution without a murmur, and he was led forthwith to investigate its origin and principles. The inquiry resulted in a perfect conviction of its divinity; and he attached himself to the same church from which he had sought by violence to estrange his wife and daughter, and for nearly half a century he continued one of its most devout and exemplary members. To his dying day religion was his favorite theme.

An only Daughter's Death.—An intelligent writer mentions the conversion of a man of the world, which, as far as means were concerned, owed its existence to the following circumstances: God laid his hand on a lovely, and I think, an only daughter, and the affliction terminated in death. When the terrible moment arrived in which the idol of his affections must die, he stood at the head of her bed almost frantic with grief, and having no consolation above what nature and education supplied, as is frequently the case, his grief terminated in rage: he was almost ready to curse the God who, as he thought, could be so cruel as to deprive him of so dear a child. His wife, an amiable and sensible woman, at the same time stood at the foot of the bed. Her eyes were suffused with tears, her hands lifted to heaven, and while every feature spoke the feelings of her soul, she exclaimed, "The will of the Lord be done! The will of the Lord be done!" These exclamations very naturally called the attention of her frantic husband from their dying daughter to herself, and as he afterwards confessed, he was on the point of wreaking his vengeance on what he then considered an unfeeling wife, and an unnatural, hard-hearted mother.

After a while, however, the storm of passion gave place to reflection. He was a man of eminence at the bar, a colonel in the army; he prided himself on being a philosopher, and he was there led to examine how his courage and philosophy had supported him in the day of trial. Here he saw reason to reflect on his conduct with shame; the more so as he contrasted it with the conduct of his amiable and pious partner. "How is this?" he could not but exclaim: "I am a man and a soldier. I boast of my courage, and pride myself in philosophy, in which I am versed, as being equal to the support of man in every emergency. But in the hour of trial I acted an unworthy part. My wife, a delicate female, and, notwithstanding my suspicions to the contrary, one of the most affectionate of mothers, was alone the magnanimous sufferer on this trying occasion. What, under circumstances so directly opposite, could lead to such contrary results?" "She is a Christian," said a still, small voice, "and I am not; surely the secret is here." This train of thought led to the most pleasing consequences. He concluded that there must be a reality in that religion which he had hitherto despised; and if so, that was the one thing needful. He conferred not with flesh and blood; but immediately began to seek the consolations of true religion, and ere long found

"What nothing earthly gives, or can destroy,
The soul's calm sunshine and the heartfelt joy."

Praying Mothers.—During the great revival of 1831, in New York, Harlan Page writes: "A case occurred last week of special encouragement to praying parents. At the close of the afternoon exercises, a meeting for religious inquirers was held in the lecture-room, and a few professors who lived at a distance stayed in the church till the evening service. Among them were two mothers, who, though strangers to each other, agreed to go to a retired pew, and spend the season in prayer. As the question arose what they should pray for, one said, 'I have a daughter who has no hope. The other replied, 'So have I an only daughter, and she is now in the inquiry-meeting, and we will pray for them.' They kneeled, and while they were still praying, one of the daughters came, found her mother, and, as soon as she could do it without interrupting her, took her by the hand, saying, 'Oh, my mother, I hope I have found Christ to be precious.' They all knelt again in prayer, and offered their united thanksgiving to God. The other daughter was hopefully converted on the following day."

"Pulling them out of the Fire."—In the memoirs of Harlan Page occurs the following instance of a final and almost desperate effort to reach the heart of one whose case seemed nearly hopeless.

To Miss N. R.

"The remark has often been made, that 'it will do no good to converse with N. R. on her state as a sinner; and you have probably yourself been brought to the same conclusion.

"I take my pen to say a few words more to you, trembling lest it should only be the means of hardening you in sin. All motives from this world would lead me at once to desist. But when I look to a dying hour, and a little beyond, into an unchanging eternity, I feel irresistibly impelled once more to expostulate with a perishing fellow-sinner. I beg you to receive it in kindness, and as probably the last lines or words addressed to you personally, which you will ever read or hear from me while you continue professedly the enemy of God.

"And now, what shall I say? Will you accompany me to that silent room? Here lies a young lady wasted by disease, and just on the confines of eternity. Approach her—the paleness of death is on her cheek. Take her by the hand—why start at its icy coldness? it is but kindred dust. Listen to her tale. 'Alas, my friend, I am dying—I am dying! My day of grace is over; my sands are almost run. In a few moments I shall be enveloped in devouring fire. I have lived in sin, rejected Christ, and now he hides his face from me, and there is no remedy. Oh, how have Christians plead with me to make God my portion; but I would not listen. I accused God of injustice, quarrelled with that sovereign love that would have wooed my heart; resisted the Holy Spirit that was teaching me my lost condition, and pressing me to accept of Christ. He called, but I refused; and now he is withdrawn from me forever. Oh, my friend, take warning from me. While you have the offers of mercy flee, to Christ. Make haste. Delay not a moment, lest you mingle your cries with me in the bottomless pit.'

"Can you look at this melancholy picture and not apply it to yourself? Death is even now at the door. There is no time to parley with Satan or your own heart. Heaven must be gained soon, or not at all. Christ now stands at the door and knocks. Oh, N., say not again, depart.

"That you may bid Him a cordial welcome, is the earnest prayer of your affectionate friend,

"H. Page."

The individual to whom this moving appeal was addressed, relates the following sequel: "I had long been awakened, but determined to let no one know it, and made every effort to *escape Mr. Page*. At length, near the close of November, I attended a little meeting where I believe all were indulging a hope except my brother and myself. After conversing with my brother, he came to me, and wished me to tell him the state of my mind. I at first said that I was in despair, but from the manner of his reply perceived that he did not give full credit to my assertion. This roused my resentment, and I at once determined not to speak again while he remained in the room. He pressed me to decide that I would without delay give my heart to Christ, but I was so angry that I would not even answer him. This conversation brought the malignity of my heart more clearly to my own view than I had ever seen it before. I could never have imagined myself to indulge such malice as I then felt towards him, and my misery was that I could assign no other reason for it but his faithfulness. Soon, as I trust, God was pleased to subdue my enmity, and my hatred to Mr. Page was *at once changed to love, for I saw in him the image of my blessed Redeemer.*"

Judson Forbes.—On the second day of June, 1856, I was called to the United States Marine Hospital to see a dying man, who had requested an interview with me. Kneeling by his side, I asked, "Do you know me?"

"Yes, Father Taylor."

"Well, my dear friend, what can I do for you?"

"Oh, I want to know what I must do to be saved. I am a great sinner. I know not what I shall do."

"Have you long felt yourself to be a great sinner?"

"Ever since I left home, a mere boy, and went to sea, my mother's prayers have been ringing in my ears. She used to pray with me every night. I have often thought what a dreadful thing it is to be a sinner, after having the instructions of such a mother. I have often desired to have religion, but at sea I had poor opportunities, and did not know how to obtain it. For some months past I have been in great distress of mind, but I have had no one to teach me the way. I have been trying to pray, but I get worse and worse. For several days past I have felt such a load of sin that it seems sometimes that my heart would burst."

"Do you think," said I, "that you hate your sins, not only on account of their consequences to you, but because they were perpetrated against a wise and merciful God?"

"Yes," he replied, "and I give up all to him.

"Even if you knew you would get well," continued I, "you would consecrate your heart and life wholly to him, and living or dying, be the Lord's without reserve?"

"Yes," said he, "I only desire to live that I may serve him."

"Do you believe that Jesus Christ died to redeem you from sin?"

"I do."

"Do you believe that God the Father accepts the price which Jesus paid for you?"

"I do."

"You believe, then, though guilty, bankrupt, and condemned, that on Christ's account you may to-day obtain the pardon of all your sins?"

"Yes, I do."

"Are you not glad that you have such an almighty and sympathizing Saviour on whom you may cast all your sins and sorrows?"

"I am glad."

"You are trusting in him now, are you not?"

"Yes;" and continued, "Oh! oh! oh!" the tears streaming down his sunken cheeks, "I never felt so before. I feel such a load taken off my heart. I feel that I could fly away to the arms of my blessed Jesus. I never before had any idea of the ability and willingness of Jesus to save me. I feel that he hath saved me. He hath cleaned me through and through. I hope to see my God in heaven before to-morrow morning."

He, however, survived two days longer, and sweetly fell asleep, trusting in an almighty Saviour. Such was the closing scene of Judson Forbes, from Wisconsin, aged twenty-four years.—*Rev. William Taylor.*

The Dying German in a Stable.—During the autumn of 1853, the City Hospital, which could accommodate about three hundred patients, was crowded to excess. One day, after visiting the wards of the sick and dying, and passing out into the back yard, a nurse said to me, "There is a very sick man in the stable," pointing to the door. I entered, and saw the emaciated frame of a tall, intelligent-looking young German. He told me he was a druggist, had been well brought up, and was doing a good business in his father-land, when he took a notion he would come to California. He had been at work in the mines, and got his leg broken. It had been too long neglected, and mortification had taken place, and he feared he never would again see his dear mother. I explained to him our guilty and exposed condition as sinners, and told him of a Friend, his Friend, one who loved him more than his mother ever did or could love him ; that his mother in Germany knew not the condition of her son, and could not help him if she did ; that this Friend knew all about him, and that he was nigh at hand ; that he was born in a stable, and was present then, in his spiritual nature, his essential Divinity, in that mean stable, and was waiting to receive him as his child.

Never before did I see a poor soul drink in the simple Gospel with such avidity. His faith seemed to follow me closely step by step, till, by the mercy of the Lord, I led him to the cross. Gazing with wonder, he at once recognized the dying Jesus as the victim slain for him. His faith took right hold of the atonement and exulted in an almighty Saviour. His countenance shone like that of Moses, as he exclaimed, " Oh, my Jesus, my Jesus, I do love thee !"

As he continued to praise God, he, every now and then, turned his beaming eyes towards me, and said, "I am so glad you came in to see me. I did not know Jesus till you came in and told me about my precious Saviour. I would like to get well that I might do something great for you."

I assured him that I was repaid a thousandfold in seeing him happy in God. His strength failing, he said, " My poor pody, he is very sick, he will soon go down ; but my spirit, he is well now, he will soon go up to my blessed Jesus." A few hours sufficed to end the mortal strife, and his spirit went up to his blessed Jesus.—*Rev. William Taylor.*

Conversion at the Mast-head.—A rough seaman, on one of his visits to his home, was greatly importuned by his parents to become a Christian. He turned impatiently from all their affectionate entreaties ; and went to seek his pleasure among his sailor companions. That night, as he lay awake upon his bed, he heard his mother's voice pleading earnestly with God for the salvation of her only son. This exasperated rather than softened the heart of the impenitent man ; and the next day he bade his home farewell, and was soon again upon the wide ocean. His parents, and their desires for his conversion, were, probably, entirely driven from his mind. But once, when he was stationed as "look-out" high on the mast, with no companions about him but the piping winds, he was made to thrill with a sudden awe and terror at what seemed to be the very voice of his mother's prayer uttered long ago in the silent night, now borne to his ears by the air of heaven, as he sailed over the lonely sea. He tried to laugh at himself for having so wild a fancy ; but again that loving cadence rose and fell on the waves of the air. He could distinguish the very words of the prayer. It was too much for the courage of the sailor. What ! was there a miracle wrought in his behalf, and should he still resist the Holy Spirit ? "God be merciful to me a sinner !" cried the mariner from amid the shrouds. "Lord, I believe, and I *will* be thy servant, if thou wilt take such a vile wretch as I am." The sailor was, from that hour, a new man ; and when next he went to visit his retired home, it was to carry to his faithful parents the joyful tidings of his conversion.

A Dream of Salvation.—A widow had a son for whose salvation she wearied the heavens by perpetual prayers. Having said and done for him, as she thought, everything that wisdom permitted, she had altogether ceased to vex him with any more personal appeals. But her heart was in continual heaviness at the thought that her only child was allowing the dew of his youth to pass without devoting himself to God. She believed fully that her Maker and Friend would make good his word to her by the final salvation of the precious soul which, with all a mother's yearning tenderness, she had intrusted to His guardian care ; but sometimes she felt her heart sinking fast and heavily under the pressure of a fear that she should not be permitted to live to see his conversion.

One morning, after the mother had almost given up the hope of a speedy change in her son, he appeared at the breakfast table with pale face and languid manner. Fearing that he might be sick, the widow questioned him with anxiety, and at length drew from him the confession that he was very much distressed in consequence of a dream which had the previous night visited him. We will give the dream in something like the youth's own words :

"I thought," he said, "mother, that I was standing at the bottom of a deep pit, from which there seemed no possible way of escape. Two vicious looking creatures, half man, half demon, stood a few feet before me, working furiously at forges. The fire flashed from the iron in their hands, and smoke and lurid flame encircled them on every side. Smoke poured from their widely distended nostrils and cavernous mouths, and the fire darted from their blazing eyes. They eyed me with malicious joy, and appeared preparing for a spring at me, as I stood cowering helplessly before them, almost within reach of their talon-like hands. I shall never forget the unutterable fear and agony with which I looked about me for some way of escape.

"The monsters grinned horribly upon me, as I did so, and then cast fearfully malicious glances from me to each other. 'He is ours,' they seemed to say, 'ours without help or hope.'

"Suddenly I saw something moving close by my face. It was a small silken cord. I looked up, and over the mouth of the pit, I saw the face of the Saviour. I knew him in a moment ; I cannot tell how, but it seemed revealed to me. He was looking down upon me and holding the other end of the silken cord. When he met my gaze, he said, in tones which I shall remember till I hear them in Heaven or at the Judgment Day, 'Take hold'! 'What! Lord, not of this little thread—it will never bear me.'

"'*Take hold!*' was the only answer. 'Oh! I cannot, I dare not ; it would break in my hand,' I persisted, in terrible agitation, for my fierce companions had dropped their work, and were in the very act of springing upon me. 'Take hold!' commanded once more the voice above me, and with a desperate grasp I seized the string, and was instantly drawn above all danger, while the fiends were howling in disappointed malignity below me. The size of the line which bore me increased continually, and in a few moments I was safe at the top of the pit. As I threw myself in a transport of joy and gratitude at my Deliverer's feet, I awoke ; but I have not yet been able to shake off the effects of that singular dream."

"Nor should you try to do so, my son," returned the widow, solemnly. "God speaks to the soul in dreams of the night—and he has now spoken in a voice of warning to the widow's only son—neglect not the vision."

Henry did not neglect it, and in less than a week from that day, his mother had the joy of knowing that her child had chosen the service of the Saviour who had rescued him from the pit.

"God willing to make His Power Known."—In the town of W., in the State of Maine, there resided a man by the name of Daniel ——. His early religious education had been very imperfect. His mother (a pious woman) had died while Daniel was yet a lad, and his father was very far from being a Christian. Upon the deathbed of the latter, he was brought to see, and heartily to repent of, all his sins, chief among which he regarded the bad manner in which he had brought up his sons. These sons he called to his bedside, and solemnly besought them to avoid leading the irreligious life that he had led. He required of each one a promise that he would make the kingdom of heaven the very first object of his search; and then, dying as he was, the poor old father struggled upon his knees to pour out his soul once more unto the Lord in behalf of his sinful sons.

The old man died and was buried; and the sons went their several ways, and, to all appearance, their father's deathbed entreaties and exhortations were to prove utterly fruitless.

But there were some that hoped against hope for better things; and many prayers were offered for the thoughtless brothers. In their youth, and while their father was robust and active, he and his sons were in the habit, in the spring-time, of *driving logs*—but that had been many years ago.

One morning Daniel thought that his father came into his room and called out, with a strong, quick voice, "Come, Daniel, the tide is almost out." Daniel leaped from his bed in haste, thinking that he was called to go and help about the logs. He afterwards said he seemed to see his father near his bed as he arose, and it was not until he was nearly dressed that he became aware that he had but dreamed. This dream-call worried him; and when he was told that it should be regarded as something more important than a common dream he was vexed, because he felt that to be in accordance with his own fears.

About this time, if we mistake not, a revival began to take place in the churches of W., and the case of these brothers was made one of especial prayer. Two of them, if no more, knew that this was so. One was not much exercised in any way by this knowledge; but Daniel was fretted exceedingly by it. He was so surly and violent at home, that few cared to speak to him. One evening his wife, or some other member of the family, pleasantly invited him to attend a meeting, and he immediately burst out in a great rage, cursing and swearing, and declaring that they needn't think they were going to get *him* prayed over into a Christian, for they could not and should not do it. So saying, he flung himself angrily out of the house. But he could not run away from the Spirit of God. He had dared to say that God had not the power to change *his* heart, and in mercy instead of wrath he was to be taught his error. As a man who is blind is sometimes led, he knows not by whom, so was Daniel led from the threshold that he crossed, in the heat of fury, straight to the house of God. He never could tell what it was that came over him; but he knew that all the anger and rancor of his heart were taken away, and when he returned to his home he went into his chamber, and kneeling down by his bed, tried, with all his heart, to pray. It was hard work for his untaught lips, and the effort brought forth a flood of tears from the rugged man's eyes. Emotions new and strange swept over him; and there he remained, trembling, weeping, and praying, till the fear that some one would come in caused him to rise and creep into bed, and try to sleep. But sleep had fled away from him. The next day, finding himself alone, he took a Bible and sat down to see what light that would throw upon his state of mind. He had uttered to no one a word of the great change which had been wrought in his feelings, and he could not at all understand what it was that had befallen him. He thought that if the Lord really *would* hear him now, and forgive him all his high-handed transgressions, that he should be most glad and grateful to devote his whole future life to the service of One so merciful and long-suffering; but it did not seem that he could ever be sufficiently sure of forgiveness and of the love of God, to speak of his feelings to any one, or to dare to enroll his name with Christians. But he would read some in the Bible, and, perhaps, he should get instruction from its sacred pages. He opened it at random ; for he knew no more where to look for anything in the Bible than a child of three years of age. What was his astonishment—what was his sudden, overflowing delight, when the very first words upon which his eyes fell were, "O Daniel, a man greatly beloved, understand the words that I speak unto thee, and stand upright, for unto thee am I now sent. . . . Fear not, Daniel, for from the first day that thou didst set thy heart to understand and to chasten thyself before God, thy words were heard."—Dan. x.

To imagine the effect these words must have had upon a man in his state of mind, it must be remembered that Daniel was totally unaware that there was a book bearing his name in the sacred volume. As he afterwards declared, an audible voice, speaking to him from the very skies, could hardly have seemed more like a direct personal address to him from God, than did the words which he then read.

They were indeed blessed words to him ; they caused him to "*stand upon his feet*," and tell in the solemn assembly all that God had done for his soul. He joined his name to the people of the living God, and although he did not prove to be quite perfect, he has given evidences of being in spirit and truth a child of the new birth. But there is a shadowy side to this story. Daniel was the only one of the brothers who was chosen, though all were called. While the revival was in progress, and after the conversion of Daniel, there was intensely earnest prayer offered for the ingathering of the other brothers, especially for the one with whom Daniel had been up to the present time associated in business. The church prayed that his brother W. might have no peace until he found it in Jesus ; that he might be followed all the day, and "disturbed in the watches of the night." It was a still, moonlight night when W. was awakened by a strange, mournful sound, which seemed to be above him, in the air. He listened. What could it mean? Was he dreaming? The tones were, part of the time, those of singing, and again they were the tones of prayer. And W. thought he recognized the voices of his departed father and mother, and that of a little niece, who had died a short time previous. He felt a chill of awe and terror creeping through his blood. He spoke to his wife—she was awake :

"Do you hear anything !"

"Yes, W., I have heard them all night ; and I think that when the spirits of the dead are thus disturbed for your sake, it is high time that you should be disturbed for yourself."

"Pshaw ! wife—the girls up stairs are up, praying and singing."

"But it is three o'clock in the morning ; and these are not the voices of our girls, as you well know."

But W. arose, and went to search. He found the girls asleep. He looked from the windows ; all around was still and calm. The pure moonlight flooded the garden and the road ; not a human being could have been anywhere near and unseen. W. returned to his bed, but not to sleep ; not until the morning broke did those mysterious voices grow silent. But they entreated all the night in vain ; for W. hardened his heart, then and afterwards. He would never listen with patience to any serious mention of the sounds which had caused him so much uneasiness when he heard them. It is not known that he ever after was personally importuned to set his face heavenward. Probably he then made his final choice, and the fear is that he will be allowed to abide by it. "My Spirit shall not always strive with man."

"Neither are your ways my ways, saith the Lord." —A good old man had several sons, none of whom were Christians. When he had, for years, tried every means for their conversion, but without effect, he prayed in his sorrow that as his life had failed to exert the right influence upon his children's hearts, he might be favored with a death so triumphant and happy that they should, by *that*, be won to enter the service of Christ. Soon after this, the faithful father was taken sick, and it was apparent that he was about to die. As he drew near to his last hours, his reason tottered, and was overthrown ; and then this saintly man, this loving Christian father, began horribly to rave. He uttered all the bitter language of despair, and went out of the world cursing and swearing in a most shocking manner.

"What an answer to a Christian's prayer for a triumphant death!" cries the reader; but *wait*. Was not the parent's desire for the salvation of his sons? Well, the young men were stricken with conviction of sin as they listened to the ravings of their dying father.

"If our father, who has lived so just and blameless a life, feels thus, and is permitted thus to fear and suffer, *where* shall *we* stand in our dying hour?"

These were the thoughts that seized upon them; and not one of them was able to rest day or night until he "looked unto Jesus," and was set free from condemnation. Their father's death *was* made the means of their conversion, though not *in the way* which he had marked out. God does things in His own time, and in His own way.

Reporter Converted.—Rev. W. P. Corbit, in his sermon to Firemen in the Academy of Music, New York, stated that one Sabbath evening a young man went to the house of God for the purpose of preparing an article for a notorious paper that assailed the church of God frequently. He went to the house of God for the first time. The minister who conducted the exercises noticed him, and prayed that he might have assistance to make effectual the word of God, and took for his text "I am not ashamed of the Gospel, for it is given of God for salvation to every one that believeth—to the Jew first, also to the Greek." In the progress of his sermon his heart glowed with holy fire and with eloquence as he described the power of the Gospel in saving the souls of men. The reporter began to tremble; his cheek paled when the minister of Christ announced that there may be some one here to-night who, like the persecuting Saul of Tarsus, might be arrested in his career, and sent out a flaming herald of the very cross which now he despised; his head fell and conviction deep and powerful seized on him. He left the sanctuary, and began to exhort his companions to forsake their evil ways and give their hearts to God; but they turned their backs on him and deserted him. He went to his father's house, and the old man spurned him from the door; but, blessed be God, the church of Jesus Christ opened her arms and bade him welcome. He was soon licensed to preach, and did go forth absolutely a flaming herald of that very cross which he had despised.

The Prodigal and his Bible.—The only son of a pious widow in the northern part of England proved ungrateful for her care, and became her scourge and her cross. He finally went to sea. When his mother took her leave of him she gave him a New Testament, inscribed with his name and her own, solemnly and tenderly entreating that he would keep the book, and read it for her sake. He was borne far away upon the bosom of the trackless deep, and year after year elapsed, without tidings of her boy. After the lapse of some years, a half-naked sailor knocked at her door, to ask relief. The sight of a sailor was always interesting to her, and never failed to awaken recollections and emotions, better imagined than described. She heard his tale. He had seen great perils in the deep, had been several times wrecked, but said he had never been so dreadfully destitute as he was some years back, when himself and a fine young gentleman were the only individuals, of a whole ship's crew, that were saved. "We were cast upon a desert island, where, after seven days and nights, I closed his eyes. Poor fellow, I shall never forget it." And here the tears stole down his weather-beaten cheeks. "He read day and night in a little book, which he said his mother gave him, and which was the only thing he saved. It was his companion every moment; he wept for his sins, he prayed, he kissed the book; he talked of nothing but this book and his mother; and at the last he gave it to me, with many thanks for my poor services. 'There, Jack, said he, 'take this book, and keep it, and read it, and may God bless you—it's all I've got.' And then he clasped my hand, and died in peace." "Is all this true?" said the trembling, astonished mother. "Yes, madam, every word of it." And then, drawing from his ragged jacket a little book, much battered and time-worn, he held it up, exclaiming: "And here's the very book, too." She seized the Testament, descried her own handwriting, and beheld the name of her son, coupled with her own, on the cover. She gazed, she read, she wept, she rejoiced. She seemed to hear a voice, which said: "Behold thy son liveth." Amidst her conflicting emotions, she was ready to exclaim: "Now, Lord, lettest thou thy servant depart in peace, for mine eyes have seen thy salvation." "Will you part with that book my honest fellow?" said the mother, anxious now to possess the precious relic. "No, madam," was the answer, "not for any money, —not for all the world. He gave it me with his dying hand. I have more than once lost my all since I got it without losing this treasure, the value of which, I hope, I have learned for myself; and I will never part with it till I part with the breath out of my body."

"Father Hull" at the Ball.—"Father Hull," now deceased, was a preacher of the old school, S. C. Conference. Passing along the highway one evening, in a strange, wicked country, he called at a good-looking house for lodgings. Weary and faint, he sat him down by the fire-side. After a while, as night began to close in, companies of well-dressed gentlemen and ladies flocked into the room. One drew out his violin and commenced playing. Away scampered the youngsters, hopping and leaping. It was "a ball!" Here sat the stranger looking silently on. At length a partner was wanted, and one ventured up and asked Mr. Hull if he would take the floor. "Certainly, madam!" said he, rising and walking out on the floor, as he spoke; "but I have long made it a rule never to commence any business till I have asked the direction of the Lord, and his blessing upon it. Will you all join in prayer with me?" As he spoke these words, he fell on his knees and began to pray. Some kneeled, others stood, all petrified with astonishment. In the mean time, being a holy, faithful man, and peculiarly powerful in prayer, he seemed to draw the very heavens and earth together. Some groaned, some shrieked aloud, and many fell prostrate, like dead men, on the floor. In short, the dance was turned into a religious meeting, from which many dated their conviction and conversion, and the commencement of a powerful revival.

The Young Convert's Prayer in the Ball-room.—In one of the interior counties of Pennsylvania, a young man whom, for the sake of distinction, we shall call B——, was convicted of sin, and found peace in believing. He was the son of one of the most respectable and wealthy inhabitants of that region of country, but his father was unhappily a bitter opposer of the religion of Christ.

About this time a splendid *ball* was got up, with every possible attempt at display, and the youth of the village and surrounding country were all excitement for the festive occasion. B—— was invited. He at once declined attending, but his father insisted that he should go. The struggle was long and anxious. At length it was decided—*he determined to go.* His father rejoiced at his decision. His friends congratulated him on having abandoned his new notions and become a man again.

The evening at last arrived. The gay party were gathered in the spacious hall. There was beauty, and wealth, and fashion. The world was there. Every heart seemed full of gladness, every voice was one of joy. B—— appeared among the rest, with a brow that spoke the purpose of a determined soul. He was the first on the floor to lead off the dance. A cotillion was formed, and as the circle stood in the centre of the room, with every eye fixed on them, what was the astonishment of the company when B—— raised his hands and said, "LET US PRAY." The assembly was awe-struck. Not a word was uttered. It was as silent as the grave, while B—— poured out his heart to God in behalf of his young companions, his parents, and the place in which they lived. With perfect composure he concluded his prayer, and all had left the room *silently,* but *one.* A young lady whom he had led upon the floor as his partner, stood near him bathed in tears. They left the room together, and not long afterwards, she was led to the foot of the cross, having been first awakened by her partner's prayer on the *ball-room floor.* They were soon married, and are still living, active, devoted members of the body of Christ. B—— is an elder in one of the churches near the city of New York.

Awakened at the Gaming Table.—A gambler at Uxbridge, Mass., while sitting at the table with the cards in his hands, was smitten almost like Saul of Tarsus. He could neither hold the cards nor play the game. His companions urged him to take another glass of liquor to quiet his nerves. He refused, and leaving them at their games, he started for home, and found no peace until he felt an inward evidence of forgiveness.

How to Believe with the Heart.*—In visiting among my people one morning, a lady informed me that a physician in the village, with whom I had some acquaintance, was confined to his room by a severe cold, and his friends had some apprehensions that it might result in his death.

I immediately went to his room to see him, and found him on his bed. He assured me that he had no apprehensions of any other serious effects from his present indisposition, than confinement from his business for a few weeks. He said he was taken with an inflammation of the lungs, and had used such thorough means to reduce it, that it had left him very weak, but he thought he should soon recover.

After conversing with him upon the general subject of religion, I requested him to take the tenth chapter of Romans, and study it as he would a medical book, and give me his opinion of its meaning when I called again.

The second time I called, as soon as I was seated, he said to me, "I cannot understand that chapter you gave me to study, when you were here last."

"What part of it, doctor, don't you understand ?"

"That part that says, 'If we will confess with our mouth the Lord Jesus, and believe with our heart, that God hath raised Him from the dead, we shall be saved.'"

"Why, my dear sir, there is no hidden meaning to that passage ; it tells us a simple truth, and must be understood just like any other plain declaration."

"What then is it to believe with the heart ?"

This I illustrated by telling him that if his wife was in New York, and a man of established reputation should come from that city, and inform him that she lay at the point of death, he would be immediately convinced of the truth of the message, while his heart would wish that it was not so ; but if a subsequent messenger should arrive and inform him that his wife had passed the crisis in her disease, and was out of danger, the feelings of his heart

* The interesting cases of Conversions recorded from this to the 321 page inclusive, are selected from that excellent book, "Incidents in a Pastor's Life," by Rev. Dr. Wisner, published by Mr. Charles Scribner.

would sympathize with his intellectual convictions, or in other words, he would believe with the heart and the understanding.

On hearing this illustration, he lay for a short time absorbed in thought, and then inquired with earnestness, "Is this all?"

I told him this was my view of the meaning of a belief of the heart, and referred him to the passage in Acts, where, on the day of Pentecost, as many as gladly received the word were baptized and added to the church.

He replied, "If this is so, then salvation is much easier to attain than I have ever supposed."

I told him it was indeed so, and that sinners often rejected it on that account. They were looking for something mysterious and difficult, and when they were told that they had only to believe with the heart, like the Assyrian leper, they would go away disappointed, and often displeased.

The next time I called to see him, I found him much more unwell, but full of joy and peace. He seemed to believe with the heart, that God had raised his Son Jesus Christ from the dead, to be a Prince and a Saviour, to give repentance and remission of sins. He continued to sink rapidly under his disease, and in a few weeks closed his earthly career, rejoicing in the simplicity of the gospel of Christ.

The dreaded Visit.—There was in my congregation a public house, in which neither the landlord nor his wife were professors of religion. It was quite a resort for the thoughtless and profane, and I dreaded visiting the place, but conceiving it to be my duty, I nerved myself up to the task. I was respectfully received and invited into the sitting-room, where I found the tavern-keeper and his wife alone. I conversed with, or rather talked to them, about the interests of their immortal souls, endeavored to show them the responsibility of their station, and urged them to give immediate attention to the things which belonged to their peace. But could get no other answer than a promise from the landlord that he would think of it. I left the house with a heavy heart, feeling that I had done them no good.

They soon left the place, and I knew nothing of them until ten years after my visit, when I received a very kind note from the man, informing me that the conversation which seemed to be so little regarded, had resulted in the conversion of both himself and wife.

The Girl who was afraid of her Parents.—Among the individuals who were present, on a particular occasion, in one of my meetings for conversation, was a young woman who was in very deep distress. On inquiring the cause of her anguish of mind, she said she was a lost sinner, and was afraid of the wrath of God.

I inquired if she did not know that Jesus came to save lost sinners.

She replied that she did, and had long known that fact.

"And why then," said I, "do you not go to him and be saved?"

"I am a stranger in this place. My mother and her husband, who is my step-father, are both angry at me for attending these meetings, and if I should become a Christian they will turn me out in the streets."

"And is this all that keeps you away from Christ?"

"I think it is all that prevents me from being a Christian."

"But you must remember the words of the Lord Jesus, that those who esteem father or mother, or even their own lives, more than him cannot be his disciples; and that if you are more afraid of the displeasure of your earthly parents than you are of the righteous displeasure of God, you must remain in a state of condemnation and death."

"Oh, I cannot do that," she exclaimed, the tears streaming down her cheeks, "I cannot do that."

"Well, miss, you must either do that, or you must be willing to be cast out from house and home for Christ's sake."

She remained for some time in great agony of spirit, and then, with a smile of joy shining through a profusion of tears, said, "I will be the Lord's."

I asked her if she had counted the cost, and meant to adhere to her purpose, though it might expose her to all that she feared.

She said she thought she had, and felt that without any reserve or condition, she had thrown herself upon the mercy of her blessed Saviour.

She returned home that evening, and to her surprise and joy

found her mother in deep distress about her own salvation, and neither parent ever made any further objections to her serving the Lord according to the dictates of her own conscience.

I have never ventured to persuade sinners that the sacrifices consequent upon their becoming pious would be less than they feared, but have endeavored to show them that they ought to prefer suffering any amount of affliction with the people of God, rather than enjoy the pleasures of sin for a season.

The Infidel Bible Class.—When I first commenced my ministry in the city of * * * * I found that there was a large class of intelligent and influential men who professed to be infidels, and kept aloof from all the means of grace. Instead of going to church on the Sabbath they would usually meet together to strengthen each other in their loose sentiments. Feeling a strong desire to bring them under the influence of the Gospel, I gave public notice on the Sabbath that the next Lord's day evening I would state the evidences upon which I received the Bible as the word of God, and if any one chose he might, in the course of the week, send me, anonymously, his objections to those evidences, or might state the reasons upon which he founded his infidelity, and if the communication was respectful and not unreasonably long, I would read it on the following Sabbath evening to the congregation, and answer it. In the course of the week I received a well-written communication, impugning the evidences I had stated as those on which I rested the claims of the Bible to our belief, and some arguments in favor of infidelity.

On Sabbath evening, I found that my house was crowded, and that the individuals for whose benefit I had instituted this kind of meeting were there. I read the communication, and answered it as clearly as I was able, and gave liberty for the continuance of the same course every week until I should give notice to the contrary.

I continued in this way to receive and answer infidel objections through the winter, and had the satisfaction of finding that my labors were not in vain in the Lord. A number of that very class were convinced of the divinity of the Holy Scriptures, and were subsequently brought into the church.

The course which I adopted operated in the following manner.

1st. It convinced infidels that ministers did not wish to stand aloof from them or call them hard names, but that we are willing to meet them, and affectionately to reason with them.

2d. When they sat down to write out their objections to the Bible, and the religion which it teaches, they found that they had not as many arguments in support of their theory as they had supposed.

3d. When some of their leading spirits would send me a communication containing what they had all been in the habit of considering unanswerable arguments against the Bible, and they saw how easily such objections were disposed of and how ill they could bear examining in the light of truth, it shook their confidence in the wisdom of their leaders, and in their own safety and made them desirous of knowing more about the Christian religion.

4th. Last, but not least, it brought them under the influence of the gospel, which was made to many of them the power of God, and the wisdom of God, unto salvation.

The Working Card.—In the fall of my first year at * * * * my church became anxious that we should have a protracted meeting, or some special effort for the salvation of sinners. For various reasons, which I need not mention here, I was opposed to a protracted meeting at that time, but in the course of the week I prepared the following card :

RESOLUTIONS,

Adopted by the bearer of this Card.

1. *Resolved*, That as I am a sinner, redeemed by the blood of Christ, I will do all that I can to save the souls for whom he died.

2. *Resolved*, That to prepare myself to do good to others, I will strive to have the same mind in me which was in Jesus Christ.

3. *Resolved*, That I will from time to time select from among my neighbors some one or more individuals with whom I will, in tenderness and affection, labor steadily, daily, if possible, or even many times a day, until God shall either bring them to Christ, or I shall be convinced that I should give them up.

4. *Resolved*, That I will carry those with whom I thus labor on

my heart, and pray for them continually, and with them frequently, if they will permit me so to do.

5. *Resolved,* That while I labor and pray for the salvation of sinners, I will depend alone on the Holy Ghost to make me successful in my work.

I had enough of these cards printed to supply every member of the church with a copy, and on the next Lord's day distributed them, with the understanding that so long as any individual should retain his card he should consider himself bound by the resolutions, and when he wished to be released from them he must return the card to me.

The next night after the distribution I was called from my bed to go and visit a distressed sinner, which was a commencement of a work of grace that continued with us all the fall and winter, and resulted, as I trust, in bringing many souls to a knowledge of the Saviour.

The Family that had never read the Bible.—In the progress of a revival of religion in my congregation, in the winter of 1830 and 1831, one of the brethren, who was visiting families in a border settlement, went into a house where he found the woman alone. On conversing with her on her religious feelings, she told him that she did not know anything about religion. He inquired if she had never attended a meeting, or read the Bible ; she said she had not since she was old enough to remember anything about it.

He then commenced giving her a brief account of the Creation, and of the fall of man, and of the plan adopted by God for his recovery. When he had proceeded as far as the fall, and its consequences upon the human family, and told her that she was herself, in consequence of it, a sinner against God, and as such exposed to his wrath in hell to all eternity, she became deeply distressed with a sense of her lost condition, and wept bitterly.

He next told her of the provision which God had made for her salvation, and exhorted her to repent and believe on the Lord Jesus Christ, that she might be saved. On hearing this she became composed and happy, and requested him to wait until she went and called her husband, adding that he needed this Saviour as much as she did.

He did wait, and when the husband came in, found him almost as ignorant as the wife, and repeated to him the epitome of the Bible history, apparently with the same effect which it had produced on the woman. He spent most of the afternoon with them in prayer and conversation, and when he came away left them both hoping in Christ.

I visited the family soon after myself, and found them hoping, and anxious to learn all that they could about the Bible, neither of them being able to read. They continued attentive to all the means of grace, and in process of time became members of the church, dating their hope back to the visit above mentioned.

They did not remain in the place a great while after they united with the church, but while they remained with us gave us no reason to doubt the sincerity of their profession, or the genuineness of their conversion.

The Woman who was afraid of her Husband.—A woman came into my meeting of inquiry in deep distress of mind, who I found upon inquiry was much alarmed about her condition as a lost sinner, but had been kept from the Saviour by fear of her husband.

I endeavored to show her that she should fear God and obey him, and then leave her husband where she had left her own soul—in the hands of the Saviour.

After a severe struggle in her mind, the Lord seemed to have caused her heart to receive the truth, and she became quiet and happy. But before she left the meeting she came to me and inquired what she should do. Her husband, she said, was a man of violent temper, and was desperately opposed to religion, and she felt really afraid to let him know what her feelings were.

I told her to go home, and as soon as she could see her husband alone, to tell him what she hoped the Lord had done for her soul, and to entreat him affectionately to go along with her in the service of her blessed Redeemer. This was just before I dismissed my meeting for dinner.

In the afternoon I had not been long in the meeting before this woman entered it with her husband, though he had never been in the habit of attending religious meetings. God had made the affectionate appeal of his wife like an arrow in his heart, which had left a wound that could only be healed by the blood of Christ. In the course of the afternoon, he, too, could rejoice in his Saviour, and went home with his wife to erect a family altar.

In a few weeks they both united with the church of which I was pastor, and up to the lastest knowledge I had of them, they were beloved and respected members.

Infidelity dreadful to the Awakened Sinner.—In 1826, when God was pouring out his Spirit on my congregation, there was living among us a young man of an active and enterprising mind, who, as he subsequently informed me, to get rid of the restraint imposed by the self-denying doctrines of the gospel, had tried to become a Universalist, but perceiving that the Bible was directly opposed to his new sentiments, had rejected the unaccommodating book, and become an infidel.

Until the revival had been in progress nearly a month, and more than one hundred were rejoicing in hope, this young man kept himself aloof from what he considered a foolish and a needless excitement. But on the 6th of December he was induced, by a sense of politeness, to accompany a lady, with whom he boarded, to an evening lecture.

He went to this meeting, however, with a full determination to keep his mind engrossed with worldly thoughts, and succeeded so well that, on his return home, he had no distinct recollection of any one truth that had been advanced.

After supper, the lady of the house, and a pious young woman who resided in the family, left the young man in the parlor, and retired to their own rooms in a distant part of the house, to have a season of prayer for the thoughtless boarder. While they were on their knees, pleading in a low tone of voice for him at the throne of grace, they were alarmed by a cry of anguish from the parlor. On repairing thither, they found the family Bible open upon the table, and the young man standing upon the floor with strong marks of agony upon his countenance. On seeing the ladies his pride rallied, and to the question, "What is the matter?" he was, as he afterwards told us, about to answer, "Nothing," but before the words had passed his lips, his heaving bosom gave vent to another cry of anguish, and he exclaimed, "Oh, I am an infidel, pray for me," and fell prostrate on the floor.

About 12 o'clock at night he requested that some of his companions of the legal profession, for he was a lawyer, might be sent for, that they, seeing his anguish, might escape the hopeless abyss into which he had fallen. At two in the morning I was called from my bed to visit him. Upon entering the room I found him upon his knees; not attempting to pray, but sustaining himself by a chair, and giving vent to the anguish of his lacerated bosom. I approached him and inquired the state of his mind, but only received the answer, "I am an infidel! I have denied my Saviour, and am now given up of God to eat of the fruit of my own doing." His soul seemed sunk in despair, while the shiverings of a strange, unearthly horror, which ran through his frame, had so prostrated his muscular powers, that he was unable to stand without support. After giving him some instructions from the word of God, and praying for him, I left him under the care of some judicious friends, and returned home.

The next evening there was a meeting of inquiry, at which there were some seventy or eighty persons, and among them was the despairing young lawyer, who came, supported by two friends. Here I again endeavored to lead him to Christ, but to every overture of mercy he would reply, "These provisions were once for me, but I have rejected them. I have sinned away my day of grace. I am an infidel!"

In this state of mind he left the meeting, and continued to tremble under a fearful looking-for of judgment and fiery indignation from the presence of the Lord, until 11 o'clock that night, when his obdurate will was humbled by the Spirit of the Lord; and the heart-rending groans of the convicted infidel were exchanged for the joyful song of the child of God.

His transition from the bitterness of a hopeless sinner, to joy and peace in believing, was sudden; but his joy, instead of being like the morning cloud and early dew, has been like the light which is shed upon the path of the just, shining more and more. He has been a pillar in the church twenty-four years, and for more than fifteen a ruling elder.

A Remarkable Revival.—The following is a brief narrative of a work of grace which occurred in the experience of Rev. William Wisner, D.D., in the winter of 1826 and 1827 :

For two years next preceding the time above mentioned, there had been fewer conversions to Christ, and less deep seriousness in our village, than at any time since my coming to that place.

In the latter part of June, arrangements were made for celebrating the fourth of July in the usual manner, but a few Christians, feeling that they could not enjoy such a celebration, resolved to meet by themselves, and observe the day as a season of thanksgiving to Almighty God for our great national blessings.

This measure was severely censured by some of the people, and many predicted a thin attendance at the sanctuary. One prominent member of my congregation remarked, that the pulpit would accommodate all who would wish to attend. But notwithstanding all the opposition, and ill-natured remarks, when the day arrived, the sanctuary was crowded at an early hour, and though seats were brought into the aisles, the congregation could not all be accommodated, and the gentleman who had predicted that the pulpit would hold all that would attend, was not only deprived of a seat, but could not get further than the door of the vestibule, where he stood on his feet through the whole service, a deeply attentive hearer of the discourse.

In the course of the next day, the general conversation in the street, and in the places of public resort, was the religious celebration of the fourth of July. Though some affected to despise it, the most were convicted in their hearts, that to be consistent we should either renounce our belief in our obligation to God for our national independence, or regard the day as a thanksgiving to him. Conversing with a lawyer, who was a prominent man in the political celebration, he said to me, "I am convinced that Christians ought to observe the day as you have, but those who have no religion will long keep it in the other way."

From this day the conversation through our village was more on the subject of religion than it had been for a long time. The people seemed to feel that if Christians regarded religion of sufficient importance to have it govern them in their public festivities, it was time for them to inquire whether they could do without it.

A female prayer-meeting, which had been neglected for many months, was revived, and a youth's prayer-meeting was established and kept up once a week. Our stated prayer-meetings were well attended, and a spirit of earnest and agonizing prayer began to prevail among the members of the church.

Our prayer-meetings now became more frequent, and when two or three Christians would meet together accidentally, or on business, they would generally spend a few moments in prayer. By the fifth of November there were sixty-five indulging hope, and some thirty-eight were added to the Church.

From this Sabbath the work seemed rapidly to decline, and continued to do so until the enemies of religion began to rejoice aloud that the excitement, as they called it, was over, and only a few young people and children had been affected by it.

On the next Sabbath I preached, with an aching heart, from the text, the triumphing of the wicked is short. At the close of the exercises, Monday was appointed as a day of humiliation and prayer, and when it came, it found the whole church with one accord in one place. Tuesday and Wednesday the little church continued instant in prayer. That evening, November 29th, at our weekly Wednesday evening lecture, two or three individuals requested the prayers of God's people, and that night one of the leading physicians in the place obtained comfort from the Lord. The next morning, as we were a few of us met at his house for prayer, his wife requested us to pray for a sister of his, who was up stairs in deep distress of mind. While we were on our knees praying for her, that she might be brought to submit herself to God, and put her trust in the crucified Saviour, she came down so full of joy and peace, that she wished us to return thanks to the Lord for snatching her as a brand from the burning. She told us that she had resisted the strivings of the spirit, and had rejoiced when she thought the revival was over ; but now she could not be thankful enough that God had not given her up to walk in her own way.

A new impulse was now given to the work. Friday and Saturday were days of much fervency of prayer, and several were brought to submit themselves unto God. On Monday evening, at my meeting of inquiry, the room was crowded with anxious sinners, and two precious souls, we had reason to hope, were in that meeting delivered from their bondage to Satan.

The next morning, as I was going into a house where the man and his wife were the night before convicted of sin, a young man came running across the street, and in great distress threw his arms around me, and besought me to pray for him. I told him I could not do so there, but I would meet him in thirty minutes at Mr. Herrick's, a merchant who had recently been converted to Christ, and pray for him. I went into the house where I had intended to visit, found the man and his wife both without hope, and told them they might meet me in half an hour at the place I had appointed for the young man. I went immediately to Mr. H.'s, and told him we would a few of us be at his house at nine o'clock, to spend an hour in prayer. I then notified two or three Christians of the meeting which I had thus unexpectedly appointed, and at nine we commenced praying with three or four, or perhaps half a dozen, Christians, and four anxious persons. As soon as we began to pray, the Spirit of God seemed to come down with great power, and three of the four anxious persons soon began to rejoice in the Lord. "When these things were noised abroad the multitude came together," and in a short time two good-sized rooms, which opened into each other, were crowded to overflowing. The Spirit continued present with his regenerating influence, and many who came to see what was doing, went away rejoicing in Christ.

At noon I endeavored to send the people away, but they would not be persuaded to disperse, and the whole day was spent in prayer and religious conversation.

When the evening came I sent them home, but not until I had promised to meet them there the next morning at nine o'clock.

That evening we had a prayer-meeting in the court-room, which was much crowded and very solemn, and several there indulged a hope of pardon and eternal life. At nine o'clock the congregation was dismissed, and we returned home with more of a disposition to pray than sleep.

Wednesday morning at nine, I met the congregation again at brother H.'s, but the assembly, by the time I arrived, was so large that we were obliged to remove to the court-house, which was filled to its utmost capacity with Christians and anxious sinners. The whole congregation of the impenitent were by this time ready to acknowledge that this was the work of the Lord, and each one felt a deep interest about his soul. We remained here, with an hour's intermission, until nine at night, when the congregation were again reluctantly sent away.

The next morning we met at the sanctuary to observe our annual State thanksgiving. The house was so greatly crowded at an early hour, that though it was large, and the aisle supplied with benches, all could not be seated. An awful solemnity pervaded the whole assembly, and for a time the only noise that was heard was the half-suppressed sobs which now and then escaped from an overburdened soul. Through the remainder of the week, the court-room was crowded from nine in the morning until nine at night with praying and inquiring souls, and very many of our leading citizens were brought to put their trust in the Lamb of God.

From the last week in September until the last week in January, there were about three hundred hopeful conversions in my own congregation, and two hundred and twenty of them became members of the Presbyterian church of which I had the charge.

There was no re-action at the close of the work, but its sweet savor remained, and was a blessing to all. I do not believe that there were three impenitent sinners in the place who would not at any time within a year, have rejoiced to have had just such another work of grace.

The Unconscious Convert.—Among the prominent members of my congregation was the leading physician of the place. He was the son of a Quaker, and though he had retained enough of the peculiarities of that sect, to be able to ward off the truths of God from his conscience, he had not enough of their commendable morality to keep him from becoming a notorious horse-racer and a gambler.

His wife was a superior woman. She was well educated, and had an independent mind, and mourned over his pernicious habits. Notwithstanding the influence of her husband, she was brought, by the grace of God, to indulge a hope in Christ, and presented herself to the session, and was approved and ordered to be received, with a number of others, on the next Sabbath.

On Saturday afternoon, she told her husband that she had been examined, and, if he had no objections, intended to make a public profession of religion. He said he had objections to her taking such a step. She told him to state them, and if she could feel that they would relieve her from her obligation to Christ, she would defer uniting with the church until they could be removed. He replied that he was dissatisfied with our confession of faith. She then got the compendium to which the candidates were required to assent, and read it article by article, and when she had got through, he told her to go on. She told him she was at the end, and had read all to which the candidates were required to give their assent. He said it could not be that she had read the whole of that confession, which I used on the admission of members. She assured him she had read every word, and requested him to examine it for himself. He left the room without saying a word, and she had no more conversation with him that evening. He was unhappy, but knew not why, and endeavored to avoid company.

Some time in the evening a man called to have him go a few miles out of town, to visit a sick woman. He sent the messenger on ahead, that he might ride alone, as he did not wish to converse with any one. While he was riding through the woods, thinking about the character of Jehovah, as he had heard it preached in the sanctuary, and explained by his pastor in private conversation, all on a sudden the subject was presented to his mind in such a manner, that he began to be filled with delight in its contemplation. "Surely," said he to himself, "such a God ought to be loved, and his moral government submitted to and delighted in," and then he was filled with joy and peace. But soon it occurred to him, that he was the enemy of this God, and might probably remain His enemy to all eternity, and be cast out from His presence. This made him unhappy. But then he thought it would be right in God to deal with him according to his sins; and then the glory of the divine perfections would fill his mind, and banish all thought of himself, and he would again be filled with joy and peace. In this way his mind alternated between joy, in view of the divine perfections, and a dread of remaining God's enemy, until he had prescribed for the sick woman and returned home.

He went to the church next morning with his wife, and saw her join herself to the Lord in an everlasting covenant, and became so delighted with the plan of salvation, that he could scarcely think of himself at all, but did not have the least suspicion that his heart had been changed, until the middle of the week, when he began to hope that he had been born again. At the next communion season, he, with thirteen other young converts, openly took the covenant of God upon himself, and became an active member of the church.

After a suitable trial, he was chosen and ordained a ruling elder, and for many years was one of my efficient helpers in bringing souls to Christ. He still lives, and is an elder in a Presbyterian church.

Fatal Advice.—In the winter of 1826, a gay and thoughtless girl from the city of New York came to reside in our village; and as her parents were members of my congregation, she came under my pastoral charge.

Soon after the arrival of the stranger, there was more than ordinary attention among my people, and she seemed to partake of the general seriousness that pervaded the circle in which she moved.

In all my instruction I endeavored to deepen her sense of guilt, and to show her that there was no help for such a sinner, but in Christ; and that the only way to avail herself of his aid, was by repentance and faith. Under this instruction she became more rationally and feelingly convinced of her lost and perishing condition; and I began to hope that she was not far from the kingdom of God. But while she was in this state of mind, she was visited by a very good young man, who, finding her much distressed, and exceedingly anxious to know what to do to obtain comfort, told her, "she must pray to God to forgive her sins, and He who heard the young ravens when they cried would hear her."

The young brother called soon after to see me, and frankly told me that he had been to see C——, and had advised her to pray.

"What," said I, "did you tell her to pray before she gave up her opposition to God?"

"Yes, I told her to pray, that God would forgive her sins, and have mercy upon her."

"And where, my dear brother, do you find any warrant in the Scriptures for such advice to an awakened sinner?"

"Does not the Apostle say that he 'will that men pray everywhere'?"

"Yes, but he adds in the same verse, 'lifting up holy hands, without wrath and doubting.' The prayer which the Apostle recommends is that which flows from a benevolent heart, and is offered up in faith."

"Well, did not Peter advise Simon to pray, that the thoughts of his wicked heart might be forgiven him?"

"Yes he did, but he told him to repent first of his great sin. This is my objection to your advice; you did not tell her to repent first, or believe first, but to pray while her heart was rankling with enmity against God. She has been wanting to do something beside repent and believe on the Lord Jesus Christ, and I am afraid you have supplied this want to the injury of her soul!"

"But do YOU never tell impenitent sinners to pray?"

"Yes very often, and show them their guilt for neglecting prayer, but I at the same time endeavor to show them, that to approach God in any other way than through faith in Christ, will only add insult to guilt. Jesus said when he was on earth, "No man cometh to the Father but through me," and for us to encourage sinners to offer up prayer in any other name, or without faith in Him is only leading them out of the way of life."

The young brother seemed to perceive his error, but was little relieved in his feelings, when he learned that the young woman had found relief in the prayer which she had offered and was full of joy

My own fears were not allayed by this change. I rather expected it, and trembled for the issue. I thought I knew something of her temperament, and of her bad instruction, and was afraid she would rest on her prayers instead of Christ.

She appeared joyful and happy a few weeks, and I began almost to hope, that my fears were groundless ; but as soon as the excitement occasioned by the novelty of her position had passed away, her interest in religious things began to decline, and she soon returned to her former course of life.

The Daily Prayer-meeting.—At a time when there was no special attention to religión in my congregation, I suggested to my elders the plan of having a daily prayer-meeting in one of the basement rooms of our church, through the fall and winter. They were pleased with the suggestion, and we adopted the following regulations, etc. : The janitor was to open the house, and keep the room warm, from nine in the morning until twelve, and from two in the afternoon until four. Any Christian who felt that he would like to spend a little time, within those hours, in prayer, was invited to go to that place, and if there should be no one there, to kneel down alone and plead with the hearer of prayer, to pour out his Holy Spirit upon our city, and if there were any there, to spend the time in united prayer with those assembled for the same object. All had the privilege of remaining as long or as short a time as they pleased.

The impenitent were informed of the meeting and invited to attend it, at any time, and at all times, when they wished to be where the people of God were assembled to pray for them.

The result of this arrangement was, that there were usually two or three Christians on their knees in that place, pleading the promises, that where that number should meet in Christ's name, he would meet with them, and that when they should agree, touching anything they might ask, he would do it for them. If a brother or a sister had only time to unite in one season of prayer, they would join that little circle, and if an impenitent sinner wished to hear the voice of prayer, he or she would visit that place. I used to go there as often as I could, and usually found from one to fifteen or twenty engaged in prayer, and oftentimes a number of impenitent persons, whom the Lord had directed to our little BETHEL.

The Almighty heard the prayers which were constantly going up from that place, and shed down his Spirit like the dew upon the mown grass, and like gentle showers that water the earth, and our basement room became the birth-place of souls, as well as a place of refreshing to the people of God. This plan consumed but little time, broke in upon no business arrangements, created no unusual excitement, and made no noise ; and yet was a means in the hand of God of strengthening the graces of his children, and of bringing many souls home to their Heavenly Father. Though there was at no time what would be called a powerful revival, yet there was a gentle work of grace going on in my congregation through the entire period of our meeting ; and its precious influence upon the church and society was visible for a long time, and, I have no doubt, was an occasion of joy among the angels in heaven.

The Woman who kept out of the Way.—In 1815, while spending a Sabbath in a place where they had no stated preaching, I put up with a deacon in the church, whose sister-in-law had come from a neighboring town to spend the Sabbath with him. She was a gay, thoughtless girl of about eighteen years of age. Knowing that her widowed mother was a pious woman, and felt anxious about her daughter, I wished to have some personal conversation with her before she went home. She seemed to be aware of my intention, and so entirely avoided me, that I had no opportunity of speaking to her, until she was ready on Monday morning to return home. When she started, I accompanied her to the door, and as I assisted her to get on her horse, I told her that I was deeply concerned for her soul ; I felt that she was in imminent danger, and entreated her to remember her Creator now in the days of her youth. She made me no answer, but rode off, and I felt that I had lost an opportunity of doing her good.

About a year afterwards, I was sent for to administer the sacrament to that church, and after the preparatory lecture, the deacons told me there was a candidate to be examined, whom I found to be the young woman who had so skillfully avoided me on a former occasion.

On inquiring what it was that first called up her attention to her lost condition, she informed me that it was the few words I said to her when helping her on her horse. That they rung in her ears all the way home, and deprived her of rest until she found it in Christ. Her successful evasion of a more deliberate conversation, was doubtless employed to bring a brief word home the more forcibly to her unguarded heart.

The Conversion of a little Child.—In the congregation where the writer was first settled, there was a little boy who had been consecrated to God in baptism at eight days old, and carefully taught the great truths of religion, as fast as his opening intellect was capable of understanding them. He never knew a day when his parents did not bend the knee morning and evening in family prayer, and had no recollection of the first time he was carried to the house of God ; nor could he remember when he did not know that he was a lost sinner, and that Jesus Christ was crucified for his salvation.

When this child was a few days short of five years old, his father took him in his arms and carried him to our Wednesday evening conference and prayer-meeting. That evening I read a chapter in the Bible, and after I had lectured upon it, gave all present an opportunity to ask questions in relation to the subject of the discourse ; when, to my surprise, the little boy, with great modesty and much feeling, made several inquiries respecting the meaning of the chapter, in a way that satisfied me he was making application of its truths to his own case.

After meeting, his father took him in his arms and carried him home, when the boy remarked that he was very glad he had been to the meeting, it made him feel so very happy.

From that evening the child appeared as if " old things had passed away, and all things had become new." His closet was his chosen retreat, in which he spent much time, and where he experienced some sore temptations from the adversary of souls. He frequently came from his place of prayer with his eyes filled with tears, and told his mother the joys or sorrows he had experienced there. When playing with his young associates, if they used bad language, he would reprove them with tears, and leaving them return to his quiet home.

At thirteen he united with the church of Christ, and has now been for sixteen years preaching the gospel, and has been a means in the hands of God of bringing hundreds to Christ.

A Revival resulting from an Oversight.—A congregation in Central New York was thrown into great disorder, and for years had its influence for good paralyzed by a quarrel between two of the leading families in the village. Various efforts had been made to settle the difficulty without effect, when the church, with the consent of the contending parties, agreed to submit the whole matter to a number of ministers not belonging to that presbytery, of whom I was one. But as the council belonged to other presbyteries than the one with which that church stood connected, on calling for the commission under which we were to act, to our surprise we were informed that their presbytery had not even been consulted on the subject. We at once agreed that we had no power to act officially in the matter, but recommended to the church and the parties, to unite with us in a season of prayer, for the gracious interposition of God's Spirit. All seemed to fall in with this proposal, and we adjourned from the place which was intended as the arena for a desperate conflict between the brethren, to a place where prayer was wont to be made. As this was about ten o'clock in the morning, we continued at the throne of grace until twelve, when we had a recess for dinner. After dinner we re-assembled, and engaged again in our supplications for the restoration of peace and love to that afflicted church. In a short time one of the contending parties came forward, and with many tears confessed that he had been awfully guilty, and begged the forgiveness of God, of the other party, and of the church, for his unchristian conduct. As soon as he sat down, the other party came and insisted that he was the guilty originator of the trouble, and that if his brother had done wrong, it was in consequence of provocations which he had given, and he wished the forgiveness of his brother, and of the church, and of God. The two principals having thus been brought to repentance, those who had become their partisans followed their example, and for a long time we sat there hearing brethren who had been engaged in an unholy strife, confessing their sins one to another, and praying one for another.

That prayer-meeting was not only the end of contention between those two families, but the commencement of a revival of religion in that place, during which many souls were, in the judgment of charity, converted to Christ.

" Compel them to Come in."—There lived in my congregation a lawyer of eminence in his profession, and of strictly moral habits ; but who was wholly devoted to his business, and heedless about the things which belonged to his eternal well-being. In a time of refreshing from the presence of the Lord, while a number of us were engaged in a prayer-meeting, I observed that one of my elders rose up suddenly and left the house. His mind, as he afterwards told me, became deeply impressed with the guilt and danger of the lawyer of whom I have been speaking, and he resolved to make one effort for his salvation. In accordance with this resolution, he went directly to the office, where he found the man whom he sought, at the writing-table, deeply engaged in preparing for court. The elder, after the common salutations, said, " Mr. I., I want you to go with me to Mr. H.'s." " What for ?" inquired the man of the bar. " We have a prayer-meeting there," said the elder, " and I want you to attend it." " Oh," said the lawyer, " I cannot possibly do that, my business is crowding me, and I must attend to it." " Your business," said the elder, " is of no importance in comparison with the salvation of your immortal soul, which you are exposing to the miseries of hell, by every moment's delay." This plain address, with the solemn and earnest manner in which it was delivered, overcame the lawyer's resolution to continue at his business, and in a few moments they both entered the prayer-meeting. We were engaged in prayer when they came in, and as soon as there was an opportunity, the elder said to me, " Mr. I. has come to this meeting, and I request an interest in the prayers of this assembly for the salvation of his soul." As it was very evident from the appearance of Mr. I., that he had no objection to the proposal of his friend, we knelt down and united all our hearts in one voice, to plead for the soul of a man who hitherto had no disposition to pray for himself. The Lord heard our prayers, and before the close of the meeting, the lawyer indulged a hope in the grace of God, through his long-neglected Saviour.

At the next communion, he, with more than seventy others, united with the church. He was subsequently chosen, and ordained, to fill the office of a deacon; in which capacity he served the church till the day of his death, which occurred about twenty years subsequent to the time of his attending this prayer-meeting.

The Infidel without a Resting Place.—Walking one day in the village where I was laboring, I met a man who I knew openly avowed himself an infidel. After the usual salutations, I said to him, "Well, Mr. B., what is the condition of your soul this morning?"

His answer was, "Oh, I am an infidel."

"I know that, Mr. B., but as a man of reflection, who understands what infidelity is, you will not pretend to me that you know the Bible is not the word of God." After a few moments' reflection, he replied, "I acknowledge that I do not know that it is not, but I do not believe it is." "Well, Mr. B., if the Bible should not be the word of God, can you be sure that there will not be just such a state of retribution beyond the grave as the Bible describes?"

"No, I am sure of nothing beyond the grave, but I do not believe there will be any retribution."

"Then, Mr. B., your reason compels you to admit, that you cannot know but, living and dying as you are, you will go to hell, and be as miserable there, to all eternity, as the Saviour represented the rich man to be."

"It is true, I can be certain of nothing beyond the grave, whether I shall exist at all there, or if I do, what will be my condition is a mere matter of conjecture."

"Keep this in mind, Mr. B., when you lie down and when you rise up, that you do not know but you shall go to hell when you die, and if you can rest with the possibility of such an end, your mind is differently constituted from mine."

We parted, and he went about his business, but, as I afterwards learned, never enjoyed any peace until he indulged a hope in Christ. In a few weeks he united with the Baptist church.

Dared not go Home before he Repented.—At a time of unsual interest in my congregation, an intelligent and well-educated boy of twelve years came to one of my elders, in great distress of mind, and inquired what he should do. The elder inquired what made him feel so distressed. The lad replied that he saw he was a great sinner in the sight of God, and was afraid that he should go to hell. He was then told that he must go home and read the Bible, and pray to God to give him a new heart.

The boy replied, with deep emotion, "Sir, I am afraid if I wait to get home, I may die by the way, and then it will be too late."

The elder felt reproved by this simple illustration of his bad counsel, and told the young inquirer that, if he was afraid to go home in his sins, he must then repent and believe in Christ, and submit himself into his hands. The boy complied with this last advice, and went home rejoicing in hope. At a suitable time, he made a public profession of religion, and has now been a member of the Presbyterian church for thirty years, and is proving the genuineness of his conversion by a well-ordered life and conversation.

Christ our Advocate.—A young lady from a neighboring town called on me, one afternoon, to inquire what she must do to be saved. I pointed out the way of salvation to her as well as I knew how, but she could find no relief to her troubled spirit.

In spite of all I could say to her, she would still cleave to the notion that she must make some progress in reform before she came to Christ.

I preached a lecture that evening to my people from 1 John ii. 1 —"We have an advocate with the Father."

In the course of my sermon, I endeavored to show my impenitent hearers what they must do if they would have Christ for their advocate, by referring to the practice in courts of justice, where a man, who employed a lawyer to prosecute or defend his cause, must give the entire management of the matter into his hand. I told them this was true of the great *advocate with the Father*. While he offered himself freely to all, he would engage for none who would not leave their soul's salvation entirely in his hands. If they would meddle with it at all, he would leave it with them, but if they would trust it with him, he would appear for them before the great white throne and be their advocate and intercessor.

After sermon, as I came down from the desk, the young lady met me, with joy beaming from her countenance, and, clasping my hand in hers, she exclaimed, " Oh, I am happy! I am happy! I have found an advocate with whom I can trust my cause!"

A Great and Speedy Result.—In the year 1830, says the Rev. William Wisner, D.D., as one of our pious young men was reading a chapter in the Bible, to a number of children who were assembled on Sabbath afternoon for religious instruction, they became so impressed with the simple reading of the word of God, that many of them were weeping before the chapter was ended, and they all seemed deeply convinced of their lost and perishing condition. This was the visible commencement of a work of grace which spread through our whole congregation. We were soon obliged to have meetings for prayer and conversation every night, when there was not regular preaching; and, often at the close of our religious meetings, which were never held later than nine o'clock, a few of our young men would assemble at one of their offices, or counting-houses, and remain in prayer most of the night. For some time, the whole moral power of the sacramental host seemed to be brought into requisition, and to bear with its whole weight upon the ranks of the impenitent. Religion was the universal theme of conversation among the righteous and the wicked, and whenever two or three Christians would meet together casually, or on business, they would not part until they had a season of prayer. There was no visible opposition to the work, all seemed convinced that it was of God, and to feel that it would be a fearful thing to be found fighting against him. Two or three left the place to get rid of the importunity of their Christian friends, and to be away from the atmosphere of religion.

On the first communion after the commencement of this precious work, one hundred and forty-four persons stood up in the sanctuary and avouched Jehovah, Father, Son, and Holy Ghost, as the God, Redeemer, and Sanctifier, of their undying souls. The season was one of overwhelming interest—it was a season of communion with Christ, and with a great company of redeemed souls, who had been recently brought into his kingdom. The young converts were rejoicing in the freshness of their first love, while older saints were sympathizing with the angels around the throne of God, over those who had recently been brought to repentance.

After the administration of the symbols of the broken body and shed blood of Christ, the communicants, with one accord, besought me to repeat the ordinance the next Sabbath, which I consented to do upon the condition that they would devote the whole week to prayer and labor for the salvation of those who yet remained impenitent. In the course of that week there were about seventy who indulged hopes, and, on the Sabbath following, about fifty more added to the church. The ordinance was repeated a third time, and, according to my present recollections, thirty more were added to the church.

At the close of this blessed work, there were more than eight hundred communicants, and only eighteen adults who did not indulge a hope in Christ, in a congregation where, fourteen years previous, there were only twelve credible professors of religion.

The True Way to put Godly Men in the Professions.—When I first took charge of the church in * * * *, all the prominent men were living without God in the world. Among this class were our two leading physicians, who, by their horse-racing and gambling, and ungodly conversation, were poisoning the morals of the rising generation, and encouraging those of riper years in the way of sin.

I felt very deeply the deleterious influence which these two men were exerting; and seeing no other remedy, I besought the Lord to send us a pious physician, that our people might have the privilege, when sick, of having a man to attend them, who, instead of having his mind filled with the race-course and the card-table, would be under the influence of the fear of God. My heart was greatly set on this thing, as a blessing I thought indispensable to the interests of religion in that place. But while I was praying for it, to my inexpressible joy the Holy Spirit came down and reclaimed the two wicked ones, and brought them into the church, and made them active and successful in counteracting the evil which they had been doing in the community. The ablest of the two, in due time, was chosen as one of our ruling elders, and became a most efficient helper in the work of the Lord.

If the Hearer of my prayer, in answering my petitions, had sent me my pious physician, we should still have had the influence of these two prominent men to contend against; but in his better way we were relieved from this evil influence, and had two pious physicians instead of one, and men who possessed the confidence of the people, instead of a stranger, who would have had for a long time but a limited influence among us.

A Remarkable Answer to Prayer.—In 1829, I was invited by the pastor of a church in a village about twenty miles from my own parish, to come out and assist him for a few days in a special effort for the salvation of his people. He thought there were indications for good in his congregation, and had made up his mind to have preaching every evening, together with prayer-meetings and family visiting through the day.

I took one of my elders with me, and went to the house of my brother, agreeably to his request. He had made an appointment for me to preach that evening. The congregation was large and solemn, and there were some indications of the special presence of the Holy Spirit. That evening my elder led our devotions in family prayer, and poured out his soul in great fervency for the conversion of sinners. He earnestly besought the Lord that he would so trouble the impenitent that they would feel constrained to awaken us in the night to inquire what they should do to be saved. After prayer we retired to rest, but about midnight the pastor came into our room and awoke us, to tell us that a number of sinners had collected at the academy, who were so distressed with a sense of their lost condition, that they had sent a request for us to visit them. On repairing to the place, the pastor and my elder, for I was not well enough to go out at that hour, found the principal of the academy, with a large number of the scholars, and some other persons, assembled to inquire what they must do to be saved. The next morning there were a number rejoicing in hope, and many more deeply bowed down under a sense of their sins. We remained there a few days, and had the pleasure of seeing many proud hearts apparently humbled at the foot of the cross.

It was the Lord who taught my brother thus to pray, and it was the Lord who answered that prayer. If Christians lived in habits of communion with God, would not his Spirit more frequently teach us what to pray for, and more frequently give us the very blessings which we ask ?

The Promise Fulfilled.—In John vii. 38, we have the following precious promise : "He that believeth on me, as the Scripture hath said, out of his belly shall flow rivers of living water."

In this passage water is the emblem of the salvation of Christ, and the promise, when divested of its figurative dress, is, that when we exercise a living faith in Christ, salvation will flow from us in broad streams like rivers.

I have often dwelt with pleasure upon this sweet promise, and have seen it fulfilled, in the providence and grace of God, but have never witnessed a more delightful exemplification of its truthfulness than in the case of an old man, who lived and died in my congregation. He had a very numerous family when he came to Christ, and received the waters of life ; or, according to the figurative language of the preceding verse, came to Christ to drink. Very soon, in answer to his prayers, and through the blessing of the Lord upon his judicious labors, his wife and five sons, and five daughters, were brought to indulge a hope in the Redeemer. The oldest son had three boys, who lived to be men, and were all Christians ; one of them is now a devoted minister of the gospel, who is turning many to righteousness. The second son died soon after his conversion, and as he lived at a distance from me I am unable to trace his history. The third son, though a feeble young man, was an active Christian, and though he was laid in an early grave, I know of many individuals who owned him as their spiritual father. The fourth son had two children, who were both members of the church. Though I am unable to trace the particular history of the other children, from what I know of the family, it would be safe to say that each of the ten streams, issuing from the pious efforts of this old man, doubled in the next generation, while some of them, in the life-time of their parents, became a broad river. Now, if we were capable of following these streams, as they flow on from generation to generation, we should find them widening and deepening, until they should not only become broad rivers but inland seas, losing themselves in the ocean of redeemed souls, who will fill the area of glory at the right hand of the Saviour at the judgment of the great day.

I have only in this estimate noticed the success of this old man in his own family, but it did not stop here. He lived to a good old age, and while he lived was a burning and shining light to all around him, and was, through every year of his Christian life, a means of turning some souls to Christ. Reader, the man whose history I have so far traced, was a plain man, of no more than ordinary talents and common education. There is no reason why you should not emulate his example, and hope for his success.

Sinners live to no Good Purpose.—An intelligent and interesting physician of strictly moral habits, called upon me one morning in my study, and told me he had come to have a little conversation on the subject of religion. I told him I was always pleased to see him, but was peculiarly so when I knew that he wished to converse upon the things which belonged to his peace. On making some inquiry respecting his feelings, I learned that he had been sick; had considered himself, and was considered by his attendant physician, for some days, to be in a critical state, but, by the blessing of God upon the means used, he was soon able to be about again. During his sickness he had no particular anxiety about himself; but when he was able to return to his office, while entirely alone, the inquiry came up to his mind, "What good purpose will be answered by your restoration to health?" This question, which seemed to come without inviting, brought his whole past life up before him, which, though it had been orderly, and what the world calls moral, he saw had been a life without God, and that his fellow-men had been none the better for his having lived among them. He felt that there was no portion of his past life which would afford him pleasure in the hour of death, and that if what remained of it was to be spent as the past had been, he might as well have died with his last sickness as to have been restored to health again. This train of thought, which was evidently caused by the operation of the Holy Spirit, convicted him of sin. He saw clearly that if his life had been a useless one, it had been a sinful one ; that, in the language of our excellent catechism, "The chief end of man is to glorify God and enjoy him forever," and as he had not made that the chief end of his life, he had not fulfilled the end of his being, and was an unfaithful cumberer of the ground in his Master's vineyard. His heart now became burdened with a sense of his guilt, and in the loneliness of his study he resolved to take the yoke of his Redeemer upon his neck, and learn of him who was meek and lowly in mind. He then knelt before God, and consecrated himself with all that he had to the service of that Saviour who came into the world to redeem sinners.

I questioned him with regard to his view of the sinfulness of his heart, the character of Christ, the ground of his hope, and the feelings which he had indulged since the change of his purpose, until I became satisfied that there was ground to hope that "old things had passed away, and all things had become new."

After some weeks he united himself to the church, and his subsequent life has fully justified the hope which I indulged for him at the interview to which I have alluded.

A Prompt Decision.—At a meeting of inquiry which I held at a time of general interest in my congregation, a young lady who had been anxious about her soul for many months, with whom I had been conversing, rose up suddenly and left the room. I could not account for this singular movement until I saw her return with a young friend, who had not attended my meeting before, during the progress of the revival. I sat down by the new comer and inquired into the state of her mind on the subject of religion. She told me that she had no special concern about herself, that she had been induced to come to the meeting by the solicitation of a young friend, and not by the promptings of her own heart.

"Are you not sensible that you are a great sinner in the sight of God ?"

"I am intellectually convinced of this fact, but do not feel it."

"Do you not know that as a sinner you are in a state of condemnation and death ?"

"I know I shall be condemned if I do not repent before I die."

"The Bible tells us that they who believe not are condemned already. The sentence of condemnation is passed upon you, and you are only waiting, like a condemned criminal, for the order of execution. How long God may suffer you to live in this condemned state, before the sentence shall be executed, is quite uncertain, but while He does spare you, it is to give you an opportunity to obtain a pardon."

"This is a new view of the subject, but it seems from the Scriptures it must be correct."

"Do you not remember that God has said in His word, 'Because sentence against an evil work is not executed speedily, therefore the hearts of the sons of men are fully set in them to do evil."

"I do, and I remember that you once preached from that text."

"Is not this your condition ? Does not your heart take encouragement from God's delay of the execution of His sentence to continue in impenitence."

"I am afraid it is even so, my sins are very great."

"Is not your conduct in this thing desperately wicked ? You are abusing the grace of God, by employing the time which He has given you to repent and obtain pardon, in sinning against Him."

"I feel that I am without excuse."

"God is yet waiting to be gracious, and it is my duty, as a minister of Christ, to offer you the pardon of your sins, and all the blessings which the Saviour has purchased for His people, if you will give your heart to Him. Will you accept of this offer, or will you reject it again ?"

"I am not prepared to give an answer at this time."

I then told her the offer was made to her by her Saviour, that I was only acting in His name, and in the nature of the case she must either reject or accept ; and I desired an answer, that she might know what she was doing.

She replied, "I am not prepared to accept, and I dare not refuse."

"Do you not see that you must either accept Christ now or reject Him again ?"

"I do see it, and feel it, too, and am truly sorry that I came to this meeting."

"Your staying away from the place of religious inquiry would not have relieved you from your responsibility, though it might have prevented you from seeing your guilt as you now see it. Every time through your life, when Christ has been presented to your mind, by preaching, reading, religious conversation, or meditation, you have rejected Him, and the guilt of all those accumulated acts is recorded on high, and I want to have you now determine whether you will reject your Saviour again, or here terminate your rebellion by submitting yourself to Him." She sat for nearly half an hour in deep thought, the agony of her mind evidently increasing all the time, when she said, "I will rebel no longer; pray for me that I may have grace to give myself up to my Saviour."

We knelt down together, and I offered a short prayer for her, but she remained on her knees, silently pleading for pardon, some minutes after I had ceased, and when she arose she came to me smiling through tears, and giving me her hand, said, "I hope I have given myself away to Christ, but I am afraid I may be deceived." At that moment she fixed her eyes on a young companion, who sat weeping in another part of the room, and running to her she caught her in her arms, and exclaimed, "Oh, Louisa! Louisa! I don't know but I am deceived about myself, but I know that Christ is willing to receive just such poor sinners as you and I are, and I do entreat you to go to him now while he is waiting to be gracious."

In a short time Louisa began to rejoice with her young friend; but the latter, while she spoke feelingly of the preciousness of Christ, would add to almost every sentence, "But I am afraid I may be deceived."

After she became a little composed in her feelings, I said to her, "Well, M——, if you should find on examining your heart, that you are deceived, what will you do ?"

"Oh," said she, "I will repent and give myself up to Him and put my trust in Him."

She soon became clear in her hope, and some time after made a profession of religion, and is now a reputable member of the church of Christ.

It is but a Moment's Work.—In a season of revival, in 1830, I found in my meeting of inquiry an old man upwards of seventy, who had for more than forty years been trying to find rest for his soul in the works of his own hands. Going about to establish his own righteousness, he had not submitted to the righteousness of God. I had been his pastor for fourteen years, and had during that time labored much with him in public and private. He was a constant attendant upon all our religious meetings, and was as exemplary in his outward walk as most Christians. He knew he could not be saved by his own works, but still hoped that his outward morality and inward anxiety would induce God to give him a new heart. After conversing with a number of other persons about their salvation, I came to this old man, and on saying a few words to him, I found him as usual, waiting for a new heart. I told him that I had labored more with him than with any other member of my congregation, and that it had done him no good; that he had lived through a number of revivals of religion, without deriving any benefit from them, and that I had made up my mind that he must then give himself up to Christ to be saved by him, or I must give him up as an old sinner, who would not have Christ to reign over him. He seemed shocked at the thought of having his pastor give him up, and with deep anguish of mind entreated me not to abandon him as an incorrigible sinner. I told him that he was an old man, who from a child had known his Master's will, but refused to do it; that his heart was constantly growing harder, and his iniquities were multiplying; that he was then in the midst of a powerful work of grace; that his Christian friends were praying for him, and his pastor, as the ambassador of Christ, was entreating him to be reconciled to God, and it seemed to me, if he suffered the present season to pass without availing himself of offered mercy, there would be no hope in his case. He entreated me to pray for him; but I told him that unless he would repent of his sins, and give himself up to Christ, prayer could do him no good, and before I could pray for him, I must have him answer the question which I had so often put to him, viz.: "Will you now submit yourself, unconditionally, into the hands of the Saviour?" After a short, though terrible, conflict with his self-righteous heart, he answered, with many tears, "By the help of God, I will." I knelt by his side, and united with him in prayer. When he arose he was full of joy and peace.

That evening, at a prayer-meeting in the neighborhood, he got up and earnestly exhorted sinners to repent and submit themselves to Christ. "Don't put it off as I have done, but do it now, *it is only a moment's work.*"

He lived about ten years after this, an exemplary and active Christian, and when I visited him on his death-bed, I found him trusting in the sinner's Friend.

Forsaking All that she Had.—In the spring of 1844, a lady came to my meeting of inquiry in great agony of mind. On inquiring what it was that disturbed her so much, she answered that she was a lost sinner.

I told her that was indeed true, but Jesus Christ came into the world to seek and to save that which was lost, and if she was sensible of her perilous condition she should go to him.

She answered, with deep emotion, while the tears were streaming down her cheeks, that there was an insurmountable obstacle in the way of her coming to Christ.

I inquired what that obstacle was which could keep her away from her precious Saviour.

She replied, "If I come to him, I must give up everything into his hands, and be willing to have him dispose of me and mine as he will; but my husband is an impenitent man, and is very dear to me, and I am not willing to give him up. He is the idol of my heart."

"My dear Mrs. D., can you take your husband out of his Maker's hand, or in any way benefit him by staying away from Christ, and thus destroying your own soul? Would it not be better for you to give yourself up to him, and in this way put yourself in a position to pray for your husband, and by your pious example lead him to the Saviour ?"

"Yes, this would be my best course ; but how can I do this, while my heart cleaves to the partner of my bosom, and I cannot give him up ?"

"But you have just admitted that he was in the hands of the Lord, and that your rebellion against your Maker could do him no good : why then should you encourage him in sin by your example ?"

"I know it is all wrong, but my husband lies so near my heart that I cannot give him up. I feel that he is my idol."

"Well, madam, you see that one of three things must then take place—either you must give up your husband, or God must take him away, or your own soul must perish."

"I know it is so ! I see it ! I feel it in my heart, and that is what distresses me."

"Well, madam, if one of these things must take place, you should make up your mind accordingly, and, as a wise woman, choose now which of the three you will prefer. If your husband stands in the way of your salvation, will you give him, with your own soul, up to Christ ? Or must he be removed out of your way ? Or will you perish ?"

She remained silent for some time, her bosom convulsed with sobs of anguish, and then, with a countenance full of joy, exclaimed, "Oh, I can give up my husband, and my own soul, too, into the hands of my blessed Redeemer. I will submit, I will be his !"

I prayed with her, and advised her to go home and examine herself, to see that her surrender was an honest and a whole-hearted one, and that her trust was alone in the mercy of God, through the blood of the Cross.

In a short time after this interview with the wife, the husband indulged a hope in Christ, and at the next communion they were both, with, as near as I can now recollect, forty others, received into the church.

Six years have since passed away, and she who feared to give up her husband is, with him, walking in the fear of the Lord, and in the comfort of the Holy Ghost.

The Woman who had no Feeling.—At a time when the Lord was pouring out his Spirit upon my congregation, I observed one morning, in my meeting of inquiry, a young lady, who was not in the habit of attending my church. I sat down by her, and told her I was happy to meet her in that place, and hoped she had come to inquire the way to her Saviour.

She replied, "I have no particular anxiety about myself. I came here this morning to gratify a friend, who was very anxious that I should accompany her to your meeting."

"But how is it, my dear girl, that you have no anxiety about yourself? do you not know that you are a lost sinner?"

"O yes, I know I am a sinner, and I know too, that if I do not become a Christian I must perish; but some how, I cannot feel any particular anxiety about my situation."

"Do you not know that Jesus Christ is just such a Saviour as you stand in need of; and that he has been waiting long, and is waiting this morning, to save your guilty soul from condemnation and eternal ruin?"

"Yes, I know it, but what can I do without feeling?"

"You can act like a rational and accountable being, with whom God has a controversy, and to whom He is making overtures of mercy. You can contemplate your lost condition, and look at the terms upon which Jesus Christ will interpose in your behalf."

"But I have always understood that we must be awakened and convicted, before we can be converted, or become Christians."

"But are you not accountable this morning, for the manner in which you treat your precious Saviour?"

"Yes, I suppose I am."

Is He not this morning waiting to be gracious to you; and does He not tell you that now is the accepted time?"

"Yes; but is it not true, that I must have more feeling than I now have, before I can become a Christian?"

"The Bible does not tell us how much we must feel in order to become Christians, but it does tell us, "To-day, if we will hear Christ's voice, not to harden our hearts, by refusing his overtures of mercy.'"

"My heart is so hard already, that religion makes but little impression upon my mind."

"Well, my child, you admit that your want of feeling does not release you from responsibility to your righteous Sovereign, and it cannot absolve me from the duty of laying the Gospel message before you. I must, therefore, as an ambassador of Christ, beseech you in his name, to be reconciled to God. Will you give up your controversy with your Maker, and become reconciled to Him this morning?"

Here she became more serious, and inquired with evident emotion, "What shall I do?"

"You know what you ought to do, and I will tell you what you must do. You must either accept Christ, as he is offered to you in the gospel, and go home a child of God; or reject him again, and go away in a state of condemnation, with his wrath abiding on you."

She now appeared to feel the full weight of her responsibility, and with tears exclaimed, "What shall I do?"

I told her that her duty was plain, and the question, whether she would go away a justified child, or a condemned sinner, must be decided by herself, and would be decided before she left the house.

I left her to make up her mind, and conversed with some other anxious persons; but before I dismissed the meeting, I returned to ask her, what answer I should give to him who sent me, when, to my great joy, I found her full of that peace which the world cannot give nor take away.

The Infidel Lady.—Returning from the funeral of a child in the city of * * * *, in 1831, I met at the house of a friend, a widow lady of middle age, and of more than ordinary intelligence. After a little general conversation, I alluded to the funeral I had been attending, and inquired whether she felt herself prepared for that great change which we must all of us sooner or later experience.

After a few moments' hesitation, she replied to my question by saying, that she was an infidel, and did not receive the Bible as the word of God.

After conversing with her long enough to satisfy myself that she had read the Holy Scriptures, and was acquainted with the common arguments which infidels have used against them, I inquired whether she believed in the existence of an infinitely wise and good God.

She replied that she did, and thought that the Bible gave a truthful account of his perfections.

I then inquired, "Do you believe that we were all created by this God?"

She replied, "Certainly I do; I believe we are all the creatures of His power." I then said to her, "Madam, as you appear to have read the Bible, will you tell me whether an unshaken belief in its divine origin, and a cordial reception of the religion which it inculcates, would not be calculated to make men better and happier, even in this world, than such a belief as you cherish?"

She answered, "It must be so; the Bible requires men to love their neighbors as they love themselves, and to do unto others as they would have others do unto them; this would make good members of society; and the belief that they were going to heaven when they died would make them happy."

"You have answered truly. The moral code of the Bible, if believed and obeyed, would regulate, in the most perfect manner, all our intercourse with each other; while its rich and precious promises, if received and relied on, as coming from God, would elevate our affections, raise us above the world, and make us happy here. But if the Bible is not a revelation from God, as it professes to be, it is one of the most impious compilations of falsehood that men have ever attempted to palm upon the world; and yet, according to your own admission, a holy, wise, and good being has formed an entire race of intelligent creatures, with such minds that a belief in this impious and lying book, will make them better and happier than to believe the truth."

She remained silent for some time, and then, with considerable feeling, replied, "I have never before thought of this subject in this light."

A short time after this conversation I preached an evening lecture in the neighborhood where this woman resided. After the public exercises, I gave notice that if there were any who wished to converse with me about their own spiritual condition, they might remain after the congregation had withdrawn. To my great joy, this widow was one who tarried for conversation. She had become convinced that she must give up her belief in the being and perfections of God, or deny what her own judgment and observation, as well as the history of the world, told her was the tendency of a belief in, and a cordial reception of, the word of God, or she must renounce her infidelity. The two first she could not do, and she had done the last; and was come to inquire what she must do to be saved. She felt that her infidelity had resulted from a depraved heart, rather than from an enlightened mind, and trembled for herself as an undone sinner. I pointed out to her, as plainly as I could, the way of salvation. I told her that Jesus Christ had come to seek and to save that which was lost; and if she would submit to him and accept of his offered mercy, she would be accepted.

After a few days she indulged a hope in Christ, and at the next communion united herself with the people of God, and for years afterwards, I knew her as a consistent Christian, adorning the doctrine of God her Saviour, by a well-ordered life and conversation.

A Word Spoken in Season.—When on a journey for my health in 1812, on a hot, sultry day, I called at a farm-house in one of the beautiful towns in Berkshire county, Mass., to procure a drink of water. There happened to be no one in the house but a young lady, apparently about sixteen years of age, to whom I was introduced by my travelling companion, and from whom I received a glass of that refreshing and healthy beverage, which flows in such rich abundance from the hills of New England.

As I arose to depart I took her hand, and said, "Permit me, my dear girl, before I leave you, to inquire whether you have yet given your heart to your precious Saviour?"

She replied in the negative, while the tear that stole down her cheek showed that she was not without feeling.

I then said to her, "My child, I am a minister of Jesus Christ, and as such it is not only my duty, but my privilege, to offer you eternal life, upon the condition of your repenting of your sins, and putting your trust in him; will you accept of this offer?"

She answered with deep emotion, "I cannot decide that question now."

I said, "You will have to decide it now. Jesus Christ is beseeching you by me, to be reconciled to God, and if you do not choose to tell me what your decision is, He will take the answer from your heart, and it will be recorded in heaven, that you have either accepted the offer of eternal life made to you by your Redeemer to-day, or that you have rejected him again."

She seemed to take a new view of her fearful responsibility, and wept convulsively; but could not be prevailed on to tell me what her decision was.

After repeating some appropriate passages of Scripture, to show her her duty and her danger, I left her, expecting to see and hear of her no more, until we should meet at the judgment-seat of Christ.

Years afterwards, on stepping upon a steam-boat in New York to go to Philadelphia, my name being called by some of my friends on board, a gentleman came up to me, and asked if my name was Wisner. On being answered in the affirmative, he inquired if I had ever been in the town of ——, in Berkshire county. I told him I had passed through it in 1812. He then informed me, that when he was coming from home, a lady requested him, if he should meet me on his journey, to say, that she was the individual who gave me the glass of water—and what I had said on that occasion sunk so deep into her heart, that she could find no rest until she hoped she had closed in with the offer of her blessed Lord—and that she wished me to accept her thanks for what was to her, truly, "a word spoken in season."

"Man Deviseth his Way, but the Lord Directeth his Steps."—When the Rev. Dr. William Wisner was first licensed to preach the gospel, he had an invitation to become the pastor of a pleasant church in a beautiful village in Western New York. He had a beloved and respected clerical friend, who had retired from the ministry, living in the place, and made up his mind to accept the invitation. He started on horseback to visit the congregation, but on the first day's journey his horse calked himself, and became so lame that he was obliged to turn back to get another horse. This made it too late in the week for him to reach the place before the Sabbath, and he made up his mind not to start again till the next week. There was a little village twenty miles from his residence, in the edge of Pennsylvania, where there was no church, and no preaching, except that of two Universalist ministers who lived in the place ; and there had not been a sermon preached there by a Presbyterian or Congregational minister for more than three years. The missionaries all shunned the place, because the population was so inveterately Universalist that they would not hear them. As he had been called there, while at the bar, to try an important ejectment cause, he thought that the novelty of hearing a lawyer preach would bring the people out to hear him, and resolved to spend his unappropriated Sabbath in that place. He went, accordingly, and having no expectation that he would get them out more than once, prepared himself to show them, in a single discourse, the total depravity of the human heart, the remedy which God had provided for fallen man, and the certainty of the eternal perdition of those who did not avail themselves of that provision. The congregation, as he expected, was large, and the Lord rolled the love of souls into his bosom, and he preached under the solemn impression that the eternal life or the eternal death of the great portion of that congregation might depend, under God, upon that single sermon. The people were attentive, and knowing, as he did, that the Universalist ministers would soon catch away the good seed, if it did not take deep root in the heart, he felt that everything depended on the influences of the Holy Ghost.

In the afternoon the congregation was still more crowded and solemn, and the preacher dwelt much upon the unwillingness of sinners to come to Christ, and the necessity of their being born again.

In the evening the house was again crowded and solemn, and some were affected even to tears, and during the last singing he made up his mind to spend one more Sabbath in that wicked place.

The next Lord's day there were evident tokens of the divine presence. One young lady and a little girl of twelve years old, were indulging a hope, and a very hardened man, who had been a Universalist, was under deep conviction of sin. Though his desire was strong to go to the place to which he had been invited, he felt constrained, by the indications of providence, to decline that invitation, and continue to labor where the Lord had set him at work.

Here he continued to labor, and the Lord continued to bless his efforts for the salvation of that people, and a little church of thirty-one members was in a few weeks gathered from among those who had been taught from their youth to believe that all men would be saved.

Though the church was too poor to think of supporting a pastor, and all who were not converted were too much opposed to the truth to render them much assistance, he continued to labor in that place for three years, partly supporting himself, and partly supported by the Hampshire and Connecticut missionary societies.

Return of a Prodigal.—As I was engaged, one cold winter morning, in conversing with a number of awakened sinners, in my meeting of inquiry, the door was opened, and a poor, bloated inebriate, thinly clad, came in trembling with the cold, and took his seat near the stove. When I had conversed with all the rest who were present, I sat down by the stranger, and inquired what his object was in visiting our meeting. To my inquiry he gave me, in substance, the following answer: "I am a poor, unhappy man ; I have been, for some years, in the habit of intemperance ; a short time since I became offended with my father, quarrelled with my wife, and left my parents and my family with the intention of returning to them no more. I came to this place without money, pawned my overcoat for my supper and lodging last night, and on hearing the bell ring this morning, and learning that there was a meeting of inquiry here, I have come to see if there is yet mercy for such a man as I am."

"Do you feel that you are a lost sinner, and justly deserve the wrath of a holy God ?" I inquired.

"I know I am. I have been religiously brought up, have a praying father, and a good wife ; but I have made a brute of myself, and have abused and forsaken my best friends."

"Have you drank anything this morning ?"

"I have not."

"Do you mean to give up drinking altogether, and be a sober man ?"

"That is my purpose, the Lord helping me."

"Do you feel your need of a Saviour?"

"I do."

"Are you willing now to forsake your sins, and give yourself up into the hands of the Redeemer to be his forever?"

"That is the desire of my heart."

The time having now come to close our meeting, I prayed for the poor inebriate, and making an appointment for a meeting in the afternoon, I took the stranger home with me to dinner. After we had dined, I learned that he was the son of a deacon in the Presbyterian Church, with whom I was acquainted, and at whose house I had spent a night soon after I was licensed to preach the gospel. I furnished him with money to redeem his coat, and kept him in my family until he indulged a hope in Christ; and then paid his fare, and put him on board the stage to return to his afflicted family.

I have subsequently heard that he got home safe, and was a reformed man, and gave his friends reason to believe that he had a good hope through grace.

The Man who was Hired to go to the Prayer-meeting.—At a time of some special interest among our people, a member of the church, who was a mechanic, had a journeyman in his shop who never went to meeting in the week time, and seldom on the Sabbath. His employer was distressed about him, and one evening endeavored to persuade him to attend the prayer-meeting. His excuse was that he could not afford to lose the time, he could earn fifty cents while he would be at meeting, and that was too much for a poor man to throw away. To overcome the influence of this hope of gain, the employer told him if he would go that evening, he would give him fifty cents for his time. The journeyman accepted the offer, and went with his employer to our little prayer-meeting. He was an Englishman, and had never attended meeting much in this country, and had, I think, never been at a prayer-meeting before in his life. He became very much interested in the meeting, and the next evening neither wanted to be paid or persuaded to attend. In the course of two or three days he became deeply interested in view of his lost and perishing condition, and attended our meeting of inquiry to know what he should do to be saved. He felt that he was the chief of sinners, and could not conceive how a holy God could ever forgive him. I referred him for encouragement to the case of Paul, who tells us that he was the chief of sinners, and yet obtained mercy, because he did it ignorantly through unbelief; but when he heard this, instead of taking encouragement from it, he wept bitterly, and said that he could not plead ignorance, as Paul did, for he believed the Bible to be the Word of God, and believed that Jesus Christ was the Son of God, and yet he had, from his childhood up, rejected him, and sinned against him with a high hand. I then told him that the blood of Jesus Christ cleansed from all sin, and if he would apply to his blessed Saviour by faith, though his soul might, by reason of its iniquities, be red like crimson, it should be made white like snow. This seemed in come measure to calm his troubled spirit, but it was several days before he could take hold on Christ as his Redeemer, but when he did he was full of joy and peace.

As soon as he found a resting-place for his own soul, his heart began to travail in pain for the companion of his bosom, and he would give himself no rest until she too was rejoicing in hope.

He still lives, and is a consistent member of an evangelical church, and furnishes an encouragement to Christians to do all that they consistently can to bring careless sinners under the means of grace. Though the method resorted to by my brother was quite a new measure, yet God seemed to smile upon it, and that half dollar was probably the means of saving a precious soul from death, and hiding a multitude of sins.

Christ's Yoke.—At one of my stated Wednesday evening lectures, I discoursed to my people from the words of the Saviour in Matt. xi. 29 : " Take my yoke upon you and learn of me ; for I am meek and lowly in heart, and ye shall find rest unto your souls, for my yoke is easy and my burden is light."

At the close of the lecture, I invited those who had made up their minds to take Christ's yoke upon them, to meet me in the basement room of the house immediately after the benediction.

When I entered the room where I had appointed to meet them, I found six individuals, who professed to have given themselves up to the Saviour that night. I examined them as carefully as I could, and thought they gave evidence of having taken Christ's yoke upon them, within the meaning of the text.

How beautifully the Lord illustrates spiritual things by temporal! He takes the objects with which we are familiar, to explain and enforce those duties which stand indissolubly connected with our eternal well-being. His figures, like illuminated diagrams, place the great truths of our holy religion so plainly and vividly before the mind, that the weakest intellect can discern their meaning, and the dullest imagination receive their impression. A man who was in the congregation at the time to which I have alluded, told me that the text made such an impression on his mind, that the whole of the next day, when he was alone and thinking on the subject, he would find himself involuntarily bowing his head, to place his neck under the yoke of Christ.

A Juvenile Home Missionary.—In my congregation, during a precious work of grace, there was a little boy of eight years old, who was among those who indulged a hope in Christ. Conversing with him in regard to his religious exercises, I inquired if he never got in the dark, and became afraid that he was not a Christian.

He replied, "Oh, yes; very often."

"Well, George, what do you do at such times?"

'Why, sir, I go to Christ and submit over again, and then I find comfort."

The little boy gave such evidence of a change of heart, that we received him into the church, but his parents soon removed into Michigan, and I did not hear from him in six years, when a man from the neighborhood where he lived gave us the following account:

The family settled in a new place, where there was no preaching, and no stated religious service of any kind. When George was fourteen years of age, he went through the settlement, and, by the consent of the parents, collected the children into a Sabbath school, of which he was for awhile superintendent and teacher; yet the school grew and prospered, and was the means of establishing the ordinances of the gospel in that place.

The Little Daughter's Request.—"A pious little girl," says Dr. Wisner, on one occasion, "who had a very hardened father in the gallery, took encouragement from the discourse, to go in search of her parent, and while her heart was lifted up to God for his salvation, she threw her arms around his neck, and with streaming eyes, and a voice almost choked with sobs, entreated him to go down and ask Christians to pray for his dying soul. The hardened sinner was overcome, and in compliance with the entreaties of his daughter, and under the strivings of the Holy Spirit, sent down in answer to prayer, he occupied the place pointed out for anxious and inquiring sinners, and went home that night with his child, rejoicing in the hope of the glory of God."

The Bible in place of the Bottle.—At a late meeting in New York, a gentleman said he was a witness for the solacing influence of the religion of Jesus Christ. Twenty years ago he was in the habit of serving the devil as faithfully as any man ever did. Often would he return home from the place of amusement "half seas over," but God had given him a pious wife, who watched her opportunity to work for his soul and for God's glory. The turning point of his life was one occasion when he went to look for the bottle which generally stood on a table, but instead of finding it, he lifted a Bible which his wife had placed there. Never could he forget that moment—that circumstance! He had never used the bottle since, and found the Bible a faithful companion under all weathers.

Conversion by Shipwreck.—At one of the prayer-meetings in Burton's old Theatre, Chambers street, a sailor in the parquette (a very old man) said that thirty-three years ago he called upon the Lord and found him near in a time of need. When his little bark was foundering, and he was lashed to a portion of the wreck, he cried out to God to take care of him, and he did so. Previous to that time he was as profane a swearer as ever stepped on the deck of a ship, but ever since then he had been preaching the Gospel, and was in hopes to meet all his shipmates in heaven, to which, God helping him, he was bound.

Jesus loves Idiots.—"*I have seen Jesus*," said a poor imbecile, who for many years had been the terror of his neighborhood, but who, under the Divine influence, had become a mild and gentle creature; "*I have seen Jesus*," was his only reply, to those who inquired what had induced a change so wonderful—and as the years passed on, and the love of Jesus showed itself in his every act, this single testimony to the power of the cross won many a stouter heart to yield to the blessed Redeemer.

"Does Jesus love foolish boy?" asked an idiotic lad of the Superintendent of the Idiotic Asylum, at Essex Hall, England. On being told that he did, the poor child could hardly contain himself for joy—"Jesus love, Jesus love me," he cried, "nobody love foolish boy before," and as time passed on, the consciousness of the love of Jesus made even the lack-lustre eye and grinning face of the boy to assume a look of intelligence, and his struggles to subdue the evil propensities of his wayward nature showed that grace had indeed found a lodgment in his heart.

The unfeeling Jailer Converted.—Two faithful preachers of the gospel in the ancient city of Philippi, delivered their message with such power and demonstration of the Spirit, that notable conversions took place, and great excitement spread among all the population. The opposers of religion were exasperated to fury. The preachers were dragged before the authorities, and in the language of an eye-witness who relates the story,—the multitude rose up together against them: and the magistrates rent off their clothes, and commanded to beat them. And when they had laid many stripes upon them, they cast them into prison, charging the jailer to keep them safely: who having received such a charge, thrust them into the inner prison, and made their feet fast in the stocks. And at midnight Paul and Silas prayed, and sang praises unto God, and the prisoners heard them. And suddenly there was a great earthquake, so that the foundations of the prison were shaken, and immediately all the doors were opened, and every one's bands were loosed. And the keeper of the prison awaking out of his sleep, and seeing the prison doors open, he drew out his sword, and would have killed himself, supposing that the prisoners had fled. But Paul cried with a loud voice, saying, "Do thyself no harm, for we are all here." Then he called for a light, and sprang in, and came trembling, and fell down before Paul and Silas, and brought them out, and said, "Sirs, what must I do to be saved?" and they said, "Believe on the Lord Jesus Christ, and thou shalt be saved, and thy house." And they spake unto him the word of the Lord, and to all that were in his house. And he took them the same hour of the night, and washed their stripes; and was baptized, he and all his, straightway. And when he had brought them into his house, he set meat before them, and rejoiced, believing in God with all his house.

A Father and his Friends Praying.—A gentleman in Boston had an impenitent son in Vermont, for whose salvation he felt extremely anxious, and calling on some of the brethren of the church, made known to them his feelings, and requested them to go with him and pray that his son might be converted to God. He prevailed on his brethren, and they joined him in prayer.

Not long after this, his son knocked at his father's door in Boston; his father went to the door, and his son, on seeing him, exclaimed, weeping, "I have come to see you, that you might rejoice with me for what the Lord has done for my soul." His father inquired at what time his mind was first arrested. He replied, on such an evening, about eight o'clock. His father remembered it was the same time at which he and his brethren engaged in prayer for his son, and he greatly rejoiced with him in the goodness of God.

"I Know What is the Matter."—A gay, dissipated young man went one day to his pious mother, and said, "Mother, let me have my best clothes, I am going to a ball to-night." She expostulated with him, and urged him not to go, by every argument in her power. He answered, "Mother, let me have my clothes, I will go, and it is useless to say anything about it." She brought his clothes; he put them on, and was going out. She stopped him, and said, "My child, do not go." He said he would; she then said to him, "My son, while you are dancing with your gay companions in the ball-room, I shall be out in that wilderness praying to the Lord to convert your soul." He went; the ball commenced; but instead of the usual gaiety, an unaccountable gloom pervaded the whole assembly. One said, "We never had such a dull meeting in our lives;" another, "I wish we had not come, we have no life, we cannot get along;" a third, "I cannot think what is the matter." The young man instantly burst into tears, and said, "I know what is the matter; my poor old mother is now praying in yonder wilderness for her ungodly son." He took his hat, and said, "I will never be found in such a place as this again," and left the company. To be short, the Lord converted his soul. He became a member of the church—was soon after taken ill—and died happy.

The Conversion of Abigail Hutchinson.—"She was," says President Edwards, "of a rational, intelligent family; there could be nothing in her education that tended to enthusiasm, but rather to the contrary extreme. It is in no wise the temper of the family to be ostentatious of experiences, and it was far from being her temper. She was, before her conversion, to the observation of her neighbors, of a sober and inoffensive conversation, and was a still, quiet, reserved person.

"She was first awakened in the winter season, on Monday, by something she heard her brother say of the necessity of being in good earnest in seeking regenerating grace, together with the news of the conversion of the young woman before mentioned, whose conversion so generally affected most of the young people here. This news wrought much upon her, and stirred up a spirit of envy in her towards this young woman, whom she thought very unworthy of being distinguished from others by such a mercy, but withal it engaged her in a firm resolution to do her utmost to obtain the same blessing; and, considering with herself what course she should take, she thought that she had not a sufficient knowledge of the principles of religion to render her capable of conversion; whereupon she resolved thoroughly to search the Scriptures, and accordingly immediately began at the beginning of the Bible, intending to read it through. She continued thus till Thursday, and then there was a sudden alteration, by a great increase of her concern, in an extraordinary sense of her own sinfulness, particularly the sinfulness of her nature, and the wickedness of her heart, which came upon her (as she expressed it) as a flash of lightning, and struck an exceeding terror upon her. Upon which she left off reading the Bible in course as she had begun, and turned to the New Testament, to see if she could not find some relief there for her distressed soul.

"Her great terror, she said, was that she had sinned against God; her distress grew more and more for three days, until (as she said) she saw nothing but the blackness of darkness before her, and her very flesh trembled for fear of God's wrath. On Saturday she was earnestly engaged in reading the Bible and other books, and continued in it, searching for something to relieve her, till her eyes were so dim that she could not distinguish the letters. She came the same day to her brother with the countenance of a person in distress, expostulating with him why he had not told her more of her sinfulness, and earnestly inquiring of him what she should do. She seemed, that day, to feel in herself an enmity against the Bible, which greatly affrighted her. Her sense of her own exceeding sinfulness continued increasing. On the Sabbath she was so ill that her friends thought it not best that she should go to public worship, of which she seemed very desirous; but when she went to bed on Sabbath night, she formed a resolution that she would, the next morning, go to the minister, hoping to find some relief there. As she awaked on Monday morning a little before day, she wondered within herself at the easiness and calmness she felt in her mind, which was of a kind which she never felt before. As she thought of this, such words as these were in her mind: "The words of the Lord are pure words, health to the soul and marrow to the bones;" and then these words came to her mind—"The blood of Christ cleanseth from all sin;" which were accompanied with a lively sense of the excellency of Christ, and his sufficiency to satisfy for the sins of the whole world. She then thought of that expression—"It is a pleasant thing for the eyes to behold the sun;" which words then seemed to her to be very applicable to Jesus Christ. By these things her mind was led into such contemplations and views of Christ as filled her with exceeding joy. She told her brother in the morning that she had seen (i. e. in realizing views by faith) Christ the last night, and that she had really thought that she had not knowledge enough to be converted; but, said she, God can make it quite easy! On Monday she felt all day a constant sweetness in her soul. She had a repetition of the same discoveries of Christ three mornings together, that she had on Monday morning, and much in the same manner at each time, waking a little before day, but brighter and brighter every time.

After this there happened to come into the shop where she was at work, three persons that were thought to have been lately converted; her seeing them, as they stepped one after another into the door, so affected her, and so drew forth her love to them, that it overcame her, and she almost fainted; and when they began to talk of the things of religion, it was more than she could bear—they were obliged to cease on that account. It was a very frequent thing with her to be overcome with a flow of affection to them that she thought godly, in conversation with them, and sometimes only at the sight of them.

She had many extraordinary discoveries of the glory of God and Christ; sometimes in some particular attributes, and sometimes in many. She gave an account that once, as those four words passed through her mind, WISDOM, JUSTICE, GOODNESS, TRUTH, her soul was filled with a sense of the glory of each of these divine attributes, but especially the last.—Truth, she said, sunk the deepest! and, therefore, as these words passed, this was repeated, TRUTH, TRUTH! Her mind was so swallowed up with a sense of the glory of God's truth and other perfections, that she said it seemed as though her life was going, and that she saw it was easy with God to take away her life by discoveries of himself.

She once expressed herself to one of her sisters to this purpose, that she had continued whole days and whole nights, in a constant ravishing view of the glory of God and Christ, having enjoyed as much as her life could bear. Once as her brother was speaking of the dying love of Christ, she told him that she had such a sense of it that the mere mentioning it was ready to overcome her.

Once when she came to me, she told how that at such a time she thought she saw as much of God, and had as much joy and pleasure as was possible in this life, and yet that afterwards God discovered himself far more abundantly, and she saw the same things that she had seen before, yet more clearly, and in another and far more excellent and delightful manner, and was filled with a more exceeding joy.

She often expressed a sense of the glory of God appearing in the trees and growth of the fields, and other works of God's hands. She told her sister that lived near the heart of the town, that she once thought it a pleasant thing to live in the middle of the town, "but now," said she, "I think it much more pleasant to sit and see the wind blowing the trees, and to behold in the country what God has made."

She was wont to manifest a great sense of her own meanness and dependence. She often expressed an exceeding compassion and pitiful love which she found in her heart towards persons in a Christless condition, which was sometimes so strong, that as she passing by such in the streets, or those that she feared were such, she would be overcome by the sight of them.

After this her illness increased upon her; and once when her brother mentioned to her the danger there seemed to be that her present illness might be the occasion of her death, it filled her with joy that almost overcame her. At another time, when she met a company following the body of one departed to the grave, she said it was sweet to her to think that they would in a little time follow her in like manner.

Others were greatly moved to see what she suffered, and were filled with admiration at her unexampled patience. At a time when she was striving in vain to get down a little food, and was very much spent with it, she looked upon her sister with a smile, saying, "O sister, this is for my good!" At another time, when her sister was speaking of what she suffered, she told her that she lived a heaven upon earth for all that. She used sometimes to say to her sister, under her extreme sufferings, "It is good to be so." Her sister once asked her why she said so. She replied, "Because God would have it so; it is best that things should be as God would have them; it looks best to me.

She was very weak a considerable time before she died, having pined away with famine and thirst, so that her flesh seemed to be dried upon her bones, and therefore could say but little, and manifested her mind very much by signs. She said she had mattei enough to fill up all her time with conversation, if she had but strength. A few days before her death some asked her whether she held her integrity still. Whether 'she was not afraid of death. She answered to this purpose, that she had not the least degree of fear of death. They asked her why she would' be so confident. She answereed, "If I should say otherwise, I should speak contrary to what I know ; there is indeed a dark entry that looks something dark, but on the other side there appears such a bright shining light that I cannot be afraid !"

She seemed to be dying for three days together ; but seemed to continue in an admirably sweet composure of soul, without any interruption, to the last, and died as a person that went to sleep, without any struggling, about noon, on Friday, June 27, 1735. She died chiefly of famine.

Conversion of Phebe Bartlett, a Child of Four Years.—She was born in March, in the year 1731. About the latter end of April, or the beginning of May, 1735, she was greatly affected by the talk of her brother, who had been hopefully converted a little before, at about eleven years of age, and then seriously talked to her about the great things of religion. Her parents now observed her very earnestly to listen to the advice they gave to the other children, and she was observed very constantly to retire, several times in a day, as was concluded for secret prayer, and grew more and more engaged in religion, and was more frequently in her closet, till at last she was wont to visit it five or six times in a day, and was so engaged in it that nothing would at any time divert her from her stated closet exercises.

She once, of her own accord, spoke of her want of success, in that she could not find God, or to that purpose. But on Thursday, the last day of July, about the middle of the day, the child being in the closet where it used to retire, its mother heard it speaking aloud, which was unusual, and never had been observed before ; and her voice seemed to be as of one exceeding importunate and engaged, but her mother could distinctly hear only these words (spoken in her childish manner, but which seemed to be spoken with extraordinary earnestness and out of distress of soul) : "PRAY BLESSED LORD, give me salvation! I PRAY, BEG, pardon all my sins!" When the child had done prayer she came out of the closet, and came and sat down by her mother, and cried out aloud. Her mother very earnestly asked her several times what the matter was before she would make any answer, but she continued crying, and writhing her body to and fro, like one in anguish of spirit. Her mother then asked her whether she was afraid that God would not give her salvation. She answered, "Yes, I am afraid I shall go to hell!" Her mother then endeavored to quiet her, and told her she would not have her cry; she must be a good girl, and pray every day, and she hoped God would give her salvation. But this did not quiet her at all—but she continued thus earnestly crying for some time, till at length she suddenly ceased crying and began to smile, and presently said, with a smiling countenance, "Mother, the kingdom of heaven is come to me!" Her mother was surprised at the sudden alteration, and at the speech, and knew not what to make of it, but at first said nothing to her. The child presently spoke again, and said, "There is another come to me, and there is another—there is three;" and being asked what she meant, she answered, "One is, *thy will be done*, and there is another, *enjoy him for ever*;" by which it seems that when the child said there is three come to me, she meant three passages of her catechism that came to her mind.

After the child had said this, she retired again into her closet, and her mother went over to her brother's, who was next neighbor; and when she came back, the child being come out of the closet, met her mother with this cheerful speech, "I can find God now!" referring to what she had before complained of, that she could not find God. Then the child spoke again, and said, "I love God!" Her mother asked her how well she loved God, whether she loved God better than her father and mother. She said "Yes." Then she asked her whether she loved God better than her little sister Rachael. She answered, "Yes, better than anything!" Then her eldest sister, referring to her saying she could find God now, asked her where she could find God. She answered, "In heaven." Why, said she, have you been in heaven? "No," said the child. By this it seems not to have been any imagination of anything seen with bodily eyes that she called God, when she said, "I can find God now." Her mother asked her whether she was afraid of going to hell, and if it was that that had made her cry. She answered, "Yes, I was; but now I shall not." Her mother asked her whether she thought that God had given her salvation. She answered, "Yes." Her mother asked her when. She answered, "To-day." She appeared all that afternoon exceeding cheerful and joyful.

The same day the elder children, when they came home from school, seemed much affected with the extraordinary change that seemed to be made in Phebe; and her sister Abigail standing by, her mother took occasion to counsel her now to improve her time to prepare for another world; on which Phebe burst into tears, and cried out "Poor Nabby!" Her mother told her she would not have her cry, she hoped that God would give Nabby salvation; but that did not quiet her, but she continued earnestly crying for some time; and when she had in a measure ceased, her sister Eunice being by her, she burst out again, and cried "Poor Eunice!" and cried exceedingly; and when she had almost done, she went into another room and there looked upon her sister Naomi, and burst out again, crying "Poor Amy!" Her mother was greatly affected at such a behavior in the child, and knew not what to say to her. One of the neighbors coming in a little after, asked her what she had cried for. She seemed, at first, backward to tell the reason; her mother told her she might tell that person; upon which she said she "cried because she was afraid they would go to hell."

At night, a certain minister that was occasionally in the town was at the house, and talked considerably with her of the things of religion; and after he was gone, she sat leaning on the table, with tears falling from her eyes; and being asked what made her cry, she said that it was "thinking about God." The next day being Saturday, she seemed a great part of the day to be in a very affectionate frame, had four turns of crying, and seemed to endeavor to curb herself and hide her tears, and was very backward to talk of the occasion of it. On the Sabbath, she was asked whether she believed in God; she answered yes; and being told that Christ was the Son of God, she made ready answer, and said, "I know it."

From this time there has appeared a very remarkable abiding

change in the child : she has been very strict upon the Sabbath, and seems to long for the Sabbath-day before it comes, and will often in the week-time be inquiring how long it is to the Sabbath-day, and must have the days particularly counted over that are between before she will be contented. And she seems to love God's house, and is very eager to go thither. Her mother once asked her why she had such a mind to go. Whether it was not to see fine folks. She said no, it was to hear Mr. Edwards preach.

She seems to have very much of the fear of God before her eyes, and an extraordinary dread of sin against him ; of which her mother mentioned the following remarkable instance. Some time in August, the last year, she went with some larger children to get some plums in a neighbor's lot, knowing nothing of any harm in what she did ; but when she brought some of the plums into the house her mother mildly reproved her, and told her that she must not get plums without leave, because it was sin ; God had commanded her not to steal. The child seemed greatly surprised, and burst into tears, and cried out, "I will not have these plums !" And turning to her sister Eunice, very earnestly said to her—"Why did you ask me to go to that plum tree ? I should not have gone if you had not asked me." The other children did not seem to be much affected or concerned ; but there was no pacifying Phebe. Her mother told her she might go and ask leave, and then it would not be sin for her to eat them, and sent one of the children to that end ; and when she returned, her mother told her that, as the owner had given leave, now she might eat them, and it would not be stealing. This stilled her a little while, but presently she broke out again into an exceeding fit of crying. Her mother asked her what made her cry again ; why she cried now, since they had asked leave ; what it was that troubled her now ; and asked her several times very earnestly, before she made any answer ; but at last said it was because—"BECAUSE IT WAS SIN." She continued a considerable time crying, and said she would not go again if Eunice asked her a hundred times ; and she retained her aversion to that fruit for a considerable time, under the remembrance of her former sin.

Captain Scott, the Preacher.—Soon after Lady Huntington fitted up her chapel at Oathall, a regiment of soldiers was quartered in the vicinity. The captain, a gay officer, went out one day on a sporting frolic, and was forced by a violent shower to seek shelter under a shed with a farmer and his laborers, with whom he soon entered into conversation; the farmer was a Christian man, and the talk took a religious turn. His remarks surprised and interested the officer, and he asked where so much had been learned about divine things.

"In that hall yonder," answered the farmer, "where there is a famous man, a Mr. Romaine, preaching for Lady Huntington; you would do well to go and hear him for yourself."

Captain Scott, moved by all the circumstances, determined to do so, and on the following Sabbath bent his steps thitherward. On entering the hall, the devout and serious air of the congregation forcibly impressed his mind. He was now in the presence of one who seemed to him to speak as man never before spoke, and they were truths just suited to his case. He afterwards made the acquaintance of Mr. Romaine in London, whose prayers and instructions confirmed him in his resolutions to seek with all diligence to make his calling and election sure; and as he had proved himself a brave officer on the plains of Minden, so did he become valiant in a better service, even a heavenly.

"I went last Monday," said Fletcher, "to meet Captain Scott, one of the fruits that have grown for the Lord at Oathall—a captain of the truth—a bold soldier of Jesus Christ. God hath thrown down before him the middle wall of bigotry, and he boldly launches into an irregular usefulness. For some months he has exhorted his dragoons daily; for some weeks he has preached publicly at the Methodist meeting-house at Leicester, in his regimentals, to numerous congregations. The stiff ones pursue him with hue and cry, but I believe he is quite beyond their reach. God keep him zealous and simple. I believe this *red coat* will shame many a black one. I am sure he shames me."

Whitefield invited him to come to London, and "bring his artillery to Tabernacle-rampart."

Captain Scott was an accomplished man, of an ancient and

respectable family, with flattering prospects of worldly advancement; but worldly honors now ceased to charm him: he quitted the army for the ministry, and for twenty years was one of the supplies at the Tabernacle, and his new labors were crowned with abundant success.

Another of the first-fruits of Oathall was an old man of a hundred years. He had long been serious, and had often complained that church-preaching was not like church-prayers; and though no friend to "new measures," old Abraham determined one day to go and hear for himself what kind of stuff they had at the chapel. He listened with the profoundest attention and delight while Mr. Venn discoursed of the love of Christ, and could hardly contain himself for joy. "Ah, neighbor," he exclaimed, as soon as the services were over, tapping the shoulder of one who sat next to him, "this is the very truth of God's word, which I have been for ever seeking, and never found before. Here will I abide."

Lady Huntington at Brighton.—Lady Huntington went frequently to the obscure lodgings of a poor soldier's wife, carrying her food to eat and raiment to put on, and inviting her to "the Lamb of God, who taketh away the sin of the world." The woman's room was next to a public bakehouse, where the people who worked at the oven overheard the pious conversation of a lady through a crack in the ceiling. When her visits became known, other poor women begged to come in and be taught also, until a little company assembled daily, with whom she prayed, read, and explained the Scriptures. One day a blacksmith, notorious for his wickedness, swore he would go to the meetings, and accordingly forced himself in behind the women. When Lady Huntington entered and saw a man in the corner, she was about to ask him to withdraw, but on second thought concluded to go on as usual. Her simple, direct, and affectionate exhortations touched the conscience of the bold blasphemer. He who came to scoff went away with the cry, "Lord, what shall I do to be saved?" A radical change took place in his character, and for nearly twenty-nine years he lived to adorn the doctrine of his Lord and Saviour.

One day as Lady Huntington was walking out, a lady suddenly

accosted her, " Oh, madam, you are come." Surprised at so abrupt an address from an entire stranger, she feared the woman was deranged. "What do you know of me?" asked the countess. " Madam, I saw you in a dream three years ago, dressed as you now are," answered the stranger, and then related other circumstances connected with the dream. Singular as these circumstances were, an acquaintance was formed between them, and Lady Huntington became instrumental in the conversion of her new-found friend, who died a year afterwards in the triumphs of faith.

Her jewels were sold for six hundred and ninety-eight pounds, and with this she erected a neat house of worship, which was opened in 1760. Here Romaine, Venn, and other godly men labored with apostolic zeal, and though their work was often evil-spoken of, the Lord "added to the church daily of such as should be saved."

The Power of Christian Meekness.—Mr. Cennick was rather below the middle stature, of a fair countenance, and though by no means robust in health, he knew little of timidity. The spirit in which he discharged his ministry may be seen in a letter he wrote to a friend: " We sang a hymn, and then the devil led on his servants; they began beating a drum, and then made fires of gunpowder: at first the poor flock was startled; but while God gave me power to speak encouragingly to them, they waxed bolder, and very few moved. The mob then fired guns over the people's heads, and began to play a water engine upon brother Harris and myself, till we were wet through. They also played an engine upon us with hog's-wash and grounds of beer-barrels, and covered us with muddy water from a ditch; they pelted us with eggs and stones, threw baskets of dust over us, and fired their guns so close to us that our faces were black with the powder; but, in nothing terrified, we remained praying. I think I never saw or felt so great a power of God as was there. In the midst of the confused multitude, I saw a man laboring above measure, earnest to fill the buckets with water to throw upon us. I asked him, 'What harm do we do? Why are you so furious against us? We only come to tell you that Christ loved you, and died for you.' He stepped back a little for room, and threw a bucket of water in my face. When I had recovered myself, I said, 'My dear man, if God should so pour his wrath upon you, what would become of you? Yet I tell you that Christ loves you.' He threw away the bucket, let fall his trembling hands, and looked as pale as death; he then shook hands with me, and parted from me, I believe, under strong convictions."

A Gospel Knight-errant.—Rev. Howel Harris, one of Mr. Whitefield's energetic followers, was a man of extraordinary powers of body and mind. Harris used to relate of himself, that being once on a journey through Wales, he was subjected to great temptation to desert his Master's cause, when he said, "Satan, I'll match thee for this;" and "so I did," he used to add; "for I had not ridden many miles before I came to a revel, where there was a show of mountebanks, which I entered, and just as they were commencing, I jumped into the midst of them and cried out, "Let us pray," which so thunderstruck them that they listened to me quietly, while I preached to them a most tremendous sermon, that frightened many of them home." Mr. Rowland Hill greatly delighted in this anecdote, and often said that amidst somewhat similar scenes he had been enabled successfully to attack the kingdom of Satan.

Reverence in Sacred Things.—Dr. Stonehouse is said to have become one of the most elegant preachers of the kingdom, and for the grace of propriety perhaps he was mainly indebted to Garrick, whose famous criticism will bear repeating.

Being once engaged to read prayers and preach at a church in London, he prevailed upon Garrick to go with him. After the service, the actor asked the preacher what particular business he had to do when the duty was over.

"None," said the other.

"I thought you had," said Garrick, "on seeing you enter the reading-desk in such a hurry. Nothing can be more indecent than to see a clergyman set about sacred business as if he were a tradesman, and go into church as if he wanted to get out of it as soon as possible." He next asked the doctor what books he had before him.

"Only the Bible and Prayer-book."

"*Only* the Bible and Prayer-book?" replied the player; "why, you tossed them backwards and forwards, and turned the leaves as carelessly, as if they were those of a daybook and ledger."

The doctor acknowledged the force of the criticism by henceforth avoiding the faults it was designed to correct.

The Little Girl and her joyful News.—Who can tell the results of a single sermon, or trace the consequences of one conversion? When Mr. Whitefield was preaching in New England, a lady became the subject of divine grace, and her spirit was peculiarly drawn out in prayer for others. But in her Christian exercises she was alone; she could persuade no one to pray with her but her little daughter, about ten years of age. She took this dear child into her closet from day to day, as a witness of her cries and tears. After a time, it pleased God to touch the heart of the child, and to give her the hope of salvation by the remission of sin. In a transport of holy joy she then exclaimed, "Oh, mother, if all the world knew this! I wish I could tell everybody. Pray, mother, let me run to some of the neighbors and tell them that they may be happy and love my Saviour too." "Ah, my dear child," said the mother, "that would be useless, for I suppose that were you to tell your experience, there is not one within many miles who would not laugh at you, and say it was all delusion." "Oh, mother," replied the dear girl, "I think they would believe me. I must go over to the shoemaker and tell him; he will believe me." She ran over, and found him at work in his shop. She began by telling him that he must die, and that he was a sinner, and that she was a sinner, but that her blessed Saviour had heard her mother's prayers, and had forgiven all her sins; and that now she was so happy that she did not know how to tell it. The shoemaker was struck with surprise; his tears flowed down like rain; he threw aside his work, and by prayer and supplication sought for mercy. The neighborhood were awakened, and within a few months more than fifty persons were brought to the knowledge of Jesus, and rejoiced in his power and grace.

"Strike, but Hear."—It is related of the Rev. Howel Harris, a distinguished Welsh evangelist in the time of Whitefield, that on one excursion he did not take off his clothes for seven days and nights, being obliged to meet his little congregation in solitary places at midnight, or by daylight in ravine or cleft, in order to avoid the persecuting vigilance of their enemies. "One man," says Harris, "was obliged to pay Sir Watkins Wynn twenty shillings, several of my poor hearers five shillings, and one who paid the same sum before, was fined seven shillings more; and this is the third time my poor sheep of this fold have been thus served."

Honorable exceptions, however, were there among the Welsh magistrates. Harris having made an appointment to meet the peasantry near Garth, in Breconshire, the residence of Sir Marmaduke Gwynne, that gentleman, frightened by the reports concerning him, resolved on the occasion to do his duty as a magistrate, and stop proceedings of so disorderly and mobbish a character. Regarding the missionary as neither more nor less than a firebrand to church and state, Mr. Magistrate Gwynne prepared for a resolute attack, but wisely enough said to his family on going out, "I'll first *hear* the man myself, before I commit him." Accordingly he mingled with the congregation, lying in wait to pounce upon the preacher at every next word. "Why, he's neither more nor less than an apostle," cried Gwynne inwardly, his stout heart melting under the manner and earnest language of the man of God. The riot act lay asleep in his pocket, and at the end of the discourse he marched up to the rude platform, shook the preacher warmly by the hand, confessed his intention, asked his pardon, bade him preach while he lived, and took him back to Garth to supper. Henceforth the countenance of the Gwynne family smiled on the new movements. Regardless of public or private censure, Sir Marmaduke stood stoutly up for the evangelists, and used all his influence for promoting the spread of the gospel in the regions round about. One of his daughters afterwards married Charles Wesley.

The Indian Conjurer.—The following instance is extracted from the diary of David Brainerd: "This day received into communion the conjurer, murderer, etc., mentioned in my diary of August 8, 1745, and February 1, 1746, who appears to be such a remarkable instance of divine grace that I cannot omit to give some brief account of him here. He lived near, and sometimes attended my meeting at the Forks of Delaware, for more than a year; but was, like many others of them, extremely attached to strong drink, and seemed to be in no degree reformed by the means which I used with them for their instruction and conversion. At this time he likewise murdered a likely young Indian, which threw him into some kind of horror and desperation, so that he kept at a distance from me, and refused to hear me preach for several months together, until I had an opportunity of conversing freely with him, and giving him encouragement that his sins might be forgiven, for Christ's sake. After this he again attended my meetings sometimes.

"The first genuine concern for his soul was excited by seeing my interpreter and his wife publicly profess Christ, at the Forks of Delaware, July 21, 1745; which so prevailed upon him, that with the invitation of an Indian who was a friend to Christianity, he followed me down to Crossweeksung, in the beginning of August, in order to hear me preach; and there continued for several weeks in the season of the most remarkable and powerful awakening among the Indians; at which time he was more effectually awakened, and brought under great concern for his soul. He continued constantly under the heavy burden and pressure of a wounded spirit, until at length he was brought into acute anguish and utmost agony of soul, which continued that night and part of the next day. After this he was brought to the utmost calmness and composure of mind; his trembling and heavy burden were removed; and he appeared perfectly sedate, although he had to his apprehensions scarcely any hope of salvation.

"I observed him to appear remarkably composed; and therefore asked him how he did. He replied, 'It is done, it is done, it is all done now.' I asked him what he meant. He answered, 'I can never do any more to save myself; it is all done for ever. I can do no more.' I queried with him, whether he could not do a little more, rather than go to hell. He replied, 'my heart is dead. I never can help myself.' I asked what he thought would become of him then. He answered, 'I must go to hell.' I asked him if he thought it was right that God should send him to hell. He replied, 'Oh, it is right. The devil has been in me ever since I was born.' I asked him if he felt this when he was in such great distress the evening before. He answered, 'No ; I did not then think it was right. I thought God would send me to hell, and that I was then dropping into it ; but my heart quarrelled with God, and would not say it was right he should send me there. But now I know it is right ; for I have always served the devil ; and my heart has no goodness in it now, but it is as bad as ever it was,' etc. I thought I had scarcely ever seen any person more effectually brought off from a dependence upon his own contrivances and endeavors for salvation, or more apparently to lie at the foot of sovereign mercy, than this man did under these views of things.

"In this frame of mind he continued for several days, passing sentence of condemnation upon himself, and constantly owning that it would be right he should be damned, and that he expected this would be his portion for the greatness of his sins. Yet it was plain that he had a secret hope of mercy, though imperceptible to himself, which kept him not only from despair, but from any pressing distress : so that, instead of being sad and dejected, his very countenance appeared pleasant and agreeable.

"It was remarkable, that he seemed to have a great love for the people of God ; and nothing affected him so much as the thought of being separated from them. This seemed to be a very dreadful part of the hell to which he saw himself doomed. It was likewise remarkable, that in this season he was most diligent in the use of all the means for the soul's salvation ; although he had the clearest view of the inefficiency of means to afford him help.

"After he had continued in this frame of mind more than a week, while I was discoursing publicly, he seemed to have a lively soul-refreshing view of the excellency of Christ and the way of salvation by him, which melted him into tears, and filled him with admiration, comfort, satisfaction, and praise to God. Since then he has appeared to be a humble, devout, and affectionate Christian ; serious and exemplary in his conversation and behavior, frequently complaining of his barrenness, his want of spiritual warmth, life and activity, and yet frequently favored with quickening and refreshing influences. In all respects, so far as I am capable of judging, he bears the marks of one 'created anew in Christ Jesus to good works.'

REVIVAL INCIDENTS.

Traits and Anecdotes of Whitefield.

"No preacher whose history is on record, has trod so wide a field as did Whitefield, or has retrod it so often, or has repeated himself so much, or has carried so far the experiment of exhausting himself, and of spending his popularity, if it could have been spent, but it never was spent. Within the compass of a few weeks he might have been heard addressing the negroes of the Bermuda islands, adapting himself to their infantile understandings, and to their debauched hearts; and then at Chelsea, with the aristocracy of rank and wit before him, approving himself to listeners such as the lords Bolingbroke and Chesterfield. Whitefield might as easily have produced a Hamlet or a Paradise Lost, as have excogitated a sermon which, as a composition, a product of thought, would have tempted men like these to hear him a second time; and as to his faculty and graces as a speaker, his elocution and action, a second performance would have contented them. But in fact Bolingbroke, and many of his class, thought not the hour long, time after time, while, with much sameness of *material* and of language, he spoke of eternity and of salvation in Christ. . . . Floods of tears moistened cheeks rough and smooth; and sighs, suppressed or loudly uttered, gave evidence that human nature is one and the same when it comes in presence of truths which bear upon the guilty and the immortal without distinction." Indeed, so simple was his natnre, that glory to God and good will to man had filled it; there was room for little more. Having no church to found, no family to enrich, and no memory to immortalize, he was simply the ambassador of God; and inspired with its genial piteous spirit—so full of Heaven reconciled and humanity restored—he soon himself became a living gospel. Coming to his pulpit direct from communion with his Master, and in the strength of accepted prayer, there was an elevation in his mien which often paralyzed hostility, and a self-possession which made him amid uproar and confusion the more sublime. With an electric bolt he would bring the jester in his fool's cap from his perch on the tree, or galvanize the brickbat from the skulking miscreant's grasp, or sweep down in crouching submission and shamefaced silence the whole of Bartholomew fair; while a revealing flash of sententious doctrine, of vivified Scripture, would disclose to awe-struck hundreds the forgotten verities of another world, or the unsuspected arcana of their inner man. "I came to break your head, but, through you, God has broken my heart," was a sort of confession with which he was familiar; and to see the deaf old gentlewoman who used to mutter imprécations at him as he passed along the streets, clambering up the pulpit stairs to catch his angelic words, was a sort of spectacle which the triumphant gospel often witnessed in his day. Whitefield was remarkable for *a devotional spirit.* Probably no man ever lived nearer to God. Had he been less prayerful, he would have been less powerful. When he came before his auditors, he looked like one who had been with God. This it was which won for him the title of *seraphic*—he was a human *seraph,* and burnt out in the blaze of his own fire. Usually for an hour or two before he went into the pulpit, he claimed retirement. In this claim he was imperative, and would not be interrupted in his seasons of hallowed intercourse with God.

On one occasion, when a young minister, afterwards exceedingly popular and useful, was visiting him, he was sent for to visit a poor woman who had been so dreadfully burnt that she could not survive many hours. He went immediately, and prayed with her. He had no sooner returned, than she called out, "Oh! where is Mr. Whitefield?" Urged by her entreaty, her friends requested him to visit her a second time. He complied, and again prayed with her. The poor afflicted woman continued still to desire his presence. When her friends came for him a third time, "I begged of him," said the young clergyman, "not to go; for he could scarcely expect to do any good. 'Your nerves are too weak, your feelings are too acute to endure such scenes.' I shall never forget his mild reproof: 'Leave me; my Master can save to the uttermost, to the *very uttermost.*'"

While he was always ready to receive reproof, he was when called to the duty, ready to give it, and often in a way which his friends did not expect. A censorious professor of religion, knowing the doctrinal differences between the two men, asked Whitefield if he thought they would see Mr. John Wesley in heaven. His answer was truly admirable: "No, sir, I fear not; for he will be so near the throne, and we shall be at such a distance, we shall hardly get sight of him."

It is said, that when he was once travelling in company with a Christian man, they had occasion to stay for a night at a road-side tavern. After they had retired, they were greatly annoyed by a company of gamblers, who were in an adjoining room. Whitefield could not rest, and told his friend that he would go into the room and reprove them for their conduct. The other remonstrated against his doing so, but in vain. He went; and unhappily, his words fell apparently powerless upon them. Returning, he laid down to sleep. "What," asked his companion, "did you gain by your trouble?" Whitefield characteristically answered, "A soft pillow."

In his intercourse with general society, Mr. Whitefield never forgot his dignity as a servant of Jesus Christ. When he was in the zenith of his popularity, Lord Clare, who knew that his influence was considerable, applied to him by letter, requesting his influence at Bristol at the ensuing general election. To this request Mr. Whitefield replied, that in "general" elections he never interfered; but he would earnestly exhort his lordship to use great diligence to make his own particular "calling and election sure."

Mr. Whitefield was greatly distinguished, even from early life, for neatness in his person, order in his apartments, and regular method in the management of all his affairs. He was accustomed to say that a minister should be "without a spot;" and on one occasion remarked, that he could not feel comfortable if he knew that his *gloves* were out of their proper place.

On one occasion, as Mr. Whitefield was preaching in Boston, a violent storm of thunder and lightning came on. In the midst of the sermon it attained so alarming a height that the congregation sat in almost breathless awe. The preacher closed his note-book, and stepping into one of the wings of the desk, fell on his knees, and with much feeling and fine taste repeated :

"Hark, THE ETERNAL rends the sky!
A mighty voice before him goes—
A voice of music to his friends,
But threatening thunder to his foes:
'Come, children, to your Father's arms;
Hide in the chambers of my grace,
Till the fierce storm be overblown,
And my revenging fury cease.'—

"Let us devoutly sing to the praise and glory of God this hymn, Old Hundred."

The whole congregation instantly rose, and poured forth the sacred song, in which they were accompanied by the organ, in a style of simple grandeur and heartfelt devotion that was probably never surpassed. By the time the hymn was finished the storm was hushed. The remainder of the services were well adapted to sustain the elevated feeling which had been produced ; and the benediction with which the good man dismissed the flock was universally received with streaming eyes, and hearts overflowing with tenderness and gratitude.

It is said that Whitefield would sometimes rise in the sacred desk, and for a minute or two looking in silence around his vast audience, as if salvation or perdition teemed in every cast of his eye, would burst into tears, while the swift contagion, before he uttered a word, had reached every heart that could feel, and dimmed every eye that could weep.

No doubt there was a connection between the tears of Whitefield and his piety ; but it must not be supposed that he was always "the weeping prophet ;" he could smile as well as weep. A venerable lady in New York, known to some yet living, speaking of the influence which first won her heart to God, said that " Mr. Whitefield was so cheerful that it *tempted her to be a Christian.*"

His voice, accompanied by his look from crossed eyes, and proceeding from a man of his robust frame, produced wonderful effects. It is said that when once preaching in a graveyard, two young men conducted themselves improperly, when he fixed his eyes upon them, and with a voice resembling thunder, said, "Come down, ye rebels."

They instantly fell, neither of them being inclined again to come into contact with such a look, or to hear such a voice.

He was once preaching to a vast crowd of people in Southern Pennsylvania, which was at that time ignorant and uncivilized. He was incessantly disturbed by their noise, and twice reproved them with great severity. At length he was so overcome by their noisy and irreverent conduct, that he stopped short, dropped his head into his hands, burst into a flood of tears, and exclaimed, " Oh, Lord God, I am ashamed that these people are provoking thy wrath, and I dare not reprove them a third time." Such was the effect of his conduct and feeling, that his audience became perfectly quiet, and remained so till the end of his discourse.

The late Sir George Beaumont, no mean authority on such a subject, thus familiarly speaks : " Oh, yes ; I heard that young gentleman this morning allude to 'roaring Whitefield,' and was amused at his mistake. It is a common one. Whitefield did not roar. I have been his auditor more than once, and was delighted with him. Whitefield's voice could be heard at an immense distance ; but that was owing to its fullness, roundness, and clearness. It was a perfectly sound voice. It is an odd description, but I can hit upon no better ; there was neither crack nor flaw. To describe him as a bellowing, roaring field preacher, is to describe a mountebank, not Whitefield. He had powers of pathos of the highest order. The tender, soft, persuasive tones of his voice were melodious in the extreme. And when he desired to win, or persuade, or plead, or soothe, the gush of feeling which his voice conveyed at once surprised and overpowered you."

From a memorandum in which Mr. Whitefield recorded the times and places of his ministerial labors, it appears that from the period of his ordination to that of his death, which was thirty-four years, he preached upwards of *eighteen thousand sermons.* It would be difficult to imagine how many thousand miles he travelled. When he ascertained that his physical powers began to fail, putting himself on what he called "short allowance," he preached *only once on every week-day, and three times on the Sabbath.* In view of his various journeyings in the slow and inconvenient modes of travelling then in use, his thirteen voyages across the Atlantic, and all that he accomplished, it appears that few men ever performed so much labor within the same period.

On one occasion, he was seized with inflammatory sore throat, that was followed by quinsy, assuming an almost fatal aspect. One physician prescribed silence and warmth, and the preacher "promised to be very obedient," but a few days afterwards, another recommended a perpetual blister : this proposal roused him, and he determined to try his own remedy—perpetual preaching. The remedy itself was painful, but he said, "When this grand catholicon fails, it is all over with me."

When he was brought to live on the "short allowance of preaching but once a day, and thrice on Sunday," he broke through the restraint, and preached three times, which, he says, "somewhat *recovered*" him, after he had been for a week at the gates of the grave.

In a letter to Hervey, he says, "Fear not your weak body, we are immortal till our work is done. Christ's laborers must live by miracle ; if not, I must not live at all, for God only knows what I daily endure. My continual vomitings almost kill me, and yet the pulpit is my cure ; so that my friends begin to pity me less, and leave off that ungrateful caution, 'Spare thyself.' I speak this to encourage you."

He preached once at Portsmouth, Me., when apparently at the point of death. On that day, as he wrote, "My pains returned;

but what gave me most concern was, that notice had been given of my being engaged to preach. I felt a divine life, distinct from my animal life, which made me, as it were, laugh at my pains, though every one thought I was taken with death. My dear York physician was then about to administer a medicine. I on a sudden cried out, 'Doctor, my pains are suspended; by the help of God I will go and preach, and then come home and die.' With some difficulty I reached the pulpit. All looked quite surprised, as though they saw one risen from the dead. I indeed was as pale as death, and told them they must look upon me as a dying man, come to bear my dying testimony to the truths I had formerly preached to them. All seemed melted, and were drowned in tears. The cry after me, when I left the pulpit, was like the cry of sincere mourners when attending the funeral of a dear departed friend. Upon my coming home, I was laid upon a bed on the ground, near the fire, and I heard them say, 'He is gone.' But God was pleased to order it otherwise. I gradually recovered."

In another account, he himself says: "In my own apprehension, and in all appearance to others, I was a dying man. I preached—the people heard me—as such. Expecting to launch into eternity, and to be with my Master before the morning, I spoke with peculiar energy. Such effects followed the word, I thought it was worth dying for a thousand times. Though wonderfully comforted within at my return home, I thought I was dying indeed. . . . . Soon after, a poor negro woman would see me. She came, sat down upon the ground, and looked earnestly in my face, and then said, 'Massa, you just go to heaven's gate, but Jesus Christ said, Get you down, get you down; you must not come here yet; but go first, and call some more poor negroes.' I prayed to the Lord, that, if I was to live, this might be the event."

Before his last sermon some one said to him: "Sir, you are more fit to go to bed than to preach." Whitefield's reply was: "True, sir;" but, turning aside, he clasped his hands together, and looking up, said: "Lord Jesus, I am weary *in* thy work, but not *of* thy work. If I have not yet finished my course, let me go and speak for thee once more in the fields, seal thy truth, and come home and die." When he was retiring to his chamber on this last evening of his life, many were so desirous to see and hear him, that he stood on the stairs with a lamp in his hand, and there gave them a tender spiritual address.

Three hours before his death, he said: "I cannot breathe; but I hope I shall be better by and by; a good pulpit sweat to-day may give me relief; I shall be better after preaching." Mr. Smith said to him: "I wish you would not preach so often." He replied: "I had rather wear out than rust out." Mr. Smith said he was afraid he took cold in preaching yesterday. He said he believed he had; and then sat up in bed, and prayed that God would be pleased to bless his preaching where he had been, and also bless his preaching that day, that more souls might be brought to Christ.

It will be observed from the above extracts, that some of the "household words" of the Christian world, are the words of Whitefield.

As a proof the power of Mr. Whitefield's preaching, Mr. Newton said, that a military officer at Glasgow, who had heard him preach, laid a wager with another, that at a certain charity sermon, though he went with prejudice, he would be compelled to give something. The other, to make sure that he would not, laid aside all the money out of his pockets; but before he left the church, he was glad to borrow some, and lose his bet."

"A very peculiar providence," says Whitefield, "led me very lately to a place where a horse-stealer was executed. Thousands attended. The poor criminal had sent me several letters, hearing I was in the country. The sheriff allowed him to come and hear a sermon under an adjacent tree. Solemn, solemn! After being by himself about an hour, I walked half a mile with him to the gallows. His heart had been softened before my first visit. He seemed full of solid, divine consolation. An instructive walk! I went up with him into the cart. He gave a short exhortation. I then stood upon the coffin—added, I trust, a word in season—prayed—gave the blessing, and took my leave. Effectual good, I hope, was done to the hearers and spectators. Grace, grace!"

Benjamin Randall was born in Newcastle, New Hampshire, in 1749. In his twenty-second year he was brought under the ministry of Whitefield, by which means he became deeply convinced of sin, and was soon after converted to God. He is considered the founder of the denomination of Freewill Baptists, which now comprises from eleven to twelve hundred churches, more than a thousand pastors and licentiates, and upwards of fifty thousand communicants.

On one of his visits to Bristol, he began a series of sermons on the evening before the commencement of the fair. His text was: "Ho, every one that thirsteth, come ye to the waters; and he that hath no money, come ye, buy and eat; yea, come buy wine and milk without money, and without price." Isa. lv. 1. The congregation was large, and thus he began: "My dear hearers, I fear that many of you are come to attend Bristol fair. So am I. You do not mean to show your goods until to-morrow; but I shall exhibit mine to-night. You are afraid purchasers will not come up to your price; but I am afraid my buyers will not come down to mine; for mine," striking his hand on the Bible, "are 'without money, and without price.'"

He tells us, among many similar facts, of the conversion of a Mr. Crane, who was afterwards appointed steward of the orphan-house in Georgia. This gentleman had one evening determined to visit the theatre, and set out for Drury-lane; that house being crowded, he resolved to go to Covent-garden; that also being so full that he could not obtain admittance, he changed his plan, and resolved on being entertained with one of Whitefield's sermons, and hastened to Tottenham Court-road chapel. It pleased God to impress the word on his heart, and he became an eminent Christian. So truly is the prediction verified: "I am found of them who sought me not."

Among his congregation one day was a young man named Tuppen, about eighteen years of age. He had been educated by a pious mother in the strict observance of the external parts of religion, but was entirely destitute of its power. He attended not so much from curiosity, as from the intention to insult and interrupt the preacher. He tells us, "I had, therefore, provided myself with stones in my pocket, if opportunity offered, to pelt the preacher ; but I had not heard long, before the stone was taken out of my heart of flesh ; and then the other stones, with shame and weeping, were dropped one by one out upon the ground." Mr. Tuppen became an excellent Christian minister, and labored as a pastor for some years in Portsmouth. He then removed to the city of Bath, where he originated a congregation, and built a house for public worship. He was succeeded in this important sphere by the late distinguished William Jay, who labored there for about sixty-four years.

Towards the close of one of his discourses, after a solemn pause, Mr. Whitefield thus addressed his numerous audience : "The attendant angel is just about to leave the threshold, and ascend to heaven. And shall he ascend, and not bear with him the news of one sinner, among all this multitude, reclaimed from the error of his ways ?"

With this exclamation, he stamped with his foot, lifted up his eyes and hands to heaven, and with gushing tears cried aloud, "Stop, Gabriel ! stop, Gabriel ! stop, ere you enter the sacred portals, and yet carry with you the news of one sinner converted to God." He then, in the most simple and energetic language, described a Saviour's dying love to sinful man, so that almost the whole assembly melted into tears.

To certain of his admirers in Dublin, he wrote : "This morning I have been talking with dear Mr. Adams, and cannot help thinking that you have run before the Lord, in forming yourselves into a public society as you have done. I am sincere when I profess that I do not choose to set myself at the head of any party. When I came to Ireland, my intention was to preach the gospel to all ; and if it should please the Lord of all lords to send me thither again, I purpose to pursue the same plan. For I am a debtor to all of every denomination, and have no design, if I know anything of this desperately wicked and deceitful heart, but to promote the common salvation of mankind. The love of Christ constrains me to this."

After preaching in Oxmantown Green, Dublin, he thought to return home by the way he came, but, to his great surprise, a passage through the barracks was denied ; and he was compelled to pass from one end of the green to the other, through thousands of Roman Catholics. He was unattended ; for a soldier and four preachers who came with him had fled from the scene of danger, and he was seriously attacked by the mob. They threw volleys of stones upon him from all quarters, and he reeled backwards and forwards till he was almost breathless and covered with blood. At length, with great difficulty he staggered to the door of a minister's house near the green, which was kindly opened to him. For a while he continued speechless, and panting for breath ; but his weeping friends having given him a cordial, and washed his wounds, a coach was procured, in which, amidst the oaths, imprecations, and threatenings, of the rabble, he got safe home, and united in a hymn of thanksgiving with his friends. In a letter written to a friend soon after this event, he says, "I received many blows and wounds ; one was particularly large, and near my temple : I thought of Stephen, and was in hopes, like him, to go off in this bloody triumph, to the immediate presence of my Master."

In one of the services held by Mr. Whitefield in Yorkshire, a deep solemnity was created by providential circumstances. He had mounted the temporary scaffold to address the thousands before him. Casting a look over the multitude, he elevated his hands, and in an energetic manner implored the divine presence and blessing. With a solemnity peculiarly his own, he then announced his text, "It is appointed unto men once to die, but after this the judgment." Heb. xi. 27. After a short pause, as he was about to proceed, a wild, terrifying shriek issued from the centre of the congregation. A momentary alarm and confusion ensued. Mr. Whitefield waited to ascertain the cause, and requested the people to remain still. Mr. Grimshaw hurried to the spot, and in a few minutes was seen pressing towards the place where Mr. Whitefield stood. "Brother Whitefield," said he, manifesting in the strongest manner the intensity of his feelings, and the ardor of his concern for the salvation of sinners, "you stand among the dead and the dying. An immortal soul has been called into eternity ; the destroying angel is passing over the congregation ; cry aloud, and spare not." The awful occurrence was speedily announced to the congregation. After the lapse of a few moments, Mr. Whitefield again announced his text. Again a loud and piercing shriek proceeded from the spot near where Lady Huntingdon and Lady Margaret Ingham were standing. A thrill of horror seemed to escape from the multitude when it was understood that a *second* person had fallen a victim to the king of terrors. When the consternation had somewhat subsided, Mr. Whitefield gave indications of proceeding with the service. The excited feelings of many were wound up to their highest point. All was hushed ; not a sound was to be heard ; and a stillness like the awful silence of death spread over the assembly, as he proceeded in melting strains to warm the careless, Christless sinner, to "flee from the wrath to come."

Some one, we believe a bishop, complained to George II. of the popularity and success of Whitefield, and entreated his majesty in some way or other to silence him. The monarch, thinking, no doubt, of the class described by the martyr Latimer, as "unpreaching prelates," replied with jocose severity, "I believe the best way will be to make a bishop of him."

It has generally happened that the most effective public speakers, whether secular or sacred, have been accused by a fastidious class, of *vulgarisms*. So with Cicero, Burke, and Chatham ; so with Patrick Henry and Daniel Webster ; and to turn to eminent preachers, so with Luther, Latimer, and Whitefield. The reason was, that intent on the greatest good to the greatest number, they used what Dr. Johnson, after Daniel Burgess, called "market language." Dr. William Bates, an accomplished and courtly non-conformist minister, in the seventeenth century, once complained in the presence of his faithful but unpolished friend Daniel Burgess, that he found very little success in his work as a minister ; when his aged brother smartly replied, "Thank your velvet mouth for that—too fine to speak market language."

Among the crowds in Boston was a somewhat remarkable gentleman of that city. He was a man of ready wit and racy humor, who delighted in *preaching over a bottle* to his ungodly companions. He went to hear Whitefield, that he might be furnished with matter for a "tavern harangue." When he had heard enough of the sermon for his purpose, he endeavored to quit the church for the inn, but "found his endeavors to get out fruitless, he was so pent up." While thus fixed, and waiting for "fresh matter of ridicule," the truth took possession of his heart. That night he went to Mr. Prince full of terror, and sought an introduction to ask pardon of the preacher. Whitefield says of him, "By the paleness, pensiveness, and horror of his countenance, I guessed he was the man of whom I had been apprised. 'Sir, can you forgive me?' he cried in a low, but plaintive voice. I smiled, and said, 'Yes, sir, very readily.' 'Indeed,' he said, 'you cannot when I tell you all.' I then asked him to sit down; and judging that he had sufficiently felt the lash of the law, I preached the gospel to him."

Among other converts won at Norwich, was the afterwards popular and useful minister of Christ, the Rev. Robert Robinson, of Cambridge, England. When he was walking one day with several companions who had agreed that day to take their pleasure, the first object which attracted their attention was an old woman who pretended to tell fortunes. Robinson was informed, among other things, that he would live to a very old age, and see his children, grandchildren, and great-grandchildren growing up around him. "And so," said he when alone, "I am to see children, grandchildren, and great-grandchildren. I will then," thought he, "during my youth, endeavor to store my mind with all kinds of knowledge. I will see and hear, and note down everything that is rare and wonderful, that I may sit, when incapable of other employments, and entertain my descendants. Thus shall my company be rendered pleasant, and I shall be respected, rather than neglected, in old age. Let me see, what can I acquire first? Oh, here is the famous Methodist preacher, Whitefield; he is to preach here, they say, to-night; I will go and hear him."

From these strange motives, as he told the celebrated Rev. Andrew Fuller, he went to hear Whitefield preach. That evening his text was, "But when he saw many of the Pharisees and Sadducees come to his Baptism, he said unto them, O generation of vipers, who hath warned you to flee from the wrath to come? Matt. iii. 7. "Mr. Whitefield," said Robinson, "described the Sadducees' character; this did not touch me; I thought myself as good a Christian as any man in England. From this he went to that of the Pharisees. He described their exterior decency, but observed, that the poison of the viper rankled in their hearts. This rather shook me. At length, in the course of his sermon, he abruptly broke off; paused for a few moments; then burst into a flood of tears, lifted up his hands and eyes, and exclaimed, 'Oh, my hearers, *the wrath's to come! the wrath's to come!*' These words sunk into my heart like lead in the water; I wept, and when the sermon was ended retired alone. For days and weeks I could think of little else. Those awful words would follow me wherever I went: 'The wrath's to come! The wrath's to come!'"

At Gloucester lived the Rev. Mr. Cole, an old dissenting minister, whom Whitefield, when a boy, had been taught to ridicule; and when he was once asked what profession he would engage in, replied, "I will be a minister, but I will take care never to tell stories in the pulpit like old Cole." Twelve years afterwards, the old minister heard the young one preach, and tell some story to illustrate his subject, when the venerable servant of Christ remarked, "I find young Whitefield can tell stories now as well as old Cole." The good man was much affected with the preaching of his young friend, and was so humble, that he used to subscribe himself his curate, and went about in the country preaching after him. One evening, while preaching, he was struck with death, and asked for a chair to lean on till he had finished his sermon. Having done this, he was carried up stairs and died. When the fact was told to Whitefield, he said, "O blessed God, if it be thy holy will, may my exit be like his!" How striking is this fact when looked at in connection with the circtances of his own removal from earth.

Mr. Whitefield wrote to Rowland Hill, referring to the withholding of his degree, for preaching: "I wish you joy of the late high dignity conferred upon you—higher than if you were made the greatest professor in the university of Cambridge. The honorable 'degrees' you intend giving to your promising candidates [allowing some of his fellow-students to preach in the various places which he had visited], I trust will excite a holy ambition, and a holy emulation; let me know who is first honored. As I have been admitted to the degree of doctor for near these thirty years, I assure you I like my field preferment, my airy pluralities, exceedingly well. For these three weeks last past I have been beating up for fresh recruits in Gloucestershire and South Wales. Thousands and thousands attended, and good Lady Huntington was present at one of our reviews. Her ladyship's aid-de-camp preached in Brecknock street, and Captain Scott, that glorious field officer, lately fixed up his standard upon dear Mr. Fletcher's horse-block at Madeley. Being invited thither, I have a great inclination to lift up the Redeemer's ensign next week in the same place; with what success, you and your dearly beloved candidates for good old methodistical contempt shall know hereafter. God willing, I intend fighting my way up to town. Soon after my arrival there, I hope thousands and thousands of volleys of prayers, energetic, effectual, fervent, heaven-besieging, heaven-opening, heaven-taking prayers, shall be poured forth for you all. Oh, my dearly beloved and longed-for in the Lord, my bowels yearn towards you. Fear not to go without the camp; keep open the correspondence between the two universities. Remember the praying legions—they were never known to yield. God bless those that are gone to their respective *cures*—I say not *livings*, a term of too modern date. Christ is our life; Christ is the Levite's inheritance, and Christ will be the true disinterested Levite's lot and portion and all."

While Whitefield's ministry at the Tabernacle was at its height of popularity, Foote, a comedian of eminent talent for mimicry, who was frequently in difficulties on account of his love of ridicule, by which indeed his life was shortened, employed his wit to bring the distinguished preacher into contempt. One of his biographers says, that "very pressing embarrassments in his affairs compelled him to bring out his comedy of '*The Minor*,' in 1760, to ridicule Methodism, which, though successful, gave great offence, and was at last suppressed." Of this miserable piece of buffoonery, it may be enough to say, that Foote, and the agents employed at the Tabernacle and Tottenham Court-road chapel to collect materials for the accomplishment of their object, were so disgracefully ignorant of the inspired writings, as not to know that what they took for Mr. Whitefield's peculiar language was that of the word of God.

Preaching from the words "Wherefore, glorify ye the Lord in fires," Isa. xxiv. 15, he says, "When I was, some years ago, at Shields, I went into a glass-house, and standing very attentively, I saw several masses of burning glass of various form. The workman took one piece of glass, and put it into one furnace, then he put it into a second, and then into a third. I asked him, 'Why do you put that into so many fires?' He answered me, 'Oh, sir, the first was not hot enough, nor the second, and therefore we put it into the third, and that will make it transparent.' 'Oh,' thought I, 'does this man put his glass into one furnace after another, that it may be rendered perfect? Oh, my God, put me into one furnace after another, that my soul may be transparent, that I may see God as he is.'"

A correspondence, indeed we may say friendship, had for years existed between Whitefield and the eminent philosopher Dr. Benjamin Franklin. The following, from a letter of Whitefield, August 17, 1752, shows his fidelity to the eminent citizen and statesman: "I find you grow more and more famous in the learned world. As you have made a pretty considerable progress in the mysteries of electricity, I would now humbly recommend to your diligent, unprejudiced pursuit and study, the mystery of the new birth. It is a most important, interesting study, and when mastered, will richly answer and repay you for all your pains. One, at whose bar we are shortly to appear, hath solemnly declared that, without it, we cannot enter into the kingdom of heaven. You will excuse this freedom. I must have *aliquid Christi*—something of Christ, in all my letters."

GREAT AWAKENING OF 1857-'8.

ON the 14th of October, 1857, the financial disorder which had prevailed with increasing severity for many weeks, reached its crisis in an overwhelming panic that prostrated the whole monetary system of the country, virtually in one hour. The struggle was over.

While the conflict for life was yet intense, a humble individual, unheard of in Wall Street, had been prompted to do something for the relief of the distressed merchants of the city.* He was a downtown missionary, one of the feeble few whom Divine mercy, kinder to us than ourselves, had spared to this church-deserted quarter of the city. This missionary, sustained by the Reformed Protestant Dutch Church, in William Street, to explore the surrounding field, visit the sick and the poor, and bring in the inhabitants and strangers to the house of God, according to the statements published, while walking down town one day, conceived the thought that an hour of prayer could be profitably employed by the business men, confining no one to the whole hour, but coming in and going out at

* We believe it was soon after the institution of daily Business Men's prayer-meetings that a prominent business man in this city was reported to have expressed himself in the following manner:

"Prayer never was so great a blessing to me as it is in this time! I should certainly either break down or turn rascal, except for it! When one sees his property taken from him every day, by those who might pay him if they were willing to make sacrifices in order to do it, but who will not make the least effort, even for this end, and by some who seem designedly to take advantage of the times, in order to defraud him—and when he himself is liable to the keenest reproaches from others if he does not pay money, which he cannot collect and cannot create—the temptation is tremendous to forget Christian Charity, and be as hard and unmerciful as anybody. If I could not get some half hours every day to pray myself into a right state of mind, I should certainly either be overburdened and disheartened, or do such things as no Christian man ought."

their convenience. He mentioned the idea to one or two persons but no one thought much of it; yet he resolved to carry it out The appointed time came; three persons met in a little room on the third floor, in the Consistory building in the rear of the church, and prayer was there offered. Mr. Lamphier (the missionary) presided, and one clergyman was present. The next meeting was composed of six persons. The next of twenty persons. The next meeting was held in the middle room, on the second floor, and now on every Wednsday noon, the Business Men's Prayer-meeting attracted increasing numbers. Its striking fitness and evident usefulness were noticed in the newspapers, secular and religious, and the suggestion was earnestly made, that it should be opened every day, instead of weekly. This was promptly done, and the meeting-room overflowed and filled a second, and eventually a third room in the same building; making three crowded prayer-meetings, one above another, in animated progress at one and the same hour. The seats were all filled, and the passages and entrances began to be choked with numbers, rendering it scarcely possible to pass in or out. The hundreds who daily went away disappointed of admission, created a visible demand for more room, and the John Street Methodist Church and lecture-room were both opened for daily noon prayer-meetings, by a committee of the Young Men's Christian Association, and were crowded at once with attendants. Meetings were multiplied in other parts of the city, and the example spread to Philadelphia, to Boston, and to other cities, until there is now scarcely a town of importance in the United States, save a few in the South, in which the Business Men's Daily Prayer-meeting is not a flourishing, and we may hope, an established institution, and a leading agency in the unprecedented awakening of public interest in religion, which now casts all the other wonders of the age into shade.

To trace the origin, or rather the original agencies, of this divine work, is a deeper task than we here propose. We should be led, more immediately, to consider the Revival Conventions, and Synodical Visitations of Churches, the Sabbath-school Conventions and Systematic Visitations of parishes, which have been held in various parts of the country for some two years past. We should then find that only a few of the more recent and general symptoms of the Divine movement in the heart of the church had been touched, and the linked succession of events would lead us farther and farther back, from one past revival to another, and from one instrumentality to another, until we had lost sight of the present state of things from which we started, among the endless ramifications of its complex origin. Generally, we must regard the century in which we live, or perhaps rather the last hundred and twenty-five years, as an epoch decidedly characterized by revivals, and by the increasing recognition, cultivation, and expectation of revivals, until the last half-century, and still more eminently the last quarter-century, has presented to view such a succession and general distribution of spiritual refreshings, and such a general increase of believing prayer and sustained, systematic, evangelical effort among Christians, as to encourage the hope that a period of loftier aim and steadier progress —in other words, of permanent "revival"—may be even now setting in, ushered by this glorious and inspiring manifestation of the Divine presence.

But we return to our simple task, to throw together the more immediate, open, and prominent beginnings and characteristics of a work of grace which we hope is but begun, and which certainly at this present writing (the first week in April, 1858,) shows no signs of abatement. Of course nothing can be farther from the character of history, than such a premature notice of events just opening to view. Yet without these vivid contemporaneous notices, history, if not left wholly without materials, would lose half its light. It should be remembered however, that at so early a stage of the work, a large part even of its earliest and most interesting features, have as yet found no opportunity to reach the public eye. Such as we find we can give.

First in order, we have taken the Noon-day Prayer-meetings, not deciding the degree of priority to which this movement is entitled among the instruments of the present state of things, but regarding them simply as the first and most remarkable public demonstration of the national awakening. The remaining pages will be mainly a compilation of records and reports, in the language of others.

Among the beginnings of the Revival in this City is to be mentioned the enterprise of "Systematic Visitation." Some time ago, a plan was set on foot, which was adopted by a large number of churches, of various denominations, in this city and Brooklyn, for the purpose of promoting attendance at divine service on the Sabbath, by *systematic visitation* of assigned neighborhoods. Each church that entered into the enterprise was allotted a certain bound, or parish, of which it was the center, in which *every house* was to be visited and the religious condition of every family inquired into The districts at first chosen to be visited were chiefly poor and low neighborhoods, where both the temporal and spiritual destitution of the people were painfully apparent. Parents were solicited to go either to the church in the district, or to some other out of it which they might prefer instead, and to send their children to the Sunday, the Mission, or the Industrial School. In this way thousands of persons, many of whom were formerly degraded and vicious, have been reclaimed to a better moral character and a higher social standing. Gradually this scheme of visitation was extended so as to include the respectable and fashionable streets, as well as the "highways and hedges," until finally no "passover" was written even on a brown-stone front, and Fifth avenue itself was not left to be exempt. And from the reports that have been presented, the results of these efforts, as seen among the higher classes of society, have been of equal interest with those in the lower. The number of rich people, who were found never to attend any church, was enormous. Another of the antecedents of the revival, has been an increased activity in the Sunday Schools. Many of the Sunday Schools, particularly of this city, have, within a very recent period, doubled, and in some instances, tripled their membership ; and many conversions have occurred among the young people who attend them as scholars. Many new Mission Sunday Schools have been established in various parts of the city, sustained by individual churches in the neighborhood.

In the city of New York a similar religious feeling has never before been known. About twenty-five years ago a revival of great power occurred in New York. Public religious meetings were then held in unusual places, and at unusual hours, and were throngingly attended, but we believe that *mid-day prayer-meetings*, held in the centre of the business circles of the city, and sustained largely by the most prominent business men, are novelties that were not then known. In fact, if the idea even of a single meeting of the character of any of the dozen or more that are now held daily in different parts of the city, had been proposed six months ago, with any probability that it would be attended to such an extent as soon to require a multiplication of rooms to accommodate the increasing congregations, the idea would have been regarded as hardly less than preposterous.

And it is a precisely similar feeling to that which is exhibited at these meetings in this city, that is now spreading throughout the country.

THE NOONDAY PRAYER-MEETINGS.—The Noon Prayer-Meeting held daily in the Methodist Church in John-street, was opened in February last, after the three rooms in the Consistory Building of the Reformed Dutch Church, in Fulton Street, were found to be too small to accommodate the increasing multitudes who were desirous of assembling at noon at some convenient place down town for devotional exercises similar to those in the Dutch Church. The meeting is composed daily of about two thousand persons, consisting of two audiences—one in the main audience-room and the other in the basement.

This meeting is more under the control of young men than that held at the same hour in the Dutch Church in Fulton Street, and is hardly ever conducted by a clergyman or an old man. The number of ladies who attend is comparatively few, and they sit chiefly in the galleries

PRAYER-MEETING IN BURTON'S OLD THEATRE.—A few years ago there suddenly arose, in one of the thriving cities of Western New York, an imperious popular demand for theatrical entertainments, which refused to be assuaged until it had been professionally ministered unto by a full company of actors. There being no theater in the place, a *church* was hired for the winter season, and was soon, by the combined efforts of carpenters and scene-painters, changed into a theatre.

On the 17th of March, Burton's old theatre, in Chambers street, lately one of the most popular places of resort for the lovers of pleasure in our country, was thrown open at mid-day for prayer, and crowded with a solemn assembly. These meetings were continued for eighteen days, until the building passed into the hands of the U. S. Government: more densely thronged, and sought by greater numbers unable to obtain an entrance, than any theatrical exhibition, perhaps, that was ever thrown open in New York. The crowd in attendance is thus described:

> "Half an hour before the time appointed for beginning the exercises, the house was packed in every corner from the pit to the roof. By noon, the entrances to the hall were so densely thronged that it required great exertions to get within hearing distance, and no amount of elbowing could force an entrance so far as to be able to get a sight of the stage. People clung to every projection along the walls; they piled themselves up on seats, and crowded the whole stage beneath, and above, and behind the curtain. The street in front was lined with carriages. The audience was composed principally of business men; there were about two hundred ladies, and not less than fifty clergymen."

The meeting was initiated by the merchants doing business in Chambers street, in the immediate vicinity of the theatre, and is continued under their supervision, the expenses being all defrayed by their contributions. When they had the first interview with Mr. Burton in relation to the leasing of the house, he expressed a perfect willingness to let the building for religious purposes, and asked the gentlemen who had the negotiation in charge if they would pray for him.

Rev. T. L. Cuyler, who conducted the first meeting, addressed the audience as follows:

"At the request of a Committee of the Young Men's Christian Association, I have come to conduct the service to-day. At last we may congratulate the defenders of the stage that a theatre has become a school of virtue, and not a school of vice—a house of prayer, and not a haunt of profanity—a spot for the real tears of penitence, and not the scene of fictitious grief over the fictitious sorrows of the stage. For this let us give God the glory!

"This is not the first time that a theatre in New York has been used for a daily prayer-meeting. In 1831, the old Chatham-street

Theatre, a haunt of obscenity, blasphemy, and vice, was purchased by a committee for purposes of worship. It was during the height of the great revival of 1831, that two gentlemen called on the lessee of the theatre and proposed to buy his lease. 'What for?' said he. 'For a church.' 'A w-h-a-t?' 'A church,' replied the gentlemen. The astonished man broke into tears, and exclaimed, 'You may have it, and I will give $1,000 toward it.' The arrangement was completed. At the close of a morning rehearsal, the beautiful hymn, 'The Voice of Free Grace,' was sung, and Mr. Tappan announced to the actors that that very evening there would be preaching *on that stage!* A pulpit was placed on the very spot where dying agonies had often been counterfeited in tragic mockery; and in front of the footlights of the stage seats for the inquirers were arranged.

"The first prayer-meeting in the theatre (which was christened 'Chatham-street Chapel') was attended by 800 persons. Among those who offered prayer were the late Rev. Hermon Norton, and the late Zachariah Lewis, one of the first editors of *The New-York Commercial Advertiser*. On the 6th of May the house was consecrated to the service of God. The Rev. Mr. Finney preached from the text, 'Who is on the Lord's side?' In the evening, the crowd was so great that many were unable to get into the building. For seventy successive nights Mr. Finney preached there to immense audiences. The *bar-room* was changed into a *prayer-room!* and the first man who knelt there poured forth these words, 'O Lord! forgive my sins. The last time I was here, Thou knowest I was a wicked actor on this stage. O Lord, have mercy on me!'

"For three years this house was used for revival meetings, and Mr. Finney continued to preach there until the erection of the late Broadway Tabernacle. That glorious revival of 1831 brought into the churches of this city many of our most active and faithful Christians, many of those who are now most prominent in the benevolent movements of the day. May the present awakening be equally fruitful in enriching God's church, and blessing a sinful world!

"To-day, for the second time in the history of New York, we set apart a disused play-house for a house of worship. Oh! what soul-tragedies may have been enacted in this very building! From youder 'pit' how many may have gone down to the pit of everlasting despair! Let our services here be as solemn as eternity! Let us invoke the presence of God's Spirit! and may this former habitation of the Tempter be the very habitation of God—the very gate of heaven to souls seeking after Jesus!

"I probably shall offer the united petition of every Christian here present, when I say, 'Come, Lord Jesus, come quickly.'"

At the doors, tracts were given away every day as the meetings were dismissed, "Issued by the Lessee of Burton's Theater, in behalf of the Committee of Merchants."

Daily meetings for prayer are held, between the hours of 12 and 1 o'clock, at the Mission Chapel in Centre street, near the Tombs. The attendance at the meeting was at first comparatively small, but has since rapidly increased, and now includes a number of persons whose previous character was not only doubtful, but openly vicious; many of whom have expressed serious concern of mind, and have come forward for prayers.

Many mechanics who work in the vicinity, and who have only half an hour to spend at noon from the labors of the day, come into the meetings blackened with smoke and dust of the forge and anvil, and participate attentively in the exercises. Many others, who cannot spend even half an hour, come in and go out at shorter intervals, so that the audience is continually changing during the hour. Many laborers, whose homes are in the upper part of the city, but whose work brings them into this vicinity, spend their noon recess in the chapel.

Numerous colored persons also are present every day, and take seats, without any seeming objection on the part of their white neighbors. The entire demeanor of the meeting, composed as the congregation is of persons in the lower classes of society, is reverent and thoughtful.

A few days since, a boy, thirteen years of age, was converted at this place through the agency of the meeting. His father was the keeper of a low groggery in the vicinity of the Five Points, who died a few months since in a fit of delirium tremens. His grandfather is well known as having been proprietor of many of the lowest dens of vicious resort in the city ; and yet this boy, with such antecedents, and with such an education and family associations, gives evidence of a true and genuine conversion. His elder brother also was recently converted, though not at this chapel. A Sabbath school is connected with the Mission, which numbers an average of about 150 children, in addition to which, a regular Bible Class for adults has been opened.

In Duane street a meeting has been in operation several weeks. It is a Union Meeting, and was started by Mr. Pratt, the missionary who labors in that portion of the city. The church is in Duane street, just west of Hudson, a very favorable location for a large meeting.

Prayer-meetings have been held in the Baptist Mariners' Church, No. 224 Cherry street, from 11 to 12 o'clock a.m., and will be continued.

THE FLYING ARTILLERY.—Among the Methodist agencies in the Revival, is a Prayer-meeting Association, composed of many of the prominent laity of the denomination, a retired merchant being its leader. They go around to different churches on Sunday, and in many instances initiate the work. The exercises consist of short prayers, hymns, and exhortations. Among the most energetic members of the Prayer-meeting Association is ex-Alderman Wesley Smith. Mr. Smith became a church member about three years ago, and has ever since led a very exemplary life. The ex-Alderman, together with ex-Councilman Jonathan Purdy, another member, are especially zealous in their exhortations. The Prayer-meeting Association are achieving great success. In consequence of their zeal in the work, the profanely inclined have christened them "The Flying Artillery of Heaven."

At the Union meeting at Mission Hall, No. 27 Greenwich street, a gentleman stated that he was transacting business with some parties yesterday, and asked a very profane friend to go with him to prayer-meeting. He went, and came away fully convinced of his great sinfulness, and asked the prayers of the meeting for him. Mr. Leland stated that a friend and himself were talking with a sea captain a few days ago, and thought it would not be amiss to say a word to him. They asked him if "he did not think it time for him to seek his soul's salvation?" The Captain said he had thought of it. The Captain, he said, went down to his ship ; in his state-room he knelt, and then beseeched and received the blessing.

Noon-day prayer-meetings have been held daily at one of the large printing offices in this city since the 6th of March with increasing interest. At the commencement of the meetings there were but four or five converts, with very few participants in the exercises, and now the number ranges as high as twelve or fourteen. The interest manifested at those meetings is very great. One of the recent converts says : "What are we to expect when printing offices are converted into religious chapels ? It is, as far as my knowledge extends, unprecedented in the history of any country, and will, no doubt, astonish many a reader." As the meetings are held between the hours of 12 and 1 o'clock, some of the men go without their dinner for the sake of attending them.

On Monday, April 5th, there was opened for the first time, a people's prayer-meeting at 333 East Twelfth street, a few doors west of the Novelty Works. More than one hundred persons were present, and it was a pleasing sight to notice the presence of a very large number of mechanics, right from the workshop, who had gathered to ask the blessing of God.

Several gentlemen who were desirous to open a new house of prayer for the accommodation of down-town business men, applied to the proprietors of the Merchants' Exchange for the use of the Rotunda. It would cheerfully have been granted, but for the fact that there is no suitable time in the day when a prayer-meeting could be held there.

A business men's Union prayer meeting, was opened in the store No. 69 Broadway, near Wall street, on Monday afternoon, April 5th, at half-past three o'clock, for the accommodation of those who cannot attend at mid-day.

The attendance of the prayer meetings at the rooms of the Young Men's Christian Association in Waverley Place, has increased so as to require the use of the reading room on the second floor of the building.

It is contemplated to open another meeting at the City Assembly Rooms, in Broadway.

The Union prayer meeting in South Brooklyn, continues to grow in interest, and attracts very general attention. The two large rooms in the rear of the Strong-Place Baptist Church, are well filled by audiences deeply imbued with the prevalent feeling.

A Union prayer meeting is held in the lecture room of the Fleet street M. E. church, near Fulton avenue, Brooklyn, every afternoon at half-past four o'clock.

A weekly bulletin of the various locations of Union prayer meetings in the city, has been posted at steamboat and ferry landings, railroad depots, newspaper offices, and other public places throughout the city.

NOONDAY PRAYER MEETINGS THROUGHOUT THE UNION.

The Philadelphia *Press*, a secular Journal, says :—

"As was announced in the last number of the *Press*, the daily prayer meetings at Jayne's Hall, are held in the main room of that capacious edifice. The room heretofore occupied contained seats for about three hundred persons, and when it was decided upon to remove into the large hall, it was with no expectation that the room would be filled. When the hour had about half elapsed yesterday, during which the mid-day meeting is held, we entered the hall, and, to our amazement, found it densely crowded, every seat being occupied, including the settees in the aisles, and a large portion of the immense galleries, and those who left for want of room upon the main floor are said to have exceeded the number who could not gain admission on the day previous, when the meeting was held in the small room adjoining. There were certainly not less than three thousand persons who entered the hall during the hour, and our reason for announcing it as an epoch is the fact that it was conceded by those present, who have reason to know, that it was the largest meeting convened for the simple purpose of prayer to God, that has ever been assembled in this country."

A gentleman from Philadelphia described to the Fulton street meeting, the absorbing interest and feeling manifested in the great meetings at Jayne's Hall. When at one of these meetings, the request was made that persons desirous of prayers should rise or raise their hands, a hard-featured man, long an infidel, scoffer and violent enemy of Christ and of all good, rose in the midst of the assembly, with both hands stretched above his head, and tears streaming down his cheeks!

A noon-day meeting is held in the Mariners' Church, on Water street, near the wharf.

Efforts have been made to assemble the members of the Fire Department to listen to the preaching of the Gospel, and this movement has not been without decided success. On one occasion nearly 2,000 regular or exempt firemen attended at the National Hotel, in Market street.

A great Revival is in progress in Newark, which is continually increasing in extent and fervor. Morning prayer meetings are held at eight o'clock, and a meeting has been started at noon.

The Union prayer meetings are attended to overflowing. Some stores in the chief business streets are closed, with a notice on the door: "Will re-open at the close of the prayer meeting." There is quite a religious interest among members of the Fire Department, with a probability that some of the engine houses will be shortly opened for prayer meetings.

Rev. H. C. Fish, writes to the Newark *Daily Advertiser*, with respect to the number of hopeful conversions in that city: "As a matter of permanent record and grateful remembrance, I have thought it well to ascertain *facts* on this point, as fully as possible. Inquiries have been addressed to thirty pastors and preachers in the city, as to the *probable* number of conversions within the limits of their respective congregations. The figures show an aggregate of 2,685. Several ministers have not been reached; and it is fair to put the number un-reported at, say, 100; which would make an aggregate of some 2,800 hopeful conversions."

Rev. Dr. Scott of Newark, states that the conversion of persons of the strongest and maturest mind in the community, is among the characteristics of the work of grace in Newark. If he had attempted to select from his congregation forty-five of its strongest minds, he would have generally taken the forty-five who had united with his church by profession.

At Paterson, N. J., a Union prayer meeting is held daily between four and five in the afternoon, and in some of the churches extra meetings every evening.

In Plainfield, Union prayer meetings are held daily.

In Hoboken, the Union prayer meetings at the Town Hall are largely attended, and all the churches are receiving accessions to their membership. The Presbyterian and the Baptist churches in West Hoboken, have both held meetings every evening this month.

In Jersey City, nearly all the churches have evening meetings, and large numbers have already professed conversion. A Union prayer meeting is held at the Lyceum, in Grand street, every morning, between the hours of seven and nine, which are animated and interesting. A prayer meeting is also held at the rooms of the Young Men's Christian Association, from half-past five to half-past six o'clock every afternoon.

In Albany the following Union prayer-meetings are held daily; two in the morning, two at noon, two in the afternoon, and one in the evening. There is a number of church meetings every evening beside. A correspondent writes:

" The meridian prayer-meetings have commenced in this city with the same crowds that attend elsewhere. Other hours have been added. At 4 p. m. to 5 meetings convene in the Fourth Presbyterian church, and from 5 to 6 at the rooms of the Young Men's Christian Association. Many are added to the churches. In Troy and Schenectady, near by, similar movements have been made, with similar gracious effect."

A prayer-meeting for the Legislature of this State has been instituted in the rooms of the Court of Appeals, at Albany, which is continued every morning. A correspondent of the New York *Commercial Advertiser*, after referring to the crowded daily prayer-meetings held in Albany, speaks of the remarkable movement in the Legislature as follows:

" Yesterday, [March 19th,] some members of the Legislature commenced meeting for prayer at 8½ in the morning, at the room of the Court of Appeals. It is opposite the Senate Chamber, and the voice of supplication and praise to the Almighty, is now heard early in the halls of our capitol. It was commenced with but six persons, but at the fifth meeting the number present filled two rooms, and the interest has increased from that time until now."

In Troy, the prayer-meetings of the Young Men's Christian Association, and one held in the meeting house of the Rev. Dr. Duncan Kennedy, on Second street, are well attended by merchants, clerks, and professional men, all seeming to exhibit a deep and abiding interest in their spiritual welfare. Meetings have been held in the various churches daily and nightly, and it is estimated that several hundred converts registered upon the rolls of membership. It seems to have taken a decided hold upon the young men of the city, very many of whom, it must be confessed, stood sadly in need of some redeeming influence. Among the most marked of the conversions is that of a man, well known in our city, who, after a career of hitherto unsubdued social recklessness in this community, being likewise regarded as wholly irreclaimable, is said to have earnestly taken up the standard of the cross. I instance this particular case because I deem it a perfect parallel with that of Mr. Orville Gardner, it having attracted comparatively as much attention hereabouts.

A letter from Hudson states:

"I am happy to state that the four evangelical churches in this city—the Reformed Dutch, the Rev. Dr. Demarest; the Baptist, the Rev. Mr. Smith; the Methodist Episcopal, and the First Presbyterian, the Rev. Mr. Leavitt—have inaugurated a Union prayer-meeting for each day in the week, from 4 to 5 o'clock, and that with one accord. The people came to them as doves to their windows. The room was thronged yesterday beyond precedent, and near 100 had only standing places. The scene was one of solemnity, deep and strong. Men, women, and children fill the seats to their utmost capacity, in an orderly and devout manner.

At Poughkeepsie Union prayer-meetings are held daily at 4 p. m., and are largely attended. It is now nearly three weeks since these meetings were commenced, and still the numbers in attendance increase daily. Religious service is held in several of the churches every evening, and all the others are holding extra meetings. Up to this time, about *three hundred* persons have confessed conversion, in the several churches in this city, and many more are seeking the Saviour.

At Peekskill, eight weeks ago, a 5 o'clock prayer-meeting was commenced in the lecture-room of the Methodist Church, which has since been very largely attended. A week subsequent to the appointment of these meetings, evening exercises were appointed, which, owing to the large attendance, have been held in the body of the church. A number of young men and women connected with the Sabbath School were the first converts, since which the work has progressed with greater power, and the number of conversions, including both old and young, has reached 300. Of these many are connected with the fire department, and others are workmen in foundries. In the New School Presbyterian Church about fifty conversions, have taken place. Peekskill has had the name of having a larger number of irreligious persons, who were openly wicked, than any other town of equal size along the river.

In Kingston, Ulster County, New York, a Union prayer-meeting was recently established in the basement of the Methodist church, which soon drew an attendance too large to be accommodated by the room, and which has since been transferred to the large lecture-room of the Reformed Dutch Church, which in its turn, has also become too small.

A correspondent in Rondout writes: "The Presbyterian church is now having meetings daily, between 12 and 1 o'clock; the principal business men of the village attend."

In Utica, in December last, the pastors of the various evangelical churches united in holding weekly Union prayer-meetings in the different churches. The interest and numbers in attendance increased so rapidly that, at the third meeting, held in the First Presbyterian church, the house was filled, including the galleries, with a deeply-interested audience. Such was the feeling in the community that, two or three weeks since, daily morning prayer-meetings were appointed in one of the large churches in the central part of the city under the direction of the Young Men's Christian Association.

The meetings have continued with great interest and a constant increase of numbers. Now, every morning the body of the house and galleries are filled full with worshippers, and frequently some have to stand. All evangelical Christians are united in this work as one man.

At Schenectady, two daily prayer-meetings are held. The revival has been in progress for nearly three months, and is still continuing with success. Every bell in the city has sounded evening after evening, and every church been filled during this time. Converts have come in with surprising rapidity. Union College has been blessed in a manner never known. Places of resort for dissipation have been thinned out. Many of the oldest inhabitants say that there was never such a time known.

At Syracuse, a daily meeting is held in Convention Hall, a place which has been heretofore the scene of much political noise and strife.

In Buffalo, Grace church has been opened for daily prayer-meetings, from 8 to 10 a. m. Similar meetings are also held every day in the Lafayette street church. Among the Presbyterians, at Dr. Thompson's church, as many as fifty have professed faith in Christ. The interest is largely increasing in Dr. Chester's, Dr. Heacock's, the Rev. Mr. Corning's, and the Rev. Mr. Rankin's churches. For months past, in the Rev. J. Hyatt Smith's church, Baptist, there has been much interest. In the Methodist churches the revival has been quite powerful. Between forty and fifty have professed religion in the Niagara street church; about the same number in Grace and Pearl street church; and about one hundred in the church at River Side. In the German church some fifteen or more have professed religion.

In Geneva a revival of great stillness, depth, and solemnity has manifested itself in the Presbyterian church under the pastoral care of the Rev. H. Winslow. About an equal number of each are subjects of the work, including many in the Sabbath school who are quite young. The revival is extending in the other congregations in this place, and a daily Union prayer-meeting is held in the Dutch Reformed Church, which is filled every morning.

A correspondent in Pen Yann writes: "For about three weeks we have had what is called a 'People's prayer-meeting,' from 8 to 9 o'clock a. m., in the basement room of the Methodist church. The room has been crowded with Christians from all our evangelical churches.

In Pittsburgh, two daily prayer-meetings are held between the hours of 11½ and 12½ o'clock. The attendance at one of these meetings numbers about 700, and at the other about 300. The interest in this city has manifested itself chiefly within a few weeks past, and the daily prayer-meetings are of recent appointment. The churches in the neighborhood are also sharing in the revival, and gathering its fruits.

In Cleveland, several morning prayer-meetings are held in the basements of the different churches, which are largely attended by business men, who stop at the meetings as they go to their stores ; the united attendance is about 2,000. Great interest exists, not only in the churches, but in the community generally. Plymouth Congregational Church has been for some time past occupied with extra meetings, which have increased in frequency and interest, till now there are *five daily*—commencing at six o'clock in the morning, and closing at nine in the evening. These gatherings are designed to meet the necessities of the different classes in the congregation, and the community generally. Eight hundred persons have been recently received into the evangelical churches of the city.

The Cincinnati *Gazette* says, "that the attendance at the daily prayer-meetings in this city is so large that the room in which they are held is not sufficient to accommodate the multitudes that flock to the place. The large lecture-room of the First Presbyterian church has been thrown open, and day-meetings will be organized in several other rooms in the basement."

Noonday Union prayer-meetings have been commenced in Indianapolis, Ia. There is much religious interest pervading the whole town. Let all the Christians of the State (says the *Witness*) unite at noon to pray for their capital, that God will work mightily here, where the strongholds of Satan are.

In Chicago, noon prayer-meetings are held each day at the Brick church, formerly First Presbyterian, corner of Clark and Washington streets. A similar service has been commenced at Metropolitan Hall. The Hall was full at the first meeting. Most interesting morning and noon prayer-meetings are held at the First Baptist church, with preaching service in the evening, at which very striking manifestations of the Spirit's power are seen. A letter received from Chicago, under date of March 24, says : "The religious interest now existing in this city is very remarkable. More than 2,000 business men meet at the noon prayer-meeting. The Metropolitan Hall is crowded to suffocation. The interest in the First Baptist church is beyond anything ever known in this city, and exceeds anything I have ever seen in my life. Some who have come to the city on business, have become so distressed about their condition, as sinners against God, that they have entirely forgotten their business in the earnestness of their desire for salvation. I am amazed to see such evidences of God's grace and power manifested among men. Every section of the country is alike favored by the Lord. I might add that the First Baptist church have daily meetings from eight to nine in the morning, twelve to one at noon, and six and a half o'clock evening. The church to-day have had an all-day meeting."

At Detroit, morning prayer-meetings for business men, both at the Baptist church and the old Congregational, are crowded by the business men of all denominations. In nearly all the churches a quickening interest has been manifest. The First Baptist church has had meetings, under appointment, every morning for two weeks. The number of inquirers is on the increase, and numerous conversions have taken place. In the Congress-street Methodist church, over 140 conversions have taken place.

At Louisville, Ky., the daily Union prayer-meeting numbers 1,000 in attendance. One writer says, "The spirit of God seems to be brooding over our city, and to have produced an unusual degree of tenderness and solemnity in all classes. Never since our residence in the city have we seen so fair a prospect for a general and thorough work of grace as is now indicated."

In St. Louis, Mo., an unusual interest has recently been manfested in the churches and in the business circles of the city. Daily prayer-meetings are held, which are well attended by all classes of people, and great seriousness exists; all the churches are crowded. All classes of society appear to feel the influence. A lady of wealth, and heretofore among the leaders of fashion, was lately converted, and united with the Baptist church.

A gentleman from Ohio lately stated, that by adding his personal observations to those of a friend, he could say, that from Omaha City, Nebraska, to Washington, *there was a line of prayer-meetings along the whole length of the road;* so that, wherever a Christian traveller stopped to spend the evening, he could find a crowded prayer-meeting, across the entire breadth of our vast republic.

At Washington, five daily prayer-meetings are held, at half-past six, ten, and eleven, a.m., and at five and seven, p.m., in the rooms of the Young Men's Christian Association, and in the churches. Some members of Congress have met to arrange for the formation of "a Congressional Union Prayer-meeting." A correspondent writes as follows of the meeting in the First Presbyterian church: "The church can scarce contain the people. Requests are daily preferred for an interest in the prayers offered, and the reading of these forms one of the tenderest and most affecting features of the meetings. Particular pains are taken to disclaim and exclude everything like sectarian feeling. General astonishment is felt at the unexpected rapidity with which the work has thus far proceeded, and we are beginning to anticipate the necessity of opening another church." Not less than 1,000 persons are in attendance at some of the meetings for prayer.

In Baltimore, daily prayer-meetings are held, by the Young Men's Christian Association. They are well attended, and considerable interest appears to manifest itself at every service. In addition to the meeting held at the rooms of the Association, Fayette street, at 12 o'clock, there are two others held during the day—one at the German Reformed church, and the other at Harmony Hall. The young men of the Seventh Baptist church set apart Tuesday as a day of fasting and prayer. Several other churches have done likewise, and are holding daily meetings. In addition to these, a general business men's prayer-meeting is held, similar to those in New York.

In Richmond, Va., a daily prayer-meeting has been recently established.

In Lynchburg, Va., a revival is in progress, resulting in many conversions, chiefly of young men.

A daily morning prayer-meeting is held in the rooms of the Young Men's Christian Association, Great St. James street, Montreal, for the special benefit of business men. A daily Union prayer-meeting is held in the same city, in the American Presbyterian church, between the hours of four and five, p.m.

In Boston, Prof. Finney of Oberlin College, well known as a revival preacher, has been laboring, during the past winter, as in the preceding. In addition to the usual meetings in the different churches, daily prayer-meetings are now held as follows: At the South Baptist church, from eight to nine, a.m.; at the Old South chapel, half past eight to half-past nine, a.m., and for business men from twelve to one, p.m.; also at Salem-street church, same hour; at Park-street vestry, and Church-street Methodist vestry, at three o'clock; at the Meionaon (Tremont Temple), four to five p.m.; at the Young Men's Christian Association rooms, half-past five to half-past six. Several of the churches have meetings every evening. Dr. Kirk preaches two evenings in the week in Mount Vernon chapel.

The business men's prayer-meetings, which many of the chief merchants in the city leave their counting-rooms to attend, are of a character never before known in Boston or Massachusetts. A correspondent, in speaking of the character of the work, says:

"It is not excitement. There is none of that wildness so often manifested in seasons of religious interest. The work has reached the 'Black Sea,' our Five Points. 'Publicans and sinners' are awakened, and are entering the prayer-meetings of their own accord. Some of them manifest signs of sincere repentance, and a movement is on foot to make them a home, to place them where vice shall not find nor temptation allure them."

Parents residing out of Boston, who have sons in business in that city, whom they would like to be visited by some of the members of the Christian Association for religious conversation, are requested to send the required information to C. D., Box No. 2,259, Boston.

At one of the prayer-meetings a few days ago, an instance was mentioned of a man who, under deep conviction, burned up his cards, and in a day or two was converted. At another meeting a gentleman arose and said, that "he had been reading infidel books for the last few years; but that, during the previous night, on his bended knees, alone, he was enabled to make a complete surrender of himself to God, and found peace." One pious merchant in Milk street brought in three or four of his clerks, and at the close of the meeting introduced them to some of the young men, who walked home with them to tell them of the blessedness of serving God.

The noonday meeting on the corner of Ferry and North streets, Boston, is attended by an unusual number of persons who have been hitherto profligate and abandoned. Considerable money has been subscribed to provide homes for those who have been converted and reformed.

At the Unitarian church, of which the Rev. Dr. Robbins is pastor, Union prayer-meetings are held every Tuesday evening, which are densely crowded. The services are conducted alternately by the Rev. Messrs. Robbins, Ellis, and Coolidge.

In Springfield, the noon prayer-meetings exhibit an increasing interest. Inquiry-meetings are held by nearly every pastor in the city.

In Lynn, working-men's prayer-meetings are held daily at the First Baptist church, between the hours of one and two o'clock, and a young man's prayer-meeting is daily held at the rooms of the Young Men's Christian Association for one hour, commencing at half after five, p.m. The attendance and interest at these meetings are increasing.

At New Bedford, a combined business men's and young men's meeting has been successfully added to the services which now occur at almost every hour of the day and evening. A new and very moderate estimate of presumable conversions in New Bedford is 800; a less cautious computation might run the number up to nearly a thousand.

In Haverhill, Mass., the daily prayer-meeting crowds one of the churches. So profound has been the impression of the Spirit, that in some instances half the assembly have been observed silently weeping. Some of the most hardened men in the place have been recently renewed. One of the pastors recently went the rounds of his parish, and found not a single house in which there were not either inquiring souls, or believers wrought to the intensest solicitude for the irreligious.

At New Haven, every morning at eight o'clock, one of the largest churches in the city is crowded to excess, and every afternoon at five another—with those who go to pray and those who are seeking the way of life, together with some careless ones who go first from curiosity, but not always in vain. There is a Young Men's Prayer-meeting every evening at half-past eight o'clock, in the large hall of the Institute building. One night, about forty requested prayers for themselves.

The revival in Yale College is probably without a precedent, so far as numbers interested are concerned. In fact, it is said to include nearly all the students; among the converts are some who have been very bitter scoffers, and who were tolerably well armed with the philosophy of the infidel.

Large daily Prayer-meetings are held at Hartford. A noteworthy feature of the revival at Hartford, is that prayer-meetings have been held in several fire-engine houses. The attendance has been large, the persons present being chiefly members of the companies.

In New London, a Union mid-day prayer-meeting is held in the vestry of the First Baptist Church in State street. The rules of the New York meeting in the North Dutch Church, have been adopted.

At Bethel, Connecticut, a Union meeting is held from four to five o'clock, every afternoon, attended by farmers, mechanics, and storekeepers, who suspend business entirely for the hour. Upwards of two hundred persons have been converted during the last two months. A Young Men's Prayer-Meeting has been established, and is well attended. About one hundred and fifty of the converts have attached themselves to the Congregational church.

In the city of Portland, Me., morning and noon prayer-meetings have been held for some time past in the vestries of the Free street and Union churches, and which more recently have become so crowded that it has been found necessary to adjourn them to the churches for larger accommodations. In the vestry of the Congregational church, of which the Rev. Dr. Dwight is the pastor, a morning prayer-meeting is held every day at eight and nine o'clock. The morning, afternoon and evening prayer-meetings are attended by crowds. In the evenings the church bells summon thousands to the various churches, and the religious interest is on the increase.

In Concord, New Hampshire daily prayer-meetings have been recently appointed, at which the attendance thus far has been very encouraging. In many of the churches more than usual interest is manifested, and the general state of things is hopeful.

In Providence, a time of religious interest like the present was never before known. Nearly every church has been awakened and the conversions are numerous. The morning prayer-meetings, commenced some weeks ago in Franklin Hall, have increased in attendance until filled to overflowing, and arrangements were required for multiplying facilities for those pressing to gain admission. An additional morning meeting has been opened in the vestry of the Richmond street Meeting-house. A five o'clock meeting has also been commenced in the vestry of the First Baptist Meeting-house, and another at the same hour in the vestry of the Beneficent Congregational Meeting-house on Broad street. All of them are fully attended, and are evidently making a strong impression. It is a fact obvious to common observation that more persons of both sexes are at this moment engaged in religious inquiry than at any former time in the history of our city; and when men are seen leaving their business to engage for an hour in social devotions, they indicate a feeling that necessarily affects others, and tends to draw the minds of the thoughtless to the vital question of the soul's highest welfare. Thus far, these meetings have been free from all appearance of unhealthy excitement.

The revival appears to be extending in Northern New England, which has been comparatively slow to feel the influence of the general mevement. In Portland, where the interest has been for some time deep and remarkable, it is greatly increasing. In addition to meetings before named, two large public halls have been opened for mid-day prayer.

The same spirit is prevailing in all the surrounding towns. The watchmen in Portland were holding prayer-meetings in the watch-houses. In Skowhegan, men shut up their stores and go to prayer-meetings at ten o'clock in the forenoon. A man in Bath had converted his bar-room into a place of prayer. All along on the river, the work of God is going on.

In Vermont and New Hampshire, special religious interest is awakened in Brattleboro, Bellows Falls, Claremont, Dartmouth College, Haverhill, Northfield, St. Albans, Burlington, Castleton,

Middlebury, Derby, and Manchester. In most or all of these places, there are daily prayer-meetings ; at Burlington they are held daily at noon.

A supplement, containing the important intelligence and pointed appeals copied from American religious papers, concerning the great awakening in the United States, which appeared in the Montreal *Witness* has been issued and widely distributed through the city of Montreal, and a copy has also been sent to every Protestant minister in Canada.

SPIRIT OF THE MEETINGS IN NEW YORK.

The following card is posted in a conspicuous manner at the John street, and other meetings of the kind.

YOUNG MEN AND YOUTH

ARE "AT HOME" HERE,

AND MUST NOT

HESITATE TO TAKE PART.

Other notices are put up in these meetings for the proper regulation of the exercises. The following rules are not adopted entire at all the meetings, but will serve to show the general spirit and mode of proceeding in all.

"*Order of Exercises and suggestions for the Government of the Business Men's Daily Union Prayer-Meeting, No.* 44, *John street.*

" 1st.—Hymn, not over four stanzas.

" 2d.—Reading Scriptures, never over fifteen to twenty verses.

" 3d.—Prayer by Leader.

" These three exercises, not to occupy over twelve minutes ; then the meeting to be left open for prayer or exhortation. No person to pray or exhort over three minutes, nor pray and exhort the same day. At half-past twelve o'clock the leader will ask any who wish the prayers of the meeting for themselves to rise without speaking, and remain standing a few seconds—a half minute being allowed for this. At the touch of the bell will begin a season of two minutes' silent prayer, to be broken by the leader asking some brother by name to lead in prayer.

" It is desired that no more than two consecutive prayers or exhortations should follow each other.

"When a verse of any hymn is desired to be sung, let it be announced distinctly, that all may find it, as it may not be familiar to each one, and never over two verses at a time.

"Whoever leads the meeting, or takes part in the exercises, must remember it is very desirable that they do not begin in low tones, but throughout, speak distinctly, with their voices somewhat raised, and facing the larger part of the audience from where they may be seated.

"When special requests for prayer are read by the leader or made by the audience, let them not be disregarded by the one who next leads in prayer.

"The pastors of the Churches, the Sabbath Schools, Bible Classes, and the Churches of our cities and land, should be made the *special* subjects of prayer for the last half hour each Saturday, that the Sabbath succeeding may be a great day in Zion.

"Young men are expected to take part.

"The leader will announce the closing hymn punctually five minutes before one—any one having the floor yielding immediately—and ask for the benediction from any clergyman present.

"A collection to defray necessary expenses will be taken Wednesdays and Saturdays, while singing the closing hymn.

"All notices must be written plainly, and pass through the Committee before reading. Union notices will be gladly read; but those of denominational character will be declined.

"The leader will strike the bell whenever the rules are disregarded, or he wishes to gain the floor, if others are before him, in order to direct the exercises at any time.

"The singing will be led by *one* person near the desk, so there may be no confusion in this regard.

"No controverted points discussed or announcements of what denomination the brother may belong to must be made upon the floor.

"It must be understood that those who cannot remain the whole hour should come and go as suits their convenience.

"N. B.—The Trustees of the Church, request that the use of tobacco be dispensed with during the hour.

"Those coming early will please *fill* seats forward. All should take seats immediately upon entering the house, as far up in the pews as possible. When all seats are filled, walk down the aisle near the desk and stand, so that none may be kept out. Standing at the stove, near the door, should be avoided by all.

"By order of the Committee on Devotional Meetings of the New York Young Men's Christian Association."

These rules are strictly enforced. A person who overruns his time, either in prayer or remark, is promptly called to order by the stroke of the bell, and he is expected to consider this reminder as no discourtesy, and immediately to obey it by taking his seat.

It is among the benefits of the present revival which can hardly fail to endure, that we have been taught how to conduct prayer-meetings. There is something in this primitive "assembling of ourselves together," which is adapted to act powerfully upon our religious life through the principles of our social nature, if we but know how to seize upon it. To prescribe an awakened state of religion in the souls of the people, as the infallible condition of a good prayer-meeting, is a sort of "begging the question." This is precisely what we solicit a good prayer-meeting for. The animated daily prayer-meetings which are springing up and multiplying all over our country, with a press of general earnestness which compels the restriction of every person participating, to three or five minutes, set before the Christian mind a vivid illustration of the proper method of these means of grace. We shall be likely to remember hereafter, that if we would meet to edification, we must unite in a vigorous effort to crowd the hour with brief, terse, pointed utterances, of prayer, sentiment, or exhortation, from the greatest variety of speakers. If there were no such thing as weariness of flesh or spirit, and nothing else to do but sit the livelong day, and every one had the tongue of an angel—still the five-minute rule would be necessary in substance for a good prayer-meeting. Rapid succession is essential to the *union* of many utterances in one unbroken chain, of many notes in one expressive melody, of many individuals in the collective majesty of a "public." A succession of prolonged tones may be each never so sweet, or soft, or grand, and may vary throughout the widest compass of the scale; but they are not music, for the want of connection and unity. Instead of a dialogue, it is a series of soliloquies, and the wonderful product of the social principle by which mere *men* become that sublime object MAN, and can in that character hold exalted converse, the whole with each, and each with the whole—is lost.

ADDRESSES.

MR. BEECHER.—I am ashamed of myself, positively, to be an object of more faith than my Saviour ; yet I have persons coming to me every day of my life, with their wants and troubles, and when I think of the injustice of coming to me thus, instead of going to Christ, I feel just like pushing them away. How eagerly they believe every statement I make ; how they hang upon my sympathy, and hope I will let them come again to-morrow. I say to myself, if you would only come to Christ with half the faith that you come to me, you might be rejoicing in half an hour. Suppose now, that, instead of a man, sinful and erring like yourselves, you should put in my place the august form of the Lord Jesus Christ, full of benignity glorious with goodness, and with a sweetness that is more than any mother ever knew for her darling child, waiting patiently, bending over you and saying, "Come unto me and take my yoke upon you ;" "learn of me and ye shall find rest to your souls," "for he that cometh unto me I will in no wise cast out." Suppose you should hear Jesus Christ saying, "I have been out to seek and search for lost men, and I have found you, and I am persuading you to come to me, believe me I love you, that I love you now." If there is a man that has one thought toward God, it is because the love of God is drawing him sympathetically to himself. It is a blessed thought that Jesus Christ is longing for you, and I would that you might turn still more earnestly to Jesus Christ and say, "Lord, I believe thee, I believe thou lovest me ; I believe thou desirest to make me thine, and from this hour it shall be the object of my life to please thee, and the one firm object of my life to serve thee." Wont you try the effect of that, some of you, to-day? Try it at once, even now, while I am speaking.

A gentleman who stood in the doorway said that, some weeks since a merchant came here from Albany, and called on one of our New York merchants to buy some goods. At 12 o'clock the New

York merchant looked at his watch, and asked to be excused for an hour. The other objected, as he was in haste to get through with his business. He replied that he must go to prayer-meeting ; it was of more importance than to sell his whole stock of goods. The gentleman from Albany inquired if he could not pray enough at morning and night, without leaving his business at noon ? The merchant said he could not ; and by persuasion and gentle force he induced his friend to go to the prayer-meeting with him. That man went into that meeting, became interested, and came out a converted man, went home to Albany, and immediately started those prayer-meetings there which have been so blessed of God.

A young man said he was walking up West street, a day or two since, when he saw a sailor sitting upon the steps of a store, who, as he looked at him, sprang up and grasped his hand, when he found it was an old schoolfellow from Connecticut. After some conversation, he asked his new-found sailor friend if he was a Christian, and the answer had struck him as very forcible ; it was, "By God's grace, I am."

That young man was the only Christian on board the ship, and he was now on the sea, the only servant of Christ among so many who were, perhaps, sending up blasphemies instead of prayers, and he hoped the brethren would remember him in their prayers, that he might be kept, and enabled to preach Christ wherever he went.

The Rev. J. P. Thompson, (colored,) Pastor of the Zion Church, in Leonard street, wanted to say a word. He had been engaged in this work since he was a boy, and he was now nearly 40 years of age. "I have striven since I was 14 years of age to live right and to love God ; I believe I love him, I *know* I do. I have been to this house before, and my heart has been so full of love to God—especially the first time I came here—that I had to return to my own place, corner of Leonard and Church streets, and bless God." He was happy to say that there had been a continuous outpouring of the spirit of God in his church since New-Year's eve. Both white and colored had been converted there ; and out of some three hundred, sixty or seventy had been saved.

After the singing, Mr. Beecher said :

It takes the summer whole months to ripen fruit ; but the sum mer of God's love does not require weeks nor months. There is no reason that the fruit that blossoms here right in the beginning of this meeting should not ripen and fall before the close of it. In the days of the Apostles, in the early periods of the Gospel, when there was simplicity of faith in the hearers, men were converted so quick that it was like a shot ; the report and the explosion were almost simultaneous. And so when the preacher and the hearer are of one accord, I think that in such an atmosphere as that, souls may be converted before one golden hour rolls by. Let us begin, then, in the conviction that souls may be converted here now. Will some brother that has this spirit pray ?

Mr. Beecher related an instance of the conversion of a sea captain a few days ago, from "a word fitly spoken" by a man who had business relations with him. The word led him to go to prayer-meeting, where he was so much affected that he went home, locked his door, got down on his knees, and did not rise until he had evidence that God had pardoned his sins. That single word saved that man, and who could tell where the end would be when that Christian captain should have preached the Gospel of Christ around the globe !

A man in the parquette, who had spoken before, now prayed. His prayer, like his exhortation, was principally composed of Scripture quotations.

Mr. Beecher—My Christian brother, you forget to pray for the only thing we ask prayers for. Let some other brother pray for the subjects of these requests.

A clergyman on the stage prayed for them.

Mr. Beecher—When persons have an old hope that does not keep them warm, they should always do as men do with their garments—go and get a suit that does. An old hope that keeps a man talking and talking, is not worth anything ; Jesus Christ is worth a great deal. Gather manna every morning ; never gather enough for two.

The Leader—I reserve to the last a petition which I shall read, and for which I shall offer prayer by and by. We will spend two minutes in silent prayer. At the close of that time, I will thank some brother to lead audibly in prayer.

The silence which ensued was peculiarly solemn and impressive, and was broken by prayer by the Rev. Mr. Nott, of the Broome street Baptist Church.

A woman in the gallery told how God had heard her prayers for the conversion of her only son, and reminded young men of the anxiety of their praying mothers.

The other message, continued a speaker, with which I am charged, and which I am happy to discharge, comes from the United Christians at Elmira, in this State. I had the pleasure of meeting with them yesterday. They have discarded their ordinary place of worship, and now meet in the large Presbyterian Church. Mr. Smith said the meetings there had the same characteristics as those here—quietness and power. The work seemed like a rising tide, insensibly but powerfully rising higher and higher, reaching all classes of persons. The message which the brethren of Elmira had sent was that delightful prophecy of Zaccariah, who records, "That the inhabitants of the city shall encourage each other," &c.

A gentleman in the corner of the room said that, a few evenings since he had been at a meeting some eight or ten miles from the city, where a lady rose and asked liberty to speak, which was granted. Her heart was full of anxiety for her two sons, and she poured out her petitions to God as only a mother could. After she closed, she turned to him and asked him to bear her petition to this meeting, that those two sons might be gathered into the fold of God. He would like to ask those present if they realized the fact that eternity was before them ; on the one hand everlasting life, and on the other everlasting damnation. If this house was in a blaze, and the cry was "Fire !" all would rush for the door. "But there is an eternal fire pursuing you—oh ! fly to Jesus Christ, and find rescue from the danger."

Mr. Hart said he could not describe his feelings to-day. He thought of the time when, a lad, he used to trip up to the old church on this spot. The pulpit was on the wrong end now. He heard there the silvery voice of the sainted Summerfield, as he poured forth his tones so lovingly. There was also the stalwart Elder Merwin, whom the old men would remember, whose strong voice was not to be forgotten ; and he could now point to the man who used to lead the choir, Mr. Daniel Ayres, (who sat close to the pulpit,) or rather, who used to be *led* by a blind woman, whose name was Hannah Baldwin. Her eyes were closed, but her tongue was loose. How she sang, as she sat in the highest seat! Preacher and singers had all gone to that happy land where there was no blindness. We, said he, wait a little longer—how little, none can know.

A gentleman in the centre of the house said that, on last Saturday he had resolved to confess his sins and come to the Saviour. On Sunday he did go to God, but could find no rest. His brethren talked and prayed with him. He had often thought prayer a "humbug," but then he saw right into his brother's heart. He went to the altar, but could get no relief. When his friends asked him if he felt better, he almost said "Yes;" but something within told him to say the truth. On Monday he read his Bible, and prayed all day, yet went to bed without relief. But on Tuesday morning all seemed clear to him. He wanted to tell his friends that religion was a fact to him.

Mr. Hart said he would invite any who wished a special interest in the prayers of the meeting to rise. Quite a number rose in various parts of the house.

Two minutes were then spent in silent prayer. After which Mr. W. E. Dodge prayed specially for those who had shown that they needed an interest in the Saviour.

A young man in the gallery said he wanted to say a few words, not to those who were old soldiers of the Lord, because he felt like a child just beginning to walk, but to those who were seeking Christ. "If you are seeking Christ," said he, "do not be *ashamed* of it. It is a design of the devil to make you ashamed to allow your wants to be made known. Heed him not, but come to the Saviour without delay."

A gentleman on the west side of the house quoted the passage, "Quench not the Spirit!" There is no doubt, he remarked, but we may so grieve the Spirit as to drive him away from us entirely. In times like these we should be especially careful. He instanced the case of a young lady who had made a profession, but was not living a Christian life. She awoke one morning very early, indeed, feeling a strange impulse to pray. At last she yielded to the impulse, and fell upon her knees at the bedside. There the morning sun found her—ready to answer to the call of "Follow me." "I will follow thee through good report and evil report." If she had neglected the impulse, it might have been the last call of the Spirit to her soul.

Mr. Dodge said he knew it was against the order to speak and pray both, but he wished to relate the case of a lady moving in high social position in this city. A few Sundays ago a poor Christian woman, who was a friend of hers, called on her to talk with her about her spiritual condition. She received her very kindly, and a few days after, the poor Christian woman was surprised to see her friend come to her with tears in her eyes, feeling very anxious about her soul. Then the lady was apparently in good health, but last Friday God came to that house, and last night the pastor stood by her dying bed, and asked if "Jesus could not make a dying bed feel soft as downy pillows are?" "Oh, yes! Oh, yes!" she said—and went to heaven.

A gentleman near the door offered a short prayer, after which the final hymn was given out, commencing,

"Before Jehovah's awful throne,"

being the hymn appointed to be sung at all the meetings on Tuesday. The tune was "Old Hundred," the whole congregation rising and uniting their voices, producing a strong effect.

At one of the meetings, a gentleman said that in Manchester, N.H., where a minister preached from the text, "Go out and bring in the lame, the halt, and the blind," a young lady went out, and at the next meeting brought in four young ladies; and in a short time, three out of the four were converted.

A gentleman rose and stated that he had been requested by a lady to solicit the prayers of that meeting in behalf of her daughter-in-law, who had become a drunkard, and who, in consequence, had been for some time separated from her kind and tender husband. She had been found, the previous day, in the yard at the back of the house, in a state of beastly intoxication, and was at that moment in a house close to the place of meeting under the care of that mother-in-law.

He also told of a gambler who, on a recent Sunday morning, had his attention attracted by the sound of a church bell, upon which he reasoned with himself, and eventually concluded that the church bell was a call for him as much as for any person else. He knelt behind a fence, and prayed to God to strengthen him, and to give him grace and faith, and he is now with the people of God, living at peace with his formerly troubled conscience.

Another gentleman said he knew of a distiller in this city who, a day or two ago, became uneasy as to the condition of his soul. He went to his minister and asked him what he must do to be at peace with God. "Believe in the Lord Jesus Christ," was the reply. "I cannot, I am a distiller," was the response. "Well, then," said the minister, "you must give up your salvation or your distillery." He went home, slept, and in the morning informed his partner that he must give up his distillery and save his soul. This man was now living a different life, believing in God, and trusting in him to supply all his wants.

Some general observations were made as to the importance of canvassing the neighborhood thoroughly, and bringing larger numbers to hear the gospel.

Another speaker said that he had been in a hotel next door, and invited eight men to come into the meeting who were playing billiards. He had no doubt that many others might be brought in in that way.

"Prayers are requested for a minister's son in Joliet, Illinois, who is away from home and friends.

The writer offered a similar case last Tuesday. Those prayers have been answered in the undoubted conversion of the young man in whose behalf they were asked."

Of the noonday meetings in New York, one visitor says: All were crowded, and almost every opportunity to speak or pray was sought by several earnest competitors. In the Chambers street meeting, many of the addresses were from persons, young and old, who had just given themselves to God. Among the many requests for prayer, was one from a young lady in behalf of her impenitent brother, now on his death-bed, and in despair. Two minutes silent prayer was announced, and many supplications, tears and sobs responded to the affecting appeal.

A sailor in the orchestra said that before prayer was offered he wanted to say that he and his brother had a quarrel some six months ago. Since that time he had found Christ precious to his soul, and he wanted prayer offered for his brother, that he might be brought into the right way, and be as happy as he was.

A gentleman in the upper circle said that a sea-captain, a friend of his, who had just come into port, informed him that he met five ships as he was coming in, and they all reported having prayer-meetings on board at 12 o'clock every day.

Another gentleman in the upper circle said that a very short time ago he wes an unbeliever. He used to stay at home on Sunday and read the Sunday newspapers, but having been induced to attend one of these meetings to gratify curiosity, he did so, and last Sunday he was not able to sit in his chair or to rest contented at home. He went to church and heard his sins laid before him. Now he had got the Saviour's cross and was resolved to cling to it.

Another man on the stage said he had come to the city upon very urgent business, but he found the good work going on here, and he resolved at once to remain here.

An opportunity was then given for all to rise, or otherwise signify their desire for the prayers of the people. In response to this, nearly two hundred persons, of both sexes, asked to be prayed for.

A gentleman in the parquette wished to speak for his son less than three days old. He was a much-blessed father in the conversion of two children, son and daughter, of whom he did not suspect anything until she asked, " Father, are certain attitudes of the will towards God conversion?" He was detained from his counting-room until after 11 o'clock. He ran in and said, " Henry, is there anything to-day?" to which the reply was made, " Father, I'm converted; at half-past nine o'clock to-day the Spirit of God was opened to me. My heart was so full that I had to turn the key in the door and run to John street." They say that he came up with the pen behind his ear: so easy is it for those young men to find the kingdom " to-day."

An old gentleman in the dress circle offered an earnest prayer for the owner of the building, the petition being responded to by numerous " amens!" in the audience.

Still another voice ascended from the parquette, in prayer for Mr

Burton, that the great Father might let him know that there was a God.

While the prayer was being offered, Mr. Burton was within a short distance of the speaker, and manifested considerable emotion.

The sound of distant singing was now heard, when Mr. Beecher said, "Brethren, do you hear that? Stop a moment and listen to that: that is the singing in the old bar-room of this theatre! Let us spend two minutes in silent prayer and thanksgiving!" With one accord 3,000 heads were bowed, and for two minutes no sound was heard save the singing from the old bar-room, and the ripple of the gas at the footlights. No more impressive scene was ever produced within those walls.

REQUESTS FOR PRAYER.

"A Christian merchant earnestly desires the prayers of God's people for his co-partners in business, and for all the young men in their employment unconverted to God."

"An anxious wife is praying earnestly at this hour for her husband, who once made a profession of religion, but is now fearful that he never was born of the Spirit, and is in darkness. She asks for an interest in your prayers in his behalf."

"A mother earnestly solicits an interest in the prayers of all Christians for a husband who once professed religion, but who has now backslidden from God."

One of the worst cases that I have ever read—because a man that has backslidden—not that has apostatized and knows it, but that has backslidden and thinks that he is a Christian, just enough to keep him from being one—that is one of the most desperate of all cases.

"The prayers of those who are accustomed to intercede with God, are requested by a San Franciscan, that the Almighty would visit the city of San Francisco with a gracious outpouring of his Spirit. Remember your brothers and fathers on the Pacific coast in your secret prayers. 'He *can* save even to the uttermost.'"

"The prayers of this meeting are asked by a grandson, who has recently been converted, for an aged grandfather, whose hairs are silvered by age, and who has passed the years of 'threescore and ten. Pray, brother Beecher, that he may be converted."

"The prayers of this meeting are requested for a young lady who scoffs at religion.

"Don't forget her, brethren. She has no one to pray for her but the writer of this. Oh, pray for her."

An elderly gentleman, in the centre of the house, offered prayer, remembering the young lady's case.

"The prayers of Christians are requested for a young man—the son of a clergyman—who is an idle jester on the subject of religion, and who has, within the last hour, been heard to ridicule these meetings, and to jest upon these subjects."

"A lady, eighty-seven years of age, who has always lived a worldly life, and who seems bent upon going into eternity trusting in her own righteousness, declined an earnest invitation of the writer to accompany him to this meeting: but she seemed unusually impressed when told that between 1 and 2 o'clock to-day, the prayers of this congregation of several hundreds of persons, would be offered up to God in her behalf. The writer, on leaving her, requested her to pray for herself at the same hour of the day."

"Prayers are requested for a young man who has thus far resisted all persuasions to attend these meetings, and who is in these rooms to-day for the first time."

"A sister, who has been praying daily three years for the conversion of an only brother, asks an interest in your prayers."

"A brother requests the earnest prayers of this meeting in behalf of a loved but thoughtless sister, that she may be led to think more of the things which pertain to her peace, and to choose that good part which shall not be taken away from her."

"A young man, connected with one of the general government offices in this city, having become deeply impressed concerning the salvation of his soul, while attending the glorious Union prayer-meetings in this house, earnestly requests to be remembered by the people of God here assembled, in their prayers, to the end that he may find peace in Jesus. Also, he would ask for the supplication of this people in behalf of her whom he so deeply loves, his affianced wife, who is also earnestly inquiring the way to heaven."

"Prayers are requested for a sister who is given to intemperance."

"A few praying souls in Spring street Presbyterian Church, deeply bewailing the spiritual desolation of that Zion, beseech you to unite with them in wrestling and importuning on her behalf. Brethren and sisters, pray for us, and if you can, come over and help us."

"I wish to state that I feel myself a great sinner, and that there is no hope for me. I feel lost forever. Although I am young in years, I feel old in sins, and know not what to do to be saved. I feel that the spirit of God has left me altogether, and if I remain in this state what will become of my soul? May God have mercy on me! Hell stands staring me in the face. Would to God that I may become converted. Pray particularly for me, and I will try to pray for myself."

"A widow asks for the prayers of the brethren and sisters for a son brought up under careful religious instruction, who last night *cursed his mother*—that he may this day be brought to the feet of Jesus."

"A young man desires prayers for a friend who is a professor, but does not know whether he is saved or not."

"The prayers of Christians are most earnestly requested by a son in behalf of an aged father, nearly seventy years old. A family of ten children are praying morning, noon, and night for him."

"It is earnestly requested by a group of four persons, who will be present at the meeting in Burton's theatre this morning, that Mr. Burton may be specially remembered in our petitions, and may God answer prayer, even so as to surprise him who has desired it for himself."

"Oh! pray for me. I was touched with the prayer of Mr. Beecher in this place on Monday. I am one of those who have not a father or mother—no Christian friends. Hated and despised by my own sex, I have felt abandoned. I am yet in a hopeless condition in life, but I have prayed that he who conversed with the woman of Samaria may reveal himself to my soul. Will you present my case to 'Our Father which art in heaven,' when you pray; and when you pray for me, remember all abandoned young women, made so by the heartlessness of unprincipled men, and kept so by the pitiless prejudice of our own sex.

"MARTHA."

The above was written in a neat, legible hand.

COMMUNION BY TELEGRAPH.

Among the remarkable and beautiful features of the new revival, it is delightful to observe how "the Holy Spirit seems to occupy with Divine power and glory, all the common channels of man's intercourse with man. No speech so humble and secret—no organ of intelligence so vast, so swift, so new and wonderful—but the Spirit claims them all for its service. The electric telegraph conveys the thrill of Christian sympathy, with the tidings of abounding grace, from multitudes to multitudes in every city simultaneously assembled, in effect almost bringing a nation together in one praying concourse. The Press, which speaks in the ear of the millions, is taken possession of by the Spirit, willing or unwilling, to proclaim His wonders, and go everywhere preaching the word, in its most impressive, its *living* forms and examples. These communications and means of grace and general awakening, on their present scale, are altogether of modern date—a new thing, and under God, a mighty thing, in the religious world. The barest statement in figures, which is all we are able to give, for the most part, of the wide outpouring of God's mercy upon our land, is more eloquent of divine love than the voice of an apostle. It carries mingled invitation, encouragement, and rebuke, in thrilling tones to every laggard church and hesitating Christian." The revival reports of the New York *Tribune* (to which we are largely indebted in this volume), while they continued, were the cause of much awakening among the millions which that immensely circulated paper reaches daily. It is a wonder of wonders, to behold such organs employed on such errands, and to such purpose. A pastor at a distance writes to one of the religious papers :

"The glorious summary, with the editorial remarks on the "Great Revivals," in your paper of the 4th instant, stirred my soul so powerfully, that I felt that something more *must be done* in our village. I accordingly called on the Presbyterian minister in the place, and proposed increased efforts in our churches. The result is, that meetings have been increased, the influences of the Spirit are falling like dew upon us, and we have every indication that the three denominations will be greatly revived, and we hope, sinners converted."

But the telegraph, as a means of grace and awakening! Shortly after the noon-day meetings began to multiply, simultaneous correspondence by telegraph was commenced between those in different cities.

TO THE PHILADELPHIA UNION PRAYER-MEETING IN JAYNE'S HALL.

NEW YORK, *March* 12, 1858—12½ *o'clock, p. m.*

CHRISTIAN BRETHREN—The New York John street Union Meeting sends you greeting in brotherly love:

"And the inhabitants of one city shall go to another, saying, Let us go speedily to pray before the Lord, and to seek the Lord of Hosts—I will go also."

"Praise the Lord—call upon his name—declare his doings among the people—make mention that his name is exalted."

BENJ. F. MANIERRE,
CEPHAS BRAINARD, } *Leaders.*

To this dispatch, the following reply was received and read to the meeting in John street:—

To GEORGE P. EDGAR, for John street meeting:

PHILADELPHIA, *March* 13, 12½ *o'clock, p. m.*

Jayne's Hall Daily Prayer-Meeting is crowded; upwards of 3000 present; with one mind and heart they glorify our Father in heaven for the mighty work he is doing in our city and country, in the building up of saints and the conversion of sinners. The Lord hath done great things for us, whence joy to us is brought. May He who holds the seven stars in his right hand, and who walks in the midst of the churches, be with you by His Spirit this day.

Grace, mercy and peace be with you.

GEO. H. STUART, Chairman of Meeting

At many of the telegraph offices in this city, as also in other places, messages have been sent to all parts of the country, announcing conversions, and that many of them have been exceedingly tender and touching. Some have been as follows: "Dear mother, the revival continues, and I, too, have been converted." "My dear parents, you will rejoice to hear that I have found peace with God." "Tell my sister that I have come to the cross of Christ." "At last I have faith and peace." Many young men, engaged in business in this city, have sent such news to their homes in New England. Many of the dispatches mention that letters, containing more full information and details, will follow by mail.

The following is the order of closing hymns agreed upon to be sung in concert at all the prayer-meetings in the various cities and towns where they are held for the week designated:

Monday, March 29—"I love thy kingdom, Lord."
Tuesday, March 30—"Before Jehovah's awful throne."
Wednesday, March 31—"Jesus at thy command."
Thursday, April 1—"Jesus shall reign where'er the sun."
Friday, April 2—"How divine, all love exceeding."
Saturday, April 3—"Jerusalem! my happy home!"

Demand for Hymn-Books and Tracts.—One of the incidental effects of the large religious meetings held every day in various quarters of the city has been to increase to an unusual degree the demand for hymn-books to be used in the devotional exercises of the meetings, and tracts to be distributed by persons who take an active part in promoting the movement. The hymn-book in general use in the prayer-meetings is a little collection, common in Sunday schools, that can be bought for a few cents, and thus scattered in great numbers through the pews at a trifling cost. The depository of the Tract house is thronged daily with ladies and gentlemen selecting and purchasing tracts and books for distribution among their friends and in destitute localities of the city.

The whole perplexity how to have good church music, is solved by hearing one hymn sung in the Chambers street or John street prayer-meeting. The observer will be struck with the unity of time and movement throughout that vast and unschooled chorus. Not a voice can be heard to "drag," on the most familiar air that has been drawled out in sleepy meetings for a hundred years. Every note is *awake*, prompt and eager in its rhythmical place. The physical imperfections of voice and ear, which, in a choir of from twenty to fifty persons, might be almost intolerable, are as little thought of as the hoarser notes in the thunder of the ocean or the roar of the forest.

GOOD NEWS.

At one of the great meetings for prayer, held at midday in the city of New York, a gentleman from Philadelphia rose and read the following hymn. He stated the singular fact that it was written by a young man in Scotland, whose mind had become shattered and broken, but which, on the single subject of religion, still remained calm and clear. The Sun of Righteousness shed a holy light into that darkened mind, and filled that troubled soul with peace. In one of his tranquil and happy moods he wrote the following lines. After this explanation, the speaker proceeded to read them, and the effect upon the crowded audience was thrilling.

Where'er we meet, you always say,
  What's the news? what's the news?
Pray, what's the order of the day?
  What's the news? what's the news?
Oh! I have got good news to tell;
My Saviour hath done all things well,
And triumphed over death and hell,
  That's the news! that's the news!

The Lamb was slain on Calvary,
  That's the news! that's the news!
To set a world of sinners free,
  That's the news! that's the news!
'Twas there His precious blood was shed,
'Twas there He bowed His sacred head;
But now He's risen from the dead,
  That's the news! that's the news!

To heav'n above the Conqueror's gone,
  That's the news! that's the news!

He's passed triumphant to His throne,
  That's the news! that's the news!
And on that throne He will remain
Until, as Judge He comes again,
Attended by a dazzling train,
  That's the news! that's the news!

His work's reviving all around—
  That's the news! that's the news!
And many have redemption found—
  That's the news! that's the news!
And since their souls have caught the flame,
They shout Hosanna to His name;
And all around they spread His fame—
  That's the news! that's the news!

The Lord has pardoned all my sin—
  That's the news! that's the news!
I feel the witness now within—
  That's the news! that's the news!
And since He took my sins away,
And taught me how to watch and pray,
I'm happy now from day to day—
  That's the news! that's the news!

And Christ the Lord can save you, too—
  That's the news! that's the news!
Your sinful heart He can renew—
  That's the news! that's the news!
This moment, if for sins you grieve,
This moment, if you do believe,
A full acquittal you'll receive—
  That's the news! that's the news!

And now, if any one should say,
  What's the news? what's the news?
Oh, tell them you've begun to pray—
  That's the news! that's the news!
That you have joined the conquering band,
And now with joy at God's command,
You're marching to the better land—
  That's the news! that's the news!

The following hymn was read by the Rev. Mr. Cook, at the noon prayer-meeting in the Ninth street Reformed Dutch Church. "*Just as I am,*" has been much blessed in the revival in this city: perhaps this form of invitation may carry peace to some soul, with the Holy Spirit's blessing.

"JUST AS THOU ART."

Counterpart of the beautiful hymn, "*Just as I am.*"

Just as thou art—without one trace
Of love, or joy, or inward grace,
Or meetness for the heavenly place,
O, guilty sinner, come.

Thy sins I bore on Calvary's tree;
The stripes thy due were laid on me,
That peace and pardon might be free—
O, wretched sinner come.

Burdened with guilt, would'st thou be blest?
Trust not the world; it gives no rest:
I bring relief to hearts opprest—
O, weary sinner, come.

Come, leave thy burden at the cross;
Count all thy gains but empty dross;
My grace repays all earthly loss—
O, needy sinner, come.

Come, hither bring thy boding fears,
Thy aching heart, thy bursting tears:
'Tis mercy's voice salutes thine ears;
O, trembling sinner, come.

"The Spirit and the bride say, Come,"
Rejoicing saints re-echo, Come;
Who faints, who thirsts, who will, may come;
Thy Saviour bids thee come.

TO PARENTS IN THE COUNTRY.

The "Committee on Devotional Meetings" of the New York Young Men's Christian Association have issued a circular, addressed to parents in various parts of the country, who have children in business in this city. The object of the circular is to gain from the parents the address (either business or residence) of young men who are not connected with the Christian Association, or with any of the churches in the city, and who would be profited by a friendly call from some member of the Committee for the purpose of religious conversation. If any father or mother will send a letter addressed "E.,' Box No. 3,841, giving the necessary directions, the person designated will receive a personal invitation to attend the daily noon prayer-meetings, and similar meetings held at other hours of the day in various parts of the city for the benefit of young men. The Committee say in their circular, "Information from any of our friends at a distance, as to what is being doing among them, sent to the above address, will be gratefully received."

RELIGIOUS TRACT CARDS.

Printed cards, of which the following is a copy, have been extensively circulated among the attendants at the John street meetings :

"The following lines were copied from a very old moss-covered tombstone in Devonshire, England. Who the author was is not known to the person who has caused them to be printed on this card. The Day of Judgment will reveal the fact, and also another fact, viz., whether the reader has been led to love the Saviour or reject him :

'Christ is the Way, the Truth, the Life divine ;
Seek thou on earth to take this Christ as thine :
For he that lives in Christ, in Christ shall die,
And dwell with Christ in Heaven eternally.' "

A card, with the title "Come ! Come ! ! Come ! ! ! Let him that heareth say come," has been issued for gratuitous distribution.

Escapades of ill-taught zeal have been surprisingly rare in all these great and enthusiastic meetings. This is owing to the solemnizing power of the Spirit of God, and the weighty earnestness which He imparts. It was reported that some enthusiastic youth cried out in the Chamber street meeting one day, that "Edwin Forrest, *the greatest actor in America*," had been converted. Whether Mr. Forrest be a "great" man in any sense or not, is a matter of no consequence to Christians. His soul is as precious as any other man's, and that is all. "Not many mighty are called," for the Spirit of God has no need of their might. Requests of special prayer for the conversion of distinguished personages, such as Archbishop Hughes, President Buchanan, and the like, which are sometimes presented, are open to a like criticism. No Christian who has "faith as a grain of mustard seed" in the infinite power of the Captain of Salvation, will be peculiarly concerned for the conversion of any man because he is great in this world. All such things as these are follies of the unregenerate mind, that furnish the adversary of revivals with real scandals on which to build a multitude of fictitious ones, against a lively religion.

THE POLICEMEN'S MEETING.

The Policemen of the Seventeenth Ward, some fifty in number, having lately intimated through their captain, Mr. Hartt, a desire to attend a religious meeting appointed specially for their own benefit, were invited to assemble on Monday, March 29th, in Dr. Hiscox's Church, in Stanton street (Baptist).

At half-past two o'clock the church was crowded, principally by the families and acquaintances of the policemen. Capt. Hartt sat at one side of the communion table, and Capt. Steers of the Nineteenth Ward at the other. Capt. Coulter of the Twenty-second Ward, Seabring of the Ninth, Sergeant Johns of the Metropolitan Police Office, and Police Surgeon Ives, were also present. Half the body pews were filled with policemen in uniform. Drs. Hiscox, Lathrop and Smith, the Rev. Messrs. Sanderson, Thompson and Horton, were in the pulpit.

Dr. Hiscox, previous to announcing the second hymn, said that the first suggestion of this meeting came, so far as he was aware, from Capt. Hartt. It was the first religious meeting of policemen which he had ever known. All the pastors of the Ward had been invited to be present, and most of them complied with the invitation.

Dr. Smith of the Seventh avenue and Fourteenth street Church, said that a few days ago, while he was out of town, two policemen came to his house to see him. On his return, he was told of it; he could not remember that he had done anything which required their presence, but one of his servants was considerably anxious. How surprised and delighted was he when they came again, and he found that they had come as representatives of the force, to invite him to participate in a meeting like this ! * * * But a little time and their names would be stricken not only from the police force, but from the book of the living. Let them make this the first purpose of their minds—to seek the means of salvation, and then they would hear how to obtain eternal life.

The Rev. Mr. Horton, Tract Missionary of the Ward, said the inhabitants of the Ward who belonged to nobody's parish belonged to his. Policemen had peculiar responsibilities, and no where was enjoyment of the gospel of Jesus Christ more necessary than in a policeman. The idea had been imbibed in some public minds that it was incompatible with the duties of a policeman to have a Christian heart under his coat. It seemed to them that the mild principles of the Saviour would not fit men to carry the stern mandates of the law into execution. But Cornelius was not a worse centurion for his Christianity.

Dr. Hiscox said they had come to speak to them of the soul's salvation, and to exhort them to become reconciled to God, and hoping that they might meet again in a better life. They were here not as officers and men, but as poor helpless sinners in the sight of God. Could he take them back of the church and unveil the dead to them, would they be able to tell who wore broadcloth, and who wore sackcloth ? They would leave this church in a few moments. They would soon leave this world. He rejoiced to know that some of them had hopes of another and a better life, and desired that all their names might be written in the Lamb's book of life. Might they go home, gather their households around them, and resolve that they would give their hearts to God. Let them do their duties faithfully to their God, and they would do them well to this city and to their fellow-men. The peculiar dangers to which they were exposed had particularly struck him. Poor Anderson ! Hardenbrook ! At what unexpected hour might the news come to us that some of them had fallen in the discharge of their duty. If the voice should come to-night, could they say : " There is my home and portion fair"—my friends, my treasures, my hopes in heaven ? No class of the community saw the fruits of sin more sadly realized than they—revelry, desperation, crime, and iniquity. Their life was in strange contrast with the harmony of the house of God. They saw the works of sin. Now, was it better to gather where the scoffers and transgressors sat, or to sit in the house of God? Which was better—to serve God or to forget him? Let them make sure of an inheritance in the rich blessings of eternal life. May heaven's richest blessings lead them and their children to the cross of Christ, and all they loved be gathered with them into the covenant of sovereign grace. Eternity would soon be all that was left us; time would soon pass like a dream of the night; the body would moulder into dust; the soul and God would be all that would be left, and they would be eternal. Shall we neglect the soul and forget God? Might the mercy of our God be their support here amid the trials of life, and sustain them in all its dangers. He thanked them for their care of our homes and our interests—watchmen for us and our welfare by day and by night; and when we bowed down to worship at our household altars, we would remember them, and when in our sanctuaries we met to worship, where they were almost forbid by necessity to come, we would remember them, and pray that we may meet them in a fairer and a better land, where sin should not corrupt its purity or pollute its joy, and where nothing unholy should ever come.

Capt. Hartt.—I can but feel, my dear friends, to return thanks in behalf of our brother officers to you, and, most of all, to the ministers who have spoken to us. I could but feel that their words of kindness and mercy were like the dew of Heaven. How different from that which we are constantly called upon to experience! And let me say we are policemen, and we feel that, like a leper spotted of old, we are almost shut out of the house of the Lord, and so we thought we would obtain the consent of the Commissioners of Police to come here, and then we set about to find out how we should bring it about. It was not a little difficult to get up these notices, for it was altogether a new thing. When we went after them, I think that the Lord had prepared the way, and prepared the hearts of all for it. The time has not yet come for the lion and the lamb to lie down together, and there is not any appearance of it for a long time to come. Let me ask you now, as we are about to separate, and, as our reverend brother says, we may never meet again, let me ask you what is our answer to the great question? Is your answer this: "I will arise and go to my father." Are you ready to set out to-day and serve the Lord—to make that your portion? Are you ready to join yourself to the hosts of Israel? Are you ready to go, or not? We shall all answer this question, most assuredly. In the first place I said to myself that I didn't feel like going to the judgment without extending to you an invitation to go with me. Let me ask here, are you ready to-day; shall it be said of you and me that we are on the road to ruin? Let me say that we have known many in this very ward. For a long while they have gone down, till at last they are bound by the strong arm of the law, and to-day they are clothed in the zebra-cloth. So it may be with us; we may go a long time, but at the last an injured God will call us to judgment, and we shall be met at last as the angel met the prophet of the Lord, when he told him to curse Israel, so that we cannot turn aside. Oh, may the Lord so deal with us, that we, policemen, may not be left out, but gathered in one bundle, the bundle of eternal life, and be welcomed to the city of life everlasting.

Dr. Smith expressed an earnest desire that the meeting should be continued, and after a prayer and benediction, the first policeman's meeting ever held was ended.

The second religious meeting for Policemen was held April 7th, at the Stanton street Baptist Church, the Rev. Messrs. Hiscox, Stewart, Sawyer, Roach and Dodge participated in the exercises.

The Rev. Mr. Roach related an effecting incident which occurred not long ago. A lady was on the point of going forward for prayers, when her husband said, "not to-night, wife, not to-night, the cards are out for Friday, wait till after the party and then we'll go forward together." She didn't go forward, but on Friday night, while her guests were dining at her house, that interesting lady expired, and they arrived in time only to see her corpse, and the agony of her husband.

Sergeant Johns of the Metropolitan Police Office, said that he thanked God that he found the Saviour some eighteen months ago, in the John-street Church. One day, when he was patroling Broadway, he was using God's name very profanely, and an old woman came along—it was in front of Trinity Church—and stopped. The policeman who was with him asked her if she wanted anything of them, and she said that she had stopped to hear that officer swear so. It made a great impression upon him. Some time after that he moved into a house with a neighbor who was a good Christian woman. Then he began to go to church, and he said :—"At last I said, I can't stand it any longer ; I can't go home without going to that altar ;" and I said to my companion, "Wife, let us go and lay off the cares of this world." The most trouble to me is, I am sometimes a little nervous ; but I tell you I do love the Lord, and I tell you my whole heart's desire is to serve Him. Many and many a prayer I have offered up for you, my brother officers. I mean to continue to offer them up, and wish that every man in the department was a Christian. O what a police we would have ! How the city would rejoice ! I hope you will pray for me ; I will remember you. I make it a duty to pray for all classes, all sects and denominations, even the heathen—even those who are shut up in prison. Pray for me that I may be faithful even until death.

A policeman's wife spoke of the trials of policemen's wives. She said that, instead of lying down quietly at night to sleep, they were tossed about with cares and anxiety. The policeman's wife did not know at what moment her husband might be brought in a lifeless corpse. It was her constant prayer that policemen might be saved. She did hope that prayer-meetings for policemen might be continued.

A policeman from Brooklyn said that he felt rather embarrassed at appearing in this house with his uniform on. Sixteen years ago he gave his heart to God ; he had since turned to the ways of the world, but now desired to return again, and he asked the prayers of all present.

After the meeting a large number of the laws and ordinances of the State and Corporation in relation to the observance of the Sabbath were examined.

THE FIRE DEPARTMENT.

The New York Young Men's Christian Association have issued a circular to the officers and members of the Fire Department of this city, the object of which was to invite them to attend some of the various prayer-meetings, and disignating the hours and places at which the meetings are held. The following is a copy of the circular :

" *To the Fire Department of our City :*

"GENTLEMEN: Through your worthy foreman, we would beg to present our kind regards to you as a department and as individuals. We know full well that your calling is a self-sacrificing one (for we have in our ranks many who in days past and at present the Fire Department were proud to recognize as fellow-members), and one, the prosecution of which subjects you to dangers and hardships, and at the same time gives an opportunity of displaying that noble heroism which entitles you to the respect and admiration of our fellow-citizens.

"You will agree with us, we think, that there are many among you who, by force of circumstances, do not have all the advantages of moral and religious enjoyment, which every one so much needs, and without which he is a great loser.

"To have these pleasures the 'House of God' should not be neglected; it is a fact, we think, that many noble and generous-hearted young men seldom attend church, not from want of early education by faithful parental care in this direction, or present denial of the advantages flowing from attention to those matters which pertain to the future interests of all. We recognize the reason of non-attendance upon these duties to be the force of habit.

"We would be happy to have so many of you as may be able, attend the 'Central Presbyterian church" (Broome street, opposite Centre Market), on Thursday evening, March 18, at 7½ o'clock, to listen to addresses from the Rev. A. A. Wood, of the Central Presbyterian church; the Rev. Thomas Armitage, of the Norfolk-street Baptist church, and the Rev. R. M. Hatfield, of the Forsyth-street Methodist church.

"We assume that it has not escaped your notice of late that all the people are giving more attention to these things than in times past. We hope it will be but a short time before every young man in our city will call his neighbor 'brother.'

"Come as suits your convenience best, whether in fire or citizens' dress, but Come! Come!! Come!!! 'let him that heareth, say, Come.'

"We inclose a few slips, which might be placed upon the tables of your Committee Rooms, if you see proper. Our Reading-rooms are open daily, from 8 A.M. to 10½ P.M. All are welcome who may feel inclined to visit them. The librarian in attendance will furnish documents, and give all needed information regarding our Association."

By invitation of several prominent members of the Fire Department, and other gentlemen interested in its welfare, Rev. William P. Corbit, pastor of the First Mariner's (M. E.) church in this city, preached a sermon on Sunday evening, at the Academy of Music, to the firemen of New York. The audience was undoubtedly the largest ever addressed, within walls, upon a religious topic, in this country. The capacious building was never more crowded. Long before the commencement of the exercises every seat was taken, and finally all the standing room in the aisles and doorways was densely packed, and hundreds were unable to obtain an entrance. Mr. Corbit spoke for an hour and twenty-five minutes, in a very ornate and flowery style, as appears by the report. The audience signified their approbation, on one occasion, by a grand round of applause. Nothing less than a *wisdom from above*, can meet the exigencies of a time of religious awakening, and enable men truly to work with, and not against the divine Spirit. Prayer should be offered continually for the imparting of such wisdom to all who lead or minister in divine things.

THE PHILADELPHIA FIREMEN.

The following is a statement of the numbers who attended public worship, upon a recent occasion, at National Hall. The list of fire companies, and the number in attendance, were : Good Will Engine Company, 210; Good Will Hose, 75; Good Intent Hose, 29; Warren Hose, 70; Western Engine, 52; Spring Garden Engine, 60; Spring Garden Hose, 25; Fairmount Hose, 42; American Engine, 34; American Hose, 30; West Philadelphia Hose, 45; Taylor Hose, 30; Munroe Fngine, 29; Weccacoe Engine, 115; Robert Morris Hose, 39; Cohocksink Hose, 64; Empire Hook and Ladder, 39; Reliance Engine, 30; Washington Engine, 70; Washington Hose, 40; Columbia Engine, 64; Columbia Hose, 64; Friendship Engine, 30; West Philadelphia Engine, 60; Schuylkill Hose, 30; Vigilant Hose, 30; Diligence Hose, 50; Humane Hose, 20; Mechanic Engine, 30; Southwark Engine, 30; Assistance Engine, 40; South Penn Hose, 30; Independent Hose, 51; Union Hose, 29; Niagara Hose, 25; Pennsylvania Hose, 30; William Penn Hose, 50. Total, 1,779.

On a recent Sabbath evening the members of the Fire Department of Poughkeepsie, assembled in the Mill-street church, and were addressed by the Rev. Mr. Holman, with great acceptance.

PRAYER MEETINGS IN STORES.

In connection with the stores and counting-rooms of several of our most prominent merchants, private prayer-meetings have been organized within a few weeks past for the benefit of the clerks and other employees. They are held in some retired place in the building, secure from public intrusion, and have been of great interest and profit to those who have attended. Some years ago a young man from New England came to this city, and was employed as a clerk in a dry-goods house down town. Shortly after his engagement, he came to his employer with the statement that some of the clerks were seriously interested in the subject of personal piety, and requested that a small upper room in the building might be set apart and furnished, to be used exclusively as a place of retirement to which the various individuals connected with the establishment might resort for religious conversation, reading of the Scriptures, and prayer. This request was immediately granted, and the room was used for years for this only purpose, resulting in the conversion of a large number of the persons who during that time came in and went out of the employ of the establishment.

THE FREE ACADEMY.

A weekly prayer-meeting has been held at the Free Academy since the Fall of 1852. It was organized by two members of the Senior Class and three of the Junior, all of whom have since graduated, and some of whom have entered the profession of the ministry. The meetings have been continued every week since that time, except during vacations, and at several periods twice a week. They are held on Friday afternoons, lasting an hour after the close of the day's exercises. They are under the management and control of the students, the Professors making it a point neither to interfere nor to intrude. It is noticeable that the students who have taken an interest in the exercises, have generally been those who were prominent and successful in their classes, and of whom an unusually large proportion, after graduation, have entered the Christian ministry. Conversions have occurred in almost every successive class in the Institution, it is thought through their instrumentality.

The prayer-meetings at the Free Academy are increasing in interest. At the meeting last week one hundred and twelve were present, being about one-sixth of the whole number in the Academy. Members of all the classes attend, and the meetings are conducted by the students, without either the supervision or the presence of the instructors.

There has been from time to time much opposition and more ridicule manifested among the students toward these religious gatherings, a somewhat singular instance of which occurred a year or two ago. On one occasion, shortly after the assembling of the meeting, a party of wild students, who remained in the building in consequence of a violent rain-storm, with thunder and lightning, determined to employ the time in the annoyance and disturbance of the meeting. They accordingly tramped heavily up and down the halls by the door, striking it with their fists as they passed ; and though they were remonstrated with, it was to no purpose. After a quarter of an hour of such injudicious sport, a vivid flash of lightning, which struck in the neighborhood, accompanied with a terrific peal of thunder, made such an impression upon the minds of three of the disturbers that they immediately desisted, and knocked for entrance to the meeting.

A PRAYER-MEETING FOR BOYS.

On Sunday afternoon a Union prayer-meeting of boys was held in the Lecture-room of the Church of the Puritans (Dr. Cheever's), on Union Square. The room was completely filled, the audience consisting chiefly of boys, with a number of their parents and friends.

The Rev. Dr. Cheever presided, and the meeting was opened with the usual order of devotional exercises, singing and prayer.

The Rev. Theodore L. Cuyler said that this was a very remarkable time. It seemed as if all that Christians had to do was to get alongside of an immortal soul, and they found him ready to be taken hold of, and waiting for salvation. There a number of boys had assembled, who offered to put their hearts in the hands of good people, and who asked them to love them. Youth is just the time to commence serving the Lord. A tree can always be well cultivated in its tender years, but when a tree gets old it is difficult and almost impossible to fix it so as to grow up properly. Early life is the season in which to be pulled out of the devil's ground, and planted in Christ's garden. Faith is very easy, but very dangerous to wait for.

Wm. E. Dodge, Esq., made a brief address to the children.

The Rev. R. Hatfield, said, that he could sympathize with the parents and friends who had brought the boys together, and who were solicitous on behalf of conversion. He related also the story of a minister who was once preaching to the inmates of a prison, each prisoner being in his cell, and not in sight of the speaker. While speaking, he asked all who had been confined there because they had obeyed their parents to rap on the doors of their cells (they not being allowed to speak). He paused, and all was silent. He then reversed the question, "How many are here because they have disobeyed their parents?" and the long corridor resounded with the raps upon the cell doors! To illustrate how happy religion could make a little boy, he told of a young English chimney-sweep, a "climbing boy," who, notwithstanding the miserable, unhappy, perilous business in which he was engaged, was heard one day when away up in a narrow flue, scraping the soot from the walls, singing those beautiful words:

> "The sorrows of the mind
> Be banished from this place," etc.

He concluded by asking all who wanted to be Christians and would like an interest in the prayers of God's people, to manifest the same by holding up their hands. Quite a large number held up their hands. He then charged them to remember what they had done.

After he concluded, prayer was offered by one of the elder boys present.

The Rev. Dr. Marsh asked the boys whether they would like to meet there again next Saturday. In response, every boy in the room held up his hand for the continuance of the "Boys' Union Meeting."

THE WAITERS' PRAYER-MEETING.

At one of our large restaurants, a gentleman had taken out a book to read while his dinner was preparing. On the arrival of the waiter with the articles he had called for, he laid down his book; when the waiter said, "Is that a Bible, sir?" "No," was the reply; "do you want a Bible?" "Yes, sir, I should like to have one." The gentleman promised to hring him one the next day; he did so, asking the waiter whether he attended any of the daily prayer-meetings. "No, sir, we have not time, being engaged here from early morning until late in the evening: but at ten o'clock we close, and then all the waiters have a prayer-meeting in one of the rooms of this house, and we know that good has resulted."

THE JEWS.

Many Jews have participated in the operations of the present revival movement. They have been in attendance at nearly all the meetings in the various parts of the city, and have presented numerous requests for prayers in their behalf. In the Twentieth Ward quite a number of Jews, of both sexes, have gone over to the profession of the Christian faith. One convert is about to go forth as a missionary among his own people. Many Jewish families have sent their children to Christian Sunday-schools. At a meeting in Burton's old theatre, a few days ago, a Jew complained that the seed of Abraham had been neglected in the prayers of his Gentile brethren. He said that a class numbering as many as thirty-five or thirty-six thousand souls in the population of this city surely had a high claim upon the interest of Christians in heart. He begged that in future they be prayed for at every meeting. In Brooklyn an entire family of Jews were recently led to embrace Christianity.

THE "PERMANENT" MOVEMENT.

A meeting of clergymen and laymen took place March 23d, at Spingler Institute, to devise means to perpetuate the present union of Christian effort among the various denominations of the city, to bring religion within the reach of the multitudes who are now practically excluded by their condition and habits from existing avenues.

It was finally, after a protracted debate, resolved that the whole subject matter be referred back to the committee, Dr. Peck, chairman, by whom the present meeting had been called, for the presentation of a more definite plan of action before a fuller representation of the clergy and laity of the various denominations, at a meeting to be called again soon by the committee.

At the last meeting, held on the 7th inst., the committee previously appointed made a report, proposing that under the supervision of a committee of ministers and laymen from each of the denominations interested, "the churches be united in *additional* efforts for the salvation of souls, by opening and sustaining places of worship, where they are needed, for the benefit of the destitute ; and it is recommended that the committee purchase and fit up a tent, which may be located, at different times, in such places as they shall deem best for the purposes specified ; to provide preaching in such tent at least once on the Sabbath, by ministers of the different evangelical denominations, alternating as regularly as practicable ; and establish Sunday Schools, and appoint Union prayer-meetings and other religious services."

At a recent meeting of the Young Men's Christian Association connected with the North Presbyterian Church (Rev. Dr. E. F. Hatfield's), corner of Ninth avenue and Thirty-first street, it was arranged to make a thorough canvass of the Sixteenth and Twentieth wards, with a view to aid in the promotion of the revival of religion manifesting itself in that portion of the city. Accordingly, about forty young men, members of that Association, entered into the work.

THE EFFECT IN THE CITY.

The "Great Revival," as all men call it, is now an absorbing topic even for ordinary conversation. The religious meetings that are held in various parts of the city during every day, are matters of common and street talk. Notices of meetings for prayer and other religious exercises have been publicly placarded in many of the places where handbills are usually posted. In many counting-rooms and stores, similar printed advertisements have been hung up, calling the attention of business men and others to the devotional convocations. In addition to these, tracts have been distributed in the cars, in the omnibuses, and in the ferry-boats, calling the attention of the chance reader to the subject of religion, quoting passages from the Scriptures, and giving notices of meetings. Such tracts have even been dropped on the pavements of the streets, for passers-by to pick up—so that "he who runs may read." The attendance on the Sabbath at the churches, has been for several weeks past, unusually large.

"SYSTEMATIC VISITATION."

This enterprise was started under the auspices of the New York Sunday-School Union. One thousand church members were called into the field as Sabbath-School teachers, and two thousand more as visitors. During the last summer, the Sabbath Schools in all portions of the city were attended as they had never been before during the warm season.

Every month during the summer brought a large number of conversions among these young people. In about one hundred and forty schools, there have been varying numbers brought under religious influences, who have publicly professed their faith in Jesus Christ, and become useful, working members of churches. These are scattered through all the evangelical denominations in the city.

The Committee on Business Men's Prayer-Meetings in the city of Philadelphia, have, with the concurrence of a large number of the pastors of different denominations in that city, issued a circular, recommending a fast day, and have selected Thursday next as the time for its observance. Measures have been taken for a similar meeting in this city.

The Young Men's Christian Association have caused to be printed and distributed at the doors of the daily prayer-meetings, and in many other ways, a variety of brief, pointed exhortations, directions for inquirers, etc., which it is hoped may accomplish silent but wide-spread good. Now is a precious seed-time, a genial season. "How shall I become a Christian?" is a single page of instruction right to the point, written for and printed by the Association, to guide any soul impressed with the importance of its eternal interest—as what soul is not, at this time?—directly and simply to Christ.

CHARACTERISTICS AND FRUITS OF THE REVIVAL THUS FAR.

The belief has been expressed by some, that the present descent of grace is without a parallel, on the whole, in the history of the church, since its primitive age. No such extensive, deliberate, and earnest turning to God, unprompted by the influence of His special messengers or by extraordinary occasions of excitement, perhaps, was ever seen in this world. From causes and instrumentalities of long, gradual, and deep-rooted growth, a novel *order of things* has come into existence, marked apparently with all the tokens of a permanent change. Nearly every city or town of importance in the Northern portion of the United States, has now its daily prayer-meetings in the midst of business hours, thronged by the men who have hitherto given their strength to the god of this world, and given to their country its preëminence in the daring, intense, and unexampled progress of worldly enterprise. Not long since, the religious press and people of New York were lamenting over the removal, in succession, of nearly all the places of worship which once blessed the lower end of the city. They little thought how soon this sad retreat of gospel institutions, before the advance of commercial enterprise, would be followed by a descent of the Spirit which should crowd not only churches, but stores and theatres in this same "business quarter," with multitudes daily, not weekly, seeking the Lord. The indications are, that the business part of the city will be likewise distinguished as the *praying* part of the city! Several large buildings, in addition to the churches, are now urgently wanted for daily prayer-meetings, and a religious paper suggests that one measure for sustaining this demand permanently, would be to *meet* it at once, by the erection or purchase of suitable houses of worship in the midst of business, in place of the dishonored and demolished structures of our fathers. "More room, more room!" is the voice of the movement in every quarter. Generally in all the commercial cities, as well as minor towns, of New England, the Middle States and the West, these meetings are opening and enlarging daily, and the telegraphic system of the country finds novel and active employment in spreading the news from day to day, and exchanging the greetings and congratulations of assembled thousands in all parts of the country. In Newark it is reported that at least three thousand souls have been hopefully converted to God; in smaller places in different parts of the country, it is asserted that scarce an unconverted adult remains; and the cities and villages in which the great awakening is in active progress, number at least *two thousand by actual count.*

Soon we may see the conflagration catching the shores of Europe, and hear like news to this from the results of the great PREACHING MOVEMENT which has been for many months going on in London and all the cities of Great Britain—perhaps itself one of the most remarkable religious phenomena of this or any other day. Why should not awakening France, Spain, and Germany, where such marked susceptibility to Evangelical truth has for some time encouraged the zeal of the handful of laborers, soon rise by communities and provinces in mass, to seek the Lord and call upon His people for the word of life? Conceive the effect of this swelling wave of Divine influence as it sweeps around the globe, upon the many families of the earth, docile Nestorians, inquiring Bulgarians, susceptible Karens, Feejee Islanders, etc., who are waiting for the kingdom of God, or already pressing into it. Will not the whole earth be shaken yet with the work of God so grandly begun upon our shores?

This is not all a supernatural matter. There is something in it for common sense to apprehend. We see in the phenomena of this revival, as plainly as our eyes can show us any other object in the world, the natural and beautiful operation of the appointed human instrumentalities in the awakening of sinners. The Gospel of Christ is as directly and surely adapted to awaken men as is an alarm of fire. Either will do it, in its way, as surely as it is uttered in earnest and with the practical evidences of sincerity. Otherwise, for neither will any man forego the comfort of his slumbers. You can not show the world the spectacle of a church in earnest, without awakening solemnity, solicitude, and tenderness on the subject of religion. You can not look on such a spectacle without being moved. The contagion of real earnestness is irresistible. The crowded Christian meeting, with its press of earnest speech and prayer, its tenderness and solemnity, its great massive weight of eternal realities incumbent on the very atmosphere of the scene, is no place for a careless man! He can not stand it. Why? Just because the Gospel, '*the power of* God *and the wisdom of* God *unto salvation,*' is actually preached, set forth and testified by living witnesses. It is preached, though no sound be heard, with a power which no eloquence or earnestness of one man could impart to the utterance. We can trace, indeed, in the history of revivals, the influence of our progress in association, since the days in which men were more massed and less individualized, and as a consequence were more controlled by single minds and less susceptible to the power of public and collective utterances, which *are* in fact mighty and eloquent in proportion as they are the voice of enlarged and strong individualities. Perhaps the day of great preachers' revivals has passed away with that of the mastery of single minds in general. We certainly witness at present a revival of unprecedented power, in which *the people are the preacher;* and this is in beautiful harmony with the nature of modern American existence. Democracy—under sin and infidelity the grimmest monster that ever made the earth to tremble—under Christ unites the intensity of individual force with the majesty of multitude and the spirit of Eternal Love.

It is true that the *novelty* of a thing is one great element of impressiveness, and doubtless a certain novelty, that is to say freshness and originality of form, always belongs to genuine manifestations of the mind, and is generally a requisite condition to any powerful effect upon the mind. But it does not follow that the continuance of our novel but most simple and appropriate means of grace—the mid-day business prayer-meetings for example—throughout the year, would soon lose any of its impressiveness on that account. The fact is, that such a persistence would itself be the greatest and most impressive novelty the church has ever yet exhibited. Neither need there be any fear that this wonderful multitude-preaching of the gospel will not develop perpetually fresher and more effective forms as it proceeds.

CHURCHES IN THE CITY.

It is not easy to obtain a definite account of the numbers added to the several churches, nor at present would those numbers be any index to the extent of the revival. The ingathering, we may hope, has but commenced. It will be more than a year, indeed, before the official aggregates of the various denominations, for the whole country, will be collected and published, so as to be compared with those of the last year, and exhibit the total increase of the churches.

In the city and suburbs of New York, the only denomination which affords us a stated report of its increase, month by month, is the Baptist. Their Pastor's Conference, held monthly, brings together an interesting view of the fruits of their labor, so far as indicated by the number of persons baptized. These, in the first three months of 1858, averaged about five hundred each month. There can be little risk in assuming that four times this number, monthly, have been received into the churches of the several denominations altogether.

Large accessions, and revival scenes of deep interest, have been witnessed in many churches of the city, a few of which may be mentioned by way of illustration.

In the THIRTEENTH STREET PRESBYTERIAN CHURCH (Rev. Dr. Burchard, pastor), one hundred and thirteen persons recently made a profession of their faith at one time. Of this number, 26 were heads of families, and 63 were children and youths : 10 were officers and teachers in the Sabbath-school, and 52 were scholars in the Bible-classes.

The NORTH PRESBYTERIAN CHURCH, in Ninth avenue, has had a very extensive revival. A marked seriousness has pervaded the congregation for more than eighteen months past. In September, 1856, a "systematic visitation" of the district was undertaken

The church has, at the present time, nearly 1,000 children and youth, in connection with its two Sunday-schools. Not less than 150 have been converted during the season, and probably more. The work of grace is constant, and the revival is, to all appearance, as progressive as at any former period, conversions occurring daily. An unusually large portion of the converts are heads of families.

The MARINER'S (PRESBYTERIAN) CHURCH, of which the Rev. Charles J. Jones is pastor, has enjoyed the presence of the Holy Spirit in a greater or less degree during the past two years. Within that time there have been 234 hopeful conversions, principally among seamen, and 25 or 30 persons are now candidates for admission to the church at the next communion season. Service is held every evening, and there are ten distinct services on the Sabbath. The gospel is preached in English and Norwegian, and in three separate dialects of the Chinese. During the last two years, persons from fifty-six different nations have been reached through the instrumentality of this church. The work is still going on here, and is apparently on the increase.

ALLEN STREET PRESBYTERIAN CHURCH.

The special religious interest connected with the services of this church manifested itself about the close of the year. The pastor says:

"I think that the origin of the work in this church may clearly be traced to the feeling awakened in the minds of brethren who attended the noon meeting held in the Reformed Dutch Church in Fulton street. At the two communions which have occurred since the commencement of the year, thirty-five have been added to the church. It is impossible to say now how many will be admitted at the next communion, for at no time since the interest commenced has there been so many new cases of conviction and conversion as now."

ELEVENTH PRESBYTERIAN CHURCH.

The work in this church commenced the latter part of December, 1857, and is still in progress. Seventy-three persons have been received into the church, and many others wait a future opportunity to profess their faith in Christ. Several members of the Fire Department and of the Police have been hopefully converted. In this church originated the effort in behalf of firemen, which promises to be extended throughout the city. The first two sermons preached to them were by the pastor.

FOURTEENTH STREET PRESBYTERIAN CHURCH.

The Rev. Asa D. Smith, D.D., is pastor of this church. For two years in succession it has been favored with a special work of grace, embracing a large number of the congregation. On the 5th of February last, a day of fasting and prayer was observed by the church, the services of which were marked by full attendance and deep solemnity. The interest thenceforward gradually deepened, but no extra services were held, with the exception of a meeting for inquirers at the pastor's house, until Monday, March 16. Then a morning prayer-meeting was commenced in the lecture-room, which is still continued, beginning at 8 o'clock, and occupying just half an hour. Large numbers attend this meeting. In connection with it, the pastor began to preach four evenings of each week, which he is still doing. The impression has been very marked in the Sabbath-schools connected with the congregation, having under their influence some 1,400 or 1,500 children. A considerable number of the children and youths are in attendance at the inquiry meetings. The pastor says: "It may be particularly noted, that some delightful fruits have appeared of the missionary labors, especially in connection with the Mission Sabbath-schools in which the church has been long engaged."

The religious interest in the Middle Reformed Dutch Church, (Rev. N. E. Smith, pastor,) began the early part of last year. In a few months between eighty and ninety were added to the church. The present year a fresh revival of religious interest has taken place, and still continues, thirty more having lately united with the church.

In the Reformed Dutch Church, corner of Broome and Greene Streets, the Rev. Peter Stryker, pastor. In the course of the past year about sixty persons have been admitted to membership.

At the last communion (March 21st,) there was an accession of fourteen by profession of faith.

MARKET STREET CHURCH.

The pastor of this church, the Rev. T. L. Cuyler, says:—"The work commenced with us before New Year; the first tokens of good date from a day of special prayer appointed by the elders of the church. The present work has gone forward very quietly, very solemnly, and we hope, very surely. It is quite too early to estimate results. The good work is still going forward. But, from present appearances, we hope to welcome at our approaching communion season, (next Sabbath,) more than fifty new members to the Lord's Supper."

In the Baptist Mariners' Church, in Cherry Street, at which the Rev. Ira Steward is pastor, since the 1st of January, meetings have been held every evening, and one hundred and one have been baptized—among them one Jew—and about forty more have been hopefully converted. Many of the converts have been seamen—among them men of twenty different nations. The congregation has increased from one hundred to five hundred; and out of a Sabbath-School numbering fifty, thirty have been hopefully converted.

The Revival in the Stanton Street Baptist Church, commenced more than eighteen months ago. For fifteen months past there has not been a week during which less than five or six persons have presented themselves as inquirers, and asking an interest in the prayers of the church. About the first of October, 1856, the work of the Spirit began to be especially manifest. During December and January, the interest increased. In February, 1857, meetings were held every evening. During the months of March and April sixty were baptized on a profession of faith in Christ. Through all the hot season, the congregations were uniformly large, with inquirers every week. As the Autumn and Winter months came, the revival began anew, with increased fervor. Eleven were baptized in February, and fourteen in March. Since the first of March, 1857, one hundred and two persons have been received by baptism, and during the eighteen months through which the Revival has continued, about two hundred.

The Norfolk Street Baptist Church, the Rev. Dr. Armitage, pastor, has participated largely in the general revival of religion. Since the first of January, seventy-seven persons have united with the church, on a profession of their faith. In addition, more than forty have been converted, and about seventy others manifest the most serious anxiety for their salvation. The ordinary services are crowded, and hundreds who wish to attend are often unable to gain admittance into the house, which is sometimes filled nearly an hour before the commencement of the exercises.

BEDFORD-STREET CHURCH.

Some months since the leading members of many of the Methodist churches in the city, well known for their exemplary piety, constituted themselves a society with the object of promoting among the people an interest in religion. Their efforts have been attended with success beyond their most sanguine expectations ; and as they labor during the entire Sabbath in a given church, and in another church the succeeding Sabbath, the organization has obtained in the levity of common remark, the name of the "Flying Artillery." The force consist of between thirty and forty, mostly middle-aged persons, among whom is ex-Alderman Wesley Smith.

Soon after its organization, the "Praying Band," or "Flying Artillery," visited this church, and occupied an entire Sabbath in prayer and exhortation. Meetings have been held every evening since, and the large church has been crowded constantly. For two weeks in March, a daily prayer-meeting was held here, which was then removed to the Baptist Church. Upward of one hundred and fifty converts have already united with the church.

FIVE POINTS MISSION.

The numbers and seriousness of the congregation attending the Sabbath evening services at this place—composed almost exclusively of residents on the Five Points—had gradually but steadily improved for several months previous to the first of January. Early in that month several persons asked the prayers of the congregation; and from that time till the present more or less have presented themselves, until upward of one hundred have been forward for prayers Of these at least seventy-five have professed conversion, and sixty have offered themselves as probationers in the church. Of the latter, most have given unmistakable evidence of a genuine reformation of life and manners; and though they had lived for years without religious or moral restraints, are now regular and constant attendants upon public worship, and are as exemplary in their lives as many persons trained under more favorable influences. The work has, at no time, been distinguished by any marked excitement; nor does it appear to have been influenced by the religious interest prevailing in the other portions of this city. The subjects of the Revival were persons invited by the Missionary, and by those who, having themselves been converted, sought out and brought their friends and companions to the house of God. There have been many interesting and affecting incidents connected with this work. Individuals who once moved in wealthy and intelligent society, but who had been degraded by dissipation, have been among the converts.

FIFTIETH-STREET CHURCH.

One hundred and twenty persons have professed conversion, and ninety-five have united "on probation" with this church. Most of them are adult persons, who before were never accustomed to attend church regularly.

NORFOLK-STREET CHURCH.

About one hundred have professed conversion during the Winter and Spring thus far. Excepting a few cases of youth, they have all been adults.

THE FIRST CONGREGATIONAL METHODIST CHURCH, Brooklyn, has had a continuous revival for eleven months past. During this time nearly one hundred and fifty persons have professed conversion, of whom over one hundred have united with this church, and about twenty with other Evangelical Churches in the neighborhood.

At the Seamen's Chapel, Cherry-street, of which the Rev. Mr. Corbit is pastor, over 150 converts have lately been made, of which number, with the exception of six, all were adults. About one-third of the entire number are seafaring men.

THE MAIN-STREET BETHEL CHURCH, BROOKLYN.

The Rev. Wm. Burnett, who labors in this church, and in the section of the city in which it is located, writes: "That a daily prayer-meeting is held in the Bethel, from 12 to 1 o'clock. On board the man-of-war North Carolina, a work of reformation, both in temperance and religion, is going on, of a truly remarkable character. We have had frequently from eighty to one hundred persons requesting prayers, and the interest still continues. I distribute Bibles and Testaments in ten different languages."

HANSON-PLACE CHURCH, BROOKLYN.

In the church of which the Rev. Mr. Law is pastor, the number of converts has reached two hundred. This is a newly-organized congregation.

DE KALB AVENUE CHURCH.

The revival influence developed itself in this church, of which the Rev. J. S. Inskip is pastor, at the height of the financial "panic." Over 150 have been converted. The work continues, and the indications are that hundreds more will soon be added to the different churches in the neighborhood. A Union prayer-meeting is held daily, alternately in the Presbyterian, Baptist, and Methodist churches.

An Episcopal clergyman of the city writes: "It is difficult to say what effect is produced in the Episcopal Church by a Revival which began outside of it. High-Churchmen view such seasons unfavorably; but Low-Churchmen at least wish them well, and hope for the best —and, more than this, open the doors and windows of their own tabernacle to let the general warmth come in, and to feel a little of the '*Spring.*' In regard to churches denominated 'Low,' it is difficult also to say how much good a general revival does, for not having a popular revival machinery in use, their members go in great numbers to other churches which have. In my own particular church all services are better attended than common, and a few persons are evidently seeking religion. In our Sunday-schools, three in number, there are some instances of recent conversions, and the Teachers'

Meetings, particularly the one for prayer on Sunday, are well attended and effective for good. No greater mistake is made about the Episcopalians, especially Low-Churchmen, than to suppose that they object to *free prayer*. I have never been connected with any Episcopal Church for fifty years past, where this opposition prevailed, and hope I never shall be. But little, perhaps nothing, is *publicly said* of a meeting for prayer where no form is used, though it has existed in one Episcopal Church for fifty years, without any cessation hardly for a week. If another examination should be made a month or two hence, more may be said of the good this Revival has done in the Episcopal Church

ST. PAUL'S CHAPEL.

St. Paul's Chapel is one of the four churches in the Parish of Trinity Church. From nine o'clock in the morning till nine o'clock at night, one or more of the churches may be found open for prayer and for preaching, and for other sacred services every day.

These continuous services are according to the system of the Protestant Episcopal Church, as laid down in the Common Prayer Book. They are, therefore, not extraordinary, being carried out in Divine Service from year to year. The number of persons *confirmed* was—last year 170, this year about 500.

Regular evening meetings for prayer and short addresses, have been held in the Church of the Ascension (Rev. G. T. Bedell, Rector). One of these evening services was of a very impressive character. The meeting commenced with singing the hymn

> "Stay, thou insulted Spirit, stay,
> Though I have done thee such despite;
> Nor cast the sinner quite away,
> Nor take Thine everlasting flight."

A series of prayers were read by the Rev. Mr. Dennison; after which the Rev. Mr. Dickson, Rector of Grace Church, delivered a short address from the text, "Lord, are there few that be saved?"

He attributed the small number of professing Christians to the low standard of Christianity among Christians themselves, to their reserve, and indifference to the salvation of others.

Another hymn was sung, commencing,

"Sing, my soul, his wondrous love,"

After which some remarks were made by the Rev. Dr. Dyer.

Two verses of the hymn commencing,

"Saviour, source of every blessing!"

were sung, and the Rev. Dr. Cutler, of St. Ann's Church, Brooklyn, addressed the congregation. He said that, twenty years ago, such a meeting as the present one would have been denounced as Methodistical, but he felt that he could almost say with Simeon of old, "Now, Lord, let thy servant depart in peace," for he had witnessed that glorious "Leviathan," the Episcopal Church, which for forty years he had lamented to see, with all its noble qualities and precious gifts, being fast in the stocks, at last launched and making full headway in the river that flows from the City of God.

The hymn beginning, "Salvation, oh, the joyful sound," was sung. The concluding prayers were read by the Rev. Mr. Dennison, who also pronounced the benediction, and the congregation was dismissed.

The singing is entirely Congregational at these services, the use of the organ having been dispensed with.

At St. George's Church (the Rev. Dr. Tyng, Rector), a strong religious interest prevails, and large numbers of both sexes are inquiring.

PERPETUATION AND EXTENSION OF THE PRESENT EFFORTS.

A Committee was formed by a meeting of ministers and laymen, held at Spingler Institute, on the 23d of March, to consider the best method of perpetuating the present providential union of the churches in efforts to save souls.

This Committee, consisting of Rev. Messrs. J. T. Peck, John Dowling, G. B. Cheever, S. D. Burchard, T. L. Cuyler, J. M. Krebs, with Messrs. Wm. E. Dodge, John R. Ludlow, Wm. C. Gilman, Mahlon T. Hewett, Horace Holden, and C. C. Leigh, report that they believe that, beside the moral power which each and all the denominations have in their separate action, there is a special force in their unity, and the outward expression of that unity, in some strong evangelical labors for the salvation of those not already reached by the established means of grace. It was felt that this joint power had, in the late revival, received a providential development and direction, which it was the manifest duty of the churches to recognize and perpetuate.

They, therefore, propose for the consideration of the Christians of New York, that a Committee of ministers and laymen, from each of the denominations interested, be appointed, to whom the supervision of this interest shall be committed.

That the churches be united in *additional* efforts for the salvation of souls, by opening and sustaining places of worship, where they are needed, for the benefit of the destitute, and that the selection of such places, and the mode of accommodating the services, be entrusted to the Committee.

That the Committee purchase and fit up a tent, which may be located at different times in such places as they shall deem best for the purposes specified; that they provide preaching in such tent, at least once on the Sabbath, by ministers of the different evangelical denominations, alternating as regularly as practicable; and establish Sunday-Schools, and appoint Union prayer-meetings and other religious services.

SURVEY OF THE UNITED STATES.*

MAINE.

At Bangor, Me., an extensive revival is in progress. The surrounding towns also partake of the excitement.

In Biddeford some of the leading citizens have been converted. During the whole winter the common topic of conversation has been the subject of religion. The revival here is distinguished for the remarkable rapidity of the work of conversion. Very clear and strongly marked convictions of sin (and in some instances the distress was well nigh overwhelming) have been soon followed by the joyful reception of Christ, and the immediate commencement of Christian duty in the closet and in the family, and in earnest efforts for the spiritual good of others. The converts are chiefly adults,

* Notices of the Awakening in the principal cities having been already given, are not repeated here.

the majority being heads of families, and many of them over fifty years of age. Among the latter is the case of a man who has been notoriously intemperate and profane.

At Deer Isle, Hancock co., females have gone three, four, and some even five miles, to attend the meetings. It was recently ascertained that one hundred and ten persons had been converted, and that in almost every house one or more are interested in the things belonging to their eternal welfare.

In Saco, a revival is in progress greater than ever before known in that place; large accessions have been made to the membership of all the churches, and the work is still going on.

Revivals are mentioned by the New York *Examiner* (which affords the greatest amount of statistics of this kind) in 88 towns, with seven or eight hundred specified conversions, the present year. The ensuing statistics are from the same source, and relate to the year 1858. The Methodist statistics are separate from these, and cannot be conveniently included. At least one-third more should be added to each State, in the average, on this account.

NEW HAMPSHIRE.

At New Ipswich, between fifty and sixty have professed conversion, including several students hitherto notoriously profane and profligate. A recent graduate of Dartmouth, who has hitherto been a follower of Voltaire, and had nearly completed an infidel poem in nine cantos, has burned his production, and avows himself an earnest seeker after religion. Several inn-keepers have banished ardent spirits from their premises, and in two instances have held prayer meetings in their bar-rooms.

At Dover, 150 hopeful conversions have occurred.

In Hampton, a very powerful revival exists—large numbers of conversions have occurred in all the churches.

In Meredith Village, a revival which promised to be of great power, and which had resulted in a large number of conversions, was suddenly arrested by a circumstance of which the Rev. C. Burnham, minister in that place, thus writes:—

"There have probably been more than 100 conversions within five miles during the winter. When the interest was at its height here, and when it seemed that the whole community was deeply interested, and were just ready in large numbers to come out on the Lord's side, the adversary of all good put a story in circulation, trivial, in itself, but yet of such a nature as to arrest attention, and it seemed to sweep through the whole region like a whirlwind, and yet there was not the slightest truth in it. There have been but one or two conversions since in our community."

The *Examiner* gives 40 towns in New Hampshire as subjects of the revival, with 425 conversions.

VERMONT.

In Rutland, 100 persons have professed conversion in the Rev. Dr. Aiken's Church, and at the close of a recent meeting, from 60 to 70 inquirers remained for special religious conversation and prayer. The church of which the Rev. L. Howard is pastor, has received forty-one by baptism, in the past few weeks, and many more were waiting to go forward in the ordinance of baptism.

In Jericho, fifty have been recently converted. Six hundred conversions are specified in 39 towns.

MASSACHUSETTS.

The number of conversions in New Bedford is estimated at 600, and at from 400 to 500 in Newburyport. In the former place, with a population of 24,000, not less than twelve daily prayer-meetings have been sustained for three months. As one of the effects of this work, one of the converts who had been a liquor-dealer, stated in a recent meeting that he had renounced the traffic, and had resolved neither to sell nor to drink a drop of liquor.

A sea captain from that place, while recently attending one of the Boston prayer-meetings, gave a very interesting account of his conversion while lying upon a wreck for four days.

In Lawrence, the interest which has, until very recently, been mainly confined to the churches, is now moving the irreligious with great power. Twenty or thirty have arisen in single church-meetings to request the prayers of believers. Daily and evening meetings are held through the week, nearly without intermission. Between thirty and forty Germans have recently joined the Central Church on profession of their faith.

At Holliston, there have been two hundred and fifty conversions.

"Never in the history of Lowell, has there been so general, and as we believe, so deep an interest in religion."

At Williamstown there were, at last accounts, some 40 conversions in College.

The work in Phillips Academy, Andover, is altogether unexampled. About thirty-five of the students are already rejoicing in hope, and the work still goes powerfully onward.

A very general interest exists in Winchester. Men gave up their business, and instead of coming to the city, stayed at home to pray. There were 75 inquirers at once, and some conversions. Since that time, the work has progressed rapidly, particularly among the young men of the town. It is thought that 250 cases, or more, of conversion have taken place in twelve evangelical societies. The revival has extended, in a greater or less degree, to nearly all parts of Worcester County.

A letter from Orange states that "the revival in that place, has been of greater power than in any neighboring locality. The town, until within a few years, has been the stronghold of error. The name of Jesus was ridiculed, humble Christians assailed and threatened in the streets, and the preacher bitterly cursed. Mr. G——, a tavern-keeper in the place, who was a Universalist, has, since his conversion, been the object of unsparing hate. He banished intoxicating drinks from his bar, opened his house to inquiry-meetings, and has not hesitated to meet 'the loss of all things.' The subjects of the revival are chiefly heads of families—the number must be nearly a hundred in the town, and still the work goes on."

In Uxbridge, among the cases of conscience is one of a gambler, who, while sitting at a table playing cards, was suddenly so impressed with a sense of the degraded life he had led, that he could neither hold his cards nor play the game. His companions urged him to take a glass of liquor to quiet his nerves. He refused and left them at once, starting for home, and shortly afterward experienced conversion.

Revivals in 147 towns, and conversions noted, between four and five thousand.

RHODE ISLAND.

At Pawtucket the revival is going on with increasing power. On a Sunday evening forty-three persons took part in the first meeting, and at the inquiry meeting which followed, forty-one spoke or prayed. Over a hundred persons have been converted.

At Warren, more than one hundred in the Baptist congregation have been hopefully converted, and many are still inquiring. Sixty of the converts are in the Sabbath-school, varying in age from 14 to 24 years. Some whole families have been found together at the feet of the Saviour. One entire Bible-class of nine young men, another of five young ladies, have been converted.

At Providence, in the First Baptist Church, some striking cases of conversion had occurred, and there are most interesting religious indications in Brown University, as well as in the city generally.

At Thurber's Pond, Providence, where a number of persons from the Fourth Baptist Church were baptized, about three thousand persons were assembled, half of whom were Irish, as Miss Carroll, who was converted from the Catholic to the Protestant faith some time ago, was one of the persons to be baptized. On entering the water, says the Providence Journal, she was saluted with cries of "kill her," "drown her," etc., the crowd being with difficulty kept behind a rope which was drawn to keep them from the shore. After the ceremony, the carriage which conveyed Miss Carroll to her residence was followed by a large crowd of Irish. The presence of the police, however, prevented any further disturbance.

Revivals 36, and numbers given of converts over 1,000.

NEW YORK.

During the last four terms nearly two hundred and forty academy students have united with some of the churches of Canandaigua.

The Baptist pastor in Union Village, writes that he has baptized 111 converts, and is expecting soon to baptize more.

"I never witnessed a revival of such extent where there was manifest so little of what may be regarded as mere sympathetic excitement. More than fifty of the number baptized are heads of families ranging from 25 to 50. One man has been hopefully converted in his 83d year."

In Westerloo, more than a hundred conversions are reported.

A letter from Catskill says, that since the revival commenced, 115 had been received into the church; more than one half being heads of families. The revival commenced at a time of religious indifference, by the conversion of a young man who was a member of the Bible-class. A prayer-meeting was established, and every member of the Bible-class has been brought to a knowledge of the truth, and made a public profession of religion.

In Olean there have been very recently 140 conversions.

The Rev. J. R. Kennedy, of Geneva, writes:

"Our little Congregational church last spring numbered only thirty, now ninety. Thus, under the providence of God this church has been trebled in less than one year."

At Genoa a Union prayer-meeting is held every morning at the Dutch Reformed Church, at which the various pastors alternate in presiding. The meetings are largely attended. At the Methodist church there are three daily meetings. At 9 o'clock a Young Men's Union Prayer-meeting is held by a class of young men, mostly new converts. At 2½ o'clock a prayer-meeting is held. At 7½ o'clock the large church is filled, and the altar and seats adjacent are crowded with inquirers.

A revival is in progress in Cold Spring, which all the different denominations have shared. I cannot state the exact number who have professed to have been converted, but I should think about 200, of whom 80 have joined the Methodist Church. The work goes on yet.

Since the commencement of the present term, a very great interest has been manifested by nearly every member of Union college, Schenectady. Public services are held in the college chapel two evenings each week, and hardly an evening passes but some one of the four classes holds a social meeting for prayer. Between thirty-five and forty attend the lectures of the Vice-President (Dr. Hickok) to young converts. But a much larger numher than this, it is estimated, have met with a hopeful change.

In Rockaway, L. I., the religious influence has been so generally felt that almost every adult person in the place has become a member of a church, and three hundred fishermen have been recently converted.

The Methodist Churches along the Hudson River report extensive revivals. Peekskill, Rondout, Poughkeepsie, and Hudson are specially noticed.

At East Greenwich, in the Methodist Church, one hundred conversions are reported, and more than fifty of them are heads of families.

At Nassau a very powerful work has heen witnessed. A clergyman writing from this place, says:

"Never since the days of Nettleton, whose labors were eminently successful in this region of country, has such a work of grace been witnessed. Over one hundred have attended the meetings for inquiry, and have sought an interest in the prayers of God's people."

In Clinton, the churches have had upward of one hundred additions.

A correspondent writing from Salem, says:

"Without any alarming event, without any extraordinary preaching, or any special effort or other means that might be supposed peculiarly adapted to interest the minds of the people, there has within a short time past been, in several towns and villages in Washington and Warren Counties, and the towns and villages along the western parts of the State of Vermont, a revival so extraordinary as to attract the attention of all classes of the community. In one town over one hundred have been brought to conviction and conversion, and the glorious work is still going on. They expect the whole town will be converted—for this they pray. This work does not appear to be confined to the churches; hundreds are converted at prayer-meetings, in private houses, in the workshops, and at their work in the fields. Men of fortune and fashion, lawyers, physicians, and tradesmen, and, indeed, all classes, ages and sexes, are the subjects of it."

Some 200 towns are named as sharing in the revival, with 6000 specified cases of conversion.

NEW JERSEY.

In New Brunswick one hundred and seventy-seven have joined the Methodist Church on probation, one hundred and twelve of whom are heads of families, among whom there are several steamboat captains, pilots, etc.

In Trenton, among the Methodist Churches, there have been upwards of one thousand seven hundred recent additions.

In Jersey City, a Union Morning Prayer-meeting has been held some two months, at half-past seven o'clock, which is well attended, and an afternoon meeting, at half-past five o'clock, under the auspices of the Young Men's Christian Association. In all the churches, perhaps as many as one hundred and fifty have been thought to have devoted themselves to the service of God since the work began.

Instances of revival in the State, over sixty ; of conversions, from five to six thousand.

PENNSYLVANIA.

At Chambersburgh, the most influential and prominent citizens have united themselves to the church. A prayer-meeting is mentioned as the largest ever known in this borough. The religious feeling is rapidly speading, and the young especially seem to be most deeply concerned.

Numerous and powerful revivals are mentioned by the Methodist papers. The work in the principal cities has been elsewhere referred to. The number of towns affected by the revival, is about sixty-five, as far as noted, with some five thousand conversions specified.

OHIO.

A great revival is in progress in Circleville. The Methodist Episcopal Church has received about two hundred and ten accessions, and the number is still increasing. Some of the other churches have also received some thirty or forty each. The great revivals in Cleveland and other cities, have already been mentioned. The work of grace has been very general, reaching at least two hundred towns, and yielding some twelve thousand reported conversions. These are largely among the Methodists.

INDIANA.

In Indiana we find about one hundred and fifty towns reported, with from four to five thousand conversions.

ILLINOIS

About one hundred and fifty towns participating: conversions specified, from three to four thousand.

MICHIGAN.

Towns sixty; conversions specified, from one thousand five hundred to two thousand.

IOWA.

The Congregational Herald says: "Never before has there been anything like the general religious interest in Dubuque that exists there now, and which there is a prospect will continue."

About sixty other places are named as sharing in the visitation, and some one thousand five hundred conversions are noted.

WISCONSIN.

Wisconsin sends about thirty names of places revived, with seven hundred and fifty or a thousand converts enumerated.

MINNESOTA.

At St. Anthony and Minneapolis, there have been from two hundred and fifty to three hundred conversions. Cheering news from all parts of the Territory.

A private letter from St. Paul, Minnesota, says: "The good work of the Lord still goes on. The interest is yet on the increase. St Paul never saw a time like the present. The Holy Spirit seems to pervade the entire community, in every department of business."

Other places named in Minnesota, ten; conversions, near one thousand.

MISSOURI.

In St. Joseph's a great revival has broken out. The churches of all the denominations have united in the effort to carry on the work. The conversions have been very numerous, including, in some instances, whole families.

The Rev. J. B. Fuller, nephew of the celebrated Rev. Andrew Fuller, of England, is producing a great excitement in Missouri, by his preaching. He is but seventeen years old, and had commanded a large salary as an actor. About fifty revivals are mentioned, and two thousand conversions.

Again and again, during the meetings at St Charles, Mo. would one and another arise and tell that a pious mother's prayers had followed them in all their wanderings and waywardness, and were now being answered ; one spoke almost identically as did John Newton, that he could almost feel the pressure of his mother's hand upon his head, as he used to feel it when that mother would kneel and commend him to the protection of a covenant-keeping God.

VIRGINIA.

In the western part of Virginia, bordering on Ohio, a general revival has appeared, similar in character to that in this vicinity. A gentleman writing from Wheeling, of the religious interest of that city, and in that section of the State, says :

"The past winter has been one long to be remembered, on account of the revivals of religion that have pervaded all the churches in this section of the country. Nothing equal to it has been known in this region of the country, even by the oldest members of our churches. In some neighborhoods almost the entire adult population is brought under its influence. I know of many churches where there are from one hundred to two hundred accessions, while there is but one church within the circuit of several counties, so far as I have heard, that has not shared to a greater or less extent in the blessed work."

Some fifty revivals are noted, with one thousand five hundred conversions.

In Maryland there are mentioned twenty-five revivals, and one thousand five hundred conversions. In the other Southern States, very sparse instances of revival are mentioned. We observe about thirty in all, with some ten thousand conversions.

In Kentucky we hear of some ninety revivals, and two thousand five hundred conversions. In Tennessee, forty revivals and one thousand five hundred conversions.

The Mobile Advertiser, says, that in this city "Services are now being held daily in the Catholic, Episcopal, Baptist, one of the Methodist, and perhaps other churches. In nearly all the congregations of this city, the converts within a few weeks have been unusually numerous."

INCIDENTS OF THE REVIVAL.

A YOUNG man who had not previously been in a church for nine years, was induced, a few days since, to attend the Union Prayer-meeting held in the Thirty-Fourth-street Methodist church, in this city, where prayers were offered for his conversion. In the evening of the same day he attended a similar meeting in the North Presbyterian church, Ninth Avenue, corner of Thirty-First street, where his case was also mentioned, and he was made the subject of special prayer. On the following day he again attended the meetings held in both these places, and on that evening experienced conversion.

At Newburyport, a pious wife entreated her dissipated husband to go to meeting with her; he replied that he would, if she would give him a pint of rum on his return. Knowing that he would have the rum whether she gave it to him or not, she agreed to his terms, and he went to the meeting. When they returned she procured the liquor for him, but he pushed it aside, saying he had found something better, and he now gives evidence of being a changed man.

A young man, in a store in Park Place, was met by a stranger, who asked him the question, "Are you a Christian?" to which, on his replying "No," the stranger said to him, "If you will pray to-night, I will pray for you." Next morning the stranger met him in the same place, and after a salutation, was surprised to learn that he had been converted since the previous day.

A young man attending a Presbyterian church in Brooklyn, received a copy of the tract-circular of the Young Men's Christian Association, accompanied with a printed card of invitation to the John-street prayer-meeting. A day or two afterward, at this meeting, he introduced himself to a member of the Association, and stated that he had experienced conversion through the instrumentality of that tract.

A law student in this city, was handed a tract by a person before unknown to him, who also gave him a card containing his address. Shortly afterward the distributor received a note from the student, saying, "I feel very serious on the subject of religion, and I hope I may be soon converted. Pray for me." His conversion took place immediately afterward.

A young man, formerly a Sunday-school scholar, recently received a tract from a gentleman, who inclosed it in a note, with a request to attend some one of the noon prayer-meetings. Shortly afterward he wrote, "I received your kind tract. I have been often warned of the dangers of city life, and have been trying to come to the Saviour. I hope I may soon be changed in heart." In a day or two afterward he called on the person who sent him the tract, and said, "I have found God."

A resident of New Haven, formerly a clerk in a bank in New York, while on a temporary visit to this city, was converted through the agency of one of the mid-day religious meetings. On his return to New Haven, he interested himself in the spiritual condition of a younger brother, who, within a week, was also converted. They are sons of a prominent minister in that city.

A gentleman who is greatly interested in the progress of the revival, recently called at the store of a friend, to whom he wished to present the claims of religion. His friend was not in, yet he, being unwilling to go away without having accomplished some good, spoke to one of the clerks—a young man about 18 years of age—to whom he was a stranger, on the same subject, and after a few days, was apprised of his conversion through the instrumentality of this conversation.

A New York merchant residing in a town in the vicinity of the city, on returning home recently after having attended a crowded prayer-meeting, determined to make an effort for the spiritual good of some of his friends and neighbors. One of these was a man who called himself an infidel. A prayer-meeting was organized, to which this man with others were invited, and after several days' attendance, rose on one occasion, and requested that prayer should be made in his behalf. To the surprise and almost astonishment of his acquaintances, he shortly afterward renounced infidelity, embraced the Christian religion, and is soon to become a member of a church. The cousin of this man was recently converted in this city, through attendance at the prayer-meetings, and two brothers and two sisters in the same family have since followed his example.

A young man stated at a prayer-meeting some weeks ago, that he had just experienced conversion. On being asked what had first arrested his attention on the subject of religion, he replied "that it was the reading of the account of the general revival of religion contained in THE TRIBUNE."

Two or three weeks since, a returned foreign missionary from the Syrian mission made an address to a Sunday school in Pittsburgh, Pa., in which he said he would put into the hands of the Superintendent a little box, made of the wood of a "cedar of Lebanon," to be given to the scholar that should commit and repeat in Sabbath-school the next two Sabbaths the greatest number of verses from the Bible. The prize was taken by a little girl, thirteen years of age. About the same time, two members of her class were converted and united with the church; and the ceremony of their admission made such an impression on her mind that she said "that she ought to have been with them." In a few days afterward, she was converted, after which she was suddenly attacked with scarlet fever and died.

The captain of one of our ocean steamers (who was one of the number immersed last month), a few years a ago, when about to start to sea in a new steamer, crossed the East River with seven or eight merchants, and went with them to a house of entertainment, where they had a jovial dinner together. A day or two ago he met with several of them and found each to be a converted man. They immediately hunted up the rest, and it was found that all were believers in Jesus. They retired together to a room belonging to a mercantile house, and spent a season in prayer and thanksgiving in view of the occurrence.

A Sunday school lad wished to join the church. His mother, for many years a neglecter of public worship, on being consulted, came and took a place beside her boy, and both have since been converted. A little girl, thirteen years old, who was six months ago in a Roman Catholic Sunday School, is now a firm Protestant and intelligent Christian, attending the church and Sunday School. A little girl belonging to the Sabbath School died a few weeks ago with the words on her lips, "I am ready," and a smile in her eye. Her father, who before spent his Sabbaths in an engine house, is now inquiring.

Rev. Mr. Adams, pastor of the Duane Street Methodist Church, says :—"Just after the great panic of last Fall commenced, a young man called on me late on Saturday night. He was the picture of distress and despair. Supposing him to be one of the many cases that daily came under my notice, I invited him in. He sat some minutes in perfect silence, and finally burst into tears. It was some time before he could control himself sufficiently to go on, and then said : 'Can you do anything for me?' I requested him to state his case. He said he was miserable beyond description—had been blessed with pious parents and a religious education, but had gone far away from the counsels of his fathers ; he had fallen into shameful sin, until his soul loathed himself, and he had been on the verge of self-destruction. 'This afternoon,' said he, 'feeling a hell within, I went out and bought poison—went into my room, and was about to take it when something seemed to say to me, "Go down and see the minister" and I have come. Will you pray for me?" He fell on his knees and cried aloud for mercy. After two hours of prayer he grew calm, and finally joyful. He gave me a package, and requested me to destroy it ; there was laudanum in it—enough to have killed half a dozen men."

The first person who renounced his sins in the Prince Street meetings, was a sailor, who was greatly addicted to gambling, and to other vices that usually accompany this. When he came to the meeting he had just left the gaming-table ; but when he returned, his first act was to consign his cards and dice to the flames. He then knelt down, prayed, and was converted. He is now at sea, sailing with a pious captain, and on board the ship daily prayer-meetings are held both in the cabin and forecastle. A man who had long been given to intemperance was among the converts, and in one of the meetings said: "No more rum shall ever touch me, by the help of God, unless it is flung on me."

The Rev. A. Cornell writes from Ionia, Mich.—"Two men came over thirty miles from the northern frontier, having heard that the Lord was with us, hoping to obtain mercy—one of them my own brother, ten years older than myself, and who had been for years so averse to Christianity that he shunned its remotest influence. The other was an Irish Catholic, whose residence was over thirty miles from here in his forest home. Having a Bible in his possession, he read, and became convicted of sin, and by weeks of prayer and agonizing struggle with his rebellious heart, he found peace in believing in Christ; and being all untaught in the doctrines of the Gospel, and no one to teach him, he conceived he might baptize himself, and so he filled a large stone trough and *immersed* himself. But not satisfied with his condition, and '*being warned of God*,' as he said, to go out of the woods where he could be taught, he found his way here, and was baptized last Sabbath. He was the most perfect specimen of one taught of God only, that I ever witnessed. Being possessed of strong mind, he had the clearest views of grace, and of his own sinfulness, and God's mercy, and was so untainted with human dogmas, that he seemed truly like a rock from its native quarry, untouched by human hands. I never witnessed a deeper and more profound love for God, connected with deep self-abasement, and adoring wonder at God's great mercy, and an unshaken confidence in a pardoning Saviour. He had no arts, no sophistry, no cant phrases common to many who have had Christian training, and yet in the doctrines of grace he was profoundly correct, and his earnest, heartfelt, simple experience and views at once dispelled from every mind all doubt that his was the work of God, and God alone."

THE REVIVAL AND THE NEWSPAPERS.

We all look for a time when the Press will be sanctified, with all its incalculable influence, to the cause of Christ's kingdom; when the authority of public sentiment will claim its active support to pure religion, as already to the conceded principles of morality.

Never before this year has such a significant and encouraging modification been seen in the tone of the secular presses on religious affairs. The following exhortation from the Springfield *Republican*, a secular paper, conducted with an eye to the doing of good as it meets opportunity, illustrates some of the ways in which the everyday press may exert a becoming influence for Christ :

"It is not our province to preach, or to exhort, but we very frankly express the opinion, that the more of our people who put themselves in the way of the influences which now prevail, the better. We have yet to see the first man who has sustained damage by becoming at heart, and in life a Christian. You old sinners, who have led a hard and careless life, put yourselves in the way of good. Go into the prayer-meetings. They will not hurt you. You young men, upon whom life is opening—you whose characters are forming, it will not harm you to incorporate into your life the Christian element. On the contrary, it will do you a world of good. You men of middle age, you hard drinkers, you swearers, you licentious men, you scoffing men, you double-dealing men, all of you, look in upon the prayer-meeting and see how it affects you. Your friends in other places are doing it, and declare themselves benefitted. Our opinion is, that it will benefit you. Try it and see."

CONVERSION OF A SAILOR.

At a prayer-meeting held in Plymouth Church, Brooklyn, the leader of the meeting announced that several seafaring men, recent converts from the Baptist Mariners' Church, were present, who were requested to speak. In response to the invitation, a young man, an American, arose and spoke as follows ;

"I am a stranger here, but I trust I am not a stranger to Christ. It is not long since I was converted, yet now I know Him, and am no longer a stranger to His love. I speak with great trembling before my brethren, because I feel my weakness ; yet I am made strong through the grace of God. When I went to sea I left behind me one of the best mothers that ever lived. She was a pious woman, and used to pray for me. She used to pray for me before I went away from home, and after I had gone she prayed more than ever Her prayer always was that I might become a Christian. In my early youth, before I went away from my father's house, I was a scholar in a Sunday-school, where I learned many lessons that I shall never forget. When I was at sea, off St. Vincent, a great storm arose. It was a tremendous gale, and many vessels were wrecked. We all thought that we should go to the bottom. There seemed to be no possibility that the ship could hold out against it, and we gave up hope. There was not a single person on board that was a Christian—none to whom I could go to seek counsel in view of preparing for eternity. I sat alone by myself, thinking what I could do. I was afraid to meet death, for I was unprepared to die. All the lessons that I had learned in the Sabbath-school came up before my mind. It seemed as if all that I had ever heard, or read, or known, flashed before me, and appeared as if it had all happened but yesterday. I thought of my religious instruction ; I thought of my mother's prayers ; I thought of the Bible ; I thought of God ; I saw my mother's tears ; I determined to pray, and I did pray. I made a vow before God, that if he would spare me, and suffer me to get ashore once more, I would consecrate all the rest of my life to his service. He heard my prayer, and we were saved. Not one of the crew was lost, although the storm proved fatal to many vessels. One of these, the bark Resolute, of New London, went down with all on board. In a day or two afterward we ran into St. Vincent, and were ashore safe. The danger was over, and so was my resolution. I forgot, in a great measure, my solemn obligation to God. There was no house of worship in St. Vincent, but if there had been I doubt whether I would have gone into it. We are always apt to forget, when peril is past, the prayers we utter when it is upon us. A short time afterward we were at St. Helena. Here there was a church, and when I saw it I began to remember what I had told God in the storm. It came upon me with great seriousness. We did not remain long at the island, but I determined, if possible, to fulfill my promise. I determined to seek and to find Christ. I began to pray, and to pray earnestly for my salvation ; and now I rejoice with great joy, and thank God with many thanks that he has shown me the way of life, and led my feet to walk in it. The prayers of my good mother are answered, for I trust that I am a child of God, redeemed by the blood of Christ."

These words were uttered with some hesitancy, occasioned by great emotion, and were listened to with intense eagerness by the congregation.

Before the meeting concluded, two other seamen narrated the circumstances of their conversion at sea.

AN OLD MAN'S PRAYER ANSWERED.

The Rev. Dr. Taylor of Newark, N. J., at one of the meetings held in the "Old Dutch Church," narrated the following circumstances "as an encouragement for parents to pray for their children :"

"Many years ago an old man, a devoted Christian, started a prayer-meeting, which is still continued, having resulted in many and glorious fruits. As a pastor it was my privilege to be with him, particularly during his last illness. In several visits made to his house I found him on the mount, looking over on to the Land of Promise. Finding nothing seemingly to mar his comfort or interrupt his joy, one morning as I went to his dwelling (he was a poor man and lived in straitened circumstances), I determined to satisfy myself whether there was nothing that gave him any trouble of heart. On entering his chamber I asked him in simple terms, 'How are you this morning ?' 'Oh, Sir,' said he, 'I am well ; why should I not be well ? I am near home. Yes, I am near home—near heaven,' I took the opportunity to ask him, 'My dear Sir, has there been nothing of late resting upon your heart as an occasion of trouble !' He spoke not a word, but turned his face over to the wall, and lay so between five and ten minutes ; then he rolled his head back upon his pillow, with his face towards me, and I saw the tears streaming down his cheeks. 'Oh, yes, Sir,' said he, 'there is one great trouble.' 'What is it ?' I inquired. 'Speak your whole mind to me freely.' 'Well,' said he, 'I have ten children, and I have prayed to God for more than thirty years that I might see one or more of them converted before I die ; but he has denied me. They are all grown up, as you know, but are not yet Christians.' 'How do you get over that trouble ? I asked. 'Ah,' he replied, 'I get over it as I get over all other troubles—by rolling it over upon Christ. I know that God means to answer my prayers, but he means to wait till I am gone. But he will do it ; I know he will ; my children will be converted.'

"This man has been in his grave for fifteen years, and I have watched over his children ever since his death ; and now to-day I am able to say that seven out of the ten have been born into the kingdom of God, and that the eighth has also just experienced conversion. This is the answer to his prayer ! God did not forget ; he only waited ; and in like manner he will answer the prayers of all parents who pray in faith for the conversion of their children. Let us, therefore, take courage, and lay hold upon the precious promises of God !"

A young man of skeptical tendencies was passing through Amity street a few days ago, and saw a child weeping bitterly. He inquired what was the matter, and it appeared that the child, whose family lived in Anthony street, had lost his way, and knew not how to get home. "Come with me," said the young man, "and I will show you the way home." But he could not persuade the lost one to accompany him. The young man left the child, and as he walked on, he thought, "that child is like me—lost—and will not be guided home." The impression ripened into conviction, penitence, and conversion.

It is stated that the captain and *entire* crew (of 30 persons) of a ship lately arrived at New York, had been converted upon the sea, without any obvious special instrumentality. Another gentleman reported five ships arrived at the same port, whose captains had been brought to Christ upon the sea.

A gentleman in Newburyport, says that the young converts have become missionaries, and go, not only from house to house, but into the neighboring towns, to hold meetings. Striking instances of conversion are occurring every day. Men go to bed careless, and wake up in the morning anxious and concerned about their souls.

DERBY & JACKSON'S

Library of Sacred Classics.

PRINTED FROM NEW AND BEAUTIFUL LARGE (PICA) TYPE.

BUNYAN'S PILGRIM'S PROGRESS, 12mo.,...$1 00
THE SAME—full gilt, sides and edges,.......... 1 50
THE SAME—half calf, antique,.......... 2 00

DODDRIDGE'S RISE & PROGRESS, 12mo.,... 1 00
THE SAME—full gilt, sides and edges,.......... 1 50
THE SAME—half calf, antique,.......... 2 00

BAXTER'S SAINTS' REST, 12mo.,.......... 1 00
THE SAME—full gilt, sides and edges,.......... 1 50
THE SAME—half calf, antique,.......... 2 00

TAYLOR'S HOLY LIVING, 12mo.,.......... 1 00
THE SAME—full gilt, sides and edges,.......... 1 50
THE SAME—half calf, antique,.......... 2 00

OTHER VOLUMES OF A SIMILAR CHARACTER TO FOLLOW.

JOHN BUNYAN! PHILIP DODDRIDGE! RICHARD BAXTER! JEREMY TAYLOR! "PILGRIM'S PROGRESS," "RISE and PROGRESS," "SAINTS' REST," and "HOLY LIVING." What Authors! What Subjects! What Books! Writers for immortality on immortal subjects, familiar to every reader from early infancy—household names and words and books for our maturer years. They will live forever, and do good to all. Old and young alike can drink at this well, "pure and undefiled," certain of refreshing draughts of pure and wholesome literature.

Copies sent by Mail post paid on receipt of price.

Address,

DERBY & JACKSON, 119 NASSAU ST., N. Y.

NOW READY,

THE LIFE AND CHOICE WORKS

OF

ISAAC WATTS, D.D.,

WITH A NEAT PORTRAIT ON STEEL.

12mo. Price $1 25.

The following are in course of preparation, uniform with the above:

DERBY AND JACKSON'S

CLASSIC LIBRARY OF SACRED AUTHORS,

COMPRISING THE BEST WORKS OF THE MOST EMINENT DIVINES; WITH BIOGRAPHICAL MEMOIRS, INTRODUCTORY ESSAYS, AND CRITICAL NOTES, ETC. BY D. A. HARSHA. THE WHOLE TO BE COMPLETED IN TWENTY-FOUR VOLUMES, 12MO., OF ABOUT 500 PP., WITH PORTRAITS ON STEEL.

THE LIFE AND CHOICE WORKS OF

JEREMY TAYLOR,
ISAAC BARROW,
JOHN NEWTON,
THOMAS SCOTT,
JOHN WESLEY,
ANDREW FULLER,
JOHN BUNYAN,
PHILIP DODDRIDGE,
RICHARD BAXTER,
JOHN HOWE,
JOHN OWEN,
MATTHEW HENRY,
ROBERT HALL,
JOHN FOSTER.

The remaining Volumes will be announced hereafter.

Copies sent by Mail post paid on recipt of price.

LIFE OF ISAAC WATTS.

INCLUDING HIS CHOICE WORKS.

BY D. A. HARSHA, A.M.

In one neat 12mo. volume, Price $1 25.

From the New York Evangelist.

Messrs. Derby & Jackson have commenced an enterprise, which, if carried forward with the same good taste with which it is begun, will deserve a very liberal patronage from the Christian public. It is the publication in convenient duodecimo volumes of a STANDARD LIBRARY OF SACRED CLASSICS. The first of the series is composed of selections from the prose works of Isaac Watts. It contains a sketch of the quiet, but not uneventful Life of Watts, several miscellaneous Essays, and seventeen Select Discourses, which have attained the highest reputation. Several of these sermons the late venerable William Jay, of Bath, pronounced "among the sweetest and most profitable sermons in the language." Those on "Death and Heaven," were the favorite reading of Dr. Doddridge, when failing health made him an exile from his native land, and he lay sinking under fatal disease at Lisbon. Those of our readers who have never met with the discourses of Dr. Watts, have a rich pleasure yet in store. We well recollect our own grateful surprise when, years ago, we first stumbled upon one of the huge quarto volumes of his sermons, and were allured on fr om page to page by the mingled pathos, sweetness, and fervency of his thoughts. His style, certainly, is open to criticism. It is too diffuse and sometimes careless, but always plain and perspicuous. It is an effort to grasp his thought, and oftentimes it is presented with a finished grace and beauty in keeping with its own pure and lofty character.

From the New York Observer.

The compiler of this volume is establishing an excellent reputation as a literary man, selecting worthy subjects and portraying them with skill. This book is well prepared. The biography is chaste, perspicuous, and discriminating; and the selection, as is claimed in the title, is choice. It is the first of a series of standard religious classics to be prepared by the same author, and we have no doubt they will be well worthy of wide circulation.

From the Albany Evening Journal.

This is the first in the series of a projected edition of the Christian Classics, and we earnestly hope that its extensive sale will reward the exertions of the enterprising publishers. It will embrace a selection of the most eminent Episcopalian and Non-Conformist writers from the period of Jeremy Taylor to Robert Hall of the present century. The sermons on which the reputation of Watts chiefly rests, are given entire, while the precious gems in other cases are taken from the controversies in which they lay embedded, and presented to the reader. What a rich feast is the perusal of this volume! If original and profound thought, vigorous illustration, chastened yet glowing sentiment, and elevated devotional feeling, please a reader, he will find all to abundance in the perusal of this admirable volume. The life of this "Master in Israel" is written with great beauty and knowledge of the state of society when Watts flourished, by Mr. Harsha, and will add fresh laurels to those which he has previously reaped in the fields of literature. For the libraries of private Christians we consider this work as indispensable, and when the series is completed, no present by churches to their pastors can be so seasonable as the interesting file of the Christian Classics.

Address,

DERBY & JACKSON, 119 Nassau St., N. Y

www.ingramcontent.com/pod-product-compliance
Lightning Source LLC
LaVergne TN
LVHW020937110826
845150LV00004B/887

9781425552022